THE TRANSLATABILITY
OF CULTURES

✛

Irvine Studies in the Humanities

Robert Folkenflik, General Editor

CONTRIBUTORS

✛

Aleida Assmann

Jan Assmann

Moshe Barasch

Sacvan Bercovitch

Lawrence Besserman

Emily Miller Budick

Sanford Budick

Stanley Cavell

Wolfgang Iser

Renate Lachmann

J. Hillis Miller

Gabriel Motzkin

K. Ludwig Pfeiffer

Klaus Reichert

Karlheinz Stierle

THE

Translatability

OF CULTURES

Figurations of the Space Between

✛

Edited by

Sanford Budick and Wolfgang Iser

STANFORD UNIVERSITY PRESS, STANFORD, CALIFORNIA 1996

Stanford University Press
Stanford, California
© 1996 by the Board of Trustees of the
Leland Stanford Junior University
Printed in the United States of America

CIP data are at the end of the book

Stanford University Press publications are
distributed exclusively by Stanford University Press
within the United States, Canada, Mexico, and
Central America; they are distributed exclusively
by Cambridge University Press throughout
the rest of the world.

A Note on This Series

This is the eighth in a series of volumes on topics in the humanities and the third in the new series published by Stanford University Press. This volume originated in a research project at the Center for Literary Studies, The Hebrew University of Jerusalem, sponsored by the German-Israeli Foundation for Scientific Research and Development.

For help with a broad range of questions, I am indebted to the Editorial Board of Irvine Studies in the Humanities, especially Leslie Rabine, J. Hillis Miller, David Smith, John Smith, and Brook Thomas. I am grateful to Dean Spencer Olin of the School of Humanities of the University of California, Irvine for his support. Joann McLean provided secretarial help for Irvine Studies. Nina Leacock, our research assistant, proofread the text and compiled the index, among other contributions. As usual, we are grateful to Helen Tartar, Humanities Editor at Stanford University Press, for her help with this volume.

Robert Folkenflik, General Editor

For Shirley Collier

Acknowledgments

The collective work brought together in this volume was made possible by the generous support of the German-Israeli Foundation for Scientific Research and Development, the Institute for Advanced Studies of The Hebrew University, the Mishkenoth Shaananim Guest House of the Jerusalem Municipality, and the Shirley Palmer Collier Endowment Fund of the Center for Literary Studies of The Hebrew University. Our colleagues in the Center for Literary Studies—too numerous to name here individually—have contributed unstintingly of their learning and enthusiasm.

Over the long haul Shirley Collier has been an extraordinary source of encouragement and strength. To her this book is gratefully dedicated.

S.B.
W.I.

Contents

Contributors

ALEIDA ASSMANN is Professor of English and Comparative Literature at the University of Constance. She has recently published *Arbeit am Ge-dächtnis: Eine kurze Geschichte der deutschen Bildungsidee.*

JAN ASSMANN is Professor of Egyptology at the University of Heidel-berg. Among his most recent books are *Akhanyati's Theology of Light and Time* and *Ma'at: Gerechtigkeit und Unsterblichkeit im alten Ägypten.*

MOSHE BARASCH is Professor Emeritus of Art History at The Hebrew University and a frequent visiting professor at Yale. He has also served as Andrew Dixon White Professor at Large at Cornell. Among his recent books are *Giotto and the Language of Gesture* and *Theories of Art from Plato to Winckelmann.*

SACVAN BERCOVITCH is Carswell Professor of English and American Literature at Harvard University. He has recently published *The Office of "The Scarlet Letter"* and *The Rites of Assent: Transformations in the Symbolic Construction of America.*

LAWRENCE BESSERMAN is Associate Professor of English at The He-brew University. His publications in medieval studies include *The Legend of Job in the Middle Ages* and *Chaucer and the Bible.*

EMILY MILLER BUDICK is Professor of American Literature and chair of the Department of American Studies at The Hebrew University. Her publications include *Fiction and Historical Consciousness* and *Engender-ing Romance: Women Writers and the Hawthorne Tradition.*

SANFORD BUDICK is Professor of English and director of the Center for Literary Studies at The Hebrew University. Among his books are *Poetry of Civilization* and *The Dividing Muse.*

STANLEY CAVELL is Walter M. Cabot Professor of Aesthetics and the General Theory of Value at Harvard University. He has recently published *This New Yet Unapproachable America* and *A Pitch of Philosophy*.

WOLFGANG ISER is Professor Emeritus of English and Comparative Literature at the University of Constance and Professor of English at the University of California at Irvine. Among his recent books are *The Fictive and the Imaginary: Charting Literary Anthropology* and *Staging Politics: The Lasting Impact of Shakespeare's Histories*.

RENATE LACHMANN is Professor of Slavic and Comparative Literature at the University of Constance. She has recently published *Gedächtnis und Literatur: Intertextualität in der russischen Moderne*.

J. HILLIS MILLER is Distinguished Professor of English and Comparative Literature at the University of California at Irvine. Among his most recent books are *Ariadne's Thread: Story Lines* and *Illustrations*.

GABRIEL MOTZKIN is senior lecturer in history, philosophy, and German literature at The Hebrew University. He has recently published *Time and Transcendence: Secular History, the Catholic Reaction, and the Rediscovery of the Future*.

K. LUDWIG PFEIFFER is Professor of English at the Gesamthochschule, University of Siegen. He has published a book on George Meredith called *Bilder der Realität und die Realität der Bilder: Verbrauchte Formen in den Romanen George Merediths*.

KLAUS REICHERT is Professor of English and director of the Center of Renaissance Studies at the University of Frankfurt am Main. His publications in Renaissance studies include *Fortuna, oder die Beständigkeit des Wechsels*.

KARLHEINZ STIERLE is Professor of Romance Languages and Literatures at the University of Constance. He has recently published *Der Mythos von Paris: Zeichen und Bewußtsein der Stadt*.

THE TRANSLATABILITY
OF CULTURES

✛

Crises of Alterity:
Cultural Untranslatability and the
Experience of Secondary Otherness

Sanford Budick

*T*o a degree that was not foreseen, the essays in this volume engage in a collective critique of a single concept. That concept is alterity or, as we frequently say—yoking definiteness with indefiniteness—"the other." Aleida Assmann bespeaks our collective perplexity at the contemporary career of this concept when she observes, "From a menacing, anxiety-provoking term, 'the other' has become the central value of postmodern culture."[1] I do not wish to suggest that the following essays all argue a single view of the value of "the other" in various antecedent cultures or of what that value has now become in an apparently global postmodernism. In fact, these essays sometimes diverge dramatically on issues basic to our inquiry. (This is the case, for example, in Jan Assmann's and Moshe Barasch's different understandings of the phenomenon of syncretism. I shall broach this difference near the conclusion of these remarks.) Yet all these essays record, or even enact, an assortment of crises in the use of the concept of alterity. What is more, I believe that reflection upon our work points toward a reconceptualization of the experience of alterity. For reasons suggested (indirectly, at least) by the following essays, I will refer to this reconceived experience as *secondary otherness*.

Critical Conditions

First, however, a word about the venue of our work. These essays were written as contributions to the final stage of a collective research project entitled "The Institutions of Interpretation." In this last stage, the topic of our discussions went by the working title "The Mutual Translation of Cultures." Over the five or so years during which the stages of our work were planned and carried out in Jerusalem, a large core group (from Israel, Germany, and the United States)[2] remained constant, so that even new members soon entered into the continuity of our concerns. Some of the fruits of the earliest stage of this project, in which the problematics were being formulated, were collected in *Languages of the Unsayable: The Play of Negativity in Literature and Literary Theory*.[3] Essays from a later stage, when the work was fully under way, were gathered in a special number of *New Literary History*, with the title *The Institutions of Interpretation*.[4] The essays in these earlier volumes have multiple concerns. One common denominator, however, which was carried over into the final phase of our work, was the testing of various terminologies for describing "otherness." Concomitant with this testing there was, I believe, a growing unease with the easiness of the terminologies proposed. It became increasingly difficult to sustain even the subliminal hope that, whether anyone had yet achieved it, the use of an adequate semiotic technology could actually prompt a consciousness of the other. For many of us, I dare say, there was a dissonant ringing in the ear, the effect not only of some of our own words but of the haranguing, lately encountered virtually everywhere in books and journals of the humanities and social sciences, against any "discourse which would exclude alterity"[5]—as if anyone anywhere had even the slimmest proposal for a discourse that could *include* alterity. Aleida Assmann notes that "the transvaluation of values that is commonly associated with postmodernism . . . is characterized by the fundamentalization of plurality," a fundamentalization that is as mystified as other fundamentalisms. "The acknowledgment of alterity," she adds, "has become the foremost ethical claim," even though what might constitute an acknowledgment of such absolutely ungraspable alterity remains opaque. (Stanley Cavell's struggle with aversive acknowledgment, noted below, directly confronts this opacity.)

In fact, the process of fundamentalizing plurality may create uniformitarian biases. Thus a holy mating of self and other often seems to be an unspoken fantasy of a large part of contemporary cultural studies. We need to raise questions, for example, about the implications of James Clifford's much-invoked version of a "mutual" translation of cultures.[6] It is true that Clifford formulates an ideal of disinterestedness when he speaks of a translation between cultures that would only be "a liberation and revivification of meanings latent in each other." Yet in practice the translation that Clifford recommends is a melting of self and other toward sameness.

(Clifford's exemplar, Maurice Leenhardt—missionary to the New Cale-
donians—is shown to have "broadened the God of European orthodoxy,"
among other ways, by making him "less transcendent" and more "to-
temic.")[7] Given the multiple local contexts of our discussions in Jerusalem—Arab and Israeli, Christian and Jewish, Jewish and German—we
were perhaps more than usually concerned with forces that press toward
cultural sameness or convergence, not least in dialogic models of self and
other.

In retrospect it seems to me that the work of clarification in which we
engaged crept up on us very much at the rate we acknowledged the particular crisis that, for our group, especially tended to contextualize discussion. This was the encounter between German and Jewish culture
which, on the one hand, had so substantially contributed to the formation
of modern institutions of interpretation (in theology, Bible criticism, ethics, psychoanalysis, Marxism, theories of revolution, arguably even in
physics) yet which, on the other hand, finally opened one of the deepest
abysses in the entire history of culture. One way or another, and whether
or not we defined our subjects specifically in "German-Jewish" terms, this
datable cataclysm in modern culture was inevitably being confronted,
however obliquely, in our individual contributions. For most of us it took
some time to acknowledge this critical condition of our undertakings. In
our discussions there was no sequential emergence of the developing line
of thought I sketch below. Yet I believe that the contours of such a conse-
quentiality very much inform what actually occurred. Forms of attention
to intellectual history and to logical explanation interact here to create specific terminologies. Indeed, what I have to say in these introductory pages
runs the risk of seeming to reduce the language of the following essays to
jargon. The best way to avert this is to ask the reader to read the essays
themselves, as soon as possible, in order to retrieve the concrete problems
that their authors address.

Gabriel Motzkin sets the stage of the crisis in which we operate when
he notes that otherness can now allegedly "be integrated into self without
confronting the absolute otherness of the other." This slippage in the term
"the other" is now virtually universal, Motzkin believes, yet the German
case of this slippage is uniquely abrupt. Since, he explains, "the self is constituted in such a way that its identity is mediated by the memory of the
other," "the absence of the memory of the other," during and (in different
ways) after the Holocaust, has alienated Germans "from their own recent
past." As a result, they seek ways of "establishing continuity in memory

around the gap in their history created by the Nazi years." (Motzkin suggests that current disturbances in Germany are partly an effect of this crisis in memory.) In non-German experience of the same crisis, Motzkin highlights parallel phenomena and their shifting complexities:

Except for the Germans, the Germans are the other for all the peoples who fought in the war on either side, even if the Germans are a different other for each of the respective peoples. And how do the peoples remember the Germans, irrespective of their attitude to the Germans of today? In all cases, the memory of the Germans is associated with the Holocaust. Thus they (the French, the Danes, or the Dutch) were fighting the people who murdered the Jews, irrespective of their attitude to the Jews.

. . . The Holocaust becomes . . . a universal myth of origin, a universal collective memory, a founding event . . . in the historical self-interpretation of the postmodern period.

As Aleida Assmann would be the first to acknowledge, the realities touched upon in Motzkin's remarks only deepen our perplexity about what it can possibly mean that " 'the other' has become the central value of postmodern culture" when "otherness" has now largely become a trick for seeming to include "the other" in our discourses of self, even while we fail to confront the absolute impossibility of embracing the otherness of the other. Ludwig Pfeiffer's essay on Japanese culture and/or the western experience of Japanese culture makes a similar point: acknowledgments of the most "radical otherness" create the illusion that we have actually, somehow, leapt over "difference." It is at this illusory juncture in our discourses of the other that crisis itself becomes our best hope.

Wolfgang Iser injected the term "crisis" into our discussions most forcefully. He did so having decided that his own essay, on Carlyle's *Sartor Resartus*, would attempt our common subject only at one remove from the framing subject itself. A decorum of dual referentiality is therefore at play in Iser's paper. His most immediate interest is "the crisis of a defunct society" after the Industrial Revolution. Yet his remarks apply with at least equal resonance (even when the symmetries are approximate) to the crisis of a defunct German culture, and perhaps even more generally to the crisis of defunct culture of the postmodern period, that is, in the vacuum of values (not merely in Germany) signaled by German fascism:

Cultural critique [is] sparked off by a crisis of culture that had not been in the orbit of those who had pleaded the superiority of their own culture. . . .

The experience of crisis splits culture itself apart, and such a process began to deepen and accelerate with the dawn of the Industrial Revolution. Fundamental differences opened up in individual cultures, not least through the experience of an all-pervading rift that divided a culture into an inaccessible past and a helplessly stricken present. A past cut off from the present is pushed back into an irredeemable pastness. . . .

Whereas a culture's "management of crisis" is ideally part of a feedback mechanism that leads to a new arrangement of "the mastery of life," Iser's meditation on Professor Teufelsdröckh's (Devil's-Dung's) crisis management ends open-endedly with Carlyle's description of Teufelsdröckh "lost in space" at Weissnichtwo (know not where), not at Eden, having himself prophesied, "*Es geht an* (It is beginning)." From this final crisis, a genesis of an unforeseeable kind has been precipitated.

From Iser's essay another question necessarily follows: What factor, inherent in the experience of culture, might trigger the crisis of culture in the first place? In fact, since no one has yet located a culture that is not, at any given moment, in severe crisis of one kind or another, the question becomes: What factor, inherent in the experience of culture, triggers cultural crisis continually?

It appears likely that the genesis Iser emphasizes has something to do with the urgent need to encounter otherness. At least some such conception, bordering on an account of crisis, is one collective implication of most, if not all, of the essays in this volume, including (at least by implication) Iser's own. "Crisis" or its equivalent emerges in this volume as a term of self-reflection. First, it names the failure of culture, in relation to otherness, that was the frame of our undertaking. Second, it predicts the disruptions of dialogue to which our discussions were sometimes subject, if only because it was painful to talk directly about our experience of this particular crisis. Third, it identifies a circle of cultural exigency and quest for otherness that is as unpredictable in its effects as it is vicious. Last, and least foreseeably, crisis functions here in its self-transformative aspect. The end of any crisis is different from its beginning, yet both the beginning and the end are parts of the crisis. Sometimes the end of a crisis may signal a wholly new beginning. In these essays the possibility is intermittently glimpsed of a crisis that might itself recast the meaning of "the other."

Even without the prompting of etymologies most of us would agree that a crisis involves a sense of imminent or immediate loss. It also entails a painful sorting out among the elements of what we consider to be reality, so that a choosing or deciding seems unavoidable. These elements of meaning are, indeed, all embedded in the Greek words *krinein*, to separate, decide, judge, and *keirein*, to cut, shear, from which "crisis" and its cognates "certain" and "shear" derive. The implications of these connections for a serious criticism, born of crisis, can be startling. Indeed, in contemplating these essays one is struck by the degree to which, in the arguments of the essays themselves, crisis and criticism (and critique) are not merely cognate words but twinborn phenomena. Perhaps this is not really surprising. A criticism that is worth talking about for any length of time cannot be the product merely of a yen for commentary. Criticism as such is itself the occurrence of a crisis in thinking and writing. What we call serious criticism is occasioned when something formerly considered significant has been lost or cut off in our understanding, so that a separation (or clarification) and decision must be made. In our group's case, what was sheared off is the claim to be able to speak of "the other." The choice of a new term was not immediately obvious, although various pointings were clearly noticeable. I will have more to say about this in a moment, but I turn first to another element of crisis: the split status of both the text and the reader.

This split makes for a large part of the formative "pain" of philosophy—"the pain of recognizing oneself in change"—which the philosopher and critic Stanley Cavell describes in his analyses in this volume. Cavell's essay is the record of a crisis in his reading of Emerson's silence on slavery (in "Fate"), mediated by Heidegger's silence (in all his philosophical writings) on the Holocaust. Cavell's experience of this crisis is all the more self-consciously painful, one might add, because no one has done more than Cavell to explain the philosophical seriousness of Emerson's thinking or to establish his status as the founding father of American thought. Cavell has shown that Emerson conceives of the self and of thinking as inherently split or what Cavell calls "aversive." Cavell develops this term from his interpretation of Emerson's sentence, "Self-reliance is [the] aversion [of conformity]":

Emerson finds that conformity is the virtue in most request—by which he means it is the primary force of our social existence. By "self-reliance" I take him, correspondingly, to mean the essay of that title, and by synecdoche, his individual body of writing. So for him to say "self-reliance is the aversion of conformity" is to say that his writing and his society incessantly recoil from, or turn away from one another; but since this is incessant, the picture is at the same time of each incessantly turning *toward* the other.

Having explained, further, that "Emerson characterizes thinking as marked by transfiguration and by conversion" in a picture of this kind, Cavell shows that Emerson was such an "other" in whose presence Heidegger stood. In a different but related turn of the same screw, he demonstrates that our reception of Emerson is necessarily "mediated by philosophers of the powers of Nietzsche and of Heidegger." In the wake of Emerson's and Heidegger's silences, grave questions necessarily threaten

Cavell's hopes for the role of the other in American culture. In particular, the entire activity of being returned to a part of one's self by "the other," which Emersonian philosophy promises, is placed in severe doubt. One possible result that Cavell hypothesizes is that "the way of philosophy I care about most is *as such* compromised."

Sacvan Bercovitch shares Cavell's sense of an American crisis. Partly because of the Emersonian heritage they have in common, Bercovitch's struggle against a self-aggrandizing "romance quest for the subversive" illuminates Cavell's crisis of an aversive thinking of alterity. The "romance quest for the subversive" pretends to the magical production of an alterity upon which it in fact has no purchase. Bercovitch is in flight from a "beatification of the subversive," which confuses "literary analysis with social action" while it enjoys an "alliance between radicalism and upward mobility in the profession." By reflecting upon Kafka's resistance to the hypostatizations within German culture, Bercovitch retraces his own attempts to elude the enticements of American "oppositional" criticism, which in effect claims to be a mechanism for summoning the spirit of otherness. Bercovitch lives out the crisis brewing in "the Emersonian re-vision of individualism as the mandate both for permanent resistance and for American identity." Yet this same crisis propels Bercovitch to a position of opposition to oppositionalism itself, since his critical condition is to remain always the interested outsider, crossing back and forth between inside and outside. For him the real issue of American-Emersonian individualism is "not co-optation or dissent," but "varieties of co-optation/dissent." Permanently the borderer, he is satisfied with "a different sense of wonder," one that is implicit in the slant he registers within the compound "co-optation/dissent." This slant on wonder, we may say, is not a subversive "open sesame" that can open the other to us. Bercovitch explains that "in its proper prosaic terms" it is only coextensive with "a critical method designed to illuminate the conflicts implicit in border crossing, and to draw out their unresolved complementarities." We cannot predict the sorts of crises that this method produces. Yet at least a method of this kind may help us elude the illusions of the subversive.

"The Self-same Song"

There is a fascinating parallel between Bercovitch's "sense of wonder" experienced in "border crossing" and J. Hillis Miller's affirmation of the phenomenon of the "unforeseeable" that is generated at the "border crossings" between cultures. Like Bercovitch's, Miller's critical method would elude pseudo-predictions—in this case by theory—about the other, especially about the other's applications of theory. Miller's paradigm for the coming into being of the "unforeseeable" is the multifarious circulation, among cultures, of the book of Ruth. For Miller Ruth is "a narrative of alienation and assimilation that can exemplify theoretical propositions about the travel of theory," particularly, that is, about its unpredictability. What interests Miller about Ruth is, then, its intercultural vicissitudes:

> What has happened to the text of Ruth (as opposed to what happens within the story) is . . . exemplary of the fate of theory. This book of the Hebrew Bible has been alienated from itself, translated from itself. It has been put to entirely new uses, uses by no means intended by the original authors or scribes. The first and foremost alienation (after all the changes that made the story of Ruth a sacred text in the Hebrew Bible) was, of course, the assimilation of Ruth into the Christian Bible. . . . Legitimating the claim of Jesus to be the Messiah . . . is its "theoretical" function in the Christian Bible.

The multicultural use of the book of Ruth is for Miller confirmation of his view that "the vitality of theory is to be open to . . . unforeseeable transformations and to bring them about as it crosses borders." In this sense, Miller's conception of the way theory travels back and forth across cultural borders is similar to Bercovitch's sense of wonder at various American border crossings—as well as to much else that seems to me of special importance in the crises of alterity witnessed in this volume. In fact, I would like to linger on this matter for a moment in order to emphasize that these "unforeseeable transformations" occur as much at the points of border crossing as they do in the perusable forms of transformation on either side of the border.

Miller testifies to his own experience of this unforeseeability (as if he were himself, with his different sorts of understanding, a kind of border crossing) when he writes, "The theoretical insight is a glimpse out of the corner of the eye of the way language works, a glimpse that is not wholly amenable to conceptualization." With regard to the collective inquiry gathered in this volume, I offer a translation of Miller's theory of this unforeseeable dimension of translating theory. It is likely that what I propose is a mistranslation of Miller's theory. Even if this is the case, however, my mistranslation will serve as confirmation of Miller's ancillary notion that mistranslation of theory, in the action of crossing borders, is inherent in theory itself. This is a large part of theory's unforeseeable quality, or wonder. The point that I wish to make, in any case, concerns the writer's and the interpreter's experiences of actively undoing foresight (subversive foresight, for example) of the other.

Among the examples Miller discusses is the "mistranslation or violent appropriation of Ruth" that occurs in Keats's "Ode to a Nightingale." Speaking of the nightingale's song, the poet speculates that this was

> Perhaps the self-same song that found a path
>   Through the sad heart of Ruth, when, sick for home,
>   She stood in tears amid the alien corn;
>   The same that oft-times hath
>   Charm'd magic casements, opening on the foam
>   Of perilous seas, in faery lands forlorn.

Miller's comment on the passage is most apt: "It associates Ruth with Keats's general presentation of the human situation as forlorn, derelict, haunted by death, even 'half in love with easeful Death' (l. 52). This pathos of alienation, however, has no biblical precedent. It is all Keats's invention. It is his translation, or mistranslation, of the story of Ruth for his own quite different purposes."

My point about the traveling of theory in these lines has to do with the fact that the last word, "forlorn," which seems to define the outer border of the new territory that Keats has reached, is tolled twice. Here are the lines, after a stanza break, immediately following the ones quoted above:

> Forlorn! the very word is like a bell
>   To toll me back from thee to my sole self!
> Adieu! the fancy cannot cheat so well
>   As she is fam'd to do, deceiving elf.

The bell, or more precisely the unseen tongue of the bell,[8] swings in opposite directions, as if from self-possession to loss and then from loss to a kind of hyper- or secondary condition of loss which may yet promise a form of self-possession. I suggest that in this two-way movement Keats recapitulates part of the cultural history of theorizing Ruth, even making a point about the border that is crossed in two directions. That is, what I am calling, by reading Keats, opposite directions of theorizing Ruth are the directly reversed meanings to which the word "forlorn" is attached. In the first movement (very much parallel to the alienation of the book of Ruth from Judaic to Christian purposes) the condition of being alienated is relocated in the Judaean territory where Ruth now abides, while what is apparently alien (the non-Judaean or gentile) is endowed with the power of the true "home." In relation to this home, the nostalgia of this nightingale song of the not-here is associated with a power of "opening" or liberating that has "faery" or magical dimensions, not least perhaps because it is a magic of being "forlorn"—forsaken in a particularly "immortal" (l. 61)

way, for the benefit of humankind. The nightingale, accordingly, is a kind
of messiah of otherness.

However, hardly have these magical sounds ceased to vibrate in our
ears when the same word tolls out with very much the opposite meaning.
Now "forlorn" is explicitly said to mean the collapse of otherness back into
mere self or "sole self" (as if back into a Judaic insularity from the gentiles
whom Jesus comes to save). Now the poet's reality is to know that he has
no access to "thee." That is, his reality is to know that he has no access to
either the nightingale or its song of a faery, alien, opening power. His fancy
is only part of himself, a deceiving "elf" (pretending to offer, or even *be*,
the alien) that cannot exceed the boundaries of the "(s)elf." Once we have
this second thought, it turns out that this grim tolling of the "sole self" was
already contained in the song of the "self-same" that the poet mistook for
the repeating "self-same song" of an "alien" power that might transport
him, liberate him, from himself. The tongue of the bell, language itself,
switches, even as "Adieu!" is a switching of tongues (commending someone to a divinity—*ad* + *Dieu*—of a different culture) across a channel divide.

Yet this Keatsian story of translation of theory does not end even here.
"Adieu!" is for Keats another signal of crisis and transformation (what
Emerson, in Cavell's reading of him, might identify as conversion). Crossing (and recrossing) the border between Keats's two theories—that is, of a
self that is negatively capable of singing the other and of a self that can only
(as Keats represents the theory) duplicate itself—produces unforeseeable
transformations. If this is the case, the large gap on the page between the
two writings of the word "forlorn" may represent a kind of escape from
representation, an "easeful Death" within life or at least within the double
tolling of language, as if located in the in-between time frame where the
crisis breaks. Of course, we can never know what this blank is. The one
thing of which we can be sure is that this other otherness is associated with
the crisis of failing to know otherness. No one who experiences this crisis
can fancy that he or she has somehow acknowledged alterity. (That would
be to cheat ourselves painfully.) Since the course of this crisis is only set in
motion when we take something like the very reverse of the view of reality
we now hold, the final results of this full round of experience could not be
more unforeseeable, or further beyond conceptualization. This secondary
achievement of alienation is alienated, with absolute severity, even from
the concept of the alien. This is no more than a secondary phenomenon, it
is true. Yet it decisively disallows imagination of the other, which also

means any allegedly outside confirmation of what we take to be knowledge or imagination of the self.

If this reading of a secondary removal of meaning (especially of the other) in Keats's poem sounds fantastic, it may be, in part, because it is closely related to the genre of the fantastic itself. A second-removal, or crisis, of alienation is characteristic not only of the genre of the fantastic as such but of its proliferations, as one element, within many other genres. Renate Lachmann usefully describes the fantastic as an interference with cultural binarisms, especially of self and other:

The transformation of the forgotten or repressed into the heterocultural . . . does not take place within the confines of a clear-cut binary model but is acted out as a permanent transgression of the boundaries between present and absent, true and false, and it is this very figure of ambivalence that makes the fantastic mode of writing a conceptual force, disturbingly interfering with the models a culture produces in order to come to terms with its "other."

If we take into account here Lawrence Besserman's explanation of the fundamental "ambivalence" that lurks within the historical relations of biblical and secular poetics, from Augustine to Chaucer at least, we glimpse this fantastical, unforeseeable element in a thousand years of European literature. Besserman portrays a kind of silent crisis engendered by the perceived impossibility of a fluid exchange between sacred and profane. Categories of "biblical" and "secular" poetics cannot serve as each other's "other." The effect of interference, within cultural binarisms, in this medieval form of ambivalence is that alterity is transformed into something disturbingly different from either biblical or nonbiblical, secular or nonsecular.

Karlheinz Stierle retrieves a long history of relations between the self and the other by unraveling the philological filaments of the term "translation" itself, in its several metamorphoses within Romance languages. In Stierle's account the term itself harbors a crisis of translation, specifically a crisis in attempting to translate the other. Translation necessarily marks the border crossing where, if anywhere, one culture passes over to the other, whether to inform it, to further its development, to capture or enslave it, or merely to open a space between the other and itself. Stierle's canvas is Romance philology, but like many others in this volume, he too has one eye on the phenomena of translation or mistranslation that constitute German-Jewish relations. Stierle openly voices this parallel concern in his closing appeal. In this epilogue, the options of European translatability that seem to him most authentic are offered as one kind of German-Jewish hope.

There is a good deal of symmetry between the kinds of failures in translation that are on Stierle's mind. He explains that the meaning of *transferre*, *translatio* was from the beginning a relation between subject and object, not between subject and subject. Translation of empire, of wisdom, of study, was until the Renaissance almost exclusively vertical and hierarchical, although it sometimes did invite an unfolding in the future and the participation of the receiver. The development of courtly love and the language of *cortoisie* marks a pre-Renaissance experiment with horizontality and mutual translation, especially in "a new communicative attitude toward women." With Petrarch (inspired by hints from Dante) a horizontal translation of translation into *renaissance* decisively emerges. Now the self is deemed capable of "looking back and forth at the same time" within a "complex copresence." Stierle is well aware that many readers are skeptical of the active participation of the beloved in Petrarch's experience (in which Petrarch often seems to be both self and other), but for Stierle Petrarch is still historically the first writer "to live in different worlds and to enjoy the complexity of this experience. The experience of the copresence of cultures is perhaps the most important aspect of what we call Renaissance. It is the fundamental plurality . . . of a new dimension of dialogue. With Petrarch begins the dominance of the horizontal over the vertical axis of *translatio*." Clearly Stierle casts his eye from Petrarch all the way to Martin Buber in extolling the possibilities of dialogue, yet he is well aware of the failures, all along the line, of models of dialogicity and/or plurality. In Montaigne's dialogic attempts Stierle detects an awareness of "the tragedy of a mutual translation of cultures." Following George Steiner, a most appropriate European-Jewish voice, Stierle dreams of reviving Dante's highest evolution of the concept of cultural translation in his version of "cortesia." This "cortesia" among cultures is an expression of art's "essential negativity," its "effort of understanding which is never in danger of blind identification" or domination because the focus of its effort is exactly to leave open "the space of understanding." Stierle acknowledges that, to be of use in our era, "cortesia" would have to be rendered within a severely chastened realism, standing before an "inconceivable mountain of guilt, disaster, and suffering." In fact, citing Steiner's wilderness-call for Dante's ideal of cultural translatability constitutes Stierle's act of identification with Steiner's utopian longing for the space that would hold off the invasions of cultures. Steiner's longing, we may add, is closely related to his crisis condition as

Jew and European, permanently relegated to a border crossing. The word "u-topia" (no-place), or its equivalent, is always the naming of a crisis in which the ground on which one stands has disappeared.

If ever there was a utopian German Jewish attempt to create a "cortesia" it was, as Klaus Reichert shows, Martin Buber's and Franz Rosenzweig's German translation of the Hebrew Bible. Reichert makes clear how central to this work was the ideal of dialogicity that is well known from Buber's *I and Thou*. In addition to reminding us that Gershom Scholem was among the first to criticize "the utopian element" in the Buber-Rosenzweig translation, Reichert explains that their goal was "to be a Jew *and* a German, self and other, without appropriation," to "keep open the distances" by, in fact, "colonizing the space between two cultures." This was to be the paradoxical realization of the two-culture theory that Rosenzweig shared with Hermann Cohen. Scholem spoke of Rosenzweig's "magic wish for a deeper and deeper marriage with the *German*: a *disaster* for the Jewish perspective." Reichert notes the parallel between Rosenzweig's longing for this marriage and Heidegger's "holy mating of the Greek and German spirit." The Bible translation was designed to convert the "alienation" of one's own language into a "renewal" in the medium of "what had been fully unfolded in another language." Reichert reminds us of the perspectives offered by Motzkin when he shows that in practice the translation was an attempt "to build up, or invent, an otherness as an offer of a new identity."

Upon the occasion of the completion of the full Bible translation in 1961, Scholem eulogized it in Jerusalem with the following words: "It was something like the present of a guest, which the German Jews left to the German people in a symbolic act of gratitude in the moment of departure. . . . The present has turned into the tombstone of a relationship, extinguished by unspeakable horrors." It helps make visible the sign of crisis under which the entire translation exists that after Scholem's speech, Buber remarked to Nechama Leibowitch, "You know, the trouble with Scholem is that he does not believe in Germany." Reichert follows Scholem in acknowledging the "fallacious" hope, the "magic wish," that a new otherness could really be created for Germans, or for Jews in their relation to Germans. He makes an additional, crucial point that has reverberations for all the essays in this volume. Even if it was manifestly impossible to reach, or create, a genuine otherness, something, he says, was in fact achieved in the space opened up by this "twofold act of negation": "Like any magic wish it reaches beyond itself. To have concretized the fundamental untranslatability of the text indicates this Beyond." Reichert is obviously more hopeful about the use of this experience of untranslatability than was Scholem. Insofar, however, as it might represent an undoing of the cheat of a hypostatized Beyond, this kind of experience is within the orbit of hope described by many other authors in this volume.

A picture of undoing the cheat of an alleged otherness, and a glimpse, as well, of the work of culture made possible by this undoing, emerges in Emily Miller Budick's account of Lionel Trilling. In Budick's view, Trilling confronted the failure, vis-à-vis the Jews, of that development of German Hegelianism called Marxism. Trilling's conception of what the Marxist dialectic could not encompass is precisely a "respect for 'being'" which Trilling experiences as a "Judaic quality." Trilling, Emily Budick explains, aims at reinstating a certain distance from being (or the other), even though being itself remains unfixable and unknowable. He works to recover "an idea of being that is not only irreducible, but nontranslatable." This kind of distance from "being" measures the gulf between the poles of any human "relationality." The distance is experienced by establishing a relationship of "resistance to essentialisms" of self and other. What Emily Budick calls Trilling's "Holocaust-inflected" speech or his respectful way of "speaking in silence" establishes the function of untranslatability in the construction of culture. It returns us to the crisis of failing to know the other. Culture can begin only from that failure, hopefully in a less than lethal form.

This critical distance, or respect, before another's being, which is not at all the same thing as knowing, or even directly acknowledging being ("the other") itself, is a vital phenomenon in the relationships among others, whether between cultures or within an internally differentiated culture. In crisis we come to recognize that this phenomenon offers no approach to otherness per se. This phenomenon is only the reflection of our need for otherness, only, let us say, a highly secondary otherness. Yet, for all that, secondary otherness of this kind is that which may enable coexistence with others as well as participation in creating culture. Further clarification of a concept of secondary otherness is available from the conversation we may hear between Jan Assmann's and Moshe Barasch's discussions of syncretism.

Secondary Otherness

I believe that Jan Assmann makes it possible for us to see that the larger element of crisis which confronts us, in various essays of this volume, is inherently the crisis brought about by trying to imagine, and necessarily failing to imagine, "the other." Assmann borrows Erik Erikson's term "pseudo-speciation" and develops, beyond it, his own salient counteraccount of a historical, psychological, and religious "secondary pseudo-speciation." He explains that by itself Erikson's term pseudo-speciation describes "the formation of artificial subgroups within the same biological species. In the human world, pseudo-speciation is the effect of cultural differentiation. The formation of cultural specificity and identity necessarily produces difference and otherness vis-à-vis other groups. This can result in the elaboration of absolute strangeness, isolation, avoidance, and even abomination." Assmann shows that the history of polytheistic and cosmotheistic religions (including cosmotheistic monotheism) is accounted for by the "principles of pseudo-speciation . . . counterbalanced by cultures of translation." The result of this counterbalancing was that religions of these kinds actively promoted translatability. They "functioned as a paradigm of how living in a common world was conceivable and communicable. The complete translatability of gods founded a consciousness of dealing with basically the same species in spite of all other kinds of cultural alterity." This paradigm, in other words, confirmed pseudo-speciation by making the grounds of translatability the pseudo-equation between self and other while at the same time, of course, abominating the pseudo-image of the other who resists translatability. In an aside, Assmann remarks that German fascism "naturalized the effects of pseudo-speciation" in its racism against the Jews.

Assmann calls attention, however, to a totally different paradigm that was also available in the ancient world. In this paradigm religion becomes a "factor of cultural untranslatability." Paradoxically, an unforeseeable "secondary" phenomenon in these religions enables, and even sustains, "normative self-definition." The difference made by this paradigm is subtle but historically real—and potentially of immense cultural significance:

Here we are dealing with what may be interpreted as an "immune reaction" of the cultural system, a tendency to build up a deliberate "counteridentity" against the dominating system. The cultural system is intensified in terms of counterdistinctivity. This mechanism may be called second-degree pseudo-speciation, to be distinguished from normal pseudo-speciation, which occurs always and everywhere. Second-degree or counterdistinctive pseudo-speciation, however, occurs mostly under minority conditions. Identity then turns normative, based on "normative self-definition." It is typically under these conditions of resistance to political and cultural domination that religions of a new type emerge which I would like to call "second-degree" or "secondary" religions. These religions defy translatability. They are entered via conversion and left via apostasy.

. . . The Jewish paradigm is the most ancient and the most typical; perhaps it is also the model and origin of all or most other cases. . . .

. . . The god of Israel . . . does not say "I am everything" but "I am who I am," negating by this expression every referent, every *tertium comparationis*, and every translatability.

Culturally speaking, the "normative self-definition" of the Jew (or the Christian) depends upon this untranslatability. This complex of ancient ideas corresponds closely to Trilling's notion of culture as that which guarantees the possibility of such independent, normative self-definition. It also confirms his historical intuition that respecting or guaranteeing being in this way is a "Judaic quality" (in Wordsworth the Christian, as well). In this view, the other cannot be or become self. Here conversion marks the border of untranslatability and implies the impossibility of imagining the other. At the same time, culture informed by this "Judaic quality" insures that conversion does not become a function of force. It may well be that Trilling's idea of culture that would guarantee this irreducible untranslatability, influenced by the Emersonian concept of aversion, is a vision of continual crisis of this sort. Culture of this kind is an encounter of safeguarded untranslatabilities, not a carrying out, or ferrying across borders, of translation. At the heart of culture in this key is the paradox that, in Assmann's terms, although identity is first engendered by counterdistinctivity and pseudo-speciation, it can become an independent "normative self-definition" because of the experience of a hyperalienation—or "secondary pseudo-speciation."

Assmann's idea of a secondary pseudo-speciation that produces normative self-definition has even a further potential which may be discovered by considering the difference between his and Moshe Barasch's views of the phenomenon of syncretism in Hellenistic Egyptian culture. For Assmann syncretism cannot be a feature of secondary religions in themselves because these kinds of religions assume the absolute untranslatability of normative self-definition. For Assmann (here following G. W. Bowersock) syncretism always requires translation into a "third language" (like Hellenism). "Syncretism," he believes, "requires or offers double membership: one in a native culture and one in a general culture." Assmann sees an important opportunity in this syncretistic hypothesis, though for him too it seems to be essentially utopian—or at least untested since Hellenistic times.

Barasch views the same syncretistic phenomena very differently. He views them, in fact, in a way that is actually conformable to Assmann's paradigm of secondary religions which are defined by absolute untranslatability and independent, normative self-definition.

The object of study that prompts Barasch's account is a funerary stele from the third or fourth century C.E. discovered in Lower Egypt. What particularly interests Barasch in the stele is that "both the combination of different techniques and the ambiguities in reading the image depicted on the stele visually manifest what was perhaps the central theme that occupied the mind of Egypt at the time—the interaction, conflictual as well as mutually complementary, of different cultures." (This recalls Bercovitch's focus on "the conflicts implicit in border crossing" together with "their unresolved complementarities.") For Barasch the feature of the stele that defines it as one particularly important kind of syncretistic work of art is "the tilting, or reversible, image." Here

the signs and traces of different and even clashing religions . . . are obscured by an ambiguity in the indication of the spiritual world to which the work of art belongs and which it expresses. It is this ambiguity that makes it possible for the object to be read in different ways, and it is in the spectator's experience that the work becomes located in the one or the other religion.

I would emphasize that Barasch believes that at any given moment the stele can only be read in terms of "one" or "the other" religion, that is, not simultaneously or in terms of both together. There is a "gap opened up by these contrasting orientations." The gap marks a border that may be crossed over by the choices made in "the spectator's reading": "he focuses on certain features and neglects, or even completely disregards, others." Barasch's discrimination of the opening of this gap of "real difference" between the two readings seems to be particularly suggestive. In fact, he locates the specific element of the stele that evokes the tilt, either of two different ways, in the spectator's response:

If the beholder focused on the fact of the sunk relief, a feature known to late antiquity only from ancient Egyptian art and considered a hallmark of that pre-Christian culture, he might have been inclined to interpret the figure as part of a pagan ritual. If, on the other hand, he focused his attention on the "round" carving within the sunk relief, he would have emphasized in his mind the Greek, western attitude, and around or after A.D. 300 this would have suggested to him a Christian meaning of the image.

I would like to reflect on a number of Barasch's points about this critical juncture, especially because of their potential explanatory power with regard to many issues in this volume. Primarily, I will try to bring together Jan Assmann's idea of secondary pseudo-speciation with the phenomena observed by Barasch. I believe Barasch describes something like the cultural function of the crisis of pseudo-speciation.

Without assigning a particular cultural meaning or allegory to "the fact of the sunk relief," we may yet see that what was depicted here in the play of emptiness and fullness had distinct importance for each of the two cultures involved. At the same time, this play was a key feature in another activity in which each culture was engaged, namely, the turning from one culture toward the other. Focusing on the traces of this turning, Barasch sees an "awareness of the 'otherness' of the surrounding culture and creed," "an interacting with other creeds and cultures," in this case built in, in two directions, in a single complex structure. It may strain belief to be asked to grant that we encounter phenomena of such complexity in a work that seems to be (as Barasch continually says) so modest. Yet it is only plausible to assume that the Terenouthis stele can embody such complexity because it stands at the junction of powerful cultural forces, forces no less powerful, indeed, than the variety of contradictory forces that press upon the book of Ruth, Keats's "Ode to a Nightingale," Montaigne's and Emerson's essays, Carlyle's *Sartor Resartus*, or the Buber-Rosenzweig German translation of the Hebrew Bible. At such junctions we may come upon the intercultural manifestations of the human need to construct consciousness in the neighborhood of an other which cannot possibly be known. For such neighboring of consciousness, which no one partner possesses, "meaning"—implying, at least, something that can finally be spelled out by an individual speller—must be too crude a term. Even without speaking of meaning, we can, however, say something more about the activity in which a neighboring of consciousness is shared among selves and others, or between cultures. In the case of Barasch's careful description of his Terenouthis example, perhaps we can also suggest where this activity might be located.

Still avoiding allegorization, we may venture to say, for instance, that the sunken relief has a remarkable function in the "interaction, conflictual as well as mutually complementary, of different cultures." I refer to the tilting feature that Barasch locates in the hollowed-out space where an either/or representation occurs. This particular hollowed-out space leads the mind of one spectator in one direction, of another spectator in another direction: either, say, to an Egyptian self-interpretation emphasizing the uniquely Egyptian feature of the hollowed-out space itself; or the very different other, Christian self-interpretation, mediated (as Barasch shows) by Greek ideas of fullness of volume, that operates somewhere in the realm of contemplation or imitation of the figure of Christ. Perhaps we can add that this latter interpretation involves specifically Christian views of the interplay of sacrifice and fulfillment. In both interpretations the hollowed-out space—of emptiness or fullness—seems to declare a negativity that is untranslatable.

While keeping in mind this dual function of the sunken relief, I wish to suggest that the interaction of different cultures that Barasch demonstrates for us in this stele closely resembles what Jan Assmann understands as the secondary pseudo-speciation that produces normative self-definition. Barasch has found, I suggest, an object that makes unmistakable the *double, two-way* occurrence of secondary pseudo-speciation.

Here I must interrupt myself to say that if the complexity of this terminology makes us wonder whether we are still speaking of things that actually occur in our lives, we may remind ourselves that a human being made this stele, with this complexity of features, at a "bloody crossroads" (to use Trilling's phrase for such encounters) where cultures meet—and may portend cultural annihilations. If we ignore or try to forget the events that may occur at that dangerous crossroads, we are giving up a portion of life itself. We do not have to send to the oracle to understand that plagues on the city ensue from such repression. In our terms this repression would be recognizable as yet another crisis of alterity, in repression. The crossroads feature of the encounter comprises both a danger and a potentiality, depending on how it is used. The need for cultural interaction of which Barasch speaks is as real as any other human need. Similarly, the pseudo-space hollowed out by the stele artist, enabling the tilt among normatively self-defined cultures, is as real as secondary pseudo-speciation itself. In each of the two cases contained in this one object, a totally untranslatable complex of another culture is speciated by the force of the hollow space or boundary. This hollow is also the space of secondary pseudo-speciation that enables mutual distancing and may set the stage for a neighboring of consciousness. In everyday realities this functioning of pseudo-entities can also be a fact of life, inhuman as this fact may seem. Our difficulty with this fact or configuration of a human reality is principally, indeed, that it seems unrelatable, as such, to anything specifically human, anything specific, that is, to anything that any one of us individually experiences. Yet this impersonal dimension of a secondary pseudo-speciation may also constitute a cultural opportunity.

I would like to recall a moment in the essays of Montaigne that also appears to be merely inhuman. This moment is especially enlightening in relation to Stierle's account of the way in which Montaigne attempted to create models of dialogicity while realizing that such models were most often doomed to demonstrating only "the tragedy of a mutual translation

of cultures." In recent essays, Joshua Scodel and Jean Starobinski have suggested that Montaigne's model of dialogicity was actually chiastic rather
than dual in nature,[9] meaning that the positions in the dialogue occupied
by self and other are each significantly self-skeptical or inherently dual and,
we may add, that these fragmentary positions themselves (all four of them)
rotate upon a space of negativity. As an example of this complex situation,
always bordering on something which is in itself not human, I instance
Montaigne's "Of Cannibals," in which the cannibalizing of a primitive culture by European culture is as much Montaigne's subject (and perhaps as
much Montaigne's own activity in writing) as the cannibalistic way of life
of the primitive culture (in which selves invade, and ingest, others). European culture fails to understand itself (its own cannibalistic ways) as well
as the normative self-definition of the primitive culture. Montaigne's
tongue in his own cheek implies at the same time that the wise primitives
are similarly impercipient.

If there is any area of hope in Montaigne's essay it may be signaled by
the offhand parenthesis (spoken as if from the gut about an unpalatable
thing which has nonetheless been ingested) in which Montaigne informs
us that, though he does not himself understand the language of the cannibals, "they have a way in their language of speaking of men as halves of
one another."[10] In Montaigne's thinking (and in many lines of thought that
his thinking inspired) this is certainly not an offhand idea. The relations
among human "halves of one another" is as consequential for his conception of a split self as it is for his notion of the way split selves can enter into
relation. The complementarities and contradictions of this highly specified
dialogicity, in other words, are chiastically structured, with all the effects
of a rotation around negativity that inhere in the figure of chiasmus. (In
"Of the Inconsistency of Our Actions," for example, he remarks that the
"supple variations and contradictions that are seen in us have made some
imagine that we have two souls"—"*zwei Seelen*," Goethe will say.[11] There
is a "gyration," notes Montaigne, around the "difference" that marks our
split condition. This split is distinctly chiastic or four-way. In Montaigne's
neat formula, "there is as much difference between us and ourselves as between us and others.")[12]

There is no easy way to sum up the meaning of this cultural complex.
This multiplex bordering on pure difference or negativity, I am suggesting,
coincides with the reciprocal secondary pseudo-speciation distinguished,
in one direction, by Jan Assmann and seen at work, simultaneously in two
directions, by Barasch. One of the benefits of noticing this constructed
framing of negativity is that it suggests that the experience of negativity is

not an automatic recognition that is always and everywhere available to thought. This recognition may, indeed, always be potential in experience or thought, yet it must be repeatedly earned, always with unforeseeable results, in a dimension of experience that is hyperalienated. By the same token, I would point out that the reciprocal potentials of this secondary pseudo-speciation are not identical with what Derrida calls differance or aporia, even if they have much to do with such phenomena. Differance undoubtedly occurs everywhere signs are used. The phenomena traced by Jan Assmann and Barasch occur only in a potential relatedness of half-selves or of cultures encountering each other as neighbors in the same object or situation.

What drives this relatedness is a crisis within pseudo-speciation or the imagining of alterity. Secondary pseudo-speciation and then secondary otherness are the effects of that crisis. These effects (as Derrida would also emphasize) can in no way be taken for the other. In human consciousness, this merely secondary otherness is a function of our failure to know the other. But the consequences of such failure are at least mutual. As a result of such mutuality, this very failure within consciousness may aid in creating the potentiality for a sharing of consciousness. (My own essay on chiasmus—in Goethe and Tasso—is concerned with how a potentiality of this sort is created.) It is as if a primary consciousness of self, together with a primary projection of self-as-other, is disallowed by the crisis of alterity, while a secondary consciousness, of a secondary otherness, as well as of a self apprehended secondarily in relation to that secondary otherness, come to the fore, creating the potentiality for an affiliation of selves. This potentiality is not realized by any individual alone. And even between individuals its realization is evanescent. Even there, it is always just coming together, just coming apart. Yet the experience of this potentiality by individuals, alone and side by side, is an impelling force of what we call culture.

It may be that a crisis experience of such secondary differentiations is implicit in Coleridge's famous description (in *Biographia Literaria*, chapter 13) of an ideal "primary imagination"—identified with the divine, absolute Self or "infinite I AM"—which must in effect be set aside for the "secondary imagination" by which we live. Whatever Coleridge meant by the relation of "primary" to "secondary imagination," it is clear in his remarks on the functioning of a secondary imagination that its divestiture of the self's projections of symbolic wholeness—as if in the creation of an other—amounts to a crisis theory of imagination.[13] "The imagination is called forth," says Coleridge, "not to produce a distinct form, but a strong working of the mind, still offering what is still repelled, and again creating what is again rejected."[14] In some measure Coleridge's secondary imagination is marked by its separation from both primary self and primary creation of otherness, both of which remain uniquely God's (the other's) capacities. Secondary imagination does not give us an infinite self or an infinite objective world produced as a human equivalent to God's other.

I refer, in closing, to the critical instability of Coleridge's term "secondary imagination" to suggest in yet one more way that the experience of secondary otherness, by whatever name we call it, is not a new invention. It has a long, indeed an ancient, history as part of culture, even if it is always an invisible part. Whenever we attempt to translate we are pitched into a crisis of alterity. The experience of secondary otherness then emerges from the encounter with untranslatability. Even if we are always defeated by translation, culture as a movement toward shared consciousness may emerge from the defeat. Thus the story of culture does not end with the experience of that which is nothing more than a secondary otherness. In fact, the multiple half-lives of affiliation known as culture may begin to be experienced, as potentialities, only there.

PERSPECTIVES
IN HISTORY

Translating Gods:
Religion as a Factor of
Cultural (Un)Translatability

Jan Assmann

Translation

*T*he Babylonians were the first to equate two gods by defining their common functional definition or cosmic manifestation.[1] We may call this method "theological onomasiology." By onomasiology is meant a method that starts from the referent and asks for the word, in opposition to semasiology, which starts from the word and asks for its meaning. Onomasiology is by definition cross-cultural and interlingual. Its aim is to find out how a given unit of meaning is expressed in different languages.

The Babylonians very naturally developed their "theological onomasiology" in the context of their general diglossia. Their constant concern for correlating Sumerian and Akkadian words brought them to extend this method into fields outside that of lexicography proper. But as long as this search for theological equations and equivalents was confined to the two languages, Sumerian and Akkadian, one could argue that it remained within the frame of a common religious culture. The translation here operates translingually but not transculturally. In the late Bronze Age, however, in the Cassite period, the lists are extended to include languages spoken by foreign peoples. There is an "explanatory list of gods" that gives divine names in Amoritic, Hurritic, Elamic, and Cassitic as well as Sumerian and Akkadian.[2] There are even lists translating theophorous proper names of persons.[3]

Among the lists from the private archives of Ugarit, a city-state on the northern Syrian coast, are quadrilingual vocabularies that contain Sumer-

ian, Akkadian, Hurritic (an Indo-European language), and Ugaritic (a
west Semitic language). Here, the translation concerns three fundamentally different religious cultures and consequentially meets with serious difficulties.[4] Sumero-Babylonian *Anum* (the god of heaven) is no problem: it
is rendered in Ugaritic by *shamuma* (heaven). But for *Antum*, his wife,
there is no linguistic equivalent in Ugaritic. It is obviously impossible to
invent a feminine form of *shamuma*. Therefore a theological equivalent is
found in the form of *Tamatum* (sea) which in Ugaritic mythology may act
as a feminine partner of heaven. The sun god, *utu* in Sumerian, *Shamash*
in Akkadian, *Shimigi* in Hurritic, is masculine; his feminine counterpart
is called *Aia* in Sumerian and *Ejan* in Hurritic. But the Ugaritic *Shapshu*,
notwithstanding its etymological identity with Akkadian *shamshu*, is a
feminine deity, for whom there has to be found a masculine counterpart.
Again, this problem requires a *theological* solution. Thus, the god Kothar,
the god of craftsmen and artisans, appears as a translation of the goddess
Aia!

    In these cases, there can be no doubt that the practice of translating
divine names was applied to very different cultures and religions. The conviction that these foreign peoples worshiped the same gods is far from trivial and self-evident. On the contrary, this insight must be reckoned among
the major cultural achievements of the ancient world. One of the main in-
centives for tolerance toward foreign religions can be identified in the field
of international law and the practice of forming treaties with other states
and peoples. This, too, seems a specialty of Mesopotamian culture. The
first treaties were formed between the Sumerian city-states of the third millenium B.C.E. With the rise of Ebla in northern Syria and with the Sargonid
conquests this practice soon extended far into the west, involving states
outside the cultural horizon of Mesopotamia. The Hittites, in the middle
of the second millenium, inherited this legal culture from the Babylonians
and developed new and much more elaborate forms of international contract.[5] The treaties they formed with their vassals had to be sealed by solemn oaths invoking gods of both parties. The list of these gods conven-
tionally closes the treaty. They had necessarily to be equivalent as to their
function and in particular to their rank. Intercultural theology thus became
a concern of international law. It seems to me probable that the interest in
translations and equations for gods of different religions arose in the context of foreign policy. We are here dealing with the incipient stages of "imperial translation" destined to reach all the politically dependent states,
tribes, and nations. Later, in the age of the great empires, official multilin-
gualism becomes a typical phenomenon.[6] The book of Esther tells us how
in the Persian empire royal commandments were sent to every province in

its own script and to every people in its own language. A similar practice seems already to be attested for the Assyrian empire. In this context belong the many bi- and trilingual royal decrees from Persia, Anatolia, and Egypt. Even the Buddhist king Asoka—roughly a contemporary of the Egyptian Manetho, the Babylonian Berossos, and the translators of the Hebrew Bible known as the Septuagint—published his edicts in Sanskrit, Aramaic, and Greek.[7]

During the last three millenia B.C.E., religion appears to have been the promoter of intercultural translatability. The argument for this function runs as follows: peoples, cultures, and political systems may be sharply different. But as long as they have a religion and worship some definite and identifiable gods, they are comparable and contactable because these gods must necessarily be the same as those worshiped by other peoples under different names. The names, iconographies, and rites—in short, the cultures—differ, but the gods are the same. In the realm of culture, religion appears as a principle counteracting the effects of what Erik H. Erikson called "pseudo-speciation." Erikson coined this term to describe the formation of artificial subgroups within the same biological species.[8] In the human world, pseudo-speciation is the effect of cultural differentiation. The formation of cultural specificity and identity necessarily produces difference and otherness vis-à-vis other groups. This can result in the elaboration of absolute strangeness, isolation, avoidance, and even abomination. Among the Papuas in the highlands of New Guinea where communication is geographically difficult, this process has led, over some 50,000 years, to the formation of more than 700 different languages.[9] Here, under laboratory conditions, the forces of pseudo-speciation could operate relatively undisturbed. Normally they are checked by other factors promoting communication and translation. The most important among them seems to be commerce, that is, cross-tribal, cross-national, and cross-cultural economy. If we look for regions in which these factors were most operative in prehistory and antiquity we must think of the Near Eastern commercial networks which already in the fourth millenium B.C.E. extended east to the Indus valley and west to Egypt and Anatolia. Along the lines and on the backbone, so to speak, of these early commercial contacts, political and cultural entities crystallized in the third and second millenia, very much according to the principles of pseudo-speciation which, however, were always counterbalanced by cultures of translation.

The profession of interpreter is attested in Sumerian texts from Abu Salabih as early as the middle of the third millenium B.C.E.[10] The term *eme-bal*, meaning something like "speech changer," designates a man able to change from one language into another. The Babylonian and Assyrian

equivalent of the Sumerican *eme-bal* is *targumannum* (interpreter), a word
that survives not only in the Aramaic *targum* (translation), but also in the
Turkish *dragoman, turguman,* and so on, that by metathesis eventually led
to the German form *dolmetsch* (interpreter).[11] In Egypt, too, interpreters
appear as early as the Old Kingdom. The nomarchs of Elephantine, the
southernmost province of Egypt, acting as caravan leaders for the African
trade, bore the title "chief of interpreters." Contacts with neighboring and
even more remote tribes were always supported by at least an attempt at
verbal communication.[12]

The practice of translating foreign panthea has to be seen in the context
of this general emergence of a common world with integrated networks of
commercial, political, and cultural communication. This common world
extended from Egypt to the Near and Middle East and westward to the
shores of the Atlantic.[13] I am not arguing that this process of intensified
interrelation and unification was a particularly peaceful one—quite the
contrary. What might have begun as occasional raids and feuds developed
into larger forms of organized warfare. We are not speaking here of peaceful coexistence. But even war has—in this particular context—to be reckoned among the factors of geopolitical unification promoting the idea of
an *oikoumene* where all peoples are interconnected in a common history,
an idea already expressed by the Greek historian Polybius.[14] And the idea
of universal peace reigning in that *oikoumene* developed along with this
process, leading to the efforts at imperialistic pacification known as *pax
ramessidica* and *pax salomonica* and ultimately culminating in the *pax romana.*

First the conviction of the ultimate identity of the culturally diversified
gods, then the belief in a supreme being beyond or above all ethnic deities
formed the spiritual complement to this process of geopolitical unification.
Polytheistic religion[15] functioned as a paradigm of how living in a common
world was conceivable and communicable. The complete translatability of
gods founded a consciousness of dealing with basically the same species in
spite of all other kinds of cultural alterity.

Conversion

Energeia: Language in Its Magical Function

This interpretation of religion as a principle counteracting the factors of
cultural pseudo-speciation seems rather paradoxical, for religion is generally held to be the most forceful promoter and expression of cultural
identity, unity, and specificity. This needs no further elaboration.[16] Assim-

ilation, the giving up of a traditional cultural identity in favor of a dominating culture, is necessarily accompanied by religious conversion, and religion is universally recognized as the strongest bastion against assimilation. Movements of resistance against political and cultural domination, oppression, and exploitation universally assume the form of *religious* movements.[17] Jewish history provides the model for these movements of liberation, and the Exodus story has been shown to be more or less universally adopted wherever people have revolted against an oppressive system.[18]

This is true, but it applies to specific political and cultural conditions which might be subsumed under the general term of "minority conditions." Minority conditions arise where a hegemonic culture dominates and threatens to swallow up a culturally and ethnically distinct group. Here we are dealing with what may be interpreted as an "immune reaction" of the cultural system, a tendency to build up a deliberate "counter-identity" against the dominating system.[19] The cultural system is intensified in terms of counterdistinctivity.[20] This mechanism may be called second-degree pseudo-speciation, to be distinguished from normal pseudo-speciation, which occurs always and everywhere. Second-degree or counterdistinctive pseudo-speciation, however, occurs mostly under minority conditions.[21] Identity then turns normative, based on "normative self-definition."[22] It is typically under these conditions of resistance to political and cultural domination that religions of a new type emerge which I would like to call "second-degree" or "secondary" religions. These religions defy translatability. They are entered via conversion and left via apostasy.[23]

I shall not recapitulate Jewish history here, which is a sequence of typical minority situations, starting with Abraham in Ur and Moses in Egypt and continuing via less mythical events such as the Babylonian exile, the situation of Judaea under the Persians, the Ptolemies, the Seleucids, and the Romans, through the various diaspora places from Alexandria to Cernovic (the historical exception, of course, being the modern state of Israel).[24] The Jewish paradigm is the most ancient and the most typical; perhaps it is also the model and origin of all or most other cases. Egypt is a far less conspicuous case, but also far less known. I shall therefore concentrate on the Egyptian example in showing how religion can work in the direction of promoting untranslatability.

Egypt entered into minority conditions only after the Macedonian conquest. The Libyan and Ethiopian conquerors had adopted the Egyptian culture rather than imposing their own. Even the Persians did not really impose their culture on the Egyptians because there were too few immigrants from Persia to form an upper class with an elite culture as the Greeks did later.[25] Under Macedonian rule, the Egyptians found themselves in very much the same situation as the Jews but without a stabilized tradition. While the Israelite tradition achieved its final state of the Hebrew canon, the Egyptian tradition had to undergo profound transformations. Some features developed under minority conditions are strikingly similar. The extreme stress laid on purity, laws, life form, and diet in many ways parallel the emergence of *halakha* in Israel. We also find the belief in the untranslatability of the Egyptian language.

Hellenized Egyptians were as active in producing Greek texts as hellenized Jews. Quite a few of these texts present themselves as translations from the Egyptian. Translation and interpretation were central among the cultural activities of Greco-Egyptian and Greco-Jewish intellectuals in the literate milieus of Alexandria and Memphis.[26] The question of translation and translatability itself became a major topic in this literature.[27] But there is also a theory of untranslatability that rejects even the principle and practice of translating gods. In Iamblichus (*De mysteriis* 2:4–5) we read, for example, that names of gods should never be translated.[28] In dealing with divine names one has to exclude all questions of meaning and reference. The name is to be regarded as a mystical symbol. It cannot be understood and for this very reason it cannot be translated. Knowledge of the names preserves the "mystical image of the deity" in the soul. For this reason we prefer to call the sun god not Helios but Baal, Semesilam (Shamash?), or Re, and the god of wisdom not Hermes but rather Thoth. The gods declared the languages of holy peoples like the Assyrians and the Egyptians holy, and communication with the gods can only take place in these languages. The Egyptians and other barbarians "always kept to the same formulas because they are conservative and so are the gods. Their formulas are welcome to the gods. To alter them is not permitted to anybody under any circumstances." The *Lautgestalt* here becomes a taboo, the phonetic form of language functioning not as a *signifiant* which stands for some *signifié* but as a mystical symbol, a kind of verbal image full of mysterious beauty and divine presence.

In opposing Celsus's view on the arbitrariness of divine names, the Christian church father Origen uses exactly the same arguments as the pagan magician and philosopher Iamblichus.[29] Both agree that there is a natural link (*sympátheia*, "sympathy") between name and deity and that the magical and "presentifying" power of language rests in the sound and not in the meaning and is therefore untranslatable. A less well known treatment of the same topos can be found in the opening chapters of treatise XVI from the *Corpus Hermeticum*. It is presented as introduction to a translation and thus deals with both translating and untranslatability.

> He said that those who read my books [Hermes Trismegistos speaks] will think that they are very clearly and simply written, when in fact, quite the contrary, they are unclear and hide the meaning of the words and will become completely obscure when later on the Greeks will want to translate our language into their own, which will bring about a complete distortion and obfuscation of the text. Expressed in the original language, the discourse conveys its meaning clearly, for the very quality of the sounds and the [intonation] of the Egyptian words contain in [themselves] the force of the things said.
>
> Preserve this discourse untranslated, in order that such mysteries may be kept from the Greeks, and that their insolent, insipid and meretricious manner of speech may not reduce to impotence the dignity and strength [of our language] and the cogent force of the words. For all the Greeks have is empty speech, good for showing off; and the philosophy of the Greeks is just noisy talk. For our part, we use not words, but sounds full of energy.[30]

The energetic theory of language is magical. The magical force of spells resides in their sound. It is the sound, the sensual quality of speech, that has the power to reach the divine sphere. The *energetic* dimension of language is untranslatable.

Conversion: Revelation Versus Evidence

One of the surest signs that we are dealing with a secondary religion is the phenomenon of conversion.[31] As long as there is the possibility of translation there is no need of conversion. If all religions basically worship the same gods there is no need to give up one religion and to enter another one. This possibility only occurs if there is one religion claiming knowledge of a superior truth. It is precisely this claim that excludes translatability. If one religion is wrong and the other is right, there can be no question of translating the gods of the one into those of the other. Obviously they are about different gods.

A very interesting borderline case is provided by the opening scene of the eleventh book in the *Metamorphoses* by Apuleius, in which Lucius prays to the rising moon and sees in a dream the goddess herself. The speech of the goddess first displays the well-known topos of the relativity of names. One people calls her by this name, the other by that name, all adoring her in their specific tongues and cultural forms. But beyond all her conventional ethnic names there is a *verum nomen*, her true name, and this one is known only to the Egyptians and the Ethiopians. Up till now it made little difference whether you worshiped Venus in the way of the Paphians, Minerva Cecropeia in the way of the Athenians, Diana in the way of the Ephesians, or Proserpina in the way of the Sicilians. But now it turns out to be of utmost importance to follow Isis in the way of the Egyptians because only they know the true name and rites. If you are really serious about it, there is no alternative: you must convert to the Isis-religion and enter into the group of the initiated.[32]

But still, Isis is a cosmotheistic deity. She belongs to the class of supreme beings who embody the universe in its totality. Her particular power and attraction lie in her double role of cosmic deity and personal rescuer; she is mistress of the stars and of luck and fate. Being a cosmotheistic deity, her name has a rich *signifié*. Presenting herself she may point to every divine role possible as a manifestation of her power. "I am this, and that, and that, . . . in short: everything," she says to her believers. The god of Israel is the exact opposite. He does not say "I am everything" but "I am who I am," negating by this expression every referent, every *tertium comparationis*, and every translatability.[33] He is not only above but displaces all the other gods. Here, the cosmotheistic link between god and world, and god and gods, is categorically broken.

This is what the enlightened and cultured among the pagans were unable to understand. It was not a problem that the Jews were monotheists: monotheism had long been established as the leading philosophical attitude toward the divine. Every cultivated person agreed that there is but one god and it little mattered whether his name was Adonai or Zeus or Ammon or whether he was just called *Hypsistos* (Supreme). This is the point Celsus made in his *Alethes Logos*. The name is "Schall und Rauch," as Goethe, another cosmotheist, put it. Varro (116–27 B.C.E.), who knew about the Jews from Poseidonios, was unwilling to make any difference between Jove and Jahve *nihil interesse censens quo nomine nuncupetur, dum eadem res intelligatur*.[34] But the Jews and the Christians insisted on the very name. For them, the name mattered. To translate Adonai into Zeus would have meant apostasy.

The translatability of gods depended on their natural evidence. They are accessible either to experience or to reason or to both in the form of indubitable, intersubjective, and intercultural data to which one can point in searching for a name in another language. What this form of natural evidence excludes is "belief": where all is "given" there is nothing to believe in. The worship of gods is a matter of knowledge and obedience but not of belief. In his book *Belief, Language and Experience*, the philosopher and indologist Rodney Needham has shown that most languages lack a word for what in the Greek of the New Testament is called *pistis* and what other languages translate as *fides, Glaube, foi* and so on; in English *pistis* is rendered by two words: *faith* and *belief*. Christian missionaries had great trouble finding words for *pistis* in the languages of the people they wanted to address.[35] In most cases they had to invent a word. Translatability rests upon experience and reason, untranslatability on belief which in itself proves to be an untranslatable concept. Paul already made the difference quite clear by stating "we are walking not by the sight (*opsis*) but by the faith (*pistis*)" (2 Cor 5.7). People walking "by the sight" could point to the visible world in telling which gods they worshiped. People walking by faith had to tell a story the truth of which rests on matters outside the visible world. They could translate the story but not the god.

Syncretism: Translation into a Third Language

In a recent book, G. W. Bowersock has proposed that Hellenism was a medium rather than a message. Hellenism provided a common language for local traditions and religions to express themselves in a voice much more eloquent, flexible, and articulate than their own. "Greek," Bowersock writes, "was the language and culture of transmission and communication. It served, in other words, as a vehicle."[36] Hellenism did not mean hellenization. It did not cover the variegated world of different peoples and cultures, religions and traditions, with a unified varnish of Greek culture. Hellenism, instead, provided them with "a flexible medium of both cultural and religious expressions." Bowersock is perhaps somewhat underrating the strong anti-Greek feelings prevailing among the native elites, especially in Judaea and Egypt,[37] and the frequent clashes and tensions between indigenous traditions and the world of the gymnasium. But he is certainly right in pointing out that the culture of late antiquity owed at least as much to indigenous influences as to the Greek heritage and that the Greek universe of language, thought, mythology, and imagery became less an alternative or even antithesis to local traditions than a new way of giving voice to them. This explains why from the Jewish and Christian points of view the differences between Greek, Roman, Egyptian, Syrian, Babylonian, and other religions disappeared. "Hellenism" became a synonym for "paganism," because it served in late antiquity as a common semiotic system and practice for all these religions. As they were translated into the common semiotic system of Hellenism, the borders between the different traditions tended to become much more permeable than they had been within the original language barriers. A process of interpenetration took place which

not only for Jews and Christians but also for the "pagans" themselves made
the differences between them much less evident than what they had in common. Hellenism, in other words, not only provided a common language
but helped to discover a common world and a "cosmopolitan" consciousness.

Nineteenth-century scholars used to refer to this process of cultural and
religious interpenetration as "syncretism."[38] The Greek term *synkretismós*
occurs only once: in Plutarch, where it refers to an archaic custom of the
Cretan people to overcome local feuds and to form a sacred alliance to
withstand foreign aggression. By way of an erroneous association with
kerannymi (to merge), which would yield *synkrasía*, the expression came
to denote the idea of a merging of gods (*theokrasía*) and then of cultures
in a more general sense. But syncretism, as opposed to "fusion," is not simply merging. It describes a kind of merging which coexists with the original
distinct entities. The local identities are not altogether abolished; they are
only made transparent, as it were. They retain their native semiotic practices and preserve their original meaning. When translated into the third
language of Hellenism, however, they assume a new kind of transparency
which smoothes down idiosyncratic differences, allows for interpenetration, and opens up a common background of "cosmotheism." Syncretism
requires or offers double membership: one in a native culture and one in a
general culture. It does not mean one at the expense of the other. The general culture depends (or even "feeds") on the local cultures.

We can distinguish three types of cultural translation: "syncretistic translation" or translation into a third language/culture; "assimilatory translation" or translation into a dominating language/culture; and
"mutual translation" within a network of (economic/cultural) exchanges.

Syncretistic translation is exemplified by what may be called "cosmotheistic monotheism." The different divinities are not just "translated"
into each other but into a third and overarching one which forms something like a common background. Syncretistic translation renders the common background visible. It presupposes a fundamental unity beyond all
cultural diversities. As far as theology is concerned, this unity is guaranteed
by the oneness of the world. The world or cosmos serves as the ultimate
referent for the diverse divinities. We may compare the unity of syncretism,
which is founded on the cosmos, with the unity of anthropology, which
is founded on "human nature" ("die Einheit des Menschengeistes," as
Thomas Mann called it).

Assimilatory or *competitive translation* is exemplified by the early instances of *interpretatio Graeca*, when Herodotus visited Egypt and formed

the opinion that "almost all the names of the gods came from Egypt to Greece." This, he adds, is what the Egyptians say themselves. What Herodotus heard in conversing with Egyptian priests must have been the Greek names. They spoke to him in Greek using the hellenized names of the gods, speaking not of Re, Amun, Thoth, and Ptah, but of Helios, Zeus, Hermes, and Hephaestus.[39] For them, it did not matter whether these gods were called Re or Helios, Amun or Zeus, Thoth or Hermes, as long as the same gods were recognized and addressed by these names. They claimed to have been the first to recognize these gods, to find out their nature by establishing their mythology and theology, and to establish a permanent contact with them: *gnosis theon*, as this particular cultural activity is called.[40] The *interpretatio Graeca* of the Egyptian gods thus turns out to be not a Greek but an Egyptian achievement. We have always assumed this translation to be a manifestation of the Greek spirit and its interpretive openness toward foreign civilizations. But it seems now much more probable that the translation of their national panthea into Greek suited in the first place the interest of the "barbarians." Morton Smith and others have shown that Greek language and learning tended already to be recognized and experienced as an elite or superior culture by oriental peoples under the Persian empire and long before the Macedonian conquest.[41] All the stories about early Greek encounters with Egyptian priests, from Solon and Hekataios down to Herodotus and Platon, show the same Egyptian tendency to impress the Greek visitors by their superior cultural antiquity.[42] What you call culture—the argument runs—and what you are so proud of has been familiar to us for thousands of years and it is from us that your ancestors borrowed it. This is a very familiar motif in "nativistic" movements of our days. Where western culture is met by primitive cultures, this is a typical reaction.[43] Greek functions in this context as the other, not as a third language. Translatability into Greek is a question of cultural competitiveness.

Mutual translation seems to apply to the Babylonian material. This type of mutual translation is based on and develops within networks of international law and commerce. The history of these networks leads us back to the very roots both of translation and of mutuality or reciprocity, namely, to the exchange of gifts as the primal form of intergroup communication. Marcel Mauss, in his classic study on "le don,"[44] was the first to point out the communicative functions of what Marshall Sahlins later called "Stone Age economics."[45] The basic function of exchange is not the fulfillment of economic needs but the establishment of community by communication, mutuality, and reciprocity. It is therefore anything but a surprise that mutual translation turns out to be the earliest type and something like the "primal scene" of cultural translatability. Translate! is the categorical imperative of early cultures. It is the overcoming of autistic seclusion, the prohibition of incest, the constraint to form alliances outside the narrow circles of house, village, and clan, and to enter into larger networks of communication.

It is revealing to translate these three types into our time. To start with the last one, *mutual translation*: Today, when these networks have finally become global, they have lost something of their primary charm. The modern situation is characterized by a strange kind of reciprocity: on the one hand, western civilization is expanding all over the world; there is hardly any place left untouched by Coca-Cola. On the other hand, cultural fragments from all places and periods are brought into the *musée imaginaire* of western culture, which is rapidly growing into a supermarket or Disneyland of postmodern curiosity. In pre- and early historical times, reciprocity and mutuality meant a process of growth and enrichment for all cultures involved; today it means loss and impoverishment. Western culture is reduced to Coca-Cola and pidgin English, native cultures are reduced to airport art. The cultural imperative, today, points in the opposite direction: to regionalism, the preservation (or invention) of dying languages and traditions, and the emphasis on otherness. This is also why assimilatory translation or competitive otherness is no longer a valid option. Mutual acknowledgment is suppressed as one culture is used as the negative foil of the other.

There remains the first type to be considered, *syncretism* as defined in terms of *double membership* and a *third language*. Such a language is something not actually given but virtually envisaged and kept up in order to provide a framework in which individual cultures can become transparent without losing their identities.

Hellenism, seen not as a message but as a medium, not as a homogenizing cover but as a flexible and eloquent language giving understandable voice to vastly different messages, preserving difference while providing transparency, might serve as a model. Hellenistic culture became a medium equally removed from classical Greek culture as from all the other oriental and African cultures that adopted it as a form of cultural self-expression. In the same way, a transcultural medium that will not amount to westernization or Americanization could provide visibility and transparency in a world of preserved traditions and cultural otherness.

Visual Syncretism: A Case Study

Moshe Barasch

I

In the centuries of late antiquity the countries on the eastern shores of the Mediterranean underwent a thorough and long-lasting inter- action of cultures which, in intensity and creative results, has not many parallels in history. Several cultures whose characters had been established and firmly articulated in the course of centuries or millennia here inter- sected. The very process of the vigorous interaction of these cultures forms a historical period in itself. It was to describe one aspect of this particular process that modern scholars coined the term "syncretism."

In a broad sense syncretism is usually understood as a merging of gods or of cults, and it thus forms part of the interaction of cultures. But the term, I hardly need stress, has been widely used and has lost any clear out- lines it may have had. In a more precise sense it means, to follow Arnaldo Momigliano, two things: "One is the positive identification of two or more gods, the other is the tendency to mix different cults by using symbols of other gods in the sanctuaries of one god, with the result that the presence of Serapis, Juno, and even Isis was implied in the shrine of Jupiter Doli- chenus on the Aventine in Rome."[1]

Scholarly discussions of syncretism are usually limited to religious stud- ies, and their main material is of course textual. What does syncretism mean for the visual arts? It is a question that must interest every student of images. Yet strange as it may seem, it is not easy to come by an answer, nor does one readily find a discussion of the problem. In many studies of individual works of art, of specific trends or motifs, scholars have occa- sionally touched on the general problem. From these studies certain phenomena may be distilled, which, not surprisingly, seem closely related to those of syncretistic texts.

One approach to an analysis of syncretistic visual images was suggested by Ernst Kitzinger, who proposed the concept of "sub-antique."[2] Kitzinger introduced this notion to describe a certain style: great imperial themes, based on classical taste and models, are represented in a style characterized by "irrational spatial relationships; proportions determined by symbolic importance rather than laws of nature; frontality; jerky and abrupt movements; hard, sharp-edged forms brought out by deep undercutting."[3] Since the late nineteenth century this style in art, as in religion and other spheres of life, has usually been explained as resulting from the conflation of Hellenic, or Roman, models and the often somewhat elusive impact of eastern cultures.[4] In fact, it occurs mainly in the eastern provinces of the Roman Empire, where the models brought from the west were copied by local craftsmen familiar with their indigenous styles. When the style resulting from this meeting of "high" culture models and "local" workmanship, at a somewhat later stage, appears in the great centers themselves, including the city of Rome, it is usually explained as an import from the East, and thus as transferring to the metropolis the mingling of cultures that was taking place in the provinces.

The concept of "sub-antique," useful as it is in many respects, has for the purpose of the present essay two important limitations. The first is that it is restricted to matters of form and thus completely disregards questions of content and meaning. Was there an iconography, a system of symbols of the cultures whose forms have quite appropriately been described by the term "sub-antique"? The notion as it stands cannot be used to explore this problem. The other limitation, though problematic in itself, is that the concept of sub-antique is not in any way concerned with the nature of the cultures conflated in the objects that Kitzinger so correctly described. Are the stylistic properties we have mentioned—the irrational relations of space, the jerky, nonorganic movements, the proportioning of the figures according to their importance—the result of non-Greek arts (in which they were leading principles), or do they rather derive from the primitive skills of low-class craftsmen?

In the following observations I do not undertake to suggest any comprehensive answers to these questions. I turn to late antique syncretistic imagery, that is, to something that may go under the label of iconography, within the limits of a specific question. However, the study of such a question may shed light on broader problems.

I have always been attracted by one particular facet of the rich and intricate iconography of late antiquity, found especially in the provincial art of the eastern countries. It is a specific ambiguity that seems characteristic of syncretism in general, and of syncretistic images in particular. What I have in mind, well known from the history of late antique religion and ritual, is what may be described as a double reading of the image, or making a double use of a representation or object. The same image, its shape unchanged or only slightly modified, could serve audiences of radically different orientations and beliefs. Adherents of one religion, people educated in one culture, would read a certain carved or painted figure in a given, firmly established, way; they would identify it as the representation of a hero or saint of their own creed. Believers in another religion would sometimes take over the very same figure (or ritual) as it stood, and transfer it into their own beliefs or customs. They would read the figure in a different way, taking it to depict something different, another event or a different hero or saint. This transfer required only a shift in reading. Without changing its form, the figure would change its meaning or identity. What takes place in such a case is a tilting or reversal of a figure's or object's meaning, without ever touching its form. This radical shift in meaning, resulting in a change of what the figure represents, derives, so it seems, from a change of audience and of context rather than of form.

II

My example is a rather modest object, a funerary stele found in Lower Egypt. In 1935 an expedition of the University of Michigan, led by Hans Petersen, excavated cemeteries at what was believed to be the site of ancient Terenouthis, in the western part of the Nile Delta. After the Second World War further excavations followed, undertaken by other institutions. A considerable part of the many objects brought to light in these excavations consisted of funerary stelae. Scholars seem to agree that all these stelae (several hundred of them) date from between 275 and 350 A.D. They are modest in size, none of them exceeding 45 centimeters in height or width. They are carved in a simple material, the kind of stone found close by. I do not intend to treat the Terenouthis stelae as a group; I shall rather concentrate on a single example, excavated in the first Michigan project and now in the Museum of Classical Archaeology at the University of Michigan (Fig. 1). Nor do I intend to provide a monograph for this object, but only to look for the clues it may provide for the understanding of syncretistic images.

Our main concern is with the meanings expressed in the stele and how

Figure 1. Funerary stele with *relief en creux*. Limestone, Terenouthis, Egypt, late third to early fourth century A.D. Courtesy of the Kelsey Museum of Archaeology, University of Michigan.

they are expressed, but it will be useful to begin with an account of some of its formal features. Even a simple description will show that here two styles, representative of two great cultural and artistic traditions, interpenetrate in a highly unusual manner, presenting us with the interaction of Hellenistic and very late Egyptian images and patterns of visual expression. In fact, on the basis of style alone it is somewhat difficult to assign the stele to one of the two cultures with confidence.

The figure, to which I shall shortly revert, strikes the spectator as Hellenistic in overall character. It is for this reason that a close look at the carving technique leads to a somewhat surprising result. Though at a first glance the stele seems to be decorated by a regular relief, what we find is, in fact, a negative relief. The technique employed is the one sometimes called *relief en creux*—that is, the figure is sunk into the stone; it does not protrude from the stele's surface (which in that case would form the "background"), but is carved *into* the surface. Since artistic techniques are often not only a "technical" matter but reflect principles and attitudes not visible in themselves, I may be permitted to make here a few comments on technique.

The so-called "sunk relief," as one knows, is a very common feature of Egyptian art; for European spectators, it has come to be considered a hallmark of Egyptian sculpture. The sunk relief, it has been said, was developed in Egypt, and it is characteristic of Egyptian art alone.[5] In Egyptian sunk relief, the figure never protrudes from the surface; it is placed in a niche, as it were, and its most forward parts only reach surface level.

The sunk relief is thoroughly non-Greek in nature. In Greek thought and art, relief is fully part of sculpture, that is, of an art whose main aim is to shape material objects that resemble bodies in having volume and protruding mass, bodies that occupy space. Greek art in general has for centuries been understood as a "body art," and for this reason sculpture was regarded as its most typical manifestation.[6] On these grounds, then, it is not surprising that Greek art, down to its many provincial Hellenistic ramifications, did not know the sunk relief. The sunk relief, Heinrich Schäfer said, "emerged from an altogether different spirit than the relief that protrudes over the surface."[7] I do not feel competent to discuss the origin of the sunk relief, or to take a stand on the question of whether, as has been suggested, it really derived from writing, which was carved into the surface.[8] Egyptologists will have to decide this matter (if there is enough material for a decision).

Reflecting on how the carving of our stele may have come about, one imagines that a provincial carver in Lower Egypt, familiar with the sunk reliefs he could see on the many great monuments that populated the country, was asked to represent a Hellenistic model. Would it not seem natural to him to transfer the main features of the model into his own professional language, as it were, and carve the figure based on a Greek model in the technique of sunk relief? This is not the occasion to take up the thorny question of whether, where, and to what extent (if at all) the ancient Egyptian technique of the sunk relief was still in use during the first centuries of the Christian era.[9] All I should like to do here is to ask whether the tech-

nique of the sunk relief itself underwent any change when it was exposed
to the Greek model.

The first thing one notes is that on our stele the figure is not pressed into
a narrow niche, as are most (though not all) figures in Egyptian sunk reliefs. In such reliefs the figure conveys a sense of being squeezed into a narrow opening, of its movements being hampered by figures or objects in
close vicinity. On the Terenouthis stele, on the contrary, the figure seems to
stand freely in a wide, open space; the raised head and the broad movement
of the arms do not in any way convey a feeling of constraint and limitation.
Now, while this sense of space surrounding the figure is surely not typical
of Egyptian art, it obviously conveys something of the Greek (classical as
well as Hellenistic) concept of sculpture, of the statue standing in the marketplace or in a garden.

The carver does not follow the Egyptian model closely in the treatment
of the figure itself, either. In the highly stylized art of the Egyptian sunk
relief the figures are either flat (forming an intermediary level between the
deeply recessing background and the upper surface of the monument), or
they are slightly raised and rounded, so that in the most projecting parts
they reach the upper surface level. The Terenouthis carver offers an interesting and original solution. He carves his figure in full volume, as it were,
but in the negative. In many parts of the figure he successfully conveys the
sense of the body's roundness (see especially the arms), though the roundness is created by carving into the stone, not by making the rounded parts
of the body project.

Summing up these observations on technique, one finds it difficult to
decide where the stele from Terenouthis (and the hundreds of other stelae
found there) actually belongs: it plainly cannot be assigned to either the
Egyptian or the Greek tradition of carving. It seems likely that in the first
place the carvers—clearly provincial craftsmen—gave the original Hellenistic model an "Egyptian" interpretation, transferring the image from the
domain of full material sculpture or high relief into the formal system of
"sunk relief." But then again they cast "Greek," round, and plastic shapes
and qualities into the "Egyptian" mold. What we see in our stele is the
product of a continuous process of translation and retranslation of shapes
and approaches from one distinct culture of art into another.

One would like to know to what extent both the anonymous carvers
of these stelae and the audiences for whom they were made were aware of
this intricate process that marks the emergence and character of the monuments we are looking at here. Unfortunately we know too little about
early-fourth-century Terenouthis society to form an opinion.

In general style the figure on our stele is not as ambiguous as in its carving technique; as a whole, it clearly betrays its origins in the tradition of Greek art. The organic character of the figure, the continuous and rhythmic movements that permeate it, the slight indication of a turning axis in its position (from right to left)—all these show that the figure comes from the domain of Greek imagery. Even though the execution is often awkward, our figure's affinity with the tradition of great Greek art is obvious at a first glance.

It is precisely because the overall character of the figure is so clearly Greek that one is surprised to find a feature that serves almost as a hallmark of Egyptian art—the feet, shown in profile, seem altogether independent of the figure's overall posture, which is frontal. Moreover, while the figure intimates a slight turn to the left, the feet turn straight to the right. The construction of the human figure out of independent parts, each represented in a typical position (thus shoulders in frontal view, feet in profile), is one of the best-known and most discussed features of Egyptian art, and it has rightly been seen as the very antipode of the Greek.

III

While it seems strange that, on the basis of technique, we have difficulties in assigning our stele to either the Greek or the Egyptian cultural tradition, another question is even more puzzling: what was the religion of the people who commissioned the stelae, and whose tombs the monuments marked? Was it Christianity or some local paganism? The modern scholars who, from different points of view, have investigated the stelae of Terenouthis have offered different answers. Even though the religious affiliation of the stelae may not have been the main issue in these scholars' studies, it is still remarkable that they differ in their views. Some consider the stelae to be Christian,[10] while others claim that they are all pagan.[11] These contradictions are significant, and they reflect a broader problem. Funerary monuments, it seems to be accepted, are usually explicit in their presentation of religious symbols, and their religious identity is, therefore, easy to define. How, then, should we understand the flat contradictions in the conclusions reached by different scholars?

The identification of the meanings the artists or patrons wished to express, and that might eventually lead us to concluding to which creed they belonged, can only be derived from a proper interpretation of the very few "symbolic" features in the stele: the Orans gesture and the boat with the rudder. The Greek inscription at the base of the stele does not offer any

clue; it only tells us that this is the stele of a certain Apion, 26 years old.[12]
We are then left with the visual motifs only, and these, as we shall immediately see, are also ambiguous.

The Orans motif—a standing frontal figure (in some rare cases also
seated) with the arms and hands symmetrically raised—is one of the common gestures of prayer and devotion. Since the last years of the nineteenth
century it has attracted the attention of scholars and has been made the
subject of several studies.[13] I shall not attempt a discussion of this important motif; I shall only briefly mention some aspects of its history that may
have a direct bearing on our present question.

It is essentially in the centuries of late antiquity that the Orans gesture
became an important, and fully crystallized, motif, found mainly in cemeteries. It has always been known, however, that its origins go further back.
As a prayer gesture it is probably already indicated in Isaiah (1.15) where
God is made to say: "And when ye spread forth your hands, I will hide mine
eyes from you; yea, when ye make many prayers, I will not hear."

In the art of early Christianity, the Orans figure belongs to the first crystallized images of the new religion. It is found in media as different in social
connotation as catacomb painting and sarcophagi, and in many areas
(from Egypt to Rome). But we also find distinct descriptions of the gesture
in early Christian literature. Suffice it to mention as early and authoritative
an author as Tertullian, who, in the early years of the third century, said
that Christians not only raise their hands but also spread them out, and
they do this in order to imitate the suffering of Christ.[14] The historian cannot help remembering that Tertullian was an African who lived not very
far from Terenouthis, and in any case in the same cultural area, although
in a highly developed urban setting. Another African Christian, Minucius
Felix, who actually must be considered a contemporary of our anonymous
carvers, also shows that the gesture was firmly established, and that it was
understood as Christian.[15] No wonder, then, that modern scholars, including historians of the art of early Christianity, saw the Orans gesture as
a Christian motif.

It is of course known that although Christian art made the Orans a
favorite figure, the motif was also current in pagan culture and society. Pagan orants were also known as sophisticated works of art, carried out in
different media: in elegant, rhetorical shapes they appear as free-standing
statues, or on sarcophagi.[16] The connotations of these pagan orants were
not too far from those of their Christian counterparts; they were understood as personifications of *pietas*. But European scholars of early Christian art and imagery, traditionally focusing on Rome, have perhaps not

Figure 2. Funerary stele with Orans figure. Limestone, Terenouthis, Egypt, late third to early fourth century A.D. Courtesy of the Kelsey Museum of Archaeology, University of Michigan.

paid sufficient attention to African, particularly Egyptian, versions of the Orans figure in late antiquity.

This is not the place to discuss Orans figures in Roman Egypt, but I should like to show an example which has particular significance for this essay. Among the funerary monuments found in Terenouthis there is a stele that is more sophisticated than many of the others. Here we see (Fig. 2) an Orans figure, standing in the open space below an aedicula supported by two columns. Here the carving is not *relief en creux*, reminding us of the Egyptian "sunk relief"; the figure protrudes from the background, forming a veritable Hellenistic relief. The dating is almost the same as that of most

Terenouthis stelae, though perhaps slightly preceding the others. No further examples are needed to show that the Orans was known in Terenouthis. What is most striking in the present context is that the Orans figure, probably representing the deceased person, is standing between a jackal, the accepted symbol of Anubis who leads the dead, and a falcon, the conventional emblem of the god Horus.[17] Whatever the further meanings and connotations of this image may be, it is obvious that here the Orans represents a pagan figure.

We should take a further step, into an earlier stage of Egyptian culture. Not being an Egyptologist (and having to rely on secondary sources), I hesitate to take it. Yet one cannot disregard the simple fact, obvious even to a non-Egyptologist, that the core of the Orans motif, the figure with the two raised hands, is a traditional feature in Egyptian art. From the third millennium B.C. onward we know the so-called Ka hieroglyph.[18] From about 2000 B.C. (eleventh dynasty) we know the puzzling wooden statue of a king wearing the sign of the two raised arms on his head.[19] The motif is found in many later monuments. I do not of course wish to suggest any conclusions. All I can say is that in Roman Egypt many ancient monuments on which this motif appeared, in one form or another, must have been easily accessible. And one is perhaps not being too speculative when one assumes that people of different layers of society must have been aware of the connotation of this Orans gesture as one of prayer and devotion.

In Roman Egypt, during the very last stage of antiquity, the Orans gesture seems to have been a matter for reflection and interpretation. The interesting testimony of Cassian is not, to be sure, direct, immediate evidence, but it can shed some light on the significance the gesture may have had. Cassian, a monk of Scythian origin, underwent a long ascetic training, mainly in Egypt, before undertaking his pioneer work in the West (Marseilles) in the early sixth century. In his *Institutions* he describes in some detail the customs of the Egyptian monks, sometimes comparing them with "ours." The Egyptian monks, he indicates, recite their prayers while standing, merely spreading their arms (possibly, we should add, performing the Orans gesture); only after that they briefly prostrate themselves on the ground. "We" (the westerners), on the other hand, continue to pray for a longer time while stretched out on the ground.[20] He also describes how prayer gestures are performed by the assembled monks who precisely imitate their abbot's actions during the common prayers.[21]

Cassian's statement, as I have said, is no direct testimony to the time and cultural level of Terenouthis, but it further supports our general impression that in late-antique Egypt prayer gestures were known, and were conceived as part of articulate rituals and as a subject worthy of reflection.

Let us now return for a moment to our stele. How did a spectator in, say, the fourth century, looking at the stele and noting the Orans figure, read the gesture? Could it not be that he identified it as a Christian gesture if he himself was a Christian, or as what we would now call a "pagan" gesture if he belonged to one of the non-Christian religious groups?

Let us now turn to the other symbolic motif, the ship with the rudder. As we remember, the figure on the stele in Terenouthis (Fig. 1) stands on a boat, perhaps about to step out of it. The boat, no less than the Orans gesture, is common in the religious imagery of both early Christianity and late-antique paganism, especially in the eastern provinces of the Roman Empire. Since it has also been studied several times, we can dispense, I hope, with most general comments and concentrate on what is essential and specific for our image.

In the treasure of metaphors and emblems available in early Christian imagination, the ship—with or without a rudder, with or without sails—played a vital part. The significance of the boat in early Christian literature is so central that one may well inquire into the reasons for this importance.[22] Whatever these were, it is clear that the boat was used in many contexts. Two of the Christian boat metaphors may contribute to the understanding of our stele.

The first is the comparison of life with a sea voyage. Hence the natural suggestion that at the end of the voyage the ship will enter a haven; if the voyage was well conducted, the haven will be safe. Lactantius (who was a precise contemporary of the Terenouthis stelae, though he lived on a different social and intellectual level) neatly sums up this metaphor:

Therefore, if you always direct your eyes towards heaven, and observe the sun where it rises, and take this as a guide of your life, as in the case of a voyage, your feet will spontaneously be directed into the way; and this heavenly light, which is a much brighter sun to sound minds than this which we behold in mortal flesh, will so rule and govern you as to lead you without any error to the most excellent harbour of wisdom and virtue.[23]

The other metaphorical context of the boat in early Christian literature is even more frequent, but its emergence is also more obscure: it is the boat as a symbol of salvation and redemption. The great example, most often used by patristic authors, is Noah's ark. Already in the New Testament (1 Peter 3.20) the ark is a lifesaving structure, related to Christ. In patristic literature the comparison of the ship with the cross is common. In the shape of the boat the sign of the cross is revealed, as Justin Martyr[24] and Minucius Felix[25] have pointed out. Finally, as is well known, the Church itself is considered a ship. True believers can entertain hope for final salvation, for the ship of the church will bring them to a safe harbor.

One further detail may also shed light on the stele from Terenouthis. I mean the fact that the salvation voyage of the boat was imagined to proceed from left to right. The equation "right = eternal life" was, as Franz Joseph Dölger points out, one with which the early Christian world was familiar.[26]

This detail brings us back to our stele. The figure is standing on, or stepping out from, a boat, and there is reason to believe that the boat is meant to be moving from (the spectator's) left to right. This is perhaps indicated by the fact that the steering rudder is on the left. In antiquity as today the rudder was known to be in the rear part of the ship.[27] This being so, a feature that is strange from a stylistic point of view may be explained by the content: I mean the feet that turn to the right. Could it not be, one asks oneself, that a rather primitive carver used the motif of the feet turning to one side to convey the idea that the figure in the boat was turning to the right?

In view of all this, one can safely assume that a Christian spectator, looking at our stele in Terenouthis in the early fourth century, would have identified it as a Christian monument.

And what about a pagan spectator of the same time and place, looking at the same stele? Would he also have identified the stele as a Christian funerary monument? Not necessarily. He may well have found in the same motif of a boat with a rudder connotations of his own, "pagan" culture and religion, whatever specifically that may have been.

The boat, usually steered by Charon, that ferries the dead to their eternal dwellings was one of the best-known images in Hellenistic and late-antique fantasy. It does not seem to have been limited to a specific area or social level but was popular in a true sense of the word. Charon, we remember, was a latecomer to the gallery of mythological figures, but by Hellenistic times everybody knew him and his boat. A measure of the popularity of the image of the ferryman and his craft are the many funerary inscriptions, or the stories about pictorial representations, such as Pausanias's description (10.28.2) of a painting by Polygnotus, and such famous literary productions as Lucian's *Charon.*[28]

The ferryman of the dead is also familiar to Egyptian tradition. For some time scholars believed that Charon was borrowed from Egypt, and they have even claimed that the name of "Charon" should be derived from Egyptian sources.[29] But whether or not Charon was indeed borrowed from ancient Egyptian lore, the pagan population of Egypt during the third and fourth centuries, one feels sure in saying, knew the image of the boat and ferryman who transports the dead to the beyond.

Coming back to the imaginary fourth-century spectator looking at our stele, a simple question must be asked: if that spectator was a pagan, and was familiar with pagan imagery, would he not have understood what the stele represented as a symbolic expression of his beliefs?

IV

So far I have tried to see what we can learn from the—admittedly rather primitive—carving of the stele in Terenouthis, and what the figural motifs of this monument can tell us about the cultural and religious links of both artists and patrons. I should like to conclude this case study with two more general comments. One is concerned with the historical conditions that prevailed in provincial Terenouthis during the third and fourth centuries, and may explain to what extent the technique and iconography of the stele reflect the broader interaction, or clash, of cultures that determined life and art in Egypt at the time; in other words, whether and to what extent the ambiguities and contradictions we see on the stele reveal and mirror the character of a period. My other comment has little to do with history. It simply asks, on the basis of a single case study (and with all the limitations that go with such a slim factual basis for drawing conclusions), whether the work of art can be read and understood in itself and from what it alone presents. It goes without saying that in these comments I can only suggest in the broadest outlines what seem to be the problems that we here face.

I shall not undertake even a very general sketch of intellectual and emotional life in Roman Egypt, particularly in provincial areas where sources are scarce; the present essay is obviously not the place to do this. But I shall briefly stress one aspect that may have an immediate bearing on our Terenouthis stele. In the Greco-Roman world, it has recently been said, Egypt was always considered a special case.[30] Greek and Roman authors always stressed the Egyptians' tenacity in clinging to their own cultural tradition, the resistance they offered to outsiders, and their way of absorbing and transforming what came from the outside world. This can also be seen in the traditions of the visual arts. As late as the third century A.D. Roman emperors could still be depicted as Egyptian pharaohs.[31]

It is well known, however, that even the intrinsic power of Egyptian tradition was not able to arrest the hellenization, or romanization, of Egypt. To be sure, cultural development in Hellenistic Egypt does not precisely correspond to that in other countries of the East. Yet whatever the particular trends that here emerged, whatever the specific syncretism of the Egyptian and Greek gods, the old Egyptian cultural tradition was replaced by something new.[32] A measure of the degree to which the new culture dislodged the old one, in the judgment of many scholars, is the decline in knowledge of the sacred language and writing. Already Clement of Alexandria tells his readers that in his day familiarity with the sacred Egyptian characters had become the preserve of a small elite.[33] But the best-known document of Egyptian estrangement from the old tradition is that strange book (which fascinated Renaissance scholars and artists), the *Hieroglyphica* of Horapollo. Composed in Greek in nearby Alexandria by an educated pagan about two generations after our stele was carved, it shows that a large part of ancient Egyptian lore, the meaning of the figures as well as the script, had become "impenetrably mysterious."[34] Whatever Horapollo may have intended, his *Hieroglyphica* shows not only how Greek interpretations supplanted ancient Egyptian meanings but also how strong was the desire to preserve at least something of the ancient Egyptian heritage.

Early Christianity in Egypt shares these characteristic features with the pagan culture of the country. First of all there is the awareness of the "otherness" of the surrounding culture and creed. The concern of Egyptian Christians with gnosticism, hermeticism, and other pagan religious trends was probably more intensive than in other countries. The African church produced some of the central early-Christian polemics against other religions, from the writings of Tertullian, Cyprian (bishop of Carthage), Minucius Felix (who was probably also an African) to those of Augustine. I do not have to show in detail, I hope, that polemics against another creed express, at least in part, a struggle against a different culture. When Origen said that Egypt is "the mother of idolatry," he had not only religious views in mind, but that composite of opinions, behavior, and artistic creations we mean by "culture."

Egyptian Christianity, however, also knew the absorption of high Greek culture and an interaction with Hellenistic thought that is largely devoid of polemics. It will be sufficient to mention Alexandrian Christian theology, mainly the work of Clement of Alexandria.[35] But the interaction with other creeds and traditions is not limited to single thinkers. It also existed in the schools. At about the same time that our stele was carved, Origen was teaching in nearby Alexandria. According to the testimony of

Eusebius, many "educated people were so impressed by Origen's universal renown that they came to his school to benefit by his skill in biblical exegesis; while innumerable heretics and a considerable number of the most eminent philosophers listened to him with close attention." And a few sentences later Eusebius tells us that Origen "found time also to give many less gifted persons a general grounding, declaring that it would stand them in good stead for the examination and study of Holy Writ."[36] This almost reads as a kind of justificatory syncretism, of the translation of what one sphere or culture produces into another one.

Even these brief and isolated illustrations will suggest, I hope, how deeply rooted our modest stele from Terenouthis is in the general culture of Egypt in late antiquity. Both the combination of different techniques and the ambiguities in reading the image depicted on the stele visually manifest what was perhaps the central theme that occupied the mind of Egypt at the time—the interaction, conflictual as well as mutually complementary, of different cultures. In this respect, it is a truly syncretistic image.

This brings us to our last observation. In speaking about syncretism in images, or of a syncretistic use of images, it will be useful to distinguish between two types. Though these types hang together, the distinction between them may shed some light both on the individual work of art and on some broader aspects of artistic creation. Some images, or complex nonverbal creations, show figures or symbols known to have originated in, and to belong to, different cultures or religions. I shall give one example that belongs to the same broad period as the stele from Terenouthis. An important text from late antiquity, the *Augustan History*, has it that Alexander Severus set up for his private prayers the images of his ancestors, and of Christ, Abraham, Orpheus, and Apollonius of Tyana.[37] Such a portrait gallery, we could say, is syncretistic "in itself," independent of any spectator; it is syncretistic in an objective sense. The individual parts—here, the figures portrayed—belong to different religions. We may be sure that the spectators looking at these images, such as Alexander Severus himself as well as the author of his biography, were fully aware that the images they saw represented figures central to different, distinct religions. In other words, they knew that the gallery was objectively syncretistic in character.

Another type of the syncretism of images follows from the spectator's approach only, from the connotations of forms and figures stored in his mind; it is these connotations that determine how he "reads" the image in front of him. In some cases, and on a certain level, the spectator's different attitudes and the cultural memories he brings to the act of experiencing the work of art may lead to a radical modification of the meaning the image in front of him is presumed to convey. Thus a Christian spectator may have discerned in the Terenouthis stele the Orans figure he knew so well from Christian religious imagery, while a spectator rooted in the Egyptian tradition may have identified the same figure as an old and common Egyptian symbol. Without changing the configuration of the object itself, then, and only by mentally placing what he sees in a different context of cultural memories, the spectator brings about a reversal of the meaning.

Late-antique cultures on the eastern and southern shores of the Mediterranean abound in switching images. Let me briefly mention one additional example. A floor mosaic from a synagogue in Gaza, produced in the early sixth century, shows the crowned figure of King David (identified by a Hebrew inscription) playing his harp, enthroned in an open landscape, and surrounded by beasts that seem charmed by his music.[38] It is not difficult to guess that a "pagan" spectator, for whom the figures of Greek mythology still had an immediate religious significance, may have read this image as an Orpheus charming the beasts with his music, while a Jewish spectator, involved in biblical imagery, will have seen here a King David playing his harp. Like the stele from Terenouthis, the David mosaic in Gaza is a "reversible" icon.

The modern student is aware that it was the original spectator, the community for which the work was made, that ultimately gave the image its precise—or, if you wish, its "correct"—meaning. But since in any "reversible image" at least two different meanings are possible, one wonders how it was read. By stressing the one or the other aspect, the Egyptian-pagan or the Christian connotations of the image, the spectator located the stele in a different cultural context and gave it a different meaning.

The "case study" here presented and the reflections it invites suggest some possible conclusions. I shall briefly outline two of them, though the problems they raise deserve detailed study.

The first conclusion is rather obvious: there are two types of works of art that may fit the category of "syncretistic." In one type, the syncretistic nature of the image is manifest; you could say, it is paraded. Alexander Severus's portrait gallery of saints, could we ever see it, would be a clear, if rather simplistic, instance of this type. The other type of syncretistic work of art is the tilting, or reversible, image. In that latter type, the signs and traces of different and even clashing religions, paraded in the first type, are obscured by an ambiguity in the indication of the spiritual world to which the work of art belongs and which it expresses. It is this ambiguity that makes it possible for the object to be read in different ways, and it is in the spectator's experience that the work becomes located in the one or the other religion.

Does the spectator experience the two types of syncretistic images in the same way? My second observation refers to the beholder's activity. In grasping the meaning of a syncretistic image that belongs to the first type, the spectator has to know whom a certain figure portrays, and to what religion a given sign belongs. His very familiarity with the symbols and images of the different religious trends of his time is a sufficient foundation for an appropriate reading of the image.

The second type, the tilting or reversible image, makes other demands on the spectator; to read it properly the beholder's activity has to be both larger in scope and different in nature. In front of the tilting image, the spectator's reading has more of an impact on the interpretation of the work than in the first type. We should remember that, at least in late antiquity, the images here described as tilting appear in places and in contexts where an openly displayed syncretism would not have seemed acceptable. Tombstones and images in the synagogue are good examples of such an orientation. Funerary art in general is well known for its traditional character, and for its intention to adhere to one distinct religion. Images in synagogues or temples have the same tendency. And yet, tilting images in themselves, as I have tried to show in the case of the stele from Terenouthis, do show elements of different cultures and religions. The gap opened up by these contrasting orientations is bridged by the spectator's reading. What happens in this reading?

It is obvious that the spectator will try to adjust the work he is looking at to the symbolic images he has inherited or accumulated in his mind. As I have already said, if the spectator who originally saw the stele from Terenouthis was a Christian, he will have read the figure carved into the slab as that of an Orans; if he belonged to one of the "pagan" groups, he probably will have tried to identify the same figure as one derived from Egyptian mythology, as that mythology was understood in late antiquity. While this is manifest, another aspect is less manifest and has received less attention.

In the process of integrating the work of art into a cultural pattern of images that the spectator brings to the experience of looking, he focuses on certain features and neglects, or even completely disregards, others in the monument before him. The image of the work of art that thus obtains in the beholder's mind may significantly differ from what is actually carved or painted in the material monument. In the case of reversible images this mental image of the work of art may well decide how it is interpreted. In the case of the David mosaic in Gaza, a pagan spectator, familiar with the figure of Orpheus the magic singer, will necessarily disregard the diadem on the figure's head, the throne on which he is sitting, and the purple in which he is clad. Such symbols of royalty would prevent him from identifying the figure within his cultural framework. The Jewish beholder, on whose mind the figure of King David is deeply impressed, will have easily accepted the symbols of royalty, but he would have had to disregard altogether the beasts that seem charmed by the figure's music; the magician charming the beasts does not fit his image of King David.

In the Terenouthis stele the carving itself could perhaps have served as a criterion for linking the monument and what it represented either with Egyptian or with Greek and western art and culture, and thus in some way also suggested whether the figure belonged to "pagan" or to Christian imagery. If the beholder focused on the fact of the sunk relief, a feature known to late antiquity only from ancient Egyptian art and considered a hallmark of that pre-Christian culture, he might have been inclined to interpret the figure as part of a pagan ritual. If, on the other hand, he focused his attention on the "round" carving within the sunk relief, he would have emphasized in his mind the Greek, western attitude, and around or after A.D. 300 this would have suggested to him a Christian meaning of the image. Whatever may have been the solution in this particular case, it is certain that the spectator's reading made a real difference. The spectator's reaction thus became part of the image itself.

Translatio Studii and Renaissance:
From Vertical to Horizontal Translation

Karlheinz Stierle

*I*s mutual translation of cultures possible without the third instance of a medium of translation as lingua franca? If it is true that in our colloquium we are doing what we are talking about, that is, translating cultures, is English then the lingua franca of our mutual translations? Assuming that is the case, is that medium of translation neutral, or does it tacitly condition the subject matter our translations are about? Does mutuality of translation, depending upon a third or hegemonic language, necessarily enter into a process of creating difference, in which the privilege of mutuality dissolves into a more general process of translations?

What English is today, a medium of translations of culture, Latin was in the first centuries after Christ. Let me explore this assumption, to which the word translation itself leads us. *Translatio* is a word of the lingua franca of the Roman Empire, which was itself a large system of translation of cultures or, one might say, a melting pot of cultures. But when the Roman Empire was no longer an empire of Rome, when by Caracalla's edict in 211 every citizen of the empire became a Roman citizen, when Romania slowly replaced Rome, then Latin as the lingua franca began to merge with local languages and dialects and to transform itself into lingua romana, which was only a common denominator for a multitude of local differences. Lingua latina was not replaced, however, by lingua romana. Instead Latin got a new function as lingua franca of intellectual communication and particularly as the language of that spiritual imperium of Christian religion which asserted itself at the very moment when the political empire began to collapse. It was in the context of the posthistory of the Roman Empire that *translatio* first acquired a prominent function.

In medieval Latin *translatio*, which has its echoes in the Romance languages as well as in English, can mean translation and displacement as well. In the Renaissance, however, with its new humanistic conception of *translation*, a separation between *translatio* and *traductio* is characteristic for the Romance languages, whereas translation in English keeps its medieval senses. French *translation* and Italian *traslazione* now refer to the displacement of material objects or symbols incorporated in objects, without any idea of structural reciprocity that might make it the kind of gift described by Marcel Mauss. Its conception remains asymmetrical, whether in time or in space, whether in a vertical or in a horizontal dimension. *Translation, traslazione* in this sense, for instance, describes the transfer of the relics of a saint from one place to another. *Traduction, traduzione*, on the other hand, are narrowing down their meaning to a specific activity of translating from one language into another.

Transferre, translatio, where it first appears in the Middle Ages as a central category of political and cultural theory, almost exclusively refers to a model of verticality. One might say that the dominance of the axis of vertical translation is basic to the medieval conception of culture and cultural exchange in western Europe. The transition from a medieval to a postmedieval model of culture can be understood as a shift from vertical to horizontal dominance. This transition will be our principal concern in the following remarks.

When in 800 Charlemagne was crowned in Rome as the emperor of the Roman Empire, this meant a *"Renovatio Romani Imperii"*[1] implying an act of translation of the Roman Empire from Byzantium to Franconia. The *translatio* itself gave rise to difficult political and religious problems. Who was the translator of this *translatio*? Was it the Pope, who had crowned Charlemagne, was it the people of Rome, or was it Charlemagne himself? Indeed, *transferre imperium* will become a central term in the political self-understanding both of the Vatican and of the German-Roman emperors.[2]

Historiography and political theory during the Stauffer period were particularly focused upon the problem of *translatio*. They both come to their culmination with the theory of world history that Otto von Freising, the uncle of Frederic I (Barbarossa), developed in his *Chronica sive historia de duabus civitatibus* (1143–46). Otto seems to be the first writer to have given the formula of *imperium transferre* a new theoretical status by transforming it into the substantive form of *translatio*.[3] He is also the first to see a correlation between *translatio imperii* and *translatio sapientiae*.[4] Thus in his *Chronica* he invents the formula of "potentiae seu sapientiae ab oriente ad occidentem translationem" (the transfer of power or learning from east to west).[5] Following Augustine, Otto understands the course of time

as the rhythm of four world empires: "Thus the temporal power passed
from Babylonia to the Medians, then to the Persians, afterwards to the
Greek and last to the Romans and under Roman name has been transferred
to the Franks [*ad Francos translata est*]."[6] This movement is at the same
time a movement through space, beginning in the east and ending in the
west of Europe. This is an old formula that Otto's teacher Hugo of Saint
Victor had reformulated: "First man was placed in the garden of Eden in
the orient such that from this origin his descendants might propagate all
over the world. Thus after the deluge the first of reigns and the center of
the world were Assyria, Chaldea and Media in the eastern parts. Then the
highest power came to Greece and at the end to the Romans living in the
west as it were at the end of the world."[7]

It is interesting to see how the formula of *translatio sapientiae* first
changes into *translatio studii sapientiae* and only then into *translatio studii*. The place of *sapientiae studium* is Paris. Thus Vincent de Beauvais
speaks in his *Speculum historiale* of Charlemagne, "qui et sapientiae studium de Roma Parisiis transtulit, quod illuc quondam a Graecia transla-
tum fuerat a Romanis" (who brought the study of wisdom, which once had
been transferred from Greece to the Romans, from Rome to Paris).[8] The
next step is made by Martin von Troppau, who quoting Vincent leaves out
sapientiae and thus creates the formula that became current in the late
Middle Ages. As Goez points out, Vincent's suggestion that *sapientia* was
transferred to Paris found an interesting follower in Alexander von Roes
who, hearing that the Pope Gregory IX might try to 'translate' the empire
to France, elaborated a theory of world order in which he tried to demonstrate that God had given *sacerdotium* to the Italians and *imperium* to
the Germans, and that Charlemagne himself had brought "studium philosophiae et liberalium artium" to Paris.[9]

Did Chrétien de Troyes know Otto von Freising's *Chronica* when,
probably in the sixties or seventies he wrote his romance *Cligés*? Or might
he have come in contact with the doctrine of Otto's teacher Hugo of Saint-
Victor? His *romanz*, apparently the second after *Erec et Enide*, begins with
a most striking theory of *translatio*, though the word is not used. After
having presented himself and the subject of his *romanz*, he proceeds to
praise the book as a medium of remembrance and translation of study: "Ce
nos ont nostre livre apris / Qu'an Grece ot de chevalerie / Le premier los et
de clergie" (We have learned this from our books that the Greeks were the
first to have had knighthood and learning [lines 28–30]).[10] Greece is the
origin of knighthood and learning, in Otto's terms of *sapientia* and *poten-
tia*. From Greece both pass to Rome: "Puis vint chevalerie a Rome / Et de

la clergie la some" (Then knighthood came to Rome and the sum of learning [lines 31–32]). From Rome they move on to *France*, leaving out the
empire that has been transferred to Germany. France does not mean the Ile
de France and Paris, however. The ideal France of King Arthur is "Engle-
terre,/Qui lors estoit Bretaigne dite" (lines 16–17). This explains why
coming to France, the movement of *translatio* has arrived at its extreme
western border and is now to last there till the end of time. This at least is
what the narrator hopes:

> Dex doint qu'ele i soit maintenue
> Et que li leus li abelisse
> Tant que ja mes de France n'isse
> L'enors qui s'i est arestee.
> Dex l'avoit as altres prestee:
> Car des Grezois ne des Romains
> Ne dit an mes ne plus ne mains,
> D'ax est la parole remese
> Et estainte la vive brese.
>
> (Lines 34–42)

God grant that this sum of knighthood and learning be maintained and that the
place pleases them, so that the honour which here has come to rest will never leave
France. God had given it to the others as a loan only. For of the Greeks and the
Romans nothing more or less can be said. The word has been taken from them and
the vivid flame is extinguished.

What is striking in this text is not only the absence of any reference to
the German claim for *translatio imperii*, but even more the fact that in this
model of *translatio* the Christian religion has no importance whatsoever.
Chrétien's conception of *translatio* is strictly secular. (There is great secular
poetry in the Middle Ages, contradicting our often too narrow conceptions
of this period.)

The passage following this one makes clear what constitutes the real
superiority of French knighthood and learning. It is their synthesis in a
larger conception, which is that of *cortoisie*. *Cortoisie* as the new distinction of the French knight implies not only a new style of communication,
a new mastery of language, but also a new communicative attitude toward
women. The finest fruit of *cortoisie* is courtly love as a highly disciplined,
self-denying, and respectful social form in which the knight venerates his
lady.

For Chrétien the new ideal of love is inconceivable without a new ideal
of language. The narrator presents himself as a translator from dead Latin
into living French or *romanz*: "Cil qui les comandemanz d'Ovide / Et l'art

d'amors an romans mist" (the one who translated into romance the Commandments of Ovid and the Art of Love [lines 1–3]). French now becomes the language of a new and lasting period of high culture. It becomes the real language or medium of *translatio studii*. To *romanz* as language, however, corresponds Chrétien's *romanz* as that literary form, invented by himself, in which *romanz* as the language of *cortoisie* comes to its highest self-expression: "De la fu li contes estrez, / Don cest romanz fist Crestiiens" (From there was the story taken out of which Chrétien made his *romanz*).[11] Here *romanz* no longer means language, but rather discourse or more precisely a literary work that is destined to open a discourse. The project of a new, everlasting culture is founded by a work that is destined to be everlasting itself. The *romanz* as work of art is the highest manifestation of *romanz* as language. On the level of its *histoire* it gives an imaginary equivalent to what the new concept of *cortoisie* means. On the level of discourse it is itself an enactment of the language of *cortoisie*.

This manifesto of a new literary form opening a new and final epoch in the history of *translatio studii* represents a revolution in the relation between Latin and vernacular language, in which for the first time the latter claims superiority. Only Anglo-Norman England could offer a basis for this new confidence. Since French was the language of the Anglo-Norman occupiers, it became socially the language of a dominant class. It is in England that French for the first time becomes a literary language.

What Chrétien's proem puts forward as a thesis is realized as fiction in the *romanz* itself. Alexander, son of the Greek emperor (meaning emperor of East Rome or Romania), decides to leave his country and to go to the far West in order to become a knight of King Arthur. No one, not even his father, can hold him back:

> Nus ne m'an porroit retorner,
> Par proiere ne par losange,
> Que je n'aille an la terre estrange
> Veoir le roi et ses barons,
> De cui si granz est li renons
> De corteisie et de proesce.
> (Lines 146–51)

No one could hold me back by imploring nor by praising that I won't go to the foreign land and see the King and his barons of whom the fame of courtesy and courage are so great.

The *translatio* from Greece to France, meaning England, is repeated by the son of the Greek emperor as a personal experience. The vertical difference

Greece-France thus becomes a difference of horizontality. Or, to put it in structural form: the vertical axis of *translatio* is projected on the horizontal axis of difference. That which bridges the two worlds, however, is *cortoisie*. King Arthur immediately allows the young prince to join him. Love is now not far from making its appearance. As soon as Alexander has seen Soredamors, one of the *damoisels* of Queen Guenièvre, he falls violently in love with her, keeping his passion secret, however, for a long time.

The happy end that brings Alexander and Soredamors together, their marriage and the birth of their son Cligés, is but the prelude to Cligés' own story. Only at this point does the political aspect of *translatio imperii*, which seemed to be totally absent from Chrétien's considerations, become relevant.

After his parents' death, Cligés, now a young knight, is following his uncle Alis, the new emperor. Alis has ceded to his counselors and, in violation of the contract that obliged him to remain unmarried, is preparing his marriage with Fenice, the daughter of the German emperor. This marriage is a purely political maneuver on the part of the counselors. It is intended to bring the two empires together and thus to reestablish the old Roman Empire. Though Fenice had already been promised to the Duke of Saxonia, the most powerful of the German dukes, the emperor immediately takes advantage of the new possibility. At Cologne, where Alis is to meet Fenice for the first time, Cligés and Fenice immediately fall passionately in love. Cligés, being Greek through his father, French through his mother, is the perfect young knight whose *cortoisie* and charm Fenice cannot resist. When finally, after a long and complicated series of adventures and after the death of Alis, they can finally marry, the axis of *translatio* is centered in a new way. The cultural supremacy of France in the sign of *cortoisie* gives to *translatio* its real meaning. Thus Chrétien's *romanz* becomes the ideal space of an imaginary *anti-translatio*. But it also proposes a new model of horizontal or mutual translation in the concept of *cortoisie*.[12] A hundred years later Pope Gregory IX for the first time will consider a *translatio imperii* from Germany to France.

Another model of *translatio*, equally formed on verticality, can be found in Marie de France's prologue to her *Lais*. Once again it is in an Anglo-Norman context that the reflection upon *translatio* arises. Like Chrétien, Marie tacitly links *translatio* with the idea of progress. A text has a semantic magnitude to be unfolded only in time. From this perspective, commentary is an essential part of the semantic dynamics of the text. "Gloser la letre" means "de lur sen le surplus metre" (to fix the surplus of their meaning).[13] This future dimension of the text needs the active collaboration of the reader. If God has given him the light of understanding, he is obliged to make use of it and thus to become an instrument of *translatio*. But study is also a medicine against melancholy. This is why Marie thought of translating a good story from Latin to French: "Pur ceo començai a penser / D'aukune bone estoire faire / E de latin en romaunz traire" (For this I began to think about how to compose a good story and to translate it from Latin into Romance [lines 28–30]). But since in that field distinction cannot be won any more, she turns to a project involving quite another risk, choosing to try her skill as a translator on a very different subject. She heard in *Breton* (the original British language) songs of a particular kind, which she remembers were called *lai*. They were songs designed to preserve extraordinary events or happenings by giving them a linguistic and musical shape. These *lai* were made "per remembrance": by virtue of their shape they will bring memory into an open future. Marie is transposing these works of an oral tradition into a written work of poetry, thus opening up a new dimension of memory. Translation here means appropriation. Marie is not so much translating but inventing the written *lai* and its new world of passionate love beyond the world of courtly love. The surplus here is not a surplus of interpretation but one of imagination. Marie's work of "translation" is manifold: she is translating an oral text into a written text, a Breton text into a French one, a past text into a present text in the context of high Anglo-Norman society. And she is presenting her text to an ongoing translation that will by successive readings unfold and widen its semantic space. Once again this translation is dominated by verticality. Mutuality does not enter into this project.

Nowhere else does the concept of *translatio* achieve such complexity as in Dante, who takes up all the concepts of *translatio* hitherto worked out. First, Dante is a passionate defender of *translatio imperii*. He has no doubt of the legitimacy of the passing of imperial power to the German emperors. In his mind it is the German emperor only who can help Italy, torn by civil wars. In *De monarchia* Dante adopts the view that there are two leaders of the Christian world: the emperor and the pope who, being the sovereign of the spiritual world only, has no ultimate power of decision in political affairs.[14]

If *translatio imperii* has displaced imperial power to Germany, *translatio studii* for Dante has taken another direction. Dante is well aware that France has become the new European center of learning and culture. He is convinced, however, that the next step of *translatio studii* will bring back to Italy the highest standard of culture. His *De vulgari eloquentia* not only confirms Chrétien's conviction that *romanz* has become a language

of the highest literary ambition. It outlines the project of creating a new
Italian language that would become the most refined, the most accom-
plished of *romanz* languages.[15]

The *Divina Commedia* is Dante's realization of this project. It culminates in Dante's relation to Virgil: "Tu se' lo mio maestro e 'l mio autore; /
tu se' solo colui da cu' io tolsi / lo bello stilo che m'ha fatto onore" (You
are my master and my author. You alone are he from whom I took the fair
style that has done me honor [*Inferno* 1.85–86]).[16] Virgil teaches Dante
how to be the epic poet of the modern world. Dante is the new Virgil. But
whereas Virgil could celebrate Rome in the moment of its glory, Dante in
the moment of Rome's deepest decay must build that ideal Rome which
will be a symbol of eternal order. Dante, Virgil's disciple, in reality tries to
surpass Virgil.

In a more specific way, however, Dante deals with the translation of the
arts in that middle part of the *Commedia* which stands in the sign of *tran-
sitio*. Purgatory as intermediary world between Hell and Paradise is the
domain of *transcendere in actu*, where the transcending nature of art in all
its manifestations is expounded. To the system of *artes liberales* Dante opposes a new system of arts which will be the origin of the modern system.
Art itself is for Dante transcendental in its essence: it leads from the visible
to the intelligible world, from time to timelessness, from actual experience
to lasting form. The other aspect of art, however is the progress of artistic
perfection in time. When in canto 11 of the *Purgatorio* Dante suddenly is
confronted with his ancient friend, the painter Oderisi d'Agobbio, this artist, who once had been outstanding in illuminating manuscripts, speaks of
being surpassed in art by another artist and generalizes this experience.[17]
There is no stable achievement of fame in art, he tells Dante. Modern art
always surpasses the art that precedes it. This is apparently the same idea
of the correlation between art and progress that we find in Chrétien and
Marie. But the sense of this idea has changed radically. There is an absolute
art which is the art of God himself, as can be seen in the scenes of humility
sculpted into the rock where pass the penitents guilty of pride (*Purgatorio*
10). This art is perfect, since it compensates for the constitutive deficiency
of its medium in an imaginary transcending.[18] Human art never will reach
the level of divine art. That is why it follows the dynamics of progress which
will always turn out to be a means of humiliation. Even the artist of highest
reputation stands under the rules of temporality.

The leading topic of the *Purgatorio*, however, is not art but rebirth.
"Ma qui la morta poesi resurga" (But here let dead poetry rise again [*Purgatorio* 1.7]), says Dante in his invocation at the beginning of the *Purga-*

torio, when he has left the realm of darkness and come back to the "chiaro mondo" again. This is the beginning of rebirth, taking its inception in an act of purification. Virgil uses a blade of grass to clean Dante's face. But the plucked reed plant has the power of renaissance: "O maraviglia! ché qual egli scelse / l'umile pianta, cotal si rinacque / subitamente là onde l'avelse" (O marvel! that such as he plucked the humble plant, even such did it instantly spring up again, there whence he had uprooted it [Purgatorio 1.134–36]). The purification is achieved when at the end of the purgatory Dante and Virgil have arrived at the earthly paradise. Here again Dante refers to renaissance in the metaphor of the newborn plant:

> Io ritornai de la santissima onda
> rifatto sì come piante novelle
> rinovellate di novella fronda,
> puro e disposto a salire a le stelle.
> *(Purgatorio* 33.142–45)

I came forth from the most holy waves, renovated even as new trees renewed with new foliage, pure and ready to rise to the stars.

Translatio imperii and *translatio studii* in their different contexts are subsumed by Dante's thinking and imagining in the form of *figura*, which is yet another aspect of *translatio*. The whole texture of the *Commedia* is interwoven with a figurative discourse, constantly intertwining the Old and New Testaments and the historical world of the past and of Dante's own times.

All these aspects of *translatio* are located vertically. But as in Chrétien's *Cligés* there is also an axis of horizontal translation upon which Chrétien's *cortoisie* comes back as *cortesia*. As in Chrétien, Dante's *cortesia* comes to its highest expression in language. It follows the idea of a rhetoric beyond rhetoric grounded in a form of life, not only in learned rhetorical skills. The paradigm of this language is to be found in the continuous dialogue between Virgil and Dante. But we find it as well when in *Inferno* 10 Dante meets his political enemy Farinata, whom he nevertheless admires as one of the great figures of Florence, or when Virgil in perfect diplomatic politeness addresses Ulysses, the enemy of Troy and perfect master of the most civilized of all languages, Greek, who would not condescend to speak even with Dante.[19]

If Dante brings the concept of *translatio* to its highest complexity, Petrarch marks a sharp break with this tradition. He replaces the idea of *translatio* with that of *rinascita*. On the political level Petrarch radically opposes the conception of *translatio imperii*. He strongly insists upon its illegitimacy. Where Dante sees a continuity of the Roman Empire, Petrarch sees disruption. His canzone to Italy violently complains against the moment when the barbarians of the north, like a new deluge, came down to Italy to ruin it.[20] For this particular vision Petrarch finds an image which proved to be extraordinarily powerful and successful for hundreds of years, that of the dark ages.[21] In using the image of darkness for the illegitimacy of *translatio imperii*, Petrarch refers to Dante's metaphysical opposition between darkness and light, which organizes the narrative structure of the *Divina Commedia*. The metaphysical opposition in Dante becomes a historical opposition in Petrarch. The light of Greek and Roman culture is obscured by the centuries of barbarism. Petrarch seems to see the beginning of a new epoch, however, where the light of antiquity might come back. Thus he is looking back and forth at the same time. It is Petrarch's decisive innovation to have replaced *translatio* by renaissance. With this metaphor, highlighting dramatically the discontinuity of times, Petrarch once again comes back to Dante. Dante's metaphorology of renaissance at the beginning and at the end of the *Purgatorio* is now used by Petrarch to mark a new epoch of culture, study, and poetry. Dante's invocation "ma qui la morta poesí resurga" becomes a historical device in Petrarch's famous sonnet 34 to Apollo, which was for a time intended to be the inaugural poem of the *Canzoniere*. In this sonnet Apollo is invoked to come back after a period of darkness and winter and to inspire the poet, who being in love with Laura, is represented by the mystical *figura* of Apollo in love with Daphne.[22]

Petrarch's hope for a renaissance of antiquity is only one aspect of a highly complex copresence. Whereas his political thought is centered upon the renaissance of Rome, matters are more complex for him when it comes to study, language, and letters. As a poet Petrarch is writing in the vernacular and is deeply rooted in a medieval tradition of lyric poetry. At the same time he is regarded as the first humanist. He is collecting manuscripts of Latin literature and poetry and he is himself trying to write in a pure classical style following Cicero. He is fascinated by the worldliness of pagan antiquity, and at the same time he is a Christian writer who is convinced that the pagan world lacked the light of Christian religion. But equally, by his discovery of landscape as a medium of projection of his own subjectivity, he is, as Jakob Burckhardt puts it, one of the first really modern men.[23] Petrarch is the first to live in different worlds and to enjoy the complexity of this experience. The experience of the copresence of cultures is perhaps the most important aspect of what we call Renaissance. It is the fundamental plurality of Renaissance that is the condition of a new dimension of dialogue. With Petrarch begins the dominance of the horizontal over the vertical axis of *translatio*.

It is not by chance that Petrarch was the first to discover the fascination of horizontality. The most striking document of this shift undoubtedly is Petrarch's letter to Dionigi di Borgo San Sepolcro on his ascent of Mont Ventoux.[24] Before Petrarch, the fascination of the mountain had been its verticality. On top of the mountain the view was lifted upward to God. When Petrarch arrives on top of the mountain, however, he is fascinated by the temptation to look down and to discover the world in its open horizontality.[25]

Renaissance is at the same time the discovery of plurality, perspective, dialogue, polyphony. Culture now means, as Leonid Batkin puts it, the culture of the communication of cultures.[26] This new experience brings about a new aesthetics of plurality.[27] A few examples may be sufficient here. The Italian *romanzo* is an ironic web of different worlds and of an ever-growing plurality of persons, situations, places, and histories. *Gargantua and Pantagruel* is, as Mikhail Bakhtin has pointed out, a carnival of voices, cultures, and languages. Marot makes the copresence of different cultural worlds the subject of his poetry, and so does Ronsard. Raphael's *Stanze della Segnatura* may be understood as the pictorial program of such a copresence of worlds and discourses. Whereas the School of Athens offers to the beholder an essential scene of dialogue and plurality of intellectual concerns, the opposite scene is dominated by a strictly hierarchical scheme under the sign of Christian dogma.

Montaigne's *Essais* are the summa of an epoch of dialogue and of an ever-growing copresence of cultural worlds.[28] In his essay "Des coches"[29] the domination of horizontality over verticality of *translatio* comes to a culmination. In this essay Montaigne is confronting two cultural worlds: "our" world of modern Europe with its technology, its need for speed, its circulating gold serving as money versus the newly discovered America of the Incas, where gold served only for ritual purposes, where the wheel did not exist, and where going by foot was the only way of human locomotion. Montaigne looks at his own culture, the modern European culture of communication of cultures, with the eyes, as it were, of an Indian. What he must then realize is the tragedy of a mutual translation of cultures, where the Indians were robbed of their gold, their land, and their culture, often also of their lives, and were forced to receive a new religion, a new technology, and poverty.[30] This confrontation is at the center of Montaigne's theory that different cultural worlds should each have their own times. For a moment he muses on how modern European history would have been changed, had America already been discovered in antiquity. Then there would have been a chance for real cultural translation between the two worlds.

Epilogue

It would seem that horizontality with all its problems has increasingly become a more central concern of culture. Whether we like it or not, we are living today in a world culture based on technology, capitalism, speed, and communication. This structuring of our world seems to be all-dominant. Looking over to the walls of Old Jerusalem I hear day and night the stream of cars driven by the rhythm of our modern world. We have learned to live in multiple cultural contexts. Most of us have the daily experience of the mutual translation of cultures within ourselves. World culture on all its stages, from banal airport culture to the most refined world cultures of art, can help to heal the wounds of difference or to repress them. But its horizontality cannot overcome the essential verticality we nevertheless live in, be it a burden, a grace or both. So difference comes up again, and even more vividly, with the weakening of our faith in modernity. How then to bridge it or to preserve it? Is difference our culture's last word, an ultimate reality, a fetish? Perhaps all three. In his admirable book on the "real presences" of art, George Steiner, arguing against the thesis of art's essential negativity and unreadability, has returned to Dante's *cortesia*. For Steiner *cortesia* is an effort of understanding which is never in danger of blind identification.[31] *Cortesia* is a highly political and diplomatic attitude, which for Dante nevertheless bore the meaning of deepest humanity. *Cortesia* leaves open the space of understanding. It is always the beginning of a possible dialogue. It means acknowledgment of difference, without making difference into a fetish. We have perhaps more in common, or we are perhaps more different, than we thought.

In every dialogue there is an interplay between distance and closeness, difference and resemblance, which reminds us of the structure of metaphor. In metaphor two poles have to work together in order to bridge a semantic gap. This is why Paul Ricoeur speaks of "métaphore vive," living metaphor. Perhaps we may come to a living difference in our translations.

Yet the point must be repeated: Jews and Germans are not only different. They have, as Gabriel Motzkin points out in "Memory and Cultural Translation," a history in common, which must again and again separate them and at the same time bring them into a particular relation of mutuality. This is not, however, primarily a question of mutual translation of culture. There is a chance, despite an almost inconceivable mountain of guilt, disaster, and suffering, that we can make this mutuality a space of living difference where something of our mysterious existence in time, which links our personal existence to the history and destiny of our peoples, may be explored.

Augustine, Chaucer, and
the Translation of Biblical Poetics

Lawrence Besserman

> While content and language form a certain unity in the original, like
> a fruit and its skin, the language of the translation envelops its
> content like a royal robe with ample folds. . . .
>   . . . To some degree all great texts contain their potential
> translation between the lines; this is true to the highest degree of
> sacred writings. The interlinear version of the Scriptures is the
> prototype or ideal of all translation.
>
> —Walter Benjamin, "The Task of the Translator"

*T*he present essay treats an important chapter in the history of the
translation of biblical poetics into the literary culture of the Middle Ages. Focusing on three crucial passages in Chaucer's *Canterbury
Tales* ("General Prologue" 1.730–42, "Sir Thopas–Melibee Link" 7.936–
64, and "Retraction" 10.1081–83) in relation to Augustine's *De Doctrina Christiana* (*On Christian Doctrine*) and *De Consensu Evangelistarum* (*On the Harmony of the Gospels*), I am primarily concerned with
the extrapolations to secular literature and literary theory that Augustine and Chaucer make from the precedent of the Bible and from what
they infer to be biblical compositional norms. Though the complex and
much-debated problem of the translation of the Bible from Hebrew or
Greek into Latin or other languages is not my focus, it will also necessarily enter into the discussion—between limits succinctly defined by
Walter Benjamin's suggestive but seemingly contradictory metaphorical
observations about secular and biblical translations and their relationship—as I consider the ways in which Augustine and Chaucer turned to
the Bible for stylistic, significative, narratological, and interpretive mod-

els suitable for "translation" into their respectively religious and secular rhetorical and poetic theory and practice.[1]

I

Our point of departure, because of its enormous influence on all medieval biblical poetics including Chaucer's, must be Augustine's seminal work on the Bible, the *De Doctrina Christiana*.[2] Begun in 396 C.E. but completed only in 427 C.E., the work blends an impressively lucid and theoretically cogent explication of the allegorical approach to biblical exegesis with an equally lucid, succinct, and elegantly formulated Bible-centered rhetorical theory, a blend of exegetical and expository methodology that Augustine elaborated for the use of Christian teachers. Even if Chaucer did not know the *De Doctrina Christiana* firsthand, his knowledge of ideas derived from it must have been considerable. A brief outline of key concepts in that work, highlighting features sometimes overlooked, will provide essential background for the discussion that follows.

At the heart of Augustine's biblical poetics are his definitions of "charity" ("the motion of the soul toward the enjoyment of God for His own sake, and the enjoyment of one's self and of one's neighbor for the sake of God") and its antithesis, "cupidity" ("a motion of the soul toward the enjoyment of one's self, one's neighbor, or any corporal thing for the sake of something other than God"), which together constitute the univocal and omnipresent theme of the Bible (3.10.15–16; pp. 88–89; Martin, pp. 87–88). Yet if everything in the Bible teaches charity or condemns cupidity, the means by which various biblical authors do so varies. Sometimes the lesson is taught literally and directly; at other times it is taught figuratively and obliquely. The way we know "whether a locution is literal or figurative," Augustine had explained, "consists in this: that whatever appears in the divine Word that does not literally pertain to virtuous behavior or to the truth of faith you must take to be figurative" (3.10.14; pp. 87–88; Martin, p. 86). This applies of course to any of the "almost shameful" passages in Scripture: "Those things which seem almost shameful to the inexperienced, whether simply spoken or actually performed either by the person of God or by men whose sanctity is commended to us, are all figurative, and their secrets are to be removed as kernels from the husk as nourishment for charity" (3.12.18; p. 90; Martin, pp. 88–89). Furthermore, when we read the Bible we may produce an unlimited number of valid interpretations of its figurative language, as long as each of our interpretations yields

a validation of the theme of charity or a condemnation of the theme of cupidity. This thematically univocal multivocity of valid interpretations of
figurative or obscure statements in the Bible, says Augustine, was God's
original intention when He inspired the Bible's human authors (3.27.38;
p. 102; Martin, pp. 99–100).

Having accounted for the difficulty of figurative language in the Bible,
and having authorized the search for doctrinal "fruit" in the "chaff" of
obscure biblical figures of speech, Augustine next addresses the problem
of occasionally obscure literal biblical terms. That figurative precedes literal in his account is an apt reminder of the fact that in the Bible, as Augustine understood it, Christian has displaced Jew—indeed, in both the Old
and New Testaments, the literal Jew is a figure for the Christian to come—
and Greek and Latin had also assumed priority over Hebrew, in authority
if not in time. Yet despite this displacement in his exposition, Augustine
recommends that the order in which we are to apply our reading strategies
to the Bible is from literal to figurative: "Having become familiar with the
language of the Divine Scriptures, we should turn to those obscure things
which must be opened up and explained so that we may take examples
from those things that are manifest to illuminate those things which are
obscure" (2.9.14; p. 42; Martin, p. 41). But when Augustine says "language of the Divine Scriptures," what "manifest" language does he intend?
Of which tongue (whether "manifest" or "obscure") is he speaking?

In the answer that Augustine finally offers to this fundamental question
we also find an explanation for the intriguing fact that the problem of the
relative status of biblical languages has been minimized in the *De Doctrina
Christiana* and its solution postponed until well into book 2, where it is
introduced, obliquely, in the context of a continuing analysis of the problematics of literal and figurative expressions. Working back from figurative
to literal, and after listing the 44 canonical books of the Old Testament and
the 27 canonical books of the New Testament, Augustine finally explains
how the literal language of the Bible is to be understood: "Against unknown literal signs the sovereign remedy is a knowledge of languages. And
Latin-speaking men, whom we have here undertaken to instruct, need two
others for a knowledge of the Divine Scriptures, Hebrew and Greek, so that
they may turn back to earlier exemplars if the infinite variety of Latin translations gives rise to any doubts" (2.11.16; p. 43; Martin, p. 42). When biblical obscurity is the result of a mistranslation from Greek or Hebrew into
Latin, Augustine says, one should consult the original text and emend
the Latin, not interpret it (2.12.18; p. 45; Martin, p. 44). But in order to
do so, we need to get back behind the Latin. We begin, however, among

"the infinite variety of Latin translations," with the *Itala*, which Augustine preferred over Jerome's Vulgate because it followed its source, the Septuagint, "word for word." By referring to a "word for word" translation of this kind, Augustine argues, "one may test the truth or falsity of those who have sought to translate meanings as well as words" (2.13.19; p. 46; Martin, p. 44–45).[3]

On the question of the status of the Bible in relation to secular texts Augustine is unequivocal, at least initially. The Bible, he asserts, contains all useful knowledge and "the books of the pagans" can add nothing (2.42.63; p. 78; Martin, p. 76). But lest it seem that he means to do away with all secular knowledge, Augustine further explains that even though the message of the Bible is uniquely divine, its mode of expression is nevertheless identical in kind to that of pagan literature. To extract the uniquely "useful" biblical meaning that always teaches charity and condemns cupidity, Augustine asserts, the proficient reader of the Bible must therefore become a competent literary critic, familiar with "all those modes of expression which the grammarians designate with the Greek word tropes" (3.29.40; pp. 102–3; Martin, p. 100–101). When Augustine resumed work on the *De Doctrina Christiana* at paragraph 35 of book 3 (in the year 427, after a hiatus of some 30 years), he proceeded to demonstrate the link between the Bible and pagan literature through a series of rhetorical analyses of Old and New Testament passages, thereby proving that "eloquence" as traditionally defined in relation to pagan literature was a self-consciously and amply witnessed feature of biblical literature, too.

Because Augustine had initially set the Bible and its plenitude of divine truth apart from and above all other writings, he is somewhat ambivalent about the blend of divine "wisdom" and everyday, pagan-style "eloquence" that his rhetorical analyses of biblical passages uncover. However, in a concluding observation about the relationship between the two key terms of his rhetorical theory, he settles the matter by elevating wisdom (which for him of course means Christian "charity") over eloquence:

What therefore is it to speak not only wisely but also eloquently except to employ sufficient words in the subdued style, splendid words in the moderate style, and vehement words in the grand style while the things spoken about are true and ought to be heard? But he who cannot do both should say wisely what he cannot say eloquently rather than say eloquently what he says foolishly. (4.28.61; p. 166; Martin, p. 165)

Immediately preceding this declaration Augustine had moved effortlessly from rhetorical analysis of the letters of Saint Paul to analysis of passages from the letters and treatises of Ambrose and Cyprian, in order to demonstrate that the three levels of style (subdued, moderate, and grand) can be correlated to the three goals of the Christian rhetorician: to teach, to delight, and to persuade to righteous action (4.18.35–50; p. 143–58; Martin, pp. 141–57).[4] Now, as the fourth and final book of the *De Doctrina Christiana* draws to a close, the rhetoric of the divinely inspired human actors of the Bible actually merges with the rhetoric of those ideal instructors in a Christian culture founded on the Bible whom Augustine was trying to educate. Whether or not Augustine succeeded in walking the thin line of finding human eloquence in the Bible without reducing the Bible to mere human eloquence, his approach to biblical poetics in the *De Doctrina Christiana* was of fundamental importance for later writers trying to understand the literary form and meaning of Scripture and its relation to religious and secular writing alike. As is generally acknowledged, Augustine's bridging of the stylistic gap between various sacred and secular texts in the *De Doctrina Christiana* influenced the reception of the Bible in the West in a deep and lasting way, directly and indirectly, through theologians like Cassiodorus, Rabanus Maurus, Hugo of Saint Victor, and Peter Lombard, and through Christian humanist poets like Dante, Petrarch, Boccaccio, and Chaucer.[5] Less often acknowledged, however, is the extent to which Augustine's complex and nuanced position in the *De Doctrina Christiana* was both preserved and, in different ways, also revised by these authors. As we shall see later on, Augustine also took up the question of the relationship between secular and biblical poetics in his *De Consensu Evangelistarum*, a work that had a similarly strong (but much less often considered) impact on the thinking of Christian authors throughout the Middle Ages and after. First, however, let us see how Chaucer addressed the same question.

II

The first passage in the *Canterbury Tales* in which Chaucer explicitly links his poetry with the Bible occurs in the "General Prologue," as the pilgrim-narrator anticipates and answers in advance the criticism of any reader or listener who might take offense at the bawdiness of some of the stories that follow:

> For this ye knowen al so wel as I:
> Whoso shal telle a tale after a man,
> He moot reherce as ny as evere he kan

Everich a word, if it be in his charge,
Al speke he never so rudeliche and large,
Or ellis he moot telle his tale untrewe,
Or feyne thyng, or fynde wordes newe.
He may nat spare, althogh he were his brother;
He moot as wel seye o word as another.
Crist spak hymself ful brode in hooly writ,
And wel ye wot no vileynye is it.
Eek Plato seith, whoso kan hym rede,
The wordes moot be cosyn to the dede.
(1.730–42; my emphasis)[6]

Literalism is defended on moral grounds. To be faithfully literal is to be honest, whereas to change the words of a story, even slightly, would make it "untrue." Chaucer's faithful adherence to the possibly "rude" speech of his characters is further authorized here by appeal to Christ and Plato. That words and deeds should be "cousins" (i.e., that they should correspond), though attributed to the very heavy artillery of Plato, was a proverbial saying in Chaucer's day; the remark "whoso kan hym rede" (let anyone who can, read him [Plato] for himself) underlines the jocularity of Chaucer's appeal to a Greek authority whom neither he nor his audience could read in order to underwrite the wisdom of a readily available proverb.[7] In combining Plato and the Bible to authorize his defense of bawdy language, Chaucer was probably following the lead of Jean de Meun.[8] But Chaucer omits Jean's philosophical and theological defense of what is mistakenly called "bawdy" or "improper" language. Instead, he presses a further extraordinary comparison between biblical and secular style: because Christ spoke "brode" (openly, frankly?) in the Bible, Chaucer may do the same in recounting the *Canterbury Tales*.

But in what sense is a literary work comparable to Scripture? Does Chaucer mean to say—taking "Christ" in line 739 as synonymous with God-the-author who "speaks" throughout the entire Bible—that there are sufficient instances of sexually explicit action and bawdy speech throughout the Bible to justify his own uses of sexually explicit action and bawdy speech? Is he implying, beyond the question of style, that the Bible and his tales are congruent at the level of content as well, and that what is frivolous or bawdy (or, in Augustine's terms, "shameful") in his poetry also has a salvific core of meaning below the surface?[9] And if Chaucer meant to imply that the laws of both biblical style and hidden meanings apply to his bawdy tales, did he also mean to imply the corollary proposition, namely, that by following the exact words of a source one can recover the original intent of its author, as Augustine had said was the case with biblical translations that followed the original biblical texts "word for word" and therefore were most likely to convey the original divine intent? Or does Chaucer mean to say—taking "Christ" in line 739 as primarily referring to Jesus, the incarnate Son of God, who acts and speaks in the Gospels, rather than to God, who speaks through all the characters in the Bible—that Christ's speeches as reported in the *sermo humilis* style of the New Testament evangelists are in some sense like the "rustic" or "bourgeois" speeches of the Miller, Reeve, Merchant, or Shipman as reported by Chaucer the pilgrim-poet?[10] Did Chaucer the poet really think they were comparable? And was the comparison in and of itself meant to justify Chaucer's stylistic procedure, without reference to the very different contents of the Gospels and his own secular compositions? Because Chaucer avoids mentioning Augustine's universally acknowledged claim about the significance of everything in the Bible ("that whatever appears in the divine Word that does not literally pertain to virtuous behavior or to the truth of faith you must take to be figurative"), and because he has put both meanings of "Christ" in play—Christ as author of the Bible and Christ as a character who acts and speaks in the Bible—which, if any, of the latter inferences takes precedence over the others remains indeterminate.

In the *De Doctrina Christiana*, as we have seen, Augustine's analysis of the Bible's style and mode of signification equated biblical and secular poetics in most respects, but Augustine held back from endorsing secular poetic practice on this account. Instead, he extrapolated from biblical precedent to Christian rhetorical practice. It remained for later writers to take the next step. As A. J. Minnis points out, it was the humanist revival of the fourteenth century that provided the intellectual climate in which "a writer could justify his own literary procedure or *forma tractandi* by appealing to a Scriptural model, without in any way offending against the great *auctoritas* of the Bible."[11] Yet the convincingly demonstrated truth of the latter statement does not, of course, prove that a fourteenth-century poet who does appeal to the precedent of a scriptural model to justify his own literary procedure will necessarily avoid "offending against the great *auctoritas* of the Bible," or even be concerned, necessarily, about avoiding doing so. For Chaucer, by reaching through the *modus loquendi* of the evangelists to the *ipsissima verba* of Christ himself, had taken a step beyond merely citing "the precedent of the *modus loquendi* . . . [of] the Four Evangelists who had recorded the life of Christ" to justify "his practice of speaking 'rudeliche and large' after the manner of the Canterbury pilgrims," as Minnis alleges.[12] By using the adverb "brode" both in reference to the diction of "Christ" as a character as well as to the *modus loquendi* of "Christ" as an author, Chaucer implied a number of things: that the Bible treats a wide range of subjects, some of which, as Augustine put it, might "seem to be shameful"; that Jesus spoke humbly and "frankly," addressing simple people in a low style, using words suited to their experience of plowing, planting, reaping, and fishing; and that Jesus spoke "clearly," "openly," and "without restraint" when addressing those same simple people in what is at times the vocabulary of violence and venality, of lust, fornication, adultery, fire, sword, and woes everlasting.[13] Within this range of implication, the precise terms of the analogy between the Bible and Chaucer's own sometimes bawdy literary creations remain obscure. Chaucer does not specify which of the implied analogies is to be preferred or which, if any, is out of bounds. If the magnitude of Chaucer's possible "offense" in drawing any of these analogies is hard to assess, the originality of his gesture of justifying bawdy language in a vernacular poem by invoking the example of Christ is clear.

III

Turning now to the second passage in which Chaucer explicitly invokes the Bible to explain and to justify secular poetic practice, we shall find that Chaucer now offers a more complete analogy between the style and content of the Bible and the style and content of one of his own literary creations. This time, however, the analogy is put forward in the introduction to a prose treatise, the "Tale of Melibee," and we turn from considering questions of diction (bawdy or otherwise) to the larger questions of narrative mode and truth content.

In the link between Chaucer's interrupted tale of "Sir Thopas" and the "Tale of Melibee" offered in its place, Harry Bailey objects to Chaucer's "drasty speche" and demands of him anything, either of "mirth" or of "doctrine," in verse or prose—anything!—just as long as it is better than "Sir Thopas." Chaucer assents, "gladly":

> by Goddes sweete pyne!
> I wol yow telle a litel thyng in prose
> That oghte liken yow, as I suppose,
> Or elles, certes, ye been to daungerous.
> It is a moral tale vertuous,
> Al be it told somtyme in sondry wyse
> Of sondry folk, as I shal yow devyse.
> As thus: ye woot that every Evaungelist,

That telleth us the peyne of Jhesu Crist
Ne seith nat alle thyng as his felawe dooth;
But nathelees hir sentence is al sooth,
And alle acorden as in hire sentence,
Al be ther in hir tellyng difference.
For somme of hem seyn moore, and somme seyn lesse,
Whan they his pitous passioun expresse—
I meene of Mark, Mathew, Luc, and John—
But doutelees hir sentence is al oon.

(7.936–52)

The "Tale of Melibee," Chaucer asserts, is a "moral tale vertuous" even though, as with the Gospel narratives vis-à-vis one another, there may be some discrepancies of detail between it and its source.[14]

Now this assertion must strike a reader as odd. To begin with, we might wonder why Chaucer thinks anyone would assume that the "morality" of a story depends upon its perfect fidelity to the words of its source rather than upon its subject and its mode of treatment—were it not for the fact that he had told us so himself, in the defense of a kind of photographic literalism in narrative that he had put forward in the "General Prologue." There, as we saw, Chaucer asserts that he is obliged to repeat the exact words of the tales that were told on the pilgrimage ("Whoso shal telle a tale after a man, / He moot reherce as ny as evere he kan / *Everich a word*" [1.731–33; my emphasis]). And Chaucer repeats the same argument, feigning reluctance and claiming that he is under duress, immediately after he has recounted the stylistically elevated but severely abbreviated "Knight's Tale" and before he begins (ostensibly) to repeat (rather than actually to invent) the sometimes obscene language used by the Miller in the immediately following "Miller's Tale" (see 1.3,167–75).[15] Furthermore, Chaucer adds, those readers or listeners who object to the "Miller's Tale" and the other "cherles tales" should skip these and choose from among the many other tales that won't offend them. Now that he has warned us, the responsibility for any possible offense is exclusively our own (1.3,176–85).

Finally, Chaucer adds with a wink, "And eek men shal nat maken ernest of game" (1.3,186). This closing advice to the reader not to take seriously what is meant only in jest serves as Chaucer's extra insurance, just in case we should read and be offended even after we have been warned to choose among the tales carefully; but it also both undercuts Chaucer's "earnest" claim that he must tell everything or else falsify his sources and his previous claim that Plato and Christ authorize his strict fidelity to the words of his sources—even his "churlish" sources.

That the axiomatic necessity of word-for-word fidelity in narrative advanced by Chaucer in relation to all of his potentially offensive tales has been modified in relation to his "Tale of Melibee" becomes clear in the following passage. I pick up Chaucer's introduction to "Melibee" where I interrupted it:

> *Therfore, lordynges alle, I yow biseche,*
> If that yow thynke I varie as in my speche,
> As thus, though that I telle somwhat moore
> Of proverbes than ye han herd bifoore
> Comprehended in this litel tretys heere,
> To enforce with th'effect of my mateere;
> *And though I nat the same wordes seye*
> *As ye han herd, yet to yow alle I preye*
> *Blameth me nat*; for, as in my sentence,
> Shul ye nowher fynden difference
> Fro the *sentence of this tretys lyte*
> After the which *this murye tale* I write.
> (7.953–64; my emphasis)

Chaucer had tried to deflect criticism in advance of telling potentially offensive tales such as those of the Miller and the Reeve by claiming that he was obliged to report these tales word for word; by declaring that, furthermore, the reader has been forewarned ("arette it nat my vileynye" [1.726]; "I moot reherce / Hir tales alle, be they bettre or werse" [1.3, 173–74]; "Blameth nat me. . . . Avyseth yow, and put me out of blame" [1.3,181, 3,185]); and by asserting, finally, that these "offensive" tales were not meant to be taken seriously in the first place. In the same way he now tries to deflect criticism in advance of telling the "Tale of Melibee" ("Therfore, lordynges alle, I yow biseche"; "blameth me nat"), but for the opposite reason: this time, Chaucer says, the narrative source has *not* been rendered verbatim (in "the same wordes . . . As ye han herd") but has been "enforced" (i.e., "reinforced" or "strengthened") with "proverbs"; and yet, even so, its "sentence" (meaning) has been faithfully reproduced.

A further connection between these two, contradictory defenses of narrative strategy is that they both adduce the Bible for support, but in contradictory ways. As we have seen, earlier Chaucer claimed that the precedent of the "brode" speech of Christ and of the evangelists who report Christ's words justified his use of "frank" language to guarantee word-for-word fidelity to his sources. Now, however, Chaucer claims that the precedent of four diverse gospel narratives of Christ's passion justifies the opposite procedure. The irony is sharp, not to say daringly intense: first the evangelists' faithful reports of Christ's words were used to justify scurrilous secular narratives; now their differing accounts of his life prove that varying the outer form of a "virtuous" story does not necessarily alter its inner meaning or "sentence." Fidelity to different aspects of the literary precedent of the Gospels yields differing results. On the one hand, when the stress is on word-for-word fidelity to a source, the outcome is an impious, entertaining fabliau like the "Miller's Tale." On the other hand, when the stress is on following the "sentence" or "essential meaning" of a source rather than its exact words, the outcome is a pious, edifying, personification-allegory like the "Tale of Melibee." As we saw in the case of the "Miller's Tale," Augustine's defense in the *De Doctrina Christiana* of the occasionally "shameful" language of the Bible and his emphasis on paying attention to the exact wording of the biblical text—even if those exact words are regularly allegorized away to make the history and customs of the Hebrews consistently yield Christian doctrine—had provided Chaucer with a ready precedent. In the case of the "Tale of Melibee," Chaucer's principal authority for the axiomatic view of the relationship between narrative form and meaning in the various Gospels would again have been Augustine, who expounded the relevant principles most fully and influentially around the year 400 C.E.—in a gap left open, as it were, by his still-to-be-completed *De Doctrina Christiana*—in a work entitled *De Consensu Evangelistarum* (*On the Harmony of the Gospels*).[16]

In the following passage, for example, Augustine's explanation of how the Gospels relate to one another as narratives recalls what Chaucer says, in summary fashion, about the "Tale of Melibee" in relation to its source:

It is sufficiently obvious that, since the truth of the Gospel, conveyed in that word of God which abides eternal and unchangeable above all that is created, but which at the same time has been disseminated throughout the world by the instrumentality of temporal symbols, and by the tongues of men, has possessed itself of the most exalted height of authority, we ought not to suppose that any one of the writers is giving an unreliable account, if when several persons are recalling some matter either heard or seen by them, they fail to follow the very same plan, or to use the very same words, while describing, nevertheless, the self-same fact. Neither should we indulge such a supposition, although the order of the words may be varied; or although some words may be substituted in place of others, which nevertheless have the same meaning; or although something may be left unsaid, either because it has not occurred to the mind of the recorder, or because it becomes readily intelligible from other statements which are given; or although, among other matters which (may not bear directly on his immediate purpose, but which) he decides on mentioning rather for the sake of the narrative, and in order to preserve the proper order of time, one of them may introduce something which he does not feel called upon to expound as a whole at length, but only to touch upon in part; or although, with the view of illustrating his meaning, and making it thoroughly clear, the person to whom authority is given to compose the narrative makes some additions of his own, not indeed in the subject-matter itself, but in the words by which it is expressed; or although, while retaining a perfectly reliable comprehension of the fact itself, he may not be entirely successful, however he may make that his aim, in calling to mind and reciting anew with the most literal accuracy the very words which he heard on the occasion. (2.12.28; p. 118; Weinrich, pp. 127–28)[17]

Here Augustine's nervously detailed balancing of divine intentions against human execution (the "exalted height of authority" that axiomatically must underlie the Gospels against the fallible human recorder who "makes some additions of his own" and may even fail to recall "with the most literal accuracy the very words which he heard on the occasion") reveals the anxious intensity of his response to a problem with profound consequences not only in matters of faith but for the literary theory and practice of a Christian author like Chaucer, and for the development of subsequent western narrative theory as well. For after confirming (in passing) the central claim of the *De Doctrina Christiana* regarding literal and figurative meaning in the Bible (i.e., that God speaks in the Bible through "the instrumentality of temporal symbols and by the tongues of men"), Augustine proceeds to place the Bible and secular letters on a new, and more explicitly equal, footing.

But if the Gospels are not absolutely consistent with one another in what they narrate, and if they share with other historical records a measure of unreliability, a margin of "human error" with regard to reported "facts," then upon what authority does the truth of the Bible and of one's faith stand?

IV

Augustine's attempt throughout the *De Consensu Evangelistarum* to explain away scores of variations among the Gospels goes well beyond theological harmonization and apologetics. For Augustine extends and extrapolates from his argument about biblical narrative modes in a most remarkable way, anticipating Chaucer's development of a similar argument in the "Sir Thopas–Melibee Link." In a crucial passage enumerating ways in which the evangelists may "seem to err," Augustine extrapolates from biblical narrative to narrative in general:

Moreover, if anyone affirms that the evangelists ought certainly to have had that kind of capacity imparted to them by the power of the Holy Spirit, which would secure them against all variation the one from the other, either in the kind of words, or in their order, or in their number, that person fails to perceive, that just in proportion as the authority of the evangelists . . . is made pre-eminent, the credit of all other men who offer true statement of events ought to have been established on a stronger basis by their instrumentality: so that when several parties happen to narrate the same circumstances, none of them can by any means be rightly charged with untruthfulness if he differs from the other only in such a way as can be defended on the ground of the antecedent example of the evangelists themselves. *For as we are not at liberty either to suppose or to say that any one of the evangelists has stated what is false, so it will be apparent that any other writer is as little chargeable with untruth, with whom, in the process of recalling anything for narration, it has fared only in a way similar to that in which it is shown to have fared with those evangelists.* And just as it belongs to the highest morality to guard against all that is false, so ought we all the more to be ruled by an authority so eminent, to the effect that we should not suppose ourselves to come upon what must be false, when we find narratives of any writers differ from each other in the manner in which the records of the evangelists are proved to contain variations. At the same time, in what most seriously concerns the faithfulness of doctrinal teaching, we should also understand that it is not so much in mere words, as rather truth in the facts themselves, that is to be sought and embraced; for as to writers who do not employ precisely the same modes of statement, if they only do not present discrepancies with respect to the facts and the sentiments themselves, we accept them as holding the same position in veracity. (2.12.28; p. 119; my emphasis; Weinrich, pp. 128–29)

Starting from the premise that all four evangelists speak only what is true even when they appear to contradict one another, Augustine moves on in this passage to a most unexpected and momentous inference and conclusion, offering nothing less than a theoretical foundation—indeed, a kind of etiological foundation myth—for the "veracity" of "narratives of any writers"; that is, for the writing of secular history and secular narrative in general. Augustine's position as the preeminent teacher of doctrine in the catholic Middle Ages would have made this striking claim about the divinely supported position of the secular writer immediately acceptable.[18] Too often, Augustine's place in the history of the development of medieval literary theory has been defined with exclusive reference to the *De Doctrina Christiana* and the idea of biblical allegory, focused on *caritas* and *cupiditas*, that Augustine formulated in that work and applied systematically in many others.[19] In light of the radical claim for the "truth" of secular narrative advanced in the *De Consensu Evangelistarum*, a general reassessment of Augustine's contribution to medieval literary theory, and of his influence on Chaucer and other medieval vernacular authors in particular, is surely in order.

For our present purposes what we may extrapolate from Augustine's claims about the veracity of discrepant secular narratives is that Chaucer had an Augustinian precedent for citing the evangelists as models to validate his strategy as a secular author who rendered the "sentence" of a source without following it word for word. Yet even if Chaucer was adapting this Augustinian idea, there is still something extraordinary in the way he applied it. For the self-importance and "seriousness" of the analogy that Chaucer draws between the Gospels vis-à-vis one another and his "Tale of Melibee" vis-à-vis its French source is, by virtue of its sheer pretentiousness, provocative of thoughts in precisely the opposite direction. That is, Chaucer's comical inflation of the "Tale of Melibee" by biblical analogy accords with the obvious additional deflationary comic touches in the link prior to the tale itself, where Chaucer returns from the lofty heights of authorial self-importance to his characteristically ironic and self-denigrating posture ("this litel tretys," "this murye tale" [7.957, 964]), and assumes once again his familiar posture as the self-effacing and apologetic narrator of the previously interrupted tale of "Sir Thopas."[20]

V

In the prose passage of "Retraction" at the end of the *Canterbury Tales* (10.1,081–92), Chaucer quotes the Bible and links it explicitly with his own compositions one last time:

Now preye I to hem alle that herkne *this litel tretys* or rede, that if ther be any thyng in it that liketh hem, that thereof they thanken oure Lord Jhesu Crist, of whom procedeth al wit and al goodnesse, / And if ther be any thyng that displese hem, I preye hem also that they *arette* [attribute] *it to the defaute of myn unkonnynge* and nat to my wyl, that wolde ful fayn have seyd bettre if I hadde had konnynge / *For oure book seith, "Al that is writen is writen for oure doctrine,"* and that is myn entente. (10.1,081–83; my emphasis)

Though the proximate object of these lines is the "Parson's Tale," they also hark back to previous tales. Earlier, with his tongue obviously in his cheek, Chaucer had referred to the lengthy "Tale of Melibee," too, as a "litel tretys." And earlier still, in the "General Prologue," he had asked to be forgiven for his failure to observe decorum in depicting his fellow pilgrims by offering a similar apology for his "unkonnyng" ("My wit is short, ye may wel understonde" [1.746]); and he had asked us not to "arette" (attribute) his bawdy tales to his "vileynye" (1.726). In addition, at the conclusion of the "Nun's Priest's Tale," the Nun's Priest had also quoted from Romans

15.4 ("For what things soever were written, were written for our learning:
that through patience and the comfort of the scriptures, we might have
hope")[21]—the same verse quoted from in this portion of the "Retraction"—as he drew an analogy between Paul's sacred text and his own secular fable of a cock and fox, encouraging his audience to search out the
fable's deeper meaning: "For Seint Paul seith that al that writen is, / To oure
doctrine it is ywrite, ywis; / Taketh the fruyt, and lat the chaf be stille"
(7.3,441–43). In Chaucer's second and final reference to Romans 15.4, the
referent of the verse remains ultimately ambiguous. Its possible objects include Chaucer's own edifying "Parson's Tale"; some (if not all) of the other
Canterbury Tales (especially the "Nun's Priest's Tale," where Paul's global
claim regarding the doctrinal pith in all scriptural writings had been adduced explicitly by the Nun's Priest to validate a seemingly trivial piece of
secular writing); and as always, the edifying works of Scripture to which
all, or some, or at the very least one of Chaucer's *Canterbury Tales* is being
compared. This second and final quotation from Saint Paul's Epistle to the
Romans thus reopens the question of privileged biblical pre-text and de-
fensive secular derivative text that Chaucer had explored in the "General
Prologue" and the "Sir Thopas–Melibee Link," even as the rest of the "Retraction" ostensibly seeks, once and for all, to close it.[22]

VI

In the three passages from the *Canterbury Tales* that I have discussed,
Chaucer speaks about the Bible in ways that reveal something quite unexpected, and generally unacknowledged, about what it meant to him in
relation to his own literary endeavors. To a large extent, these passages set
Chaucer apart from the many characters in his fiction who also quote from
or allude to the Bible in variously serious or comic ways.[23] Instead, they
link him to a tradition of learned interpretation of the Bible in the Latin
West going back to Jerome and Augustine and, indirectly but no less firmly,
with those divinely inspired authors of Scripture whose authority Chaucer's fictional exegetes challenge so provocatively.

Though Chaucer's ambivalence about the relationship between his
own works and the Bible had the most venerable Augustinian precedent,
there were similar influences nearer to home. Among his contemporaries
(or near-contemporaries) were men like Heinrich von Oyta (an influential
Austrian master of the sacred page), Nicholas de Lyra (a major influence
on late-medieval and Reformation exegesis in general and on Luther in
particular), and other late-fourteenth-century exegetes who were surpris-

ingly critical in their approach to the Bible, calling attention not only to its divine otherness but also to its human familiarity, and willing to go even further than Augustine in recognizing its literariness and its contingent textuality.[24] Having shaken off the decisive weight of Augustine's univocal method of reading the Bible allegorically—and even if they continued to rely exclusively on Jerome's Latin "Vulgate" Bible translation when christologically interpreted Old Testament passages were at issue—von Oyta, de Lyra and other fourteenth-century exegetes nevertheless also recognized that textual corruption of the Vulgate had become a serious problem. To correct their Latin Bibles in order to raise the level of their exegesis, they began looking into Hebrew and Greek biblical texts.[25] Because of new philosophical interests and approaches that flourished in the fourteenth century (summarized inadequately under the heading "nominalism"), philosophers became less likely to turn to their Bibles in their search for intellectual truth; and theologians, who in turn became less likely to turn to philosophy in their search for religious truth, consequently became even more dependent on their Bibles.[26] It was all the more important, therefore, that their Bibles be accurate and their methodology for using those Bibles be sophisticated—or, at the very least, defensible against the attacks of skeptics. One of the most important of these fourteenth-century Scripturocentric opponents of skepticism, John Wyclif, was himself a very controversial figure (though not yet considered a heretic).[27] Whether or not Chaucer knew Wyclif personally, there are many signs in Chaucer's poetry that testify to his interest in Wyclif's controversial but nevertheless fundamentally Augustinian ideas about biblical interpretation.[28]

The activities of fourteenth-century philosophers and poets who were skeptical about the Bible's unique authority, and the responses of both orthodox and heterodox opponents of these philosophers and poets were to have immediate and long-range consequences of the greatest importance. On the orthodox side, the efforts of von Oyta, de Lyra, and others fed a fourteenth-century revival of Greek and Hebrew biblical studies and a new, critical attitude to texts in general, and to the text of the Bible in particular, that helped constitute the cultural shift of the coming European Renaissance.[29] On the heterodox side, the activities of Wyclif and his disciples were, as we now realize, fourteenth-century steps leading to the Reformation side of that cultural shift.[30] The idea that Chaucer's works should be seen as major pre-Renaissance and pre-Reformation monuments of this fourteenth-century world (if not as contributory causes then at least as cultural products whose true milieu these pre-Renaissance and pre-Reformation developments provide) is not new. We have long been accustomed to the idea that Chaucer's contribution to these progressive pre-Renaissance and pre-Reformation cultural developments is evidenced by his openness to a multiplicity of secular humanist poetic influences, as well as by his sharp criticism of various forms of corruption in the church.[31] More recently, a new generation of scholars sensitive to both literary form and medieval social and economic history have found Chaucer's greatest originality and his major accomplishment as a literary artist to reside in his subtle depiction of the vexed social and economic realities of his day—and ours.[32] But if Chaucer's stylistic and thematic innovations had their social and economic correlatives, to be fully understood these complex and appealing aspects of his poetry must also be considered as evidence of his central concern with, and as facets of his response to, a problem that had bedeviled Christian culture from the time of Augustine but that had become especially troubling in the late fourteenth century: the problem of the mutual translatability of secular and biblical poetics.

The Curse and Blessing of Babel;
or, Looking Back on Universalisms

Aleida Assmann

*I*n pondering the problem of translation I thought it safe to go back to the story of Babel. I expected the story that tells of an original parting—the severing of languages, the dissemination of nations, the differentiation of cultures—to be a genuine point of departure. I could hardly expect that it would lead me to a history of universalisms. The aspect of the story that has most haunted the imagination turned out to be the one original language that was lost at Babel. The myth about multiplicity has generated a host of visions in which the shattered unity is restored. These visions of universalism are more than curious chapters in the mental archives of mankind; they are myths that have defined images of the self and the other, oriented action in history, supported institutional and political claims, motivated attitudes of aggression and tolerance. They were in fact the guiding fictions of western history.

Since we are no longer in the grip of these visions, we can afford to look at them rather than with them. What we see are various mental frameworks in which the One plays the dominant role. What has an examination of these visions to do with the problem of intercultural translation? In trying to answer this question, we become aware of an epochal turning point. Until very recently, what I would call the regulative ideal of the One was considered as the necessary framework for intercultural translation. Today, we are beginning to realize that it was precisely this ideal that has prevented it. My reason for the following excursion into the history of ideas is that one possible way to overcome mental dispositions is to remember them.

Christian Universalism: The Tower of Babel
and the Miracle of Pentecost

The story about the tower of Babel as told in Genesis 11.1–9 has a key-word. This is "one" (*ekhad*). In the original state, the whole earth was united in one language, and this language consisted of "one" (= invaria-ble?) words; the Hebrew text here uses "one" in the plural. This state of oneness is to be manifested in a name, and the name is to be represented in a colossal monument reaching up to heaven. God recognizes this act as a dangerous provocation; and seeing that the oneness of their language and words (the phrase from the beginning is repeated) is the condition for fur-ther dangerous projects, he descends to obstruct their work by multiplying their languages. The insistence on words like "one" and "name" makes it obvious that divine prerogatives are about to be usurped by man. A point of the story seems to be that the One is reserved for God, while the Many is the proper dimension for man.[1]

In the Hebrew Bible, there are obvious references to the story of Babel. These are verses in which the prophets anticipate the messianic solution to the problem of mundane confusion. Messianic unity and unanimity over-come the separation of the languages as well as the fatal split between the truth of the heart and the lie of the mouth. In the prophetic visions, the return to messianic unity is described as a process of catastrophic trans-formation, involving violent means of purification.[2] In the tradition of Christian exegesis, the references to messianic unity are replaced by a New Testament story. It is the miracle of Pentecost that entered into a typolog-ical constellation with the story of Babel. Both stories acquire their ster-eotypic meaning within this paradigmatic constellation of Old Testament and New Testament text: the earlier story is interpreted in terms of sin, punishment, curse, the latter in terms of spirit, redemption, grace. Unity, oneness, is at the core of the miracle of Pentecost. In this case, however, the differentiation of languages is not suspended, there is no return to the "one" language with the invariable words. Instead, a new dimension is opened in which unity, oneness, is miraculously achieved, this time not ma-terially from below but pneumatically from above: the realm of the spirit.

The second story takes place on the day of Pentecost at Jerusalem. This is the description of the event as rendered in Acts 2.1–11:

When the day of Pentecost had come, they were all together in one place. And sud-denly a sound came from heaven like the rush of a mighty wind, and it filled the house where they were sitting. And there appeared to them tongues as of fire, distributed and resting on each one of them. And they were all filled with the Holy Spirit and began to speak in other tongues, as the Spirit gave them utterance.

Now there were dwelling in Jerusalem Jews, devout men from every nation under heaven. And at this sound the multitude came together, and they were bewildered, because each one heard them speaking in his own language. And they were amazed and wondered, saying, "Are they not all these who are speaking Galileans? And how is it that we hear, each of us in his own native language? Parthians and Medes and Elamites and residents of Mesopotamia, Judea and Cappadocia, Pontus and Asia, Phrygia and Pamphylia, Egypt and the parts of Libya belonging to Cyrene, and visitors from Rome, both Jews and proselytes, Cretans and Arabians, we hear them telling in our tongues the mighty works of God."

The meticulous enumeration of the many ethnic communities confirms the effects of the curse of Babel; it is a faithful account of the multicultural situation in the Roman Empire. With the linguistic fall at Babel language received its materiality. A language that is not understood turns into a dense mass of sounds. It is reduced to external noise, to dross or impenetrable materiality. Its very opposite is the language spoken at Jerusalem. This language is sheer immateriality, transparency, immediacy. Its materiality is evaporated. "Pneuma" like the rush of a mighty wind penetrates and transforms matter. Pneuma suspends for a moment the linguistic curse, not in returning to an original unified language but in achieving unified and immediate understanding via the different languages.[3]

Pentecost is the feast of the Holy Spirit. To link the gospel with the Holy Spirit is to cut its bond with materiality, be it that of the written letter or of words in a particular language. The Holy Spirit guarantees truth beyond language, sense in its immateriality, immediacy, clarity, and completeness. In establishing the norm of such a spiritual core of meaning, language and writing are reduced to conventional sign systems. They are looked upon as external shells, instrumental vehicles without any inherent quality or efficacy.

The Holy Spirit is generally held to be an exclusively Christian institution. With the introduction of the concept of the Holy Spirit, Christian semiotics has changed fundamentally; a dividing line was drawn, separating the material word and letter from the immaterial meaning. This change in the sign system which occurred in the name of the Holy Spirit promoted transcendence of the written law and its letter, translation of the holy Scripture, transformation in history. In affirming the Holy Spirit as an immaterial energy, Christianity cut off its links with the letter of the law—that is, with its Jewish roots.

It is true that the breach has promoted a contradistinction on either side, the Jews themselves minimizing elements of their own tradition after they had been embraced by Christians and turned into an alien dogma. The language the apostle used to describe the miracle of Pentecost, however, did not fall from heaven like a fiery tongue. Its motifs and images belong to a background of a common Jewish mysticism which was revived in the festivities of Shavuoth. According to rabbinic understanding, prophecy was intimately linked with the Holy Spirit: "the spirit of prophecy is the Holy Spirit."[4] There are voices in the rabbinic tradition that claim that in two prominent instances the charisma of the Holy Spirit was extended to the whole people of Israel. One is the crossing of the Red Sea, when all the people sang along with Moses; the other is the consecration of the holy tabernacle through the Shekhinah. A midrash describes how, when the column of fire fell from heaven into the tabernacle, the thousands and tens of thousands who stood in the court of the desert sanctuary "all saw the great miracle and fell down on their faces . . . and the Holy Spirit rested on them and they sang a song in joy." K. E. Grözinger, who cites this description, continues: "This seems to be the tradition invoked by the New Testament to describe the miracle of Pentecost."[5] The intervention of the Holy Spirit in the desert, the singular event of ecstatic, inspired collective singing, was transformed in the Christian tradition into an event supporting an exclusive and universal claim to faith.

It is worth noting that the typological confrontation of the two stories was not used before the second half of the fourth century C.E.[6] Before it was firmly established as a homiletic topos, the theme "unity versus diversity" was discussed by Origen, who related the story of Babel to a verse in Acts 4.32 ("praising God with one heart and one soul"). In this context he made a generalization which was to set the pattern for the readings to follow: "You will find that wherever you encounter in Scripture terms like plurality, chasm, division, dissonance or the like, they are evaluated as evil [kakias]. Where you meet unity and unanimousness, however, such terms are synonymous with goodness [aretes]."[7] Likewise Augustine compared the stories of the linguistic curse and the pneumatic miracle and established the moral contrast between pride and division on the one hand and humility and unity on the other. According to his formula, "the spirit of pride dispersed the languages, the holy spirit reunited them."[8]

We have said before that a possible lesson of the story of Babel could be that One is the prerogative of God, not men. One is not only a number; it is a divine quality. In the Christian reception of the tradition, a significant change occurred. The divine quality of oneness was extended from the eternal realm of God to that of human institutions—one god, one Christ, one

Spirit, one bishop, one church.[9] The disciples and apostles were defined as agents of the Holy Spirit, promoting a unity which is not the compact material oneness (one language with invariable words) that existed before Babel but a translinguistic unity of the faith, the heart, the spirit, the church. Thus, the contrast has shifted; it is no longer the plurality of men over against the oneness of God but the plurality of the pagans over against the oneness of the Christian faith. According to Augustine, it is apt for the savage gentiles to have divided languages; "if they want one language, may they come to the church; for even in the diversity of the material languages, there is one language in the faith of the heart."[10]

The idea of a mystic, pneumatic unity of the faith "in" the very variety of the natural languages was the rock (to use an inappropriate metaphor) on which the institution of mission was founded. Or, to use another metaphor: the spiritual status of the gospel was the gold standard that permitted the use of native tongues as convertible currencies. From the very start, Christianity defined itself as a message rather than a medium.[11] For the church fathers, there was no longer one holy language of the Bible, but three: Hebrew was supplemented by Greek and Latin. This linguistic plurality created an atmosphere of linguistic relativity which facilitated the leap from scriptural to vernacular languages.[12] In the eastern church, which was not under the dominance of Latin, the affirmation of the mother tongues had already begun in late antiquity. Not only could the Holy Spirit be incarnated in any human language, but the mother tongue had a particular aptness to revive this spirit. Up to this day, the eastern liturgy retains the standard typological correspondence between the division at Babel and the unity at Jerusalem:

Once, the tongues were divided at the occasion of the tower of Babel. But now, tongues are filled with wisdom due to the glory of knowing God. There, God had condemned the sinners. Here, Christ has illumined the fishers through the spirit. There, punishment was imposed through the sounds of language. Now, the consonance of the languages is renewed for the salvation of our souls. . . . The epiphany of the holy spirit has united the divided tongues of those who were parted in strife. He has founded the unity of the believers on the trinity. . . . When he confused the languages, the Holy one divided the nations. When he distributed the tongues of fire, he summoned all to unity.[13]

The story of Babel is a myth of diversification; the story of Jerusalem is a myth not of unity (which is not to be restored) but of universalization as it is to be achieved through the languages and the course of history. From Augustine to Karl Barth, the confrontation of the two texts has elicited the stock interpretation for Christian exegesis. Rather than illuminating the hidden meaning inherent in the texts, the topos has shed on the stories the light of particular values. This textual confrontation has not only oriented Christian self-definition; it has also modeled the stereotype of the other. In linking Genesis 11 with Acts 2, the Hebrew story became a pretext for the Greek story. In doing so, it was used as the foil for the new myth of unity which was to become the central doctrine of the church. Ethnic and linguistic diversity was affirmed as a way to spiritual unity. To restore unity was the central task of the church, and it was to be achieved through mission.[14] Furthermore, the confrontation of the two stories supported a strategy of amnesia in Christian theology which covered its Jewish roots and replaced them with emphatic distinctions. The milieu of a common spirituality—the prehistory of the Holy Spirit in ecstatic Jewish mysticism—was deliberately forgotten. In its stead, polemical opposites reigned and unleashed an inexhaustible aggressive potential through history.

Eschatological Universalism: The Doors of Heaven Opening

The cabalists developed their own reading of the story of Babel. For them, the remedy for the linguistic fiasco lay not in the message but in the medium of holy Scripture. Their task was the reconstruction of the divine language of creation, the restoration of the mystical names of God in the text of the Torah. Inspired by cabalistic theories about the mystical quality of biblical language, Renaissance scholars adopted the vision of restoring Hebrew as the original and universal language. During this period, ideological disputes and schisms were widely assumed to derive from language problems. They were considered symptoms of imperfect communication and understanding, both having their roots in the corruption and pluralization of languages.[15] To restore Hebrew to universal dignity was not a philological achievement; it was an eschatological step toward cosmological insight and universal peace. Only the divine original language could provide a common heritage and a common frame for all nations of the world.

Cabalistic linguistics attempted to rediscover the language spoken by God in the act of creation. Hebrew was considered a divine language, replete with cosmological mysteries. The humanists who studied with Jewish rabbis shared the eschatological vision of an imminent messianic age of peace and illumination. Early modernity ("Neuzeit") was conceived of as a messianic age ("Endzeit"). Pico della Mirandola and Johannes Reuchlin were famous Christian Hebraists at the turn of the sixteenth century. In his book *De Verbo Mirifico* (1494) Reuchlin wrote that Hebrew was the uncorrupted original language: the speech of the Hebrews is simple, pure, holy, brief, and constant, which means that it is a language of cosmic, not communicative, power, a language exempt from time and change. It is God's language. In a letter he wrote: "The mediator between God and man was, as we read in the Pentateuch, language, yet not any language but only Hebrew. God wished his secrets to be known to mortal man through Hebrew."[16]

The fascination of Hebrew lasted through the fifteenth till the seventeenth century.[17] This one and only language from which all the other languages were poor derivatives was held to be strictly untranslatable. A language containing the mystical names of God with their magical energy of divine creation is by definition untranslatable. Cabala was founded on a semiology very different from that of the church fathers. It did not start from a distinction between outer and inner aspects of the sign, between word and meaning or letter and spirit. In the semiotics of cabala, the spirit resides within the material word and letter. Altering a single letter is considered a spiritual act which may lead to the destruction of the universe. The sound and the script were thought to be charged with spiritual energy. Cornelius Agrippa stressed this point in his *Occult Philosophy* (1510):

The profound meanings, and signs are inherent in those characters, and figures of them, as also numbers, place, order, and revolution, so that Origenes therefore thought that those names being translated into another Idiome, do not retain their proper vertue. For only originall names, which are rightly imposed, because they signify naturally, have naturall activity: it is not so with them which signifie at pleasure, which have no activity, as they are signifying, but as they are certain naturall things in themselves.[18]

Translatability, therefore, is the mark of human languages: they are convertible into each other because they are composed of conventional signs and have no activity. The one language of Hebrew lies beyond the realm of the many languages.[19]

As stressed before, the recovery of Hebrew as the primal language was related to the dawn of the messianic age. In the same vein, vernacular languages were claimed to be the messianic language, and the cabalistic qualities of Hebrew were discovered as individual mother tongues. For Jacob Boehme, his native idiom was not a conventional language. He freely applied cabalistic speculations to the German language. He claimed that this language yielded the deepest mysteries, a claim which he extended to any individual:

If you understand your mother tongue aright it will provide as profound a basis for wisdom as Hebrew or Latin; the scholars may boast with their knowledge like a conceited bride, it is all for nothing, their high art is now lying low. The spirit showeth that before the end (of this world) many a layman will know more and understand deeper than the sage doctors: because the doors of heaven are now opening.[20]

While the doors of heaven are opening, the messianic draft rushes in and transforms the conditions of the fallen universe in a pentecostal/messianic event. As the eschatological end of history was felt to draw near, any language turned into a messianic language—that is, into a genuine medium of revelation directly accessible to everyone.[21] At this messianic dawn, faith was no longer mediated through the institution of the church but propelled directly through the intervention of the Holy Spirit. In this last phase of history the spirit takes over. Radical spiritualists like Boehme and Sebastian Franck believed that as the world was precipitated toward the messianic end of universal truth, the Holy Spirit was poured into the vernaculars and into the hearts of the believers.

Enlightened Universalism: The Metaphysics of Absence

Modernity has a Janus face. One face can be called the eschatological face and identified with millennial hopes which agitated cabalists, alchemists, and spiritualists. It is oriented toward the imminent coming of the Messiah. The widely shared belief was that in one way or another messianic truth would finally hit the axis of history and transform the world in a radical way. The other face of modernity can be called the enlightened face. It looks in the opposite direction and considers the world as it is rather than as it will be. It suspends the eschatological vision and cools the fervent messianic hopes. It has promoted the process of secularization, rationalization, and disenchantment in the world. The Janus face of modernity is responsible for the complexity, the ambivalence, and the dialectic turns of the historical process.

Eschatological universalism had invoked the fiery language of the spirit, while enlightened universalism suspended, even suppressed, this source of illumination. It blocked the way to the revelation of divine mysteries and exchanged illumination and truth for a void, an absence. In a destructive atmosphere of political strife and ideological warfare, a new theory of universalism arose. Its vision was not to restore a single faith or a single language but to accept the difference of creeds and languages on the basis of an underlying unity of truth. This truth could fulfill its function only if it had a hidden or virtual status; as soon as it came to the fore and was associated with a particular claim, this would invariably mean a return to the tyranny of the One that had so catastrophically shaken the world.

The program of enlightened universalism was therefore to keep truth on the level of deep structure and prevent it from surfacing. It was to remain hidden and implicit as something to be discovered rather than revealed or claimed.

For Cusanus, the One, the truth of God, was strictly transcendent. There was no way to approach or partake of it, whether by word, letter, or spirit. The void center, the radical and unapproachable hiddenness of God, was the pivot that held the different languages and creeds in balance: "Why are there so many languages if not for the purpose of better naming the unnamable?"[22] He believed that in the multiplicity of the languages, the same content was expressed.[23] Such a statement not only has philosophical and theological weight; it has diplomatic consequences. Cusanus was active in the conciliar efforts of his time; he wrote with a vision in which the different creeds could be fused. The basis for this kind of universalism lay in his nominalism; he made a clear distinction between what modern linguists would call deep structure and surface structure. The deep structure is reserved for the unapproachable One, for God, while the material human expressions of multiplicity remain in equidistance from it on the surface. All verbal expressions and cultural signs point to the same center, which, for Cusanus, is the key to religious tolerance and peace. It was his belief that "in the many rites, there is only one religion."[24]

The so-called *philosophia perennis* can be considered as another forerunner of enlightened universalism. It was developed by speculative philosophers in the Renaissance who searched for a common truth beyond the incompatible traditions. They believed in an ancient and arcane truth that was corrupted in time and lay buried under the distorted fragments of manifest cultural expressions. This unifying truth or *prisca theologia* they hoped to uncover and revive. Their most important tool was the allegorical distinction between overt expression and covert meaning. While the allegory of the church fathers was devised to harmonize the Old Testament with the New, their task was to construct a transcultural tradition in harmonizing Christian religion with pagan lore.[25]

In this universal frame, truth is not the exclusive property of one nation but passes in history from one culture to another. To reconstruct the obscured lines of this succession is to reconvert the universal genealogy of wisdom. In this search for a hidden truth, difference, distinction, and novelty are associated with lies, while age, uniformity, and consensus are associated with truth. This attitude is clearly reflected in the following quotation from a manifesto of the Rosicrucian movement: "Thus the maxim is not: Hoc per Philosophiam Verum est, sed per Theologiam falsum, but wherein Plato, Aristotle, Pythagoras and others agree, where Enoch, Abraham, Moses, Salomo lead the way, and in particular what is confirmed by the great book of wonders, the bible, all of this comes together and becomes a sphere or globe, all the parts of which are equally distant from the center."[26] Circle and sphere are symbols of unity. The different points of the circumference are mutually translatable and interchangeable because they are in equal distance from a common center. In such a model there is no room for hierarchy, hegemony, or a privileged position, let alone an exclusive claim to truth. The only privileged position is occupied by God. The center is transcendent, which means that it lies beyond the reach of human claims. It is on this metaphysical ground of absence that diversity can be tolerated.

This idea was taken up by philosophers of the Enlightenment. When Lessing gave it its memorable shape in his parable of the ring, he could draw on a rich fund of tales from the Middle Ages onward.[27] These tales occupy the border between the heretical and the didactic and deal with the problem of multiple religions. How in a world of divided creeds is one to find out which is the true belief? In the heretical versions, the problem is solved by asserting that there is no such thing as the true religion; Moses, Christ, and Mohammed are all referred to as "impostors." In the skeptical versions, it is not religion that is rebuked but its hegemonic claim to absolute truth. In one version the world is compared to a dark chamber into which a precious pearl has fallen. The people in the room notice the falling of the pearl, and each one tries to capture the jewel for himself. Some pick up a piece of mud, others a stone or a small shard. As long as darkness prevails, it is impossible to decide who has actually found the real pearl. The decision of the question has to be suspended until the return of the Messiah, who brings light and will act as the authoritative arbiter of truth.[28] While eschatological universalism was based on the coming of the Messiah, enlightened universalism is based on the fact that he stays away. It is precisely the absence of messianic light, the status quo of a common darkness, that moderates universal claims. Messianic light and truth have to be withheld—domesticated—if wisdom and skepticism are to flourish.

Lessing's Nathan is the most prominent representative of this tradition. When he is challenged by the sultan to answer the fundamentalist question—which religion is the true one?—he answers in undermining the logic of the question. Sovereign decision is replaced by enlightened skepticism.[29] Enlightenment for Lessing does not mean religious indifference; it means religious moderation.[30] Nathan tells the story of a father who could not make up his mind which one of his three sons to honor with a precious ring. So he ordered copies to be made of the ring and gave them to his sons, suggesting to each one that he was the privileged heir. After the problem was solved for the father, it became urgent for the sons. Which of the three rings was the true one? Who was to be considered the lawful heir?

There are two possible solutions to the problem, that of the fundamentalist and that of the sage. The fundamentalist overcomes the confusion of multiplicity by a return to the One. Truth can be restored only if rivals are eliminated and false pretenders unmasked. Truth and order are founded on the tyranny of the One. The solution of the sage is founded on the metaphysics of absence: *Der rechte Ring ward nicht erweislich* (the true ring was not to be found). Under these conditions, multiplicity cannot be overcome. It has to be endured, tolerated. It is a permanent reminder of the fact that absolute truth is not for this world as we know it. To put it in a paradoxical way: it is the discovery of enlightenment that we are all groping in the dark.

The Roots of Universal Humanism

Nothing is harder for the mind than to maintain a void. There is a horror vacui which sees to it that blank spaces are quietly invaded by new essences. The space vacated by the heretics and skeptics was soon filled with positive values. When the codified revealed law was removed from the center, natural law took its place. Or, to put it the other way round, the affirmation of natural law was a way to diminish the status of revealed law. Uriel da Costa, the marrano, adopted a relativistic position to the established religions in going back to the natural law given to Noah. The seven laws that God gave to Noah were considered as a *lex naturalis* common to all mankind. The identity of a collective body is defined by its reference to a common heritage. To construct a *lex naturalis* or heritage common to mankind is to construct the identity of mankind. In this case, the name of Noah stands for a common root and a new identity. "Humanity" is a construction of enlightened philosophers who invented universalistic concepts like "natural law," "common notions," "lumen naturale," or "reason."

The roots of universal humanisms were laid long before the eighteenth century by heretics, skeptics, and spiritualists who transcended the manifest surface of their traditions in search of a common human substance. Comenius, for instance, was interested in a preverbal "alphabet of human thought." He believed that if the curtain of language and socialization was withdrawn, all distinctions of culture, language, religion, status, and gender would eventually disappear: "Those universal Notions, original and innate, not yet perverted by monstrous conceptions, the divinely laid foundations of our reason, remain the same for man and woman, for the child and the old man, for the Greek and the Arab, for the Christian and the Mohammedan, for the religious and the irreligious."[31] For Comenius as for other universalists, differences present a challenge. In one way or another, they have to be transcended. There is no chance of peace before the foundations of unity are safely laid. The only way to peace is the return to the One: "If men understand each other, they will become as it were one race, one people, one household, one School of God. . . . And then there will be universal Peace over the whole world, hatred and the causes of hatred will be done away, and all dissension between men. For there will be no grounds for dissenting, when all men have the same Truths clearly presented to their eyes."[32]

Radical spiritualists like Sebastian Franck denied the power of revelation even to God's holy word and Scripture. Franck considered it idolatry to assume that truth is enshrined in books or that the Holy Spirit resides in the Bible. The Spirit uses media that are more reliable than codified tradition. For Franck, the prominent medium of the Holy Spirit was the human heart. He was convinced that God printed his messages on the human heart rather than on paper. The heart of the individual was dignified by him as a genuine medium of revelation surpassing even the Bible.

More than a century before Comenius, Franck had already propagated the claim of "divinely laid foundations of our reason." The biblical motif of God writing his law immediately into the soft substance of the heart was taken to be a proof of the authentic and uncorrupted quality of human reason. In proverbial lore Franck discovered an oral body of wisdom which was directly derived from the divine source. "All true proverbs as they are taught by nature are truly the word of God. . . . Nature and reason [have] written them into the human hearts and put them into the mouths of all men."[33] It is significant to note how the domain of the Holy Spirit is here stretched to include both nature and reason. With the transition from the Holy Spirit to concepts like nature and reason, the path was forged for secular universalism. Radical spiritualists like Sebastian Franck have in their way promoted the project of modernity in overcoming the canonized status of revealed law and the dogma of the fallen condition of human reason. They tried to overcome the defects of Babel—dissent, difference, and alienation—by recovering the natural and universal light of human reason.

The Eclipse of Humanism

Universal humanism is itself far from universal but a phenomenon located in time and place. After having considered aspects of its rise, let us examine some of its decline. For this reason, we must make a huge leap from the Renaissance to the time after World War I. In Europe, the period between the wars was experienced as a time of profound crisis. As life-forms and traditions were shattered, there was an overwhelming urge to exchange bourgeois values for apocalyptic visions. The intellectual climate of western culture shifted again from the pole of enlightenment to that of eschatology. This time, it was not the coming of the Messiah but the imminent end of western culture that heated up the atmosphere. Under these menacing conditions, the values of western culture were either evaporated or fundamentalized. The hegemony inherent in occidental universalism came to the fore and was radicalized. The following lines read like a summary of the charges raised today against hegemonic universalism, but in fact they were written in the spirit of invigorating self-definition and self-admonition: "Whatever the nature of the crisis may be that we are facing at this historical moment—we must say that for more than 2,000 years occidental man has had the principality over all nations and races; this means—to put it in utmost clarity—that he has had the principal possibility (which in fact he often enough has not embraced) to understand all other human beings of any nation, and in this capacity is implied his actual and possible political dominance."[34] According to Theodor Haecker, the author of these lines, the crisis of the imminent end of occidental culture can be met only if occidental man recovers his faith. Haecker's book on Virgil is meant to be a breviary of occidental values and a legitimation of hegemonic humanism.[35]

In September of 1921, Thomas Mann gave a talk on Goethe and Tolstoy in his hometown of Lübeck. This talk he ended rather abruptly in a diagnosis of the current intellectual climate. In a sober but severe tone, he announced the end of an epoch. It was the epoch of liberal humanism which was begun in the Renaissance and triumphed in the French Revolution. Three years after the First World War, Mann witnessed the rapid disintegration of this tradition. He noticed that the Mediterranean and classical heritage of universalism was everywhere in Europe giving way to forms of anti-universalism—nationalism, dictatorship, and terror. Radical movements of ethnic separatism were suppressing all forms of cosmopolitanism—Jewish internationalism, Christian universalism, classical humanism.

In the twilight of liberal humanism Mann formulated his personal credo. It is the credo of a dissenter, the exact inversion of the antiliberal stance. Antiliberal values are vigor and violence, firm resolution, decision and stern commitment; Mann extols their very opposites: versatility and suppleness, deference, the prolonged stage of "not yet," the suspension of the end, and a Janus-faced irony which plays in the space between the harsh opposites. Irony is incompatible with pathos; Mann defines irony ironically as "pathos of the middle," meaning not the golden mean but the open space between fixed positions.[36] Mann invokes the god Hermes as the deity of this intermediary realm; the go-between and trickster, patron of thieves, translators, and interpreters, master of tricks and transformations.

Thomas Mann's theory of irony implies a theory of intercultural translation. It was developed at a time when European skies darkened and when in Germany the humanist tradition was eclipsed by the growth of fascism. In a review of Oswald Spengler's best-seller, *The Decline of the West*, written in 1924, Mann made his point very clearly. He reproached Spengler for his total disregard of the human spirit, calling him a "defeatist of humanity."[37] This disregard led Spengler to a theory according to which cultures evolve and decline according to strict morphological laws. These mechanisms take place in their own separate spheres; there are no interactions, translations, communications. The borderlines are without windows; there is no network of traffic, no contact, no correspondence. This view of cultural autopoiesis (to use an anachronistic, but perhaps not inappropriate term) entails a theory of the untranslatability of cultures, of radical alterity, mutual strangeness, and profound incommunicability. The only thing that the individual cultures share are the inexorable laws of growth and decline. Otherwise they are totally separate in their essences. The situation as described by Spengler is—to use Mann's words—that of a "Babylonian confusion of languages."[38]

What had Mann to put up against Spengler's scientific dogma? Nothing but his personal credo of universal humanity, a loyalty to a cultural tradition, the vision of a spiritual unity. For this vision he has no scientific evidence of the sort that Spengler claims for his model. It is only an intuition, an affect that was the fuel for his life and art.

After Universalism?

As we look back on the various forms of universalism, their differences are patent. They are sacred or secular, institutional or spiritual, hegemonic or subversive. But they all worship the One. Whether as a political goal or as a spiritual event, whether as a hegemonic claim or as a hidden mystery, the One is the unrivaled hero of all universalisms. During the last decades the One has lost its magic. The dismissal of the regulative ideal of the One is part of the transvaluation of values that is commonly associated with postmodernism. The period of postmodernity is characterized by the fundamentalization of plurality. Difference is affirmed in the form of deviance, gaps, and radical alterity. Concepts like communication and consensus have become unpopular. Bridges are no longer welcome because they hide abysses and rifts. The acknowledgment of alterity, the acceptance of difference, has become the foremost ethical claim. Difference is no longer something that has to be trivialized, tolerated, or violently overcome; it is something that has to be discovered and acknowledged. In the following statement, Wolfgang Welsch sums up the general postmodern ethos of difference: "Whether life-forms, types of knowledge, or modes of rationality are concerned, [we have come to] be immune and allergic against thoughtless transgressions, against using one type as a measure for another, against this elementary mistake in a situation of plurality, against this small beginning of terror, the end of which—for all we know—may be gross and vast."[39] One must not forget that the postmodern philosophy of difference is formulated against the background of a world that is growing ever more homogeneous, a world in which distances are rapidly shrinking as the networks of commerce and economy, of traffic and communication are spreading across the globe. While on one level technology is in the process of effecting a "really existing universalism," it has ceased to work as a regulative ideal. From a menacing, anxiety-provoking term, "the other" has become the central value of postmodern culture.

The One is dismissed from the earth on which it has no place. Attempts to resurrect it have proved illusory or fatal. Does this mean that we are back at the beginning of the story, right in the midst of Babel? The word "difference" has assumed a new meaning. It is no longer associated with corruption or judged from the point of view of unity and perfection. It is recognized as a basic human need; its manifestations, however, belong not to the level of nature and essence but to the level of cultural constructions. The same holds true for the concept of humanity. It is no longer regarded as a given, as an invariable essence to which one can appeal. Instead, it is taken to be a cultural construct. It would be shortsighted to think that with the waning of the One, the construct of humanity is to be dismissed along with it. It still has vital functions, but these have changed profoundly. Instead of legitimizing hegemonic claims or backing up universal consent, they are now precisely those of protecting difference.

As long as the concept of humanity was regulated by the One, intercultural communication was reduced to the choice of either destruction or fusion. At the end of our excursion into the history of universalisms I want to quote two authors, one who affirms the dominance of the One,

the other who affirms the copresence of the Two. The statements introduce two different modes of interaction which at the same time may stand
for two different theories of intercultural translation. The first is a maxim
by Goethe: "The most beautiful metempsychosis is the one in which we
recognize ourselves in the shape of the other."[40] In this case, the other is
used as the screen on which the self is projected. Projection is extension of
the self: the triumph of the poetic genius in his ability to assimilate the
world to the self. This type of interaction is based on empathy and associated with colonization. It aims at a dissolution of barriers; its final stage
is fusion.

Goethe's concern is the successful return to the enriched self; Hofmannsthal's concern is the sustained presence of the other. For his meditation on identity and alterity Hofmannsthal chose the language of eros.
He is careful to separate the interactional mode of the Two from that of
the One. His own terms are "embrace" and "encounter." Embrace is linked
to the mode of the One; it implies fusion, unity, extension of the self. Encounter is linked with the mode of the Two; it invokes alterity, surprise,
mystery, and awe: "I think it is not the embrace but the encounter that is
indeed the decisive erotic pantomime. . . . In the embrace, strangeness, estrangement are fatal, cruel, paradox—in the encounter, each is shrouded
in its eternal solitude as in a precious cloak."[41]

Cover Letter to
"Emerson's Constitutional Amending"

Stanley Cavell

Of the ambiguities in our title—*Translations of Culture*—I note a question concerning the priority or purity of the concepts it puts in play: Does the title conceive translation as, so to speak, something external or something internal to culture? Is the perspective one that emphasizes the stability and antagonism of human cultures (however contingent) and their datable demands for or refusals of understanding of one another; or is the perspective one that emphasizes the circulations (necessary, however imperfect) within a culture, between classes, genders, generations, individuals, among which circulation from or toward a voice "outside" is not marked off as a special arena of change, or threat to identity? Say that in the latter case the issue of culture is assimilation, in the former colonization. I believe that in the United States (hereinafter "America") the reception or appropriation over the past quarter of a century of French thought, as over the quarter of a century before that the reception or appropriation in America of logical positivism from Austria and Germany, has presented itself, and still does, sometimes as the one issue, sometimes as the other. (Along the line of culture, or cultural change, as assimilation, the question may be reached whether there must be [= ? human imagination cannot imagine the human without there being] more than one culture [language], hence perhaps whether the human can imagine itself without the possibility of exile, of an elsewhere.)

My contribution picks up an apparent assumption in both perspectives, namely that no association of talkers is a culture that lacks the power of (self-)translation, call this the power of making itself understood (in its terms) to others, and of understanding others (in their terms); where understanding implies the pain of recognizing oneself in change, in another's mark or voice, and implies the pleasure of leaving one's mark on the other. (Here the question may be reached whether colonization is, in (a)voiding the other's mark, bad translation or rather not translation at all. [Is bad philosophy philosophy? Always?]) Specifically, I present an example from America—a reading of Emerson's essay "Fate"—by way of continuing my search for terms in which to assess the question whether America has expressed itself philosophically. I call my example/reading "Emerson's Constitutional Amending."

The example is meant to work against two events, one public one private, that haunt or otherwise bear on my life: the public event, already alluded to, is the reception of French thought in American academic ("humanistic") culture since, say, the late sixties; the private event, cited in each of my two lectures in *This New Yet Unapproachable America*, is Wittgenstein's remarking to friends, in 1931, "What can we give the Americans? Our half-decayed culture? The Americans have as yet no culture. But from us they have nothing to learn." (As if it is the condition of America, in relation to Europe, always to be discovered and always to be colonized. Not Emerson's question alone; but perhaps his most single-mindedly.)

I conceive my text on Emerson's "Fate" as the middle one of a trio of texts. My text on "Fate" proposes that Emerson's philosophical silence (precisely not polemical silence) on the topic of slavery is a function of his effort to preserve (you might say to create and hence to preserve) philosophy; and it suggests that since Emerson's language is translated, through Nietzsche's, early and late, into Heidegger's lectures on Nietzsche beginning in 1936, the frightening price of Emerson's choice to preserve philosophy is to be measured against the political devastation, to say the least, of Heidegger's analogous choice.

I would like to indicate how the idea, or some idea, of the translation of culture is in turn carried forward in the first and third of my trio of texts. The first is a study of Emerson's cultural translation (prior to "Fate") of Kant's *Groundwork of the Metaphysics of Morals* in his "Self-Reliance." Kant speaks of acting for the sake of (versus acting in *conformity* with) the moral law, hence of the rational animal as *constrained* by the law, a constraint expressed as an "ought" (failing to obey which we cause ourselves shame), and finds that this expression necessitates the characterization and positing of the human as occupying two *standpoints*, say sensual and intellectual. Emerson's "Self-Reliance" translates those emphasized concepts—I am taking Emerson's translation of translation here as what he calls transfiguration and conversion, his predicates of thinking—by speaking of *conformity* to (versus self-reliance in the face of) society and its observant power of causing shame, and speaking of my being *constrained* by the *standard* (cf. standpoint) of the true man. In Emerson's translation (another Emerson translation for this mode of translation is "making the transit," as in a passage cited in the introduction to *This New Yet Unapproachable America*), the idea of constraint is precisely not expressed by an "ought." Emerson thus casts Kant's moral law otherwise than as Freud repeatedly announced it must be cast, namely, for Freud, as a figure for the punitive superego. There is also less heady evidence, lots of little details, that suggest Emerson composed "Self-Reliance" with the *Groundwork* at his elbow.

If the first text plots a movement from the old to the new world (Kant to Emerson), and the second plots a movement from the new to the old world (Emerson to Nietzsche to Heidegger), my third text rather disorients these directions. It proposes, in effect, to deliver, or say make explicit (not to say make a transit for), a further essay implicitly insistent within my second text (about Emerson's "Fate"). The third takes further an idea already quite prominent in the second—Emerson's identification of thinking as a certain form of breathing. The form is one that opposes the breath in my body—say my voice—to the ideas that fill the common air, as if the individual voice and the cosmic air are essentially equal antagonists. (This becomes Emerson's philosophical elaboration of the topic repeatedly reformulated in the opening paragraph of "Fate," that of the Spirit of the Age.)

In the third text I relate this identification to Artaud's visions of conformity and breathing as presented in Derrida's "La parole soufflée." This is the least worked out of the trio, but the general connection is not (or after a few moments not terribly) surprising, given Nietzsche's presence also in Artaud. Evidently something similar has happened to me this time in reading the Derrida of the 1960's as happened to me the last time, in Jerusalem in 1986, which produced the somewhat embarrassed, belated pages of, for me, uncanny criss-crossings I note in my contribution to our first proceedings, *Languages of the Unsayable*. My excuse for not having previously read Derrida on Artaud was, in all banality, that I hadn't sufficiently studied Artaud. (I had only read, fashionable here in the 1960's, *The Theater and Its Double*, in preparation for, or protection in, writing about theater and about film.) But I have, for less banal reasons, working on my education, recently come across, near the opening of Derrida's "White Mythology," a sentence containing these words: "Metaphor seems to involve the usage of philosophical language in its entirety, nothing less than . . . the usage of natural language *as* philosophical language." I surmise that this sentence will prove to be closer in thought than I can readily account for to the opening sentence of my "Must We Mean What We Say?": "That what we ordinarily say and mean may have a direct and deep control over what we can philosophically say and mean is an idea which many philosophers find oppressive." This surmise has constrained me to go back to Derrida's interpretation of Austin, hence to our "silent quarrel" over the role of voice in philosophy. (This material is now published as chapter 2 of *A Pitch of Philosophy*.)

This constraint is overdetermined. When I learned, in Derrida's text on Artaud, of the complexities of the word *soufflée*, most particularly that it may be translated as "spirited away," I recalled, beyond Emerson's interpretation, or I might say literalization, of the Spirit (of the Age), that in *Conditions Handsome and Unhandsome*, near the end of my discussion of Kripke on Wittgenstein's *Philosophical Investigations*, particularly objecting to Kripke's (even his) typically philosophical disdain or flight from the ordinary; and having virtually identified a comically placed sentence of Wittgenstein's with a comparably placed sentence of Emerson's; I characterize Augustine's portrait of himself as a child acquiring language (the portrait that opens and inspires the *Investigations*) as presenting the exemplary child as the *thief* of language, thus marking the permanent doubt whether language is *ours*. No doubt I was moved to this characterization of Augustine's memory of himself by another memory of himself as the thief of another valuable set of things related to the mouth, forbidden pears. This characterization, in turn, fits an alternative reading of Emerson's discerning of the air as "full of men"—in a passage I focus on in the ensuing text on "Fate"—a reading of it as announcing his (so America's) belatedness, hence as naming the ideas taken into his lungs and voice, impressing him, as plagiarized. This threat of suffocation (the air, being full, is fully spoken for, none is my own) accounts otherwise for the fervor of Emerson's insistence on and inflection of freedom as the power to *originate* our actions (in Kant, to cause them, given our immersion in the plenum of nature; in Emerson, to claim them, given our submission to the plenum of culture).

Will the juxtaposition of Emerson and Artaud provide the shock, say the genteel cruelty, I sometimes seek in order to get Emerson seriously considered as a star in the philosophical sky? Or will the juxtaposition merely confirm the suspicion that I cannot be serious about this?

Emerson's Constitutional Amending:
Reading "Fate"

W hat follows is the latest installment of a project, or experiment, of about a dozen years' standing, to reappropriate Emerson (I sometimes call this overcoming his repression) as a philosophical writer. I am aware of a number of reasons for my interest in such a project. Since Emerson is characteristically said—by his admirers as well as by his detractors—not to be a philosopher (no one known to me in the history of western thought is so obsessively denied the title of philosopher), my thought was that if I could understand this denial I would learn something not only about Emerson, and not only about American culture, but something about philosophy, about what makes it painful.

If the thought of Emerson's work as constituting philosophy—or, as I sometimes put it, as calling for philosophy—is considered, then something further could be considered. It is more or less obvious, and is given more or less significance by various philosophers that western philosophy has, roughly since the death of Kant, been split between two traditions, call them the German and the English traditions; and each of these has its internal splits. I take Wittgenstein as the culmination of one line of English-speaking philosophy arising from the work of Frege and Russell; and I take Heidegger as the culmination of one line of German-speaking philosophy arising from the work of Hegel and Husserl. I am not alone in regarding Wittgenstein and Heidegger as perhaps the two major voices of philosophy in the middle third of this century. Yet it seems to me that no one—however intelligent or cultivated—is equally at home, say equally creative, with the writing of both; so that the distance between them, in content and in procedure, remains to my mind unmeasured. I might say that, for me, to inherit philosophy now means to me to inherit it as split.

Against this rough background, the figure of Emerson represents for me (along with Thoreau) a mode of thinking and writing I feel I am in a position to avail myself of, a mode which at the same time can be seen to underlie the thinking of both Wittgenstein and of Heidegger—so that Emerson may become a site from which to measure the difficulties within each and between both.

What follows is a continuation of the work of the first chapter of my *Conditions Handsome and Unhandsome*, concerning Emerson's concept of thinking, a concept I call aversive thinking. That title alludes to a sentence of Emerson's from "Self-Reliance": "Self-reliance is [the] aversion [of conformity]." Emerson finds that conformity is the virtue in most request—by which he means it is the primary force of our social existence. By "self-reliance" I take him, correspondingly, to mean the essay of that title, and by synecdoche, his individual body of writing. So for him to say "self-reliance is the aversion of conformity" is to say that his writing and his society incessantly recoil from, or turn away from one another; but since this is incessant, the picture is at the same time of each incessantly turning *toward* the other. But why call this writing *thinking*?

Emerson characterizes thinking as marked by transfiguration and by conversion. I will merely assert here that these predicates refer essentially to the action of words, under subjection to some kind of figuration, in causing understanding or illumination on a par with that of religion—the religion always under criticism (held in aversion)—in Emerson's thought. My claim is accordingly that the sentence "Self-reliance is the aversion of conformity," when itself subjected to the operation of transfiguration and conversion, means something like: To think is to turn around, or to turn back (Wittgenstein says lead back), the words of ordinary life (hence the present forms of our lives) that now repel thought, disgust it. (Repels him, Emerson, of course, but he is also part of that life, which is therefore disgusted with itself.)

The only way to become convinced of such a reading, and its possible significance, is of course to try it out in scores of instances. We will see some cases in what follows from the essay "Fate."

Before beginning on that, I should say why it is just now in my adventure with Emerson that I choose, or feel forced, for the first time to emphasize a political theme in his work. I specify a brief answer at the close of these remarks, but I might indicate at once the general stakes in play. I have over the years ever more closely linked Emerson and Heidegger through the intermediary of Nietzsche, who is intimately, pervasively involved in the thinking of each. In *Conditions Handsome and Unhandsome*

I associate each of them in a view of the moral life I call Emersonian Perfectionism—at a moment in which the revelations of Heidegger's lasting
investments in Nazism were producing a new convulsion of response from
at least half the western philosophical world. Does Heidegger's politics—
by association, to say the least—taint Emerson's points of contact with it?

The essay "Fate" is perhaps Emerson's principal statement about the
human condition of freedom, even about something Emerson calls the paradox that freedom is necessary; we might formulate this as the human fatedness to freedom. This amounts to speaking of the human fatedness to
thinking, since "Intellect annuls Fate. So far as a man thinks, he is free. . . .
The revelation of Thought takes man out of servitude into freedom." Could
it be that the founder of American thinking, writing this essay in 1850, just
months after the passage of the Fugitive Slave Law, whose support by Daniel Webster we know Emerson to have been unforgettably, unforgivingly
horrified by, was in this essay not thinking about the American institution
of slavery? I think it cannot be. Then why throughout the distressed, difficult, dense stretches of metaphysical speculation of this essay does Emerson seem mostly, even essentially, to keep silent on the subject of slavery,
make nothing special of it? It is a silence that must still encourage his critics, as not long ago his admirer Harold Bloom and his detractor John Up-
dike, to imagine that Emerson gave up on the hope of democracy. But since
I am continuing to follow out the consequences of finding in Emerson the
founding of American thinking—the consequence, for example, that his
thought is repressed in the culture he founded—the irony of discovering
that this repressed thinking has given up on the hope and demand for a
nation of the self-governing, would be, so I fear, harder than I could digest.
    I was myself silent about this question of Emerson's silence when I
wrote an essay in 1983 mostly on Emerson's "Fate" (I called it "Emerson,
Coleridge, Kant"), my first somewhat extended treatment of an Emersonian text. It seemed to me so urgent then to see to the claim of Emerson as
a philosophical writer, in principle imaginable as founding philosophy for
a nation still finding itself, that I suppose I recurrently hoped that Emerson
had, for the moment of the essay "Fate," sufficiently excused or justified
his silence in saying there, "Nothing is more disgusting than the crowing
about liberty by slaves, as most men are." But no sooner would I see this
as an excuse or justification for silence than it would seem empty to me,
so that I could never appeal to it. Isn't the statement that most men are
slaves merely a weak, metaphorical way of feeling and of speaking, one that
blunts both the fact of literal slavery and the facts of the particular ways

in which we freely sell ourselves out? How is this conventional use of words essentially different from the sort of "[shameful capitulation] to badges and names, to large societies and dead institutions" that had so chagrined Emerson in "Self-Reliance"?

> If malice and vanity wear the coat of philanthropy, shall that pass? If an angry bigot assumes this bountiful cause of Abolition, and comes to me with his last news from Barbados, why should I not say to him, "Go love thy infant; love thy woodchopper; be good-natured and modest; have that grace; and never varnish your hard, uncharitable ambition with this incredible tenderness for black folk a thousand miles off. Thy love afar is spite at home."

It is not news that high philosophy can be used to cover low practice; nor that the love in philanthropy is tainted. Is Emerson so in doubt about the state of his own malice and vanity and anger and bigotry and charity and love that he has to clear them up before he can say clearly that he sides against slavery?

On March 7, 1854, Emerson delivered a lecture called "The Fugitive Slave Law," marking the fourth anniversary of Webster's decisive speech in favor of that legislation. Emerson's lecture goes this way:

> Nobody doubts that Daniel Webster could make a good speech. Nobody doubts that there were good and plausible things to be said on the part of the South. But this is not a question of ingenuity, not a question of syllogisms, but of sides. *How came he there?* . . . There are always texts and thoughts and arguments. . . . There was the same law in England for Jeffries and Talbot and Yorke to read slavery out of, and for Lord Mansfield to read freedom. . . . But the question which History will ask [of Webster] is broader. In the final hour when he was forced by the peremptory necessity of the closing armies to take a side,—did he take the part of great principles, the side of humanity and justice, or the side of abuse and oppression and chaos? (*Emerson's Works*, 11, *Miscellanies*, ed. J. E. Cabot, 1883)

So Emerson names and would avoid both those at home who choose to interpret the law so as to take the side on behalf of slavery near, as well as those whom in "Self-Reliance" he had named angry bigots incredibly varnishing their uncharitable ambition at home by taking the side against slavery afar. Both may count as what Emerson describes as "crowing about liberty by slaves"; and his refusal of crowing (for or against) would perhaps be what strikes one as his essential silence on the subject precisely in an essay on freedom paradoxically entitled "Fate."

The suggestion is that there is a way of taking sides that is not crowing, a different way of having a say in this founding matter of slavery. If Emerson is who I think he is, then how he finds his way to having his say, how he undertakes to think—whether, most particularly, he is serious (as opposed to what?—literary?) in his claim that "so far as a man thinks, he is free"—is as fateful for America's claim to its own culture of thinking as its success in ridding itself of the institution of slavery will be for establishing its claim to have discovered a new world, hence to exist.

We have to ask what kind of writing—philosophical? political? religious?—takes the form of the pent, prophetic prose of "Fate." Emerson speaks there also (as well as in the later "Fugitive Slave Law") of the taking of a side. His formulation in "Fate" is of the capacity, when a person finds himself a victim of his fate—for example, "ground to powder by the vice of his race"—to "take sides with the Deity who secures universal benefit by his pain." This may strike one as the formulation less of a course of action than of inaction. But take Emerson's reference in his phrase "the vice of his race" (by which a person finds himself victimized) to be specified in the description earlier in the essay of "expensive races—race living at the expense of race." But *which* vice does "expensive" suggest? The literal context of that predicate takes the races in question as the human race living at the expense of the races of animals that serve us as food: "You have just dined, and however scrupulously the slaughter-house is concealed in the graceful distance of miles, there is complicity, expensive races." It happens that we can produce evidence that this passage about human carnivorousness, and its companion human gracefulness in keeping its conditions concealed from itself, is a parable about the cannibalism, as it were, in living gracefully off other *human* races. The evidence comes from an early paragraph in Emerson's address "On Emancipation in the British West Indies," delivered in 1844, the tenth anniversary of that emancipation legislation, the year of Emerson's breakthrough essay "Experience." In Emerson's West Indies address, he remarks that "From the earliest monuments it appears that one race was victim and served the other races," and that "the negro has been an article of luxury to the commercial nations"; and he goes on to say there, "Language must be raked, the secrets of the slaughter-houses and infamous holes that cannot front the day, must be ransacked, to tell what negro-slavery has been" (*Works*, 11: 133, 134).

I propose to take "Fate" pervasively beyond the reach of the sort of textual intersection I just adduced as evidence—as something I might call a philosophical enactment of freedom, a parable of the struggle against slavery not as a general metaphor for claiming human freedom, but as the absolute image of the necessary siding against fate toward freedom that is the condition of philosophical thinking; as if the aspiration to freedom is philosophy's breath.

Doesn't the sheer eloquence of the West Indies address compromise this proposal from the outset, with its demand to rake language and ransack slaughter-houses to tell of negro slavery? And again, always again, the question returns whether Emerson in "Fate"—the same man who younger, in that earlier West Indies address, confessed himself heartsick to read the history of that slavery—isn't courting the danger of seeming to avoid the sickening facts of the slavery that continues not metaphysically afar but at home.

What is he thinking of—whom is he thinking of—when in "Fate" he says, "In the history of the individual there is an account of his condition, and he knows himself to be party to his present estate"? If the sentences of "Fate" are to be brought to the condition of slavery, are we to imagine this statement about the individual knowing himself to be party to his estate to be said to the individual who is in the condition of enslavement? What would prevent this announcement from constituting the obscene act of blaming the slave for his slavery? (My intermittent sense of this possibility, and of the fact that I had no satisfying answer to it, was brought home to me by a letter from Professor Barbara Packer, whose book *Emerson's Fall* is indispensable to readers of Emerson, following a brief conversation between us concerning Emerson's politics. She writes in her letter of her sense of what I called obscene announcement in "Fate" as something that she had yet to bring under control, and asked for my thoughts. That was in the autumn of 1989. Much of the present version of this essay, meant to collect and incorporate those thoughts, was drafted the following year.)

An implication of saying "you know yourself party to your estate"— if it is not pure blame—is that you are free to leave it. John Brown might say something of the sort, without obscenity, to a person in the condition of enslavement, given that he would be saying, if with a certain derangement, "I know the only way to exercise your freedom to leave your estate is to court death, and I'll court it with you." And Walt Whitman might say something related, as in the altogether remarkable "I Sing the Body Electric," in which he watches the man's body at auction and the woman's body at auction, and he declares his love for, his sameness with, the body— hence, he declares, with the soul—of the slave. What gives to the knowledge of American slavery the absoluteness of its pain is the knowledge that these human beings in that condition, in persisting to live, persist in taking part in every breath in interpreting and preserving what a human existence can bear. But do we imagine that Emerson, like John Brown and Walt Whitman, has a way to bear the knowledge of that pain—he who is habitually supposed to have turned aside from the philosophically tragic sense of life?

Then perhaps Emerson only means to say of us Northerners, neither slaves nor slave owners, that we are party to our estate—meaning perhaps that we make ourselves slaves to, let us say, the interests of Southern slave owners that never even paid for us. But that is not exactly news. Emerson reports in the West Indies address that when "three hundred thousand persons in Britain pledged themselves to abstain from all articles of island produce . . . the planters were obliged to give way . . . and the slave-trade was abolished." Such responses to slavery as economic boycott are evidently not Emerson's business in "Fate." Whom, then, in that mood, is he writing to? Who are we who read him then?

If "taking sides with the Deity" does not, for Emerson, (just) mean taking the right side in the crowing about slavery, the side Daniel Webster failed to take as the armies were closing on the issue, how might it be taken? Here is more context from "Fate": "A man must ride alternately on the horses of his private and his public nature. . . . Leaving the daemon who suffers, he is to take sides with the Deity who secures universal benefit by his pain." That the human being is the being who *can* take a representative—public—stance, knows the (moral, objective) imperative to the stance, is familiar and recurrent Emersonian—not to say Kantian— ground; nothing is a more founding fact for him. I read this Platonic image about riding alternately the horses of human nature, so that taking sides with the Deity is a refusal to take sides in the human *crowing* over slavery. Emerson's turn to take sides with the Deity, like and unlike the political extremity of Locke's appeal to Heaven, is not exactly a call to revolution but a claim to prophecy. (Second Treatise, sections 168 and 242.) "Leaving the daemon who suffers" means leaving one's private, limited passions on the subject of slavery, for or against.

What is the alternative horse, the public expression of a beneficial pain (given in the absence of a constituted public, since so much of the human voice, the slave's voice, is unrepresented in that public)? The alternative is, let us say, not venting your pain, but maintaining it; in the present case, writing every sentence in pain. (Freud comparably says: remembering rather than repeating something.) It contains the pain of refusing human sides, shunning argument, with every breath. The time of argument is over. —Where is pain's benefit? Is philosophy over?

At the opening of "Fate," Emerson says "We are incompetent to solve the times. . . . To me . . . the question of the times resolved itself into a practical question of the conduct of life." I have in effect said that in "Fate" the "question of the times"—what Emerson calls in his opening "the huge orbits of the prevailing ideas" whose return and opposition we cannot "reconcile," and what he describes near his close by saying, "Certain ideas are in the air"—is the question of slavery; and certain ideas in the air, accordingly, are emancipation and secession, issues producing the compromise of 1850, which concerned—besides the Fugitive Slave Act—the slave trade, and the admission of territories into the union with or without slaves. Setting out the terms for "the greatest debate in Congressional history" (*Documents of American History*, ed. Henry Steele Commager [New York, 1958], p. 319), Henry Clay prefaces his Resolutions of compromise by saying, "It being desirable, for the peace, concord and harmony of the Union of these States to settle and adjust amicably all existing questions of controversy between them, arising out of the institution of slavery, upon a fair, equitable and just basis; therefore,"—and then follow eight paragraphs, each beginning with the word "Resolved" or the words "But, resolved." Emerson in effect prefaces "Fate" by speaking, in his opening paragraph, as noted, of our incompetence to *solve* the times, and of *resolving* the question of the times; in the second paragraph he states that "The riddle of the age has for each a private *solution*"; and continuing in effect to reverse or recapture the word "resolved" Emerson says in the middle of "Fate," "Thought *dissolves* the material universe by carrying the mind up into a sphere where all is plastic"; and in the closing paragraphs he speaks of a "solution of the mysteries of human condition" and of "the Blessed Unity which holds nature and soul in perfect solution." This is not Henry Clay's imagined union.

Of course Emerson is quite aware that compared with Henry Clay, and the Houses of Congress, his words about resolution and unity will sound, at best, or at first, private, not to say ethereal. But he seems somehow also to know that he is speaking with necessity ("Our thought, though it were only an hour old, affirms an oldest necessity"), and speaking with universality (being thrown "on the party and interest of the Universe [i.e., taking sides with the Deity] against all and sundry; against ourselves as much as others"). Now necessity and universality are the marks, according to the Kantian philosophy, of the a priori, that is, of human objectivity; so if Emerson's claim is valid, it is the opposing party who is riding the horse of privacy, of what Emerson also calls selfishness, something he would have taken Henry Clay's use of the word "desirable" to have amounted to.

We of course must ask—since Emerson would also know, as well as what is called the next man, that anyone can *claim* to be speaking on the part and interest of the universe and on the side of the Deity—what the source is of his conviction in his own objectivity, his ability, as he puts it in the poem he composed as an epigraph for "Fate," to read omens traced in the air. I understand the source to be his conviction that his abilities are not exclusive, that he claims to know only what everyone knows.

Toward the close of the essay: "The truth is in the air, and the most impressionable brain will announce it first, but *all* will announce it a few minutes later." Emerson is not even saying that *he* is announcing it first, since the truth that is in the air is also, always already, philosophy; it contains not just the present cries for freedom and union and the arguments against them, but perennial cries and arguments. This is surely one meaning of the gesture that Emerson so habitually enjoys making, of listing his predecessors and benefactors—that they are the benefactors of the race, part of our air, our breath. In the essay "Fate" he cites the names of Napoleon, Burke, Webster, Kossuth; Jenny Lind; Homer, Zoroaster, Menu; Fulton, Franklin, Watt; Copernicus, Newton, Laplace; Thales, Anaximenes, Empedocles, Pythagorus; Hafiz, Voltaire, Christopher Wren, Dante, Columbus, Goethe, Hegel, Metternich, Adams, Calhoun, Guizot, Peel, Rothschild, Astor, Herodotus, Plutarch. And he says: "The air is full of men." (Emerson puts those words in quotation marks without saying who or what he is quoting. Bartlett's *Familiar Quotations* contains the line "In the air men shall be seen" in a list of rhymed prophecies attributed to Mother Shipton, according to Bartlett's editors a witch and prophetess fabricated in the seventeenth century. I'll have a suggestion about why Emerson might have wanted in this essay to associate himself with such a figure.)

I associate the men in the air with—as in Emerson's epigraph poem— "Birds with auguries on their wings" who "Chanted undeceiving things, / Him to beckon, him to warn." The "few minutes later" Emerson calculates between the first announcements of truth and, for example, his own impressionable announcings of it—which the world may measure as millennia but which are a few minutes of eternity—are equally no more than the few minutes between, for example, our reading Emerson's pages (his wings of augury, flapping as we turn them forth and back, before us, above our horizon) and our announcing or pronouncing, if just to ourselves, what is chanted from them (not crowed). I have noted elsewhere another of Emerson's master figures for a page of his writing—that of its representing a "standard," that is, a measure to aspire to, specified concretely as a flag, to which to rally oneself. This idea of a standard—by which "Self-Reliance" alludes at the same time to Kant's idea of humankind's two "standpoints"—takes pages one at a time; whereas "wings" pictures them as paired, bound symmetrically on the two sides of a spine.

As with his great reader Thoreau, Emerson loves playing with time, that is, making time vanish where truth is concerned: " 'Tis only a question of time," he says casually a few minutes later in "Fate" than, and as a kind of answer to, the earlier, more portentious phrasing, "the question of the times." (In invoking the idea of the casual, as one characteristic tone he gives his prose, I am thinking of Emerson's characteristic association of that idea with the idea of causality; as if he misses no opportunity for showing that we do not see our fate because we imagine that it is most extraordinary and not yet; rather than most ordinary, and already, like our words.)

Emerson's philosophical sentence strikes the time of conversion and transfiguration that he calls thinking, the time—past crowing—of aversion (inversion, perversion, subversion, "unsettling all things," verses, reversals, tropes, turns, dancing, chanting . . .).

Here are three successive sentences to this effect from "Fate": First, "If the Universe have these savage accidents, our atoms are savage in resistance." That is, speaking philosophically, or universally, "accidents" are opposed to "necessities," and in thus implying that slavery is accidental, or arbitrary, and resistance to it necessary and natural, Emerson takes away its chief argument. Second, "We should be crushed by the atmosphere but for the reaction of the air within the body." That is, the ideas that are in the air are our life's breath; they become our words; slavery is supported by some of them and might have crushed the rest of them; uncrushed, they live in opposition. Third, "If there be omnipotence in the stroke, there is omnipotence in the recoil." That is, every word is a word spoken *again*, or against again; there would be no words otherwise. Since recoil and aversion have been expressed at any time only by breathers of words, mortals, their strokes may be given now, and may gather together now—in a recoiling—all the power of world-creating words. The sentence introducing the three just cited asserts: "Man also is part of [Fate], and can confront fate with fate." That is, I will now say, Emerson's way of confronting fate, his recoil of fate, is his writing, in every word; for example in every word of "Fate," each of which is to be a pen stroke—a seen stroke, a stroke of genius—because a counterstroke of fate. You make your breath words in order not to suffocate in the plenum of air. The power he claims for his words is precisely that they are not his, no more new than old; it is the power, I would like to say, of the powerlessness in being unexceptional, or say exemplary. ("We go to Herodotus and Plutarch for examples of Fate; but we are examples.") This unavoidable power of exemplification may be named impressionability, and seen to be responsibility construed as responsiveness, passiveness as receptiveness.

These are various ways of looking at the idea that the source of Emerson's conviction in what I called the objectivity (I might have called it the impersonality) of his prophesying, his wing-reading and omen-witnessing, lies in his writing, his philosophical authorship, a condition that each of his essays is bound to characterize and authenticate in its own terms.

A characteristic of this authorship is announced in the opening paragraph of the quite early "Self-Reliance": "In every work of genius we recognize our own rejected thoughts; they come back to us with a certain alienated majesty." Even from those who remember this sentence, there is, I have found, resistance in taking Emerson to be naming his own work as an instance of the work he is characterizing, resistance in taking that sentence about rejected thoughts as itself an instance of such a rejected thought coming back in familiar strangeness, so with the power of the uncanny. The mechanism of this rejection and return is, I suppose, that characterized by Freud as transference, a process in which another person is magnified by our attributing to him or to her powers present in our repressed desires and who, putting himself or herself aside for a moment, gives us usably what we have shown ourselves unusefully to know. It is an interpretation of Kant's mechanism of projection he calls the sublime, reading our mind's powers in nature, in the air. Emerson's authorship enacts, I have gone on to claim, a relationship with his reader of moral perfectionism in which the friend permits one to advance toward oneself, which may present itself, using another formulation of Emerson's, as attaining our unattained self, a process which has always happened and which is always to happen.

The word "majesty" reappears in "Fate," again in a context in which the presence of a "thought and word of an intellectual man . . . [rouses] our own mind . . . to activity": " 'Tis the majesty into which we have suddenly mounted, the impersonality, the scorn of egotisms, the sphere of laws, that engage us." A "sphere of laws" into which we have suddenly mounted, as if attaining a new standpoint, suggests Kant's Realm of Ends—call it the eventual human city—in which the reception of the moral law, the constraint, as Kant names the relation, by the moral imperative, expressed by an "ought," is replaced by the presence of another, like and unlike myself, who constrains me to another way, another standpoint Kant says (Emerson says, transfiguring Kant, a new standard); this other of myself—returning my rejected, say repressed, thought—reminds me of something, as of where I am, as if I had become lost in thought, and stopped thinking. In "Experience," Emerson expresses finding the way, learning as he more or less puts it, to take steps, as to begin to walk philosophically, in the *absence* of another presence—more accurately, in allowing himself to present himself to the loss of presence, to the death of his young son. His description of his authorship in that essay takes the form—I have given my evidence for this elsewhere—of fantasizing his becoming pregnant and giving birth to the world, to his writing of the world, which he calls a new America and calls Being. In "Fate" he is giving the basis of his authorship in that passage about riding alternately on the horses of his private and his public nature. Those are descendants of the horses he invokes, in his essay on "The Poet," in naming the Poet as one whose relation to language is such that "in every word he speaks he rides on them as the horses of thought." The idea is that the words have a life of their own over which our mastery is the other face of our obedience. Wittgenstein in *Philosophical Investigations* affirms this sense of the independent life of words in describing what he does as "leading words back from their metaphysical to their everyday use," suggesting that their getting back, whatever that achievement is, is something they must do under their own power if not quite, or always, under their own direction. Alternating horses, as in a circus ring, teach the two sides of thoughts, that objectivity is not a given but an achievement; *leading* the thought, allowing it its own power, takes you to new ground.

The achievement of objectivity cannot be claimed for oneself, that is, for one's writing. As in "Self-Reliance": "I would write on the lintels of the door-post, *Whim*. I hope it may be better than whim at last." But in the necessity for words, "when [your] genius calls [you]," you can only air your thoughts, not assess them, and you must.

In Emerson's as in Wittgenstein's way of thinking, ethics is not a separate field of philosophical study, but every word that comes from us, the address of each thought, is a moral act, a taking of sides, but not in argument. In Emerson's terms, the sides may be called those of self-reliance and conformity; in Wittgenstein's terms, those of the privacy and emptiness of assertion he calls metaphysical, and the dispersal of this empty assertiveness by what he calls leading words home, his image of thinking. It strikes me that the feature of the intersection of Emersonian with Wittgensteinian thinking that primarily causes offense among professional philosophers is less the claim to know peculiar matters with a certainty that goes beyond reasonable evidence (matters like knowing the location of the deity's side, or of the ambition to insistent emptiness), and less the sheer, pervasive literary ambition of their writing, than the sense that these locations, diagnoses, and ambitions are in service of a claim to philosophical authorship that can seem the antithesis of what philosophical writing should be, a denial of rational or systematic presentation apart from which philosophy might as well turn itself into, or over to, literature, or perhaps worse.

The worse one may call esotericism, an effect it seems clear to me both Emerson and Wittgenstein recognized in themselves. Wittgenstein recognizes it in his continuous struggle against his interlocutors, whose role sometimes seems less to make Wittgenstein's thoughts clearer than to allow him to show that his thoughts are *not* clear, and not obviously to be *made* clear. They must be *found* so. Emerson recognizes his esotericism in such a remark from "Fate" as: "This insight [that] throws us on the party of the Universe, against all and sundry . . . distances those who share it from those who do not." But what is the alternative? At the close of "Experience" Emerson suggests that the alternative to speaking esoterically is speaking polemically (taking sides in argument), which for him, as for Wittgenstein, gives up philosophy, can never lead to the peace philosophy seeks for itself. (The philosopher I am reading who preceded Emerson in contrasting something like the esoteric with the polemical in considering the presentation of philosophy, as a matter internal to the present state of philosophy, is Hegel.) The dissonance between these thinkers and professional philosophers is less an intellectual disagreement than a moral variance in their conceptions of thinking, or perhaps I can say, in their concepts of the role of moral judgment in the moral life, in the way each pictures "constraint."

If slavery is the negation of thought, then thinking cannot affirm itself without affirming the end of slavery. But for thinking to *fail* to affirm itself is to deny the existence of philosophy. It is accordingly no more or less certain that philosophy will continue than that human self-enslavement will end. Philosophy cannot abolish slavery, and it can only call for abolition to the extent, or in the way, that it can call for thinking, can provide (adopting Kant's term) the incentive to thinking. The incentive Emerson provides is just what I am calling his authorship, working to attract our knowledge that we are rejecting, repressing thinking, hence the knowledge that thinking must contain both pain and pleasure (if it were not painful it would not require repression; if it were not pleasurable it would not attract it).

The linking of philosophical thinking with pain is expressed in an Emersonian sentence that seems a transcription at once of Plato and of Kant: "I know that the world I converse with in the city and in the farms is not the world I *think*" ("Experience," last paragraph). To think this other world, say the Realm of Ends, is pleasure; to bear witness to its difference from the actual world of cities and farms is pain. Here, perhaps, in this

pleasure and pain, before the advent of an imperative judgment, and before the calculation of the desirable, is the incentive of thinking that Kant
sought. The pain is a function of the insight that there is no reason the eventual world is not entered, not actual, hence that I must be rejecting it, rejecting the existence of others in it; and the others must be rejecting my
existence there.

I note that it is from here that I would like to trace Emerson's understanding of the origination of philosophy as a feminine capacity, as following his claim, toward the end of "Fate," that I excerpted earlier: "The truth
is in the air, and the most impressionable brain will announce it first, but
all will announce it a few minutes later." He continues: "So women, as
most susceptible, are the best index of the coming hour. So the great man,
that is, the man most imbued with the spirit of the time, is the impressionable man"—which seems to divine that the great man is a woman. The idea
that philosophical knowledge is receptive rather than assertive, that it is a
matter of leaving a thing as it is rather than taking it as something else, is
not new and is a point of affinity between Wittgenstein and Heidegger.
Emerson's thought here is that this makes knowledge difficult in a particular way, not because it is hard to understand exactly, but because it is hard
to bear; and his suggestion, accordingly, is that something prepares the
woman for this relation to pain, whereas a man must be great to attain it.
I grant that this may be said stupidly. It may be used—perhaps it most often
is, in fact—to deny the actual injustice done to actual women. Must it be
so appropriated? By philosophical necessity? But I associate Emerson's
invocation of the feminine with a striking remark of Hélène Cixous's, in
which she declares her belief that while men must rid themselves of pain
by mourning their losses, women do not mourn, but bear their pain. The
connection for me here is that the better world we think, and know not to
exist, with no acceptable reason not to exist, is not a world that is *gone*,
hence is not one to be mourned, but one to be borne, witnessed. The attempt to mourn it is the stuff of nostalgia. (In the closing paragraph of "Experience" I remember: "Patience, patience, we shall win at the last." I had
not until now been able to understand this as the demand upon Emerson's
writing, and his readers, to let the pain of his thoughts, theirs, collect itself.)

Is philosophy, as Emerson calls for it—we must keep reposing the question, without stopping it—an evasion of actual justice? It hasn't kept Emerson from sometimes writing polemically, as his West Indies and his Fugitive
Slave Law addresses attest. His direct idea, to repeat, is that polemic is an
evasion, or renunciation, of philosophy. How important a loss is the loss
of philosophy?

I think sometimes of Emerson, in his isolation, throwing words into the air, as aligned with the moment at which Socrates in the *Republic* declares that the philosopher will participate only in the public affairs of the just city, even if this means that he can only participate in making—as he is now doing—a city of words. As if without the philosopher's constructions, the actual human city would not merely lack justice in fact, but would lose the very concept, hence the imagination, of justice. Whether you think keeping that imagination alive is a valuable activity depends on how you think the reign of justice can come about.

I began in effect by saying for Emerson that the loss of philosophy is the loss of emancipation—of the imagination of the possibility of emancipation as such—from all forms of human confinement, say enslavement. I make explicit now, again, for a moment the thought about thinking that I claim is implicit throughout Emerson's writing (not solely in "Fate," however painfully there)—the thought that human freedom, as the opposition to fate, is not merely called for by philosophical writing but is instanced or enacted by that writing: the Emersonian sentence is philosophical in showing within itself its aversion to (turning away in turning toward) the standing conformation of its words, as though human thinking is not so much to be expressed by language as resurrected with it.

Let us accordingly transfigure once again: "In the history of the individual there is an account of his condition, and he knows himself to be party to his present estate." The days of the individual are told, counted out, in his condition by the words he suffers, and in his estate by the statements he utters: to know himself, as philosophy demands—or say to acknowledge his allegiances—is to take his part in each stating and in each silence.

In my encounter in 1983 with the essay "Fate," I did not speak of Emerson's philosophical authorship and esotericism, and I did not see the connection between Emerson's mode of thinking and his moral perfectionism, his constraint of his reader through his conviction in the magnified return of the reader's own rejected thoughts. It is as if in my desperateness to show Emerson capable of rigorous, systematic thinking, against the incessant denial of him as a philosopher, I felt I could not at the same time show his practice of thinking as one of transfiguring philosophy, in founding it, finding it, for America. I could not, as it were, *assume* his right to speak for philosophy. My primary focus in my earlier encounter with "Fate" is on Emerson's use of the term "condition," and his relation of it to the term "terms" (meaning words and meaning stipulations) and the term "dictation," which I claim shows Emerson turning the *Critique of Pure Reason* on itself, taking its fundamental term "condition" in its etymological significance as speaking *together*, so suggesting that the condition of the possibility of there being a world of objects for us is the condition of our speaking together; and that is not a matter of our sharing twelve categories of the understanding but of our sharing a language, hence the task of philosophy is not deriving privileged categories but announcing the terms on the basis of which we use each term of the language. Any term may give rise to what Wittgenstein calls a grammatical investigation, but beyond "condition" and its relatives, my earlier essay got just to the idea of "character" as, as always in Emerson, meaning the fact of language as well as the formation of an individual. But even that distance allowed me to summarize the essay's word as saying that character is fate, that the human is fated to significance, to finding it and to revealing it, and—as if tragically—fated to thinking, or to repressing thinking. Emerson—the American who is repeatedly, famously, denied the title of philosopher and described as lacking the tragic sense—writes an essay on freedom entitled "Fate" and creates the mode of what we may perhaps call the tragic essay.

If I now add the use of the word "constitution" in the essay "Fate" to the terms whose terms I demand, Emerson's claim for his philosophical authorship becomes unpostponable. Along with "condition" and "character," other philosophical terms Emerson allows the reader to find unobtrusive are "possibility" and "accident," and "impression" and "idea." "Constitution" appears in "Fate" only a few times, but its placement is telling, and the essay's array of political terms or projects magnifies its force: I cited earlier the term "resolution"; and we have heard of our being party to our estate; and then a not notably obtrusive sentence speaks of "this house of man, which is all consent, [inosculation] and balance of parts"—where "consent" worked to associate "balance of parts," with "checks and balances," and "house" thus names each of the branches of Congress. Here is an example of what I called placement:

Jesus said, "when he looketh on her, he hath committed adultery." But he is an adulterer before he has yet looked on the woman, by the superfluity of animal and the defect of thought in his constitution. Who meets him, or who meets her, in the street, sees that they are ripe to be each other's victim.

In my earlier essay I read this as the claim that most of what we call marriage is adultery, not a thought original with Emerson. Now, according to my implied hypothesis that every metaphysical claim in "Fate" about freedom, and its deprivation, is to be read also in a social register, as applying also to the institution of slavery, I read the phrase "the defect of thought in his constitution" to refer to the famous defect in the Constitution of the United States concerning those persons who are, let's say, interminably unfree, a defect which adulterates our claim to have established a just and tranquil human society, corrupts it, makes it spurious. I'll come back in a moment to the passage I mean.

From at least as early as "Self-Reliance" Emerson identifies his writing, what I am calling his philosophical authorship, as the drafting of the nation's constitution; or I have come to say, as amending our constitution. When he says there, "No law can be sacred to me but that of my nature," he is saying no more than Kant had said—that, in a phrase from "Fate," "we are law-givers," namely to the world of conditions and of objects, and to ourselves in the world of the unconditioned and of freedom. But the next sentence of "Self-Reliance" takes another step: "Good and bad are but names readily transferable to that or this; the only right is what is after my constitution; the only wrong what is against it." (The anticipation of Nietzsche's genealogy of morals is no accident.) Such a remark seems uniformly to be understood by Emerson's readers so that "my constitution" refers to Emerson's personal, peculiar physiology and to be the expression of his incessant promotion of the individual over the social. Such an understanding refuses the complexity of the Emersonian theme instanced in his saying that we are now "bugs, spawn," which means simultaneously that we exist neither as individual human beings nor in human nations.

The promise that we are capable of both is the fervent Emersonian theme to the effect that each of us is capable of speaking what is "true for all men." This capacity Emerson envisions in endless ways, often as speaking with necessity (a transfiguration of what philosophers, especially of what Kant, means by necessity). The theme is fervently announced in Emerson's various formulations of the vision that the innermost becomes the outermost. In "The American Scholar": "[The scholar] is one who raises himself from private considerations and breathes and lives on [as if they were air] public and illustrious thoughts"; in "Self-Reliance": "To believe your own thought, to believe that what is true for you in your private heart is true for all men—that is genius"—and specifically it is that which in every work of genius comes back to us with the alienated majesty of our own rejected thoughts. Speaking what is "true for all men," what in "Fate" Emerson speaks of as "truth com[ing] to our mind," is the event of insight he describes as "throw[ing] us on the party and interest of the Universe . . . against ourselves as much as others." "Throw[ing] us on the party . . . of the Universe,"—as if to say taking its part (as if taking sides with the deity)—puts me in mind of what Kant calls "[speaking] with the universal voice," which is the essential feature in making an aesthetic judgment (going beyond a mere expression of individual taste), namely that it demands or imputes or claims general validity, universal agreement with it; a claim made in the face of the knowledge that this agreement is in empirical fact apt not to be forthcoming. Moral judgment also speaks with—or rather listens to—what we might call the universal voice, in the form of the capacity to act under the constraint of the moral imperative, the imperative of the universal (of the universalizable). Emerson is, I am suggesting, appealing to something of the kind in simply claiming as a fact that we can, in thinking generally, judge the constitution of the world and of the lives complicitous with it from a standpoint "all and sundry" may be expected to find in themselves. The great difference from aesthetic and moral judgment is that the constitutional judgment demanding the amending of our lives (together) is to be found by each of us as a rejected thought returning to us. This mode of access to what I am calling constitutional judgment seems to me no less well characterized by Emerson than moral or aesthetic judgments are by philosophers generally. (If Emerson's "representativeness," his universalizing, is not to go unexamined, neither should his habitually condemned "individualism." If he is to be taken as an instance of "humanism" [as if he doesn't really mean much definite by being "thrown" on "the interest of the Universe"] then he is at the same time to be taken as some form of antihumanist, working "against ourselves," against what we understand as human [under]standing.)

It is the appeal to what we have rejected, as it were forgotten, say displaced, that gives to Emerson's writing (and to Wittgenstein's) the feel of the esoteric, of work to whose understanding one is asked to convert. It is an obvious sign of danger for professional, university philosophy, and it should be. Emerson ought to have to make his way, to bear the pain of his arrogating his right to speak for philosophy in the absence of making himself curricular, institutionalizable, polemical. Which is another way of saying that it does not follow from his institutionalized silencing that he has failed to raise the call for philosophy and to identify its fate with the fate of freedom. The fact of his call's repression would be the sign that it has been heard. The apparent silence of "Fate" might become deafening.

The absoluteness of the American institution of slavery, among the forms human self-enslavement takes, hence the absoluteness of philosophy's call to react to it, recoil from it, is announced, as I have more or less said, in the sentence cited earlier from the West Indies address: "Language must be raked, the secrets of the slaughter-houses and infamous holes that cannot front the day, must be ransacked, to tell what negro-slavery has been." I take the idea of raking language as another announcement, in a polemical context, of Emerson's philosophical authorship of what cannot be undertaken polemically.

One surface of the idea of raking language is a kind of Emersonian joke, namely that we are to respond to the fact, be responsible to it, that the largely unquestioned form or look of writing is of being raked on a page, that is, raked in parallel straight lines; and then to recognize that bringing what writing contains to light, letting these words return to us, as if to themselves, to mount suddenly to their majesty, to the scorn of egotisms, is to let the fact of them rouse our mind to activity, to turn it to the air. Perhaps we are to think that the fact of language is more telling than any fact uttered within it, as if every fact utters the fact of language: against this fatedness to language, to character, against, that is, what I earlier called our condemnation to significance, it figures that it is we who are raked. To think of language as raking and recoiling is to think of it, though it may look tranquil, as aimed and fired—at itself, at us—as if the human creature of conditions, fated to language, exists in the condition of threat, the prize of unmarked battles, where every horizon—where the air of words (of what might be said) gravitates to the earth of assertion (of what is actually said)—signifies a struggle between possession and dispossession, between speech and silence, between the unspeakable and the unsilenceable. (Here I am letting myself a little express, as earnest of wishing to describe better than I can, the anguish I sense in Emerson's language in "Fate.")

The particular direction of the raking of language I emphasize now is its office in *telling*; which is to say, in counting and recounting—"[telling] what negro-slavery has been" is how Emerson put it—hence in telling every enslavement. An origin of the word "raking" is precisely the idea of reckoning, of counting, as well as recking, paying attention. Of the endless interest there may be in thinking of language itself as a matter of counting, I confine attention momentarily here to the connection between counting or telling and the writing of the American constitution.

When in the second paragraph of "Experience" Emerson asks, bleakly, "How many individuals can we count in society?" he is directing our attention back, wherever else, to the famous paragraph containing what I earlier quoted Emerson as calling "the defect of thought in [our] constitution." That famous paragraph is the fifth—it is also just the fifth sentence—of the Constitution of the United States: "Representatives and direct Taxes shall be apportioned among the several States which may be included within this Union, according to their respective Numbers, which shall be determined by adding to the whole number of free Persons, including those bound to service for a Term of Years, and excluding Indians not taxed, three fifths of all other Persons." The paragraph goes on to specify the calculation of democratic representation, and I find the comic invoking in "Fate" of the new science of statistics, in its attention to populations, to be another allusion to the "defect," the lack of philosophical necessity, in our constitutional counting. In the large we do not see how many we are; in the small we do not know, as Emerson puts it in "The American Scholar," whether we add up to what the "old fable" calls "one Man." As if we do not know whether any of us, all and each, count. We are living our skepticism.

So again, Emerson's simultaneous use of the idea of "my constitution"—his transfiguration of these words—so that we know they name at once his makeup and the makeup of the nation he prophesies, is a descendant of Plato's use of his Republic—his city of words—to name a structure at once of the soul and of its society. That is part of my cause in finding Emerson's philosophical prose, his authorship, to earn something like Plato's description (a city of words) for itself—as I find Thoreau's *Walden* to do—hence to imagine for itself the power to amend the actual city in the philosophical act of its silence, its power of what Emerson calls patience, which he seeks as the most active of intellectual conditions. (Even one who recognizes this possibility of his or her own constitution as entering into an imagination of the constitution of the just city may find no city even worth rebuking philosophically—through the proposal of a shared imagination—but purely polemically. This condition may sometimes be pictured as a form of exile rather than of Emerson's agonized membership. Yet it is not clear how different these forms are. I have elsewhere identified Emerson's idea of American membership, his philosophical stance toward America, as one of immigrancy.)

Nothing less than Emerson's peculiar claim to amendment would satisfy my craving for philosophy. But nothing so much creates my fears for it. I am aware that I have mentioned the name of Heidegger once or twice in these remarks, but cited no word of his. And yet in my present return to Emerson's "Fate" and my sense of its tortured, philosophical silence about the tyranny of the institution of slavery—in its effort, as I have more or less put the matter, to preserve philosophy in the face of conditions that negate philosophy—I am aware of a kind of preparation for some explicit coming to terms on my part with Heidegger's relation with the tyranny of Nazism, an explicitness I have, with growing discomfort, postponed over the years.

Here is motivation for the present essay I cited at the outset. It is to pose for myself the following questions: Am I prepared to listen to an argument in Heidegger's defense that he was, after his public falling out of favor with the regime, attempting to preserve philosophy in the face of conditions that negate philosophy? If not, how am I prepared to understand, as in his 1936 lectures on Nietzsche and in his contemporaneous "Origin of the Work of Art," his call of a people to its historical destiny, and his announcement of a form of the appearance of truth as the founding of a political order? Such questions press me now not only because of the oddly late and oddly stale recent accounts of Heidegger's extensive involvements with Nazism, and the inundation of responses to these revelations by so many of the major philosophical voices of Europe, but because of the pitch to which my sense of Nietzsche's absorption in Emerson's writing has come, and of Heidegger's absorption or appropriation, in turn, of Nietzsche.

Only four or five years ago did I for the first time read all the way through Heidegger's sets of lectures on Nietzsche, delivered from 1936 to 1940, surely the most influential interpretation of Nietzsche to have appeared for serious philosophers in Europe. Emerson's presence in Nietzsche's thought as Heidegger receives it—in certain passages of Nietzsche that Heidegger leans on most heavily—is so strong at certain moments that one has to say that Nietzsche is using Emerson's words; which means that Heidegger in effect, over an unmeasured stretch of thought, is interpreting Emerson's words. Here are two instances: in volume 2 of the English translation of the Nietzsche lectures Heidegger notes that Nietzsche's "early thought . . . was later to become the essential center of his thinking." Heidegger mentions two school essays of Nietzsche's, and in a footnote the translator notes in passing that the essays exhibit the "influence" of Emerson and quotes two sentences from the longer of the essays, "Fate and History: Thought":

Yet if it were possible for a strong will to overturn the world's entire past, we would join the ranks of self-sufficient gods, and world history would be no more to us than a dream-like enchantment of the self. The curtain falls, and man finds himself again, like a child playing with worlds, a child who wakes at daybreak and with a laugh wipes from his brow all frightful dreams.

Compare this with a sentence from the next-to-last paragraph of "Fate": "If we thought men were free in the sense that in a single exception one fantastical will would prevail over the law of things, it were all one as if a child's hand could pull down the sun." Nietzsche is not "influenced" by Emerson but is quite deliberately transfiguring Emerson, as for the instruction of the future. This happens early and late. In the section from book 3 of *Thus Spoke Zarathustra* called "The Convalescent," of which Heidegger's reading is among the high points of his opening set of Nietzsche lectures, Nietzsche says this: "To every soul belongs another world: for every soul, every other soul is an afterworld." In Emerson's "Fate" we find: "The hero is to others as the world." The relation of transfiguration here is the clearer the more one goes into what Emerson means by the hero (who is in principle every soul) and into his view of how souls touch.

So I am faced with the spectacle of Heidegger's in effect—unknowingly—facing certain of Emerson's words, guiding himself in these fateful years by signs from, of all places on earth, the waste of America. How do I guide myself? Do I guide myself by the thought that since Emerson is the philosopher of freedom I can, in his mediation through Nietzsche to Heidegger, in principle trust to our eventual success in showing Heidegger's descent into the allegiance with tyranny to be an aberration—hence redeemable—of his philosophical genius? Or must I guide myself instead by the thought, that since Heidegger is so radically, unredeemably compromised, and since Emerson is mediated by philosophers of the powers of Nietzsche and of Heidegger, it is not even to be trusted that we will eventually succeed in showing Emerson's genius to be uncompromised by this mediation, so that the way of philosophy I care about most is *as such* compromised?

The Holocaust and the Construction of Modern American Literary Criticism: The Case of Lionel Trilling

Emily Miller Budick

No Jew and no Christian has a right to live and guide his actions *as though* the six million had not died in agony. For this thing did not happen far away or long ago. . . . It happened yesterday; it has not ceased happening.

—Ludwig Lewisohn

*H*ardly any conversation in American literary studies today does not concern the issue of multiculturalism—of how American culture can become truly reflective of its many different ethnic and racial voices, most prominently African American, Native American, and Hispanic. The terms *race*, *gender*, and *class* punctuate conference programs, as well as articles, books, and classroom syllabi. They are the haunting "mantra," as one recent session of the American Studies Association labeled them, of the critical discussion. By chanting these words and thus keeping them at the forefront of our moral sensibilities, we would, as scholars, make our notion of literary culture nonelitist, inclusive, democratic. In terms of the practicalities of literary criticism this means several things. First, we would read the canonical texts of the tradition (and the canonical readings of those texts) for the ways in which they have excluded competing cultural voices, thus exposing how these texts reaffirm a societal status quo characterized by nothing so much as appalling sociopolitical and economic inequality. Second, we would break the hegemony of the "tradition" by reintroducing into the canon those authors and critics whom the prevailing authorities have excluded. And, finally, we would register the potential for the individual expression and mutual translatability of all of the culture's voices—

black and white, male and female, mainstream and marginal—as they are permitted to discover and respond to and be refashioned by one another, producing what can only come to seem the genuine multivocalism of the American people.

The enterprise is inspiring, and the idea of acceding to a genuine cultural inclusiveness could not be more appealing. What, if anything, does the idea of multiculturalism exclude? And what dangers might it introduce in its very insistence not only on probing the politics of literary writing and canon formation but also on actively revising them? What, in other words, guarantees access to speaking in a democracy: the sheer publication of the nation's many voices, or a way of thinking about what it means to speak, listen, and understand one another's discourse?

In the following essay I want to record a particular moment in one unfolding of the multicultural idea, and I want to trace in that moment the acts of exclusion (rather than inclusion) by which multiculturalism gains its objectives. The moment occurs in an argument between two prominent Americanist critics, one of an older, the other of a newer generation: Frederick Crews and Donald Pease; and it centers around a third, almost legendary, literary critic who represents an even earlier generation: Lionel Trilling.[1] At issue in this intersection of literary critical voices, each with its own agenda, is the place of politics within literature and literary criticism; how and why and to what consequence the politics of a literary or critical text function, not simply within the world of writing and discourse but within the sociopolitical world itself. For as Pease and Crews struggle, via Trilling, over what emerges as the issue of Marxism in American literary culture, there is a subject that does not emerge at all, despite its inescapable pertinence to the post–World War II moment Pease and Crews are debating as well as to Trilling's writings. This subject is the Nazi Holocaust, the extermination of virtually all of European Jewry during the Second World War.[2]

Pease, Crews, Trilling (Or Is It Matthiessen?), Dreiser, and Parrington: Marxism, Nazism, and the Founding of American Literary History

Responding to a review essay by Crews that is, among other things, a response to his own work, Pease cogently summarizes the recent turn in American literary criticism away from formalist criticism to what has come to be known (following Crews's essay) as the New Americanism.[3] According to Pease, the postwar New Critics, yielding to the pressures of

World War II and the Cold War, attempted to segregate literature from politics. In so doing, they seriously neglected the sociological contexts both of the American literary canon and of their own critical writings. The New Americanists, in Pease's view, have endeavored to recover that much-maligned link between the political and the literary. They have done this largely by distinguishing between politics in the sense of a particular socioeconomic or political agenda, and politics, or ideology, in the sense of the larger belief system that informs any society or culture. Culture, the New Americanists point out, is ideological, even if a given culture (America, for example) defines itself through its rejection of certain ideologies, such as totalitarianism or fascism.

Pease anchors his critique of New Criticism and its contemporary exponents in a particular moment in Crews's essay, when Crews turns his attention to the critical writings of Lionel Trilling. In setting himself in opposition to Crews, Pease constructs the issue between them in terms of an earlier opposition in American literary critical history. This is the opposition between F. O. Matthiessen and Lionel Trilling, where, in Pease's view, the issue was Marxism. As Pease notes, Trilling's response to Matthiessen had to do primarily with Matthiessen's own response to the work of Theodore Dreiser, who, as Pease records, "had decided to join the Communist Party in August 1945."[4]

The question I raise is whether Marxism is the only, or even the primary, issue between Trilling and Matthiessen; and what, therefore, it means that Crews and Pease assume the rejection or acceptance of Marxism to be the central issue of contention between them.

Before I venture an answer to this question, let me note several factors that help justify the direction of my inquiry. First of all, Pease is hardly alone in placing contemporary literary studies against the background of the Second World War and designating Marxism, or, more precisely, the resistance to Marxism, as a major determinant of postwar literary culture. Myra Jehlen, for example, suggests in her introduction to the collection of New Americanist essays she edited with Sacvan Bercovitch that "the background for the criticism in this volume is not the twenties and thirties [when American literary criticism, in the New Americanist view, was still self-consciously ideological] . . . , but the forties and fifties. This is a crucial distinction because the forties and fifties—characterized first by war-inspired nationalism, later by the jingoism of the McCarthy period—essentially reversed the dominant ideological and cultural thinking of the twenties and thirties." Jehlen's focus on "war-inspired nationalism" and the McCarthy period (the "Cold War consensus," as Pease refers to it) is

shared by other New Americanists (Russell Reising, for example) as well
as critics of various other literary persuasions.[5]

Given the particular emphasis of the New Americanism on uncover-
ing lines of sociopolitical cultural bias (as, say, in relation to nineteenth-
century fiction and the issue of slavery), one would think that in designating the Second World War as a formative pressure on American literary
studies, New Americanist criticism would necessarily have to deal with
what was a major and unavoidable aspect of this war: anti-Semitism and
the Holocaust. To be sure, the Holocaust is often implicit in the New Americanist designation of World War II as the background for criticism of the
1950's, 1960's, and 1970's. Nonetheless, the events of the Holocaust are
almost never made explicit (the Holocaust, as such, is usually not named),
and even more rarely is the extermination of European Jewry put forward
as a subject, among others, for direct consideration. When the Holocaust
is named, it is almost invariably linked with other, related crimes and catastrophes of the era. Three Americanists who, in the course of their literary
analyses, do address the Holocaust directly are Mark Shechner, Mark
Krupnick, and Gregory Jay. Even here, however, the Holocaust pales beside Marxism and the Communist Revolution as factors in the construction of modern American literary culture. This is so even for "Jewish intellectuals" (like Trilling), Shechner observes, for whom "in the years just
following the Second World War, the shadows of 1936 (Spain, the Moscow
show trials) and 1939 (Stalin's nonaggression pact with Hitler, the carving
up of Poland) loomed even more darkly than those of the death camps in
which six million Jews lost their lives." For Jay, who is not specifically concerned with Jewish matters, the "background of the war" includes the Holocaust, but it does so along with "Hiroshima and Nagasaki"; "Auschwitz
with Hiroshima."[6]

At this juncture, let me state explicitly that I do not intend to put anyone on trial, especially not for something that might, in this context, all
too sensationalistically be called anti-Semitism. I think of my own interest
in the (non)debate concerning the Holocaust in something of the same
terms in which New Americanists have expressed their ideas concerning
the slave/race/Indian issues in authors like Hawthorne, Melville, and Poe.
In other words, I take New Historicist critical principles as legitimizing my
own suspicions about what it means that a particular conversation is or is
not taking place, or is taking place while ostensibly not taking place; and
I worry all the more that it is / is not taking place among a group of literary
scholars whose critical priorities seem to demand that such a conversation
become explicit and overt.

So I return to my question. What does it reveal about the development of American literary studies that in the Crews-Pease exchange the issue heard in Trilling's response to Matthiessen is Marxism? Further, how do we understand the emergence of Lionel Trilling as a key figure in the debate concerning the good/bad founders of American literary studies, especially given the fact that Trilling, despite his deep investment in American culture, is neither an Americanist nor a New Critic?

This latter fact about Trilling, that he is not a New Critic and that he even voices sharp objection to the New Critical enterprise, makes the New Americanist response to him puzzling to say the least, even more so when one considers that Trilling's ideas resemble no contemporary body of criticism more than that of the New Americanism.[7] "What I understand by manners," Trilling explains, "is a culture's hum and buzz of implication. I mean the whole evanescent context in which its explicit statements are made."[8] Culture, Trilling states somewhat later in his career, is the "unitary complex of interacting assumptions, modes of thought, habits, and styles, which are connected in secret as well as overt ways with the practical arrangements of a society and which, because they are not brought to consciousness, are unopposed in their influence over men's minds."[9]

Trilling's definition of the relation between the literary text and culture anticipates the contemporary definition of ideology, as put forward, for example, by Sacvan Bercovitch. Ideology, writes Bercovitch, is "the ground and texture of consensus . . . the system of interlinked ideas, symbols, and beliefs by which a culture—any culture—seeks to justify and perpetuate itself; the web of rhetoric, ritual, and assumption through which society coerces, persuades, and coheres."[10] In a moment I will suggest how Bercovitch's criticism may differ from that of many New Historicists and New Americanists. These differences may owe something to the relation of Bercovitch's ideas to Trilling's. Nonetheless, Bercovitch's definition of ideology identifies a central assumption of New Americanist criticism generally.

Trilling does not, then, as the New Americanist argument against him suggests, place the writer/critic outside society, as if literature and culture were forces on one side of a power struggle, and politics and ideology forces on the other side. Trilling specifically rejects New Criticism for the same reasons that the New Americanists object to it, because it makes the text autonomous, places it outside the cultural complex in which it exists.[11] Like Bercovitch and others, Trilling is suspicious of what he calls the evanescent (Bercovitch calls it the "transcendental") contextualization of culture, by which both Trilling and Bercovitch mean the way in which culture appeals to something outside itself to legitimate and authorize what are, finally, only the very human workings of socially constituted institutions. Therefore, Trilling shares with the New Americanists a commitment to a "hermeneutics of nontranscendence," a dialectical apprehension and explication of culture through what Bercovitch (thinking perhaps of Wolfgang Iser) calls border crossings.[12] I will have more to say about this hermeneutics of nontranscendence later.

Still, there are differences between Trilling's form of cultural criticism and that of most of the New Americanists. In order to get at these differences let me pursue further Pease's objections to Trilling and Trilling's objections to Matthiessen. These several objections have to do with the critics' apparently differing definitions of "reality." According to Pease, Trilling desired a definition of reality (at least that kind of reality represented in the literary text) that would make it independent of politics; therefore, in Pease's way of thinking, Trilling rejected Matthiessen's sense of reality, which turns out to be Dreiser's and Vernon Parrington's sense of reality as well, because it seemed to Trilling politically overdetermined. But, as I have already begun to suggest, and as Trilling makes clear in his essay entitled ("tendentiously," according to Pease) "Reality in America," he does not wish to separate politics and art. Instead, he wants to discover their relation.

It is because Trilling accepts the idea of literature as political that he does not, for example, object to Parrington's "lively sense of the practical, workaday world, of the welter of ordinary undistinguished things and people, of the tangible, quirky, unrefined elements of life"; in fact Trilling considers it Parrington's "best virtue." What Trilling resists in Parrington is the way in which "whenever he was confronted with a work of art that was complex, personal and not literal, that was not, as it were, a public document, Parrington was at a loss." Trilling describes the issue between himself and Parrington as follows:

There exists, he believes, a thing called *reality*; it is one and immutable; it is wholly external, it is irreducible. . . . Reality being fixed and given, the artist has but to let it pass through him. . . . It does not occur to Parrington that there is any other relation possible between the artist and reality than this passage of reality through the transparent artist; he meets evidence of imagination and creativeness with a settled hostility, the expression of which suggests that he regards them as the natural enemies of democracy.[13]

In thus limiting the definition of reality, Parrington, in Trilling's view, "stands at the center of American thought about American culture." This is exemplified for Trilling in the critical reception of Dreiser, especially by a critic like Matthiessen, whom Trilling otherwise admires:

This belief in the incompatibility of mind and reality is exemplified by the doctrinaire indulgence which liberal intellectuals have always displayed toward Theodore Dreiser, an indulgence which becomes the worthier of remark when it is contrasted with the liberal severity toward Henry James. Dreiser and James: with that juxtaposition we are immediately at the dark and bloody crossroads where literature and politics meet. One does not go there gladly, but nowadays it is not exactly a matter of free choice whether one does or not go. . . . Few critics . . . have ever been wholly blind to James's great gifts. . . . And few critics have ever been wholly blind to Dreiser's great faults. But by liberal critics James is traditionally put to the ultimate question: of what use, of what actual political use, are his gifts and their intention? . . . But in the same degree that liberal criticism is moved by political considerations to treat James with severity, it treats Dreiser with the most sympathetic indulgence. Dreiser's literary faults, it gives us to understand, are essentially social and political virtues. . . . The liberal judgment of Dreiser and James goes back to politics, goes back to the cultural assumptions that make politics. . . . If it could be conclusively demonstrated . . . that James explicitly intended his books to be understood as pleas for cooperatives, labor unions [etc.] the American critic in his liberal and progressive character would still be worried by James because his work shows so many of the electric qualities of mind. . . . [1] In the American metaphysic, reality is always material reality.[14]

(I will return to the material elided in [1] in a moment.) For Trilling a proof of a serious misstep in American literary criticism is Matthiessen's defense of Dreiser's novel *The Bulwark*. Matthiessen, Trilling stresses, knows full well the limitations of the "Parrington line of liberal criticism." He is also hardly insensitive to the virtues of Henry James. "Yet Mr. Matthiessen," Trilling explains, "writing in the *New York Times Book Review* about Dreiser's posthumous novel, *The Bulwark*, accepts the liberal cliché [of the Parrington line] which opposes crude experience to mind and establishes Dreiser's value by implying that the mind which Dreiser's crude experience is presumed to confront and refute is the mind of gentility . . . [2]."[15] (The material elided in [2] will be supplied shortly.)

The issue between Trilling and Parrington/Matthiessen/Dreiser, I suggest, is not simply Marxism. It is certainly not whether or not texts are ideological or political. It is rather the specific ways in which texts are ideological or political, and what a given way means for the relation between culture and particular political ideologies such as Marxism, fascism, and democracy. Trilling finds Matthiessen's defense of *The Bulwark* unacceptable because of its failure to recognize the full political dimensions of Dreiser's text. In Trilling's view, Dreiser's book is morally inadequate and even offensive, not (as Matthiessen anticipated the attack would be) because the novel's "renewal of Christianity" marks a "failure of nerve." Rather, Trilling objects to the book because it represents a "failure of mind and heart":

"We dare not," Trilling writes, "as its hero does, blandly 'accept' the suffering of others; and the Book of Job tells us that it does not include enough in its exploration of the problem of evil, and is not stern enough."[16] Matthiessen's willingness "undiscriminatingly" to defend the book on the same realist/materialist grounds on which he defended Dreiser's earlier novels brings into focus what is for Trilling most deeply distressing about the "Parrington line of liberal criticism." This is the way in which it "establishes the social responsibility of the writer and then goes on to say that, apart from his duty of resembling reality as much as possible, he is not really responsible for anything, not even for his ideas."

It is this split between social and individual responsibility that Trilling utterly rejects, the idea that the novelist's responsibility extended no further than accurately representing social inequalities and injustice, so that, in the end, he or she is "not really responsible for anything, not even for his [or her] ideas." For Trilling Dreiser's bland acceptance of the suffering of others, in particular in a book with an expressly Christian message, signaled a very specific danger, a very particular phenomenon in the history of western culture. I now supply the materials elided in [1] and [2] above:

[1] And if something like the opposite were proved of Dreiser [that he did not have social interests at heart] it would be brushed aside—as his doctrinaire anti-Semitism has in fact been brushed aside—because his books have the awkwardness, the chaos, the heaviness which we associate with "reality."

[2] It is much to the point of his intellectual vulgarity that Dreiser's anti-Semitism was not merely a social prejudice but an idea, a way of dealing with difficulties.[17]

Cultural Conversations, Hidden Agendas, and the Holocaust: Trilling's Definition of the Opposing (i.e., Aversive) Self

The "hidden agenda" of *The Liberal Imagination*, suggests Steven Marcus, expressing an idea later confirmed in Diana Trilling's memoir, is Trilling's attack on Stalinism.[18] I suggest that there is in this book a second hidden agenda as well.

I will not here go into the details of Trilling's Jewish background, except to say that his upbringing was Jewish and that his early career as a student at Columbia provides ample evidence of continuing Jewish concerns.[19] What is relevant to my argument here is the way in which Trilling recurs throughout his writings—though with considerable reserve, to be sure—to moments of anti-Semitism within the western literary tradition, even where the ostensible subject of a given essay hardly dictates that he refer to matters of Jewishness at all. Aside from the two Dreiser examples I have already cited, there are, for instance, Trilling's noting Henry Adams's "hateful" "anti-Jewish utterances,"[20] a reference to the anti-Semitism of Santayana,[21] and his comment on Joyce's objections to another writer who was anti-Semitic.[22] There are also, of course, Trilling's more sustained attentions to anti-Semitism and Jews, not only in some of his early fiction and other writings for the *Menorah Journal* but, for example, in his afterword to the republication of Tess Slesinger's *The Unpossessed*,[23] his essay on Isaac Babel,[24] and his review of C. Virgil Gheorghiu's *The Twenty-fifth Hour*.[25] Also relevant in this context is Trilling's participation in two important symposia published in *Commentary*: "The Jewish Writer and the English Literary Tradition" and "Seven Professors Look at the Jewish Student."[26] Trilling directly acknowledges the Holocaust in "Art and Fortune" when he observes that "the great psychological fact of our time which we all observe with baffled wonder and shame is that there is no possible way of responding to Belsen and Buchenwald. The activity of mind fails before the incommunicability of man's suffering."[27] He notes it as well in "The Changing Myth of the Jew," first written in 1930 but only published in 1978 in *Commentary*[28] and in "The Sense of the Past" as well as in "Wordsworth and the Rabbis."[29] Furthermore, refusing him tenure at Columbia, his colleagues labeled him a Communist, a Freudian, and a Jew. Nor was the anti-Semitism of the Hitler period irrelevant to his thinking about his experience at Columbia. As Diana Trilling put it in her memorial essay "Lionel Trilling: A Jew at Columbia," Trilling's experience is "the story of what it meant to be a Jew in the American academy before we actually let ourselves recognize what was happening in Germany and what the casual anti-Semitism in our own country would portend." She then goes on to note that even after Trilling had talked the Columbia faculty into endorsing his tenure, his former thesis advisor, Emory Neff, found it necessary to caution Trilling not to use his own success as an occasion for letting more Jews into Columbia. But, Diana Trilling continues, by then the Second World War had begun. The extermination of six million Jews would put to rest the numerus clausus at American universities as surely as it would give birth to the State of Israel.[30] Much of Diana Trilling's memoir of herself and her husband is preoccupied with describing their Jewish identity and reclaiming for her husband his rightful status as a *Jewish* intellectual.

　　I do not want to exaggerate the number of Trilling's direct references to Jews, anti-Semitism, and the Holocaust. Given the quantity of writing that he produced during his career, the number of such explicit references is relatively small. These references, however, such as they are, permit us to glimpse an element in Trilling's cultural project that might otherwise vanish from view. This element, which (because of the enormity of the events of the Second World War) I would like to call Trilling's Holocaust inflection, helps impel Trilling's resistance to the Parrington line of liberal criticism. Anti-Semitism and, later, the Holocaust forced Trilling to see that the "Jewish Question," as Marx referred to it, was not easily susceptible of a "solution" through either Marxist theory or practice.[31]

Trilling was well aware that Marxism's failure adequately to deal with anti-Semitism could be understood in several different ways. The most obvious of these was that a phenomenon like anti-Semitism, or racism or sexism, might simply not be referable to economic realities or simple power relationships, but might represent a deep-seated, non-socioeconomic hatred of one human being for another. The disillusionment of many African Americans with the Communist party in the 1940s, which forms a central feature in the fiction of writers like Richard Wright and Ralph Ellison, and the movement of African American literature away from realistic modes of representation in the contemporary period, tell their own story, I think, of the failure of Communism adequately to redress racism. That story also emerges, I maintain, in a slightly different version, in Trilling's criticism and in the subsequent inheritance of that criticism in the 1960's and 1970's. Alfred Kazin puts the case of the Jew and the Communist party very directly: "The Jews had been ruled out of existence by the Nazis and could not be admitted into the thought of those who were fighting Hitler. The Jews could not be fitted into Nazi or Communist schemes." "Like all of us old liberals," Kazin remarks later, "the Trillings lived on the edge of the abyss created in modern culture, in all our cultured minds, by the extermination of the Jews. The case of Alger Hiss seemed easier to deal with. He was a proven liar."[32] Kazin misses the degree to which Trilling does not take the "easier" route. He was not simply an anti-Marxist. Nor was this least visibly affiliated of the American Jewish critics a "non-Jewish Jew."[33] Trilling's writings are subtly pervaded by a Jewish consciousness; and they are characterized not by an economically or politically motivated refusal of Marxism, but by an awareness of the degree to which Marxist thinking had very little light to shed on, or remedy to offer for, racism and anti-Semitism.

But there are other, more complex, reasons for Trilling's resistance to Marxism as a "solution" to anti-Semitism. And these go to the heart of Trilling's literary-critical poetics. In order to get at these other reasons, let me turn for a moment to another critical conversation concerning Trilling, Marxism, and the Holocaust.

For Gregory Jay, as for Pease, Trilling is a pivotal figure in the debate between the New Critics and the New Historicists. But whereas Pease emphasizes Trilling's opposition to Marxism and hence his complicity with the New Criticism, Jay, in the name of deconstructionism, recalls Trilling's vehement opposition to the New Criticism and, going behind Marx, recovers Trilling's relationship to Hegel (making Trilling, from Jay's point of view, the true Marxist).[34] In Jay's interpretation Trilling provides an important alternative to New Historicist directions in literary criticism. "As an 'other'—Jew, Freudian, Marxist," struggling both to assimilate to the "authority within Anglo-European high culture" and to maintain "his allegiance to an 'otherness,'" Trilling, argues Jay, comes closer than the New Historicists to realizing the historicism of dialectical Hegelianism. "The modernist 'tragic vision' Trilling offers in the wake of liberalism's paradoxes and failures," writes Jay, "focuses on the view that 'the world is a complex and unexpected and terrible place which is not always to be understood by the mind as we use it in our everyday tasks.' Set against the background of the war, the Holocaust, and Hiroshima and Nagasaki, these rather deceptively simple words take on considerable resonance. The special cognitive virtue of the literary, according to Trilling, is its dialectical power to reopen the complexities foreclosed by ideologies."[35]

But, in Jay's view, Trilling regrettably swerves away from his deconstructionist position. This swerve has to do, Jay suggests, with Trilling's idea of a "self" (what Jay earlier calls "consciousness"). Here is Jay's indictment of Trilling, gentle yet decisive:

Hegel's text becomes a pretext in Trilling for affirming the ontological reality of the "performed" self, the written subject, who thus recovers from the inauthenticity of repetition and the impotence or errancy of action. . . . The threatened disappearance of the modern self . . . is remedied [by Trilling] by postulating an ontological and referential determination of writing by selfhood. . . . Style is freedom, choice, and responsibility, and Trilling can thus theorize the cohesion of the moral and the aesthetic judgment. . . . Efforts to move past the antinomies of his criticism, and of the tradition he belonged to, require a thinking of the dialectic of the literary and the historical that does not subordinate itself to either a deterministic narrative of the subject's subordination to Power or an idealistic tale of the achievement of an Absolute Freedom for Consciousness. It can only be historical, and political, if it remembers that history is a way of being that cannot simply be referred to. Our responsibility is rather to rewrite it, though it cost us our "I"'s in the process.[36]

Although the experience of the "war . . . and Hiroshima and Nagasaki" might have led Trilling to eliminate the "I" from the rewriting of history, the experience of the Holocaust, in which individuals were exterminated for no other reason than the fact of their being "I"s in the first place—individuals of specific historical and biological identity—made Jay's proposed "cost" of forfeiting the self an impossibly high price to pay. Trilling's personal commitment to a personal self, which Trilling in "Wordsworth and the Rabbis" identifies as Wordsworth's commitment to *being*, is the distinctive marker of Trilling's Jewish consciousness, especially after the Holocaust. Indeed, Trilling's essay on Wordsworth, which produces this idea of being, is very directly a commentary on the Holocaust, as I shall indicate in a moment. For Jay, as for the New Americanists, the primary victims of American New Criticism were those many "others" whom New Critical poetics eliminated from the literary canon. Therefore, in his own telling of the story of American literary history in the twentieth century, Jay retrieves Trilling as an "other."[37] What Jay will not grant Trilling, however (as he will not grant it to African American critics who have had similar difficulties with Hegel and his racism), is the specificity of otherness—that what is from the perspective of the dominant culture largely a nonspecific, almost impersonal, otherness is from the point of view of the individual not otherness but self. In the case of Trilling this selfhood was inseparably part of his Jewishness (however obliquely he defined that Jewishness), which in the 1940's had perched him, along with other Jews, vicariously on the edge of cataclysmic destruction. It is worth noting in this context (although I would resist making more of this than it is worth) that Jews are not among the "empirical others, such as Native Americans, women, and blacks" whom Jay cites in his list of American "others."[38] Nor is it irrelevant, as I mentioned earlier, that when he cites the Holocaust as a pivotal event of the Second World War, one that inevitably shaped Trilling's thinking, Jay couples it with Hiroshima and Nagasaki, and Auschwitz with Hiroshima. For Jay, Trilling's otherness is an abstraction; it is his link to a category of individuals, namely others, all of whom, for one reason or another, have suffered exclusion and even death, and whom Jay would bring into some kind of relationship with the culture at large. The one human right Jay elides is that of naming oneself in one's absolute difference from others.

I do not wish to be mistaken here. Jay's objectives are admirable. Furthermore, the catastrophes at Hiroshima and Nagasaki to which he refers are cosmically horrifying events of recent human history. They are just as deserving of our sustained critical and moral consciousness as the events of the Holocaust. By the same token, it is an important fact about Hitler's Nazism that he exterminated gypsies and homosexuals as well as Jews. But the devastation at Hiroshima and Nagasaki is different from the devastation at Auschwitz; and the relationship between Nazism and the Jews is different from the relationship between Nazism and gypsies and homosexuals. It has become, in the contemporary period, a common feature of discussions of the Holocaust to link the Holocaust with other tragedies of the Hitler period. This diffusing of the consequences of the Holocaust occurs in texts as vastly different from each other as William Styron's *Sophie's Choice*, Toni Morrison's *Song of Solomon*, Lesléa Newman's "A Letter to Harvey Milk," and the poetry of Sylvia Plath.[39] In erasing the differences among moral violations, these writers, I think, for all the value of their writing, do at least one kind of violence to moral thinking. They also effect, inadvertently perhaps, a further erasure of the Jews. New Americanist and deconstructive criticism frequently (largely unwittingly) has something of the same effect.

The "I" that Trilling is unwilling to relinquish to a full historical dialecticism is hardly simplistic. For Trilling, as for Stephen Greenblatt and many New Historicists, identity is a socially mediated construct. Nonetheless Trilling maintains an idea of being that is not only irreducible, but nontranslatable. This, according to Trilling, was the wise counsel of Wordsworthian poetry. Wordsworth, writes Trilling, did more than teach us how "to feel." He "undertook to teach us how to *be*." "What does it mean when we say a person *is*?" Trilling asks, as he leads into a reading of Wordsworth's "Idiot Boy": "Again and again in our literature, at its most apocalyptic and intense, we find the impulse to create figures who are intended to suggest that life is justified in its elementary biological simplicity, and, in the manner of Wordsworth, these figures are conceived of as being of humble status and humble heart: Lawrence's simpler people . . . Dreiser's Jennie Gerhardt . . . Hemingway's waiters . . . Faulkner's Negroes . . . and . . . idiot boys."[40]

Given that Trilling is writing "Wordsworth and the Rabbis" in the years immediately following the war, it is not difficult, I think, to understand Trilling's emphasis on the idea of "being," or to discover what motivates Trilling to associate the contemporary rejection of Wordsworth's poetry with a particular and vicious historical phenomenon: "The quality in Wordsworth that now makes him unacceptable," Trilling specifies, "is a Judaic quality."[41] Nor are the reasons for Trilling's particular formula for distinguishing between this elemental being (human beings in their biological simplicity) and the evolution of a morally responsible self particularly obscure. He writes: "How was a man different from an individual? A person born before a certain date, a man—had he not eyes? had he not hands, organs, dimensions, senses, affections, passions? If you pricked him, he bled and if you tickled him, he laughed."[42] For Trilling, the Holocaust necessitated thinking not simply about social injustice (as Marxism had undertaken to do) or about undoing ideology (as in dialectical Hegelianism, as it has been evolved by deconstruction). Rather it compelled a redefinition of the human—the person, the human being, in Trilling's specific case, the Jew.

It is not irrelevant to Trilling's relationship to Marxism that of the major figures who created modern culture, Marx was certainly one of the more virulently anti-Semitic—although, of course, T. S. Eliot, standing in various ways behind the New Criticism, and Hegel and Heidegger, standing behind deconstruction, produce similar taints. Nonetheless, this does not release us from the necessity of considering, in the case of Marx as in the case of all of these figures, how, precisely, we want to understand their anti-Semitism in relation to the cultural circulations in which they took part and which may, indeed, put that circulation beyond, say, a merely Marxist or Hegelian understanding. For Trilling, Marxism must necessarily fail before the threat of anti-Semitism because, like Nazism, it imagined the "Jewish" as a "Question" in need of a "solution" or removal: "Let us look at the real Jew of our time," writes Marx in *A World Without Jews* (part one was published as *The Jewish Question*); "not the Jew of the Sabbath . . . but the Jew of everyday life. What is the Jew's foundation in our world? Material necessity, private advantage. What is the object of the Jew's worship in this world? Usury. What is his worldly god? Money. Very well then; emancipation from usury and money, that is, from practical, real Judaism, would constitute the emancipation of our time."[43]

From Trilling's point of view, Marx's solution to the Jewish Question was only marginally better than Hitler's. He demanded the disappearance of the Jew as Jew, as of the Christian as Christian. As Ludwig Lewisohn has put it, "the world's peoples wanted us to be emancipated not *as* ourselves but *from* ourselves."[44] But what if (for whatever reasons) Jews and Christians did not wish to disappear? One is reminded here of a statement Toni Morrison made concerning African American identity. Until the contemporary period, she suggests, race made all the difference in the world to white society. Now that African Americans have claimed that difference as their own, imbued it with power and beauty, race, according to the white world, makes no difference at all.[45] With regard to Trilling's dissatisfaction with Marxism, we might say, similarly, that Marxism made no provision for Jewish difference, for the self-declared otherness and identity of a people, who might wish to exist and live as a distinct people.

Marxism made no provision for an individual who might wish to exist and live in his or her private human being, either. This question of Marxism and the individual returns me to Trilling's critique of the Parrington line of liberal criticism. To imagine reality as exclusively "material" (which is to say, socioeconomic), and to imagine, further, the text as a transparency reproducing this reality was, from Trilling's perspective, exactly not to acknowledge the writer/critic's place within the construction of culture and, therefore, his or her moral responsibility within it. It was instead to exempt the writer/critic as standing somehow outside culture, as if she or he could, or should, do no other thing than render the world back to itself. In fact, from Trilling's point of view, the Marxist definition of literary criticism doubly distanced the writer/critic from culture. In the first place, the material theory of reality declares that morality is not the province of writers to define but exists in a transcendental place outside culture (in the case of Marxist criticism, it rests with Marxist economic and political theory). In the second place, it makes it the task of writers to reflect or reveal societal ills as functions not of the writers' self-perceptions and self-incriminations, but of timeless and universal metaphysical truths about culture.

I would suggest that the event of the Holocaust contributed powerfully to Trilling's unwillingness to give up either on the idea of individual being or on personal moral responsibility. This is so not because the individual moral self epitomized for Trilling a metaphysical or religious truth beyond or outside culture to which culture might appeal and make itself accountable. Quite the contrary. Since, in Trilling's view, there is nothing outside culture to which culture can apply, and since culture is only a human construction, human beings must individually assume ethical responsibility. I will not broach here the complexities of Trilling's definition of the self. I will, however, note that by an "opposing self" Trilling does not mean an essentialist, unitary identity (which stands in an oppositional, outsider relationship to society, which then constitutes the nonself or, in contemporary terms, the other). Rather, he means a self that is definable by its resistance to essentialisms and by its relationship to other selves, within the context of culture. From the point of view of the self, these other selves do possess definitive identity. It is Trilling's hope that in a moral society every self will accord, and also be accorded, this courtesy of imagining others, and not itself, as possessing essential identity. Thus for Trilling, in "Wordsworth and the Rabbis," Wordsworth is not Christian but non-Jew, while Trilling is not Jew but non-Christian. Trilling's ideas here bear strong affinities to Stanley Cavell's idea of the "aversive" relationship between individuals within society. This relationship, as expressed by Emerson, for example, so ties together individuals within society as to transform opposition or the turn-away-from (aversion) into a turning-toward or engaging of others within the shared world of culture.[46]

In ways similar to the thinking of the New Americanists, for Trilling culture is a nontranscendent place. Cultural criticism, therefore, constitutes for Trilling what Bercovitch (as I have already noted) calls a hermeneutics of nontranscendence. For both Trilling and Bercovitch such a hermeneutics of nontranscendence empowers rather than limits human authority, and it is here that the Trilling-Bercovitch line of cultural criticism separates from other branches of the same family. In a recent reflection on his own development as an Americanist, Bercovitch makes the point as follows:

America was more than a figment of the imagination, an imperial wish-fulfillment dream brought to life in the assertion of nationhood. It was a way of imagining that expressed the mechanisms through which "reality" is made real. . . . The music of America . . . sounded to me like ideology, but it was ideology in a new key, requiring a blend of cognitive and appreciative analysis. Benjamin contrasts empathic understanding with historical materialism, an adversarial outlook of "cautious detachment" which, aware of the "origin" of culture, "cannot contemplate [its subject] without horror." I sought a mode of mediation between horror and empathy.[47]

Inspired by Walter Benjamin but resisting his despair, Bercovitch searches for a place where individuals exist, neither outside culture nor hopelessly locked into it, but in a creative, meaning-making, and, equally important, responsibility-assuming place within it. The discovery of this place of meaning-making and moral responsibility is, I suggest, exactly Trilling's aim. It marks the specific Holocaust inflection of his writing and distinguishes his aesthetic, as it does Bercovitch's, from competing forms of cultural criticism. Thus what Cornel West most objects to in Trilling (whom he sees as the god-father of contemporary neo-conservatives and whose work seems to West to lead to "an intellectual dead-end") is Trilling's "preoccupation" (West repeats this twice) "with the circumstantial and the conditioned."[48] That is, what are for Trilling and a tradition of scholars culminating in Bercovitch the circumstances and conditions that permit, indeed necessitate, moral action and personal responsibility, seem to West and others the narrowing of perspective into elitist notions of cultural conservation. But what are the uncircumstantial and the unconditioned if not the imagined transcendental ideals that West, like Trilling, is rejecting?

Political Urgencies and the Problematical
Silent Speaking of the Literary Text

The New Americanism has placed at the center of its multiculturalist agenda the politicization of literary studies—in two senses. It aims to expose unacknowledged hegemonic power and cultural bias; in other words, to reveal the concealed politics of the traditional canon. It also implements its own literary politics, which aim at producing an integrated, multivocal canon. Neither of these is an insignificant goal. In fact, both are highly laudable. Nonetheless, the question raised by the writings of such critics as Trilling, Bercovitch, and Cavell, as of such writers as Hawthorne, Emerson, Thoreau, Ellison, and James, is whether such direct political intervention as the multiculturalists propose (whether in the form of exposé or canon reform) is the only or best method of achieving the goals of multiculturalism itself. In his opposition to Marxism and in his dedication to unraveling an idea of being such as characterizes the writings of poets like Wordsworth, Trilling, I suggest, enters into a tradition of writers who did not, in any way, ignore or disregard the major social issues of their time. (Was there ever a group of American authors more politically engaged than, say, the Transcendentalists?) Nor did they dismiss the relation between politics and literature. Rather this literary tradition chose to broach political matters and incorporate them within the literary text in oblique and aesthetically mediated ways.

Nonetheless, Trilling's lack of sustained and explicit speaking out on a subject as important as the Holocaust, like his withdrawal not so much from Communism as such (that is a move for which most contemporary critics would forgive him) as from the camp of socially engaged Marxist critics, raises disturbing possibilities, which the repetition of that silence (as in the conversation between Crews and Pease) makes ever more pressing. And this, of course, goes to the heart of multiculturalism's argument with the aestheticism of a previous generation of literary critics. In his recent essay, "Emerson's Constitutional Amending: Reading 'Fate' "—published in this volume—Stanley Cavell has analyzed the analogous problem in relation to Emerson. This is Emerson's apparent silence (in his major philosophical essays) on the subject of slavery (Emerson, of course, had much to say about slavery in his political statements). Cavell understands this silence, primarily in the essay "Fate," but in "Self-Reliance" as well, as part of Emerson's effort to separate polemics from philosophy and to constitute and preserve philosophy as that which constitutes and preserves human freedom. Yet, reading back through Heidegger's evolution of Emerson's thought as that thought was mediated by Nietzsche, Cavell wonders whether philosophy has not been tainted by its silences, in relation both to slavery and to Nazi anti-Semitism.[49] Cavell's comments, I suggest, usefully apply to other nineteenth-century authors, such as Hawthorne, Melville, and Thoreau, who also did and did not speak to the subject of slavery. These comments illuminate the case of Lionel Trilling as well. They explain Trilling's investment in literature as doing its political work in some way other than that of politics as such, but they suggest as well the degree to which explanations such as the one I will offer below cannot wholly salve the pain of certain moral statements unmade.[50]

I would suggest that precisely because nineteenth-century writers such as Emerson, Hawthorne, and Thoreau, and critics like Trilling, believed (in common with the critics of multiculturalism) that culture was the nontranscendental construct of human manufacture, they resisted literary forms that seemed to them to work more by moral or religious or political fiat (however well intended and even ethically sound) than by skepticist, cultural engagement or enactment. They preferred, that is, textual process over textual message, nonmimetic evocation over realistic representation. In their view, literary texts contributed to the processes of democracy, including multicultural expression, precisely by resisting the overt declarations and overdeterminations of political ideologies.[51] For one whole tradition of American authors (the romance writers from Hawthorne through the early James and on to such twentieth-century figures as William Faulkner and Toni Morrison) such resistance to political statement included even resisting the idea of realistic representation as determining rather than evolving meaning. Trilling's experience as a Jew, his sensitivity to anti-Semitism, and his consciousness of the enormity of the catastrophe in Europe led him, I suggest, to distrust political solutions such as Marxism and literary political solutions such as Marxist theory and discourse. He placed his energies instead in the never-to-be-completed process of rearticulating respect for "being," which seemed to him the high purpose of literature. One may call this a commitment to "high" culture if one wishes, and sneer at it, but it is by no means clear that "low" culture has any better solutions to catastrophes such as the Holocaust; and perhaps even the opposite is the case.

Thus, Trilling quite explicitly rejects what he sees as sensationalistic discourse, the kind of language that, in Trilling's view, characterizes, and compromises, the "intense social awareness" of twentieth-century American fiction. Modern fiction, Trilling acknowledges, rightfully concerns itself with "the situation of the dispossessed Oklahoma farmer and whose fault it is, what situation the Jew finds himself in, what it means to be a Negro." But, in his view, this body of texts is given to irresponsible, exploitative, and ultimately dangerous rhetorical excess. An "extreme" instance of this excess, which bears directly on my argument concerning the degree to which Trilling's critical predilections were, to some degree at least, responses to the Holocaust, is a novel by John Dash, which, Trilling tells us, has "attracted a great number of readers . . . because of its depiction of Nazi brutality" and the "stark realism" of its "torture scenes." Trilling's objection to this book has to do with the way in which "pleasure in . . . cruelty is protected and licensed by moral indignation." For Trilling the task of literature is not to confirm some simple definition of morality. Rather it is to examine what "lie[s] behind our sober intelligent interest in moral politics":

I have elsewhere given the name of moral realism to the perception of the dangers of the moral life itself. Perhaps at no other time has the enterprise of moral realism ever been so much needed, for at no other time have so many people committed themselves to moral righteousness. We have the books that point out the bad conditions, that praise us for taking progressive attitudes. We have no books that raise questions in our minds not only about conditions but about ourselves, that lead us to refine our motives and ask what might lie behind our good impulses.

There is nothing so very terrible in discovering that something does lie behind.[52]

In avoiding directly political language and in pointing the moral question toward the examination of what lies behind our morality, Trilling resembles no earlier critic of American culture more than Emerson. Emerson writes in "Self-Reliance":

Whoso would be a man, must be a nonconformist. He who would gather immortal palms must not be hindered by the name of goodness, but must explore if it be goodness. . . . If malice and vanity wear the coat of philanthropy, shall that pass? If any angry bigot assumes this bountiful case of Abolition, and comes to me with his last news from Barbadoes, why should I not say to him, "Go love thy infant; love thy wood-chopper, be good-natured and modest; have that grace; and never varnish your hard, uncharitable ambition with this incredible tenderness for black folk a thousand miles off. Thy love afar is spite at home."[53]

Like Emerson (and others in the American tradition), Trilling would get behind goodness to explore whether it be goodness, and why.

Such silent speaking as Trilling practices places us on the horns of a dilemma. No matter how powerful, the silence of his speaking does not, any more than in the case of the nineteenth-century American writers vis-à-vis slavery, remove the objection that Trilling, inadvertently perhaps, may have conspired in the erasure of Jewish consciousness and memory, which is to say, given the literal extermination of six million people, in the erasure of the Jew. Nonetheless, the alternative to such silence may not be the sheer act of speaking, which could represent so much babble, incapable of achieving its goals and aspirations. This dilemma returns us to the conversation between Crews and Pease and the agenda of multiculturalism. Contemporary Americanist criticism faults New Critical readings of nineteenth-century texts for failing to locate the sociopolitical issues that generated those texts. Yet by failing to locate the sociopolitical issues—the nonpolitical dimensions of phenomena such as racism and anti-Semitism, for example—that generated New Critical readings or the cultural critical readings of a critic like Lionel Trilling, New Americanists risk replicating not the silent speaking of one literary tradition, but—at least in relation to Jews and the Holocaust—silence itself. For Trilling only respect for being as such, irrespective of one literary or cultural or political program or another, could even begin to address catastrophes like the Holocaust, and, in Trilling's view, such respect for being was the very essence of the literary text.

Discovering America:
A Cross-Cultural Perspective

Sacvan Bercovitch

When I first came to the United States, I knew nothing about America. I attribute my immigrant naïveté to the peculiar insularity of my upbringing. I was nurtured in the rhetoric of denial. To begin with, I absorbed Canada's provincial attitudes toward "the States"—a provinciality deepened by the pressures of geographical proximity and economic dependence. Characteristically, this expressed itself through a mixture of hostility and amnesia, as though we were living next door to an invisible giant, whose invisibility could be interpreted as nonexistence. The interpretation was reflected in the virtual absence of "America" throughout my education, from elementary and high school, where U.S. history ended in 1776, to my fortuitous college training at the adult extension of the Montreal YMCA, where a few unavoidable U.S. authors were taught as part of a course on Commonwealth literature. I learned certain hard facts, of course, mainly pejorative, and I knew the landmarks from Wall Street to Hollywood; but the symbology that connected them—the American dream which elsewhere (I later discovered) was an open secret, a mystery accredited by the world—remained hidden from me, like the spirit in the letter of the uninitiate's text.

A more important influence was the Yiddishist–left wing world of my parents. I recall it as an outpost barricaded from the threat of assimilation by radical politics and belles lettres, an immigrant enclave locked into a Romantic-Marxist utopianism long after its disillusionment with Stalin, and fortified by the alleged spiritual values of art in the face of utter cultural estrangement. It was there, far more than at school, that I learned the strategies of denial. Their object in this case was Canada. I cannot recall a single reference to national matters in serious conversation. Literary discussions ranged from Sholom Aleichem to Franz Kafka, with polemical excursions to Yiddish contemporaries published in the local newspaper, *Der Keneder Odler* ("The Canadian Eagle," a mixed metaphor, carrying cross-cultural ironies for me even then). Politics consisted in a conflict of imaginary options for world revolution, extending from Trotsky's lost cause to the visionary boundaries of anarchism. It seems appropriate that I should have graduated from high school not to college, but, for several years, to a socialist kibbutz in what used to be called the Arabian desert.

The harvest of these experiences was an abiding suspicion of high rhetoric, especially as a blueprint of the future, and an abiding fascination with the redemptive promises of language, especially as a source of personal identity and social cohesion. Still, nothing in my background had prepared me for my encounter with a secular modern nation living in a dream. "I hear America singing," writes Whitman, and concludes: "The United States are themselves the greatest poem." So, too, Emerson: "America is a poem in our eyes." I arrived at a similar conclusion, but from a different perspective and to a different effect. My experience of the music of America (as I came to think of it) was closer to the epiphany of otherness recorded in Kafka's "Investigations of a Dog." The canine narrator of that story tells us that one day in his youth a group of seven dogs appeared before him, suddenly, "out of some place of darkness," to the accompaniment of "terrible" and ravishing sounds:

At that time I still knew hardly anything of the creative gift with which the canine race alone is endowed . . . for though music had [always] surrounded me . . . my elders had [never] drawn my attention to it. . . . [A]ll the more astonishing, then . . . were those seven musical artists to me. They did not speak, they did not sing, they remained generally silent, almost determinedly silent; but from the empty air they conjured music. Everything was music, the lifting and setting of their feet, certain turns of the head, their running and standing still, the positions they took up in relation to one another, the symmetrical patterns which they produced. . . . [M]y mind could attend to nothing but this blast of music which seemed to come from all sides, from the heights, from the deeps, from everywhere, surrounding the listener, overwhelming him. . . . I longed to . . . beg [the musicians] to enlighten me, to ask them what they were doing. . . . [Their music] was incomprehensible to me, and also quite definitely beyond my capacities. . . . I rushed about, told my story, made accusations and investigations. . . . I was resolved to pursue [the problem] indefatigably until I solved it.

The pursuit unfolds as a series of ingenious inferences, deductions, and explications extending to virtually every aspect of "dogdom," from the higher laws of "universal dog nature" to the specialized issue of "soaring dogs" (how do they "remain for the most part high up in the air, apparently doing nothing but simply resting there?") and the still-controversial "rules of science" for getting food: should you bring it forth by "incantation" or "water the ground as much as you can"?[1] Nothing, it seems, escapes observation, except the presence of human beings.

Kafka's story is a great parable of interpretation as mystification—facts marshaled endlessly to build up contexts whose effect, if not intent, is to conceal or explain away. It is also a great parable of the limitations of cultural critique—*limitations*, not just illusions, for in fact the story conveys a good deal about the dog's world, in spite of the narrator's inability to transcend it; or rather, as a function of his nontranscending condition. In this double sense, negative and ambiguous, Kafka's "investigations" apply directly to my own as an Americanist. The general parallels may be drawn out through a Chinese box of skewed interpretive positions: dog vis-à-vis human, Russian-Jewish immigrant vis-à-vis French Canadian Montreal, Canada vis-à-vis the States, and eventually "America," as I came to understand it, vis-à-vis the cultural norms and structures it represents.

These are not precise symmetries; but they point to certain common principles of exegesis. I begin with the negative implications. First, to interpret is not to make sense of a mystery out there. It is to discover otherness as mystery (something "overwhelming," "incomprehensible"), and then to explain the mystery as the wonders of an invisible world, a realm of meaningful "silence," resonant with universals. Second, to investigate those wonders is not to come to terms with the new or unexpected. It is to domesticate the unknown by transferring the agency of meaning from the mystery out there to realities we recognize, and so to invest the familiar— ourselves, or our kind—with the powers of a higher reality: "universal laws," the view of eternity, the canine principles of music. Third, to establish the laws and rules of that higher reality is not to break through the limitations we experience. It is to deny our conditions of dependency by translating those limitations into metastructures of culture, history, and the mind. As for motives, we may infer from Kafka's parable that they are self-defensive or self-aggrandizing, and that in either case interpretation is a strategy for repressing the actual worlds around us which expresses itself through yearnings for a world elsewhere.

We might call this the hermeneutics of transcendence. The possibilities it offers for self-aggrandizement (repressing otherness for purposes of control or incorporation) are not far to seek: one need only think of the manifold uses of "he" for God and/or humanity. But this is to interpret from the vantage point of dominance. From the dog's subordinate point of view, or the scholar's, to magnify the categories of our containment is to diminish our capacities for understanding.[2]

A negative prospect, as I said, especially since it is Kafka's donné that we have no choice but to interpret. However, it is complemented in the parable by the *enabling* ambiguities of limitation. As the title suggests, "Investigations of a Dog" points not only to the dog's attempts to describe Kafka's world, but, at the same time, to Kafka's attempts to describe dogdom. And the result, as I interpret it, is not a double impasse. It is a model of cross-cultural criticism. Its terms are reciprocity, as against dichotomy: not canine *or* human, but the contingencies of both, as revealed (in degree) through the re-cognition of limitation. We might call this the hermeneutics of nontranscendence. It may be said to reverse traditional comparativist methods by its emphasis on the historicity of archetypes and essences. Its aim is not to harmonize "apparent" differences (in the manner of pluralist consensus) but on the contrary to highlight conflicting appearances, so as to explore the substantive differences they imply. This entails the re-cognition of universals as culture-specific barriers to understanding; it is grounded in the faith that barriers, so specified, may become (within limits) avenues of discovery; and its logic may be briefly stated. If dreams of transcendence are indices to the traps of culture, then inquiry into the trapping process may provide insight both into our own and into others' actual nontranscending condition. Such insight is problematic, provisional, and *nourished* by a frustrating sense of boundaries. It denies us access to apocalypse, but it helps make our surrounding worlds visible.

I would like to think that my own investigations as an Americanist show the benefits of this approach. For purposes of analysis, I review these thematically rather than chronologically. My subject is the discovery of an other America, in the double sense of Kafka's parable: negatively, as cultural otherness, and ambiguously, as a set of cultural secrets, the other America hidden from view by interpretation. Emerson's American Scholar grows concentrically toward transcendence, in an expanding circle from nature to books to representative selfhood. My own unrepresentative (not to say eccentric) experience may be described as a series of increasingly particularized border crossings: first, into America proper; then, into the interdisciplinary field of American Studies; and finally, into the special area of American literary scholarship.

I crossed into the States with a Canadian's commonsense view of the Americas: two continents, North and South, each of them a mosaic of

nations—which is to say, a variety of European models of civilization—
joined by the semitropical bush countries of Central America. How could
I *not* see "America" as a cultural artifact? I knew that that sort of definition
applied to all national identities—except Canada, which by consensus was
"a country without a mythology."[3] But if Canada was an exception that
proved the rule, America was its antithesis, the example par excellence of
collective fantasy. Consider the claims of Puritan origins. By comparison,
myths of other national beginnings were plausible at least. The mists of
antiquity cover the claims of Siegfried and King Arthur and the exiled Trojan heroes who sired Virgil's Rome. Scripture itself authorizes Joshua's
claims to Canaan. But we *know* that the Puritans did not found the United
States. In fact, we know that by 1690, 60 years after the Great Migration
and a century before independence, not even the colony of Massachusetts
was Puritan. Nonetheless, the belief in America's Puritan ur-fathers was
evident everywhere three centuries later, at every ritual occasion, from
Thanksgiving Day to July Fourth, throughout the literature, from Harriet
Beecher Stowe to Thomas Pynchon, and in every form of literature, including endless debates about whether or not the Puritan legacy was a
good thing.

My study of Puritanism started out as an investigation of what appeared to me a cultural secret. I expected to discover the creation of a national past, the invention of a Puritan tradition commensurate with the
needs of a modern republic. Instead, as I traced the act of creation back
through the nineteenth into the eighteenth and seventeenth centuries, I
found that its roots lay with the Puritans after all.[4] The tradition *had* been
made up, as suspected, but it was built out of historical materials, selected
for historical reasons. The fantasy of Puritan origins had worked because
these Puritans represented (among other things) the movement toward modernity, because they associated that movement with their prospects in the
New World, and because they developed a rhetoric that joined both these
aspects of their venture, cultural and territorial, in a vision that was simultaneously distinctive, expansive, spiritual, and secular. Their major
legacy was neither religious nor institutional. The Puritans are not particularly responsible for the Calvinist strain in the United States, or for civil
religion, or for any particular democratic forms, not even the town meeting. They did not invent guilt, or the Protestant work ethic, or individualism, or contract society. All of these were in varying degrees part of the
New England Way, and together they might be said to express its movement into modernity. But the distinctive contribution, it seemed to me, lay

in the realm of symbology. The Puritans provided their heirs, in New England first and then the United States, with a useful, flexible, durable, and compelling fantasy of American identity.

I mean "compelling" in a descriptive, not a celebratory, sense. My discovery pertained to the historicity of myth, and the secret it yielded applied as well to my Canadian geography of the New World: what I had considered to be my neutral, commonsense view of the territory out there as an extension of various European civilizations. To see America as myth was to historicize the Canadian identity—to see in it the contours of another, complementary myth. I refer to the dominant vision of Canada: a "loose scattering of enclaves or outposts of culture and civilization," protected from a "hostile bush-country" by the Royal Canadian Mounted Police.[5] The Mountie is a symbolic figure in this design, of course. But the design itself represents a distinctive national fantasy, which I now saw as a variation of the same myth of conquest that had shaped the growth of the United States.

"Canada" was the *colonial* version of the myth, a story told by invaders who claimed authority for conquest from abroad—from European royalty and civilizations centered in England and France.[6] "America" was the indigenous *imperialist* inversion. It relocated the seat of empire from the Old World to the New; it reversed the very meaning of "newness" from its colonial status of dependency to a declaration not just of independence but of superiority; and in this new sense it sanctified the "empty continent" as itself constituting the natural-divine patent for conquest. Gradually, the imperial counterpart to the bush-country police became the frontiersman, living in harmony with nature and yet the harbinger of civilization, a paradox explicable by the fact that the frontier itself had been transformed from its colonial sense of "barrier" into an imperial summons to expand.

The issue, then, was not a clash of opposites, Canadian facts versus American fantasies. It was a juxtaposition of myths, colonial vis-à-vis imperial, each of them a borderland of fantasy and fact. The colonial version had issued in "Canada," a country with a mythology elsewhere, systematically decentered and characterized, accordingly, by a rhetoric of absence: non-Indian, non-European, non-American, nonmythological. The other, imperial issue was America. As I followed its changing terms of identity (Puritan errand, national mission, manifest destiny, the dream), the windings of language turned out to be the matter of history. America, an act of symbolic appropriation, came alive to me as the twin dynamics of empire: on the one hand, a process of violence unparalleled (proportionately) by even the Spanish conquistadores, and sustained into the twentieth century by a rhetoric of holy war against everything un-American; on the other hand, an unleashing of creative energies—enterprise, speculation, community building, personal initiative, industry, confidence, idealism, and hope—unsurpassed by any other modern nation.

It amounted to a demonstration from within of Walter Benjamin's thesis about barbarism and civilization. Polemicizing against the tradition of empathy in historical studies—which literary critics have inherited as the tradition of aesthetic appreciation[7]—Benjamin presents "the triumphal procession" of "cultural treasures" through a contrast between "the great minds and talents who created them" and "the anonymous toil of their contemporaries. There is no document of civilization," he concludes, "which is not at the same time a document of barbarism." To some extent, my view of America is a cross-cultural variation of that outlook, with certain differences in emphasis and approach. Benjamin was seeking to historicize art's claims to transcendence, but he tended not so much to challenge those claims as to insist on a complicity of opposites: "great minds" and "anonymous toil," cultural treasures and the inhumanity of power. My approach was geared to the dynamics of complicity, which in this case called the opposition itself into question. What I discovered in America was the simultaneity of violence and culture formation. America, as its meanings gradually unfolded to me, was interchangeably a cultural treasure of barbarism, a barbaric dream documented by a procession of "great minds and talents," and an interpretative process through which the worlds out there had been triumphantly repressed—first, by myths of their inhabitants ("savage," "primitive") attended by facts of genocide; and then by symbols of the land ("virgin," "wilderness") attended by the creation of the United States as America.

So what began as English graduate studies in the United States became instead a trail into the myth and symbol thickets of American Studies. I encountered in its foundational documents a scholarly achievement commensurate with the cultural creation of America: Perry Miller's intellectual construction of national origins out of the esoteric writings of forty Protestant sectarians; F. O. Matthiessen's aesthetic construction of a national literary tradition out of the masterpieces of five self-declared "isolatoes"; Frederick Jackson Turner's historical construction of the national character out of a frontier West that largely excluded its native inhabitants, not to speak of the nation's non-westering immigrants. In all of these monumental works, as well as in their successors, an extraordinary capacity to analyze intricacies of thought, emotion, and imagination seemed bound up with an extraordinary unwillingness to extend analysis beyond the intricacies themselves. The America they revealed appeared out of nowhere—"out of some place of darkness," or rather a *spirit* of place,[8] variously labeled nature, the New England mind, the Spirit of '76, pioneer democracy—like the seven musical performers in Kafka's story.

I registered the anomaly as a cultural secret of academia. American Studies, as it had developed from the 1940's through the Cold War decades, seemed a method designed *not* to explore its subject, somewhat as the dog's investigations, though conjured up by the music, are deliberately, exclusively, and astonishedly focused elsewhere—on the wonders of canine artistry ("the lifting and setting of their feet, certain turns of the head . . . the positions they took up in relation to one another, the symmetrical patterns which they produced"). The analytic tools of American Studies consisted of the same materials, the same patterns of thought and language, that Americanists had set out to investigate. This was empathic history with a vengeance. As in Kafka's story, analysis was the celebration of a mystery.

Nonetheless, their work had a compelling range and force, which I attributed to a daring act of transgression: the application of aesthetic criticism to what by tradition belonged to the province of cognitive criticism. I refer to the familiar distinction between art and artifact, *Kultur* and culture, that reaches back through German romanticism to the theological separation of sacred from secular. Theology, we know, had actually mandated separate methods of exegesis for that purpose: one method for unveiling the meanings of the Bible, proceeding from text to transcendent text, and from one divinely inspired (if perhaps anxiety-ridden) authority to the next; and another, profane method, an empirical approach suitable to ordinary books concerning the empirical truths of this world. The modern literary equivalent for that dichotomy, based on the sacralization of art, is the opposition between text and context. The latter is the arena of cognitive criticism, since "context" designates the world pro-fana, the "background" areas surrounding the temples of genius, a secondary reality illuminated by "secondary sources." Aesthetic criticism is designed to reveal the richness, the complexity, and the (unfathomable) depths of the "primary text" in its own "organic" terms. This so-called intrinsic method may draw on matters of context—psychology, sociology, philosophy, science—but only insofar as they serve the ends of appreciation. It may even reach outside the strictly aesthetic to the realm of spirit (moral truths, universal values) provided that what it finds there is reincorporated, truth and beauty entwined, into the metacontextual pleasures of the text.

American Studies seemed to have developed through a reverse strategy
of incorporation. It drew methodically on contextual matters—it actively
elicited cognitive analyses (of the American "mind," "heart," and "character")—but it required these to conform to the principles of aesthetic
appreciation. If America was not literally a poem in these scholars' eyes,
it was a literary canon that embodied the national promise. The Puritans
had discovered America in the Bible; Jacksonians discovered the Bible in
the Declaration of Independence and the Constitution; American Studies
added to this Biblia Americana the national literary classics. It may even
be said to have concentrated upon them as the key to it all, somewhat as
Christian typologists had discovered the secrets of Holy Scripture, Old and
New, in stories of Christ. What followed was a series of investigations of
the country's "exceptional" nature that was as rich, as complex, and as
interdisciplinary as America itself—a pluralist enterprise armed with the
instruments both of aesthetic and of cognitive analysis, all bent on the appreciation of a unique cultural artifact. Aesthetic instruments had a privileged place here because it was as art, by modern consensus, that the spirit
most fully revealed itself. But the instruments of cognitive analysis were no
less important. It was their task to reconstitute history itself as American;
and, as we might expect, they did so most appreciatively when they repressed the adverse facts of American history, or else, more emphatically
still, represented these as a violation of the nation's promise and original
intent.

The music which thus came, in Kafka's words, "from all sides, from the
heights, from the deeps, from everywhere," sounded to me like ideology. I
sometimes thought of it as Muzak, and I recognized in its strains a long
series of scholarly ventures in culture formation, the nationalist project of
modern literary history that had been baptized over a century before in the
trinitarian faith of *Volksgeist*, world spirit, and the sanctity of art. One
extreme application, or distortion, of this genre was the aesthetics of fascism. Another extreme was the humanist enterprise (mingling chauvinism,
utopianism, and social critique) of Georg Gottfried Gervinus, Francesco
de Sanctis, and Desiré Nisard. American Studies stood at the latter extreme, of course, and no doubt it was the humanist difference that allowed
me to appreciate the insight it embodied into the dynamics of culture.
Without quite articulating it as a principle of analysis, American Studies
taught by example, in practice, that rhetoric is not a surface coating, "mere
metaphor," upon the deep structures of the real. It is substantially, fundamentally, what the real is, even (or especially) when the rhetoric serves
to repress and deny. The dog's interpretations mask the rules of music, but

they reveal the world he inhabits. Among other things, culture is how people interpret and what they believe.

A simple lesson, but it required time, observation, and participation to absorb. My outsider's view of American Studies was that its America was a barbaric context made text, empathically, by Americanists. My American experience persuaded me that the poem was in some important sense an accurate representation of the ways things worked. America was more than a figment of the imagination, an imperial wish-fulfillment dream brought to life in the assertion of nationhood. It was a way of imagining that expressed the mechanism through which "reality" is made real. Like other modern nations, America was an imagined community. It was also a process of symbol making through which the norms and values of a modern culture were internalized, rationalized, spiritualized, and institutionalized—rendered the vehicle, as the American *Way*, both of conscience and of consensus.

The music of America still sounded to me like ideology, but it was ideology in a new key, requiring a blend of cognitive and appreciative analysis. Benjamin contrasts empathic understanding with historical materialism, an adversarial outlook of "cautious detachment" which, aware of the "origin" of culture, "cannot contemplate [its subject] without horror."[9] I sought a mode of mediation between horror and empathy. Accordingly, I turned to the more flexible, nonpejorative definitions of ideology available in anthropology: ideology as the web of ideas, practices, beliefs, and myths through which a society, any society, coheres and perpetuates itself. I hoped that ideological analysis, so conceived, would allow me both to exploit the insights of American Studies and to revise its outlook. American Studies had set out the interactions between symbol and fact, rhetoric and history, by synthesizing their different forms of discourse. I wanted to separate those forms (and their functions) in order to investigate the conditions of synthesis making. To that end, I hoped that ideological analysis would allow me to negotiate between the world and the word in such a way that the word, "America," might be contextualized, recovered for purposes of cognitive criticism, while the world of America might be apprehended in its fantastic textuality, as the development of an empowering and (within limits) genuinely liberating rhetoric and vision.

Necessarily, this set me at odds with the dominant concepts of ideology in the field. I thought of these as three models of the hermeneutics of denial: (1) *The consensus model,* adopted by the leading schools of literary and historical scholarship during the Cold War decades. This denied that America had any ideology at all, since ideology meant dogma, bigotry, and repression; whereas Americans were open-minded, inclusive, and eclectic. (2) *The official Marxist model*, imported into academia during the Depression, and revived in the 1960's. This denied that ideology had any truth-value, since it was by definition false consciousness, the *camera obscura* of the ruling class. (3) *The multicultural model*, a medley of various indigenous themes, from the melting pot to the patchwork quilt, melded together or interlaced with various forms of neo-Marxism. This denied that America had an ideology, on the grounds that there were *many* ideologies, all in flux: republicanism, agrarianism, free enterprise, consumerism, liberalism, working-class consciousness, corporate industrialism, and so on, to the point where it came to seem the other side of consensual open-endedness.

Against that background my concept of ideology was intended to insist on: (1) the ideological context of commonsense eclecticism; (2) the truth-value of ideology, as a key not to the cosmos but to culture, which mediates our access to cosmic truth; and (3) the de facto coherence of American culture, as for example in the ideological symmetries underlying the models of multiculturalism and consensus. The symmetries seemed to me transparent in the relation I spoke of between the world and the word: the changing, conflictual, and yet continuously sustaining relation between the United States—in all its multifarious "realities" (pragmatic, agrarian, consumerist, etc.)—and the abstract, unifying meanings of America. Heterogeneity was not the antithesis to those abstractions; it was a function of hegemony. The open-ended inclusiveness of the United States was directly proportionate to America's capacity to incorporate *and exclude*, and more precisely to incorporate by exclusion. The culture seemed indefinite, infinitely processual, because as America it closed everything else out, as being either Old World and/or not-yet-America. And vice versa: the process by which it closed out everything un-American was also the spur toward an ideal of *liberal* inclusiveness, a vision of *representative* openness that eroded traditional barriers of nationality, territory, language, and ethnicity, and eventually, perhaps, would erode even the barriers of race and gender—which is to say, would open the prospects of liberalism to women and blacks as it had to the Irish, the Jews, and the far-flung regions of Alaska and Hawaii.

I am describing a broad, deeply ingrained symbolic strategy; one need only think of the reciprocities between inclusive and exclusive representation in the concept of a national errand or of a continental manifest destiny. But my concern here lay with a specific academic enterprise. It seemed to me that the process by which the United States had become America was nowhere more clearly displayed than in the bipolarities of American Studies: on the one hand, a multiculturalism (or experiential pluralism) that rendered invisible the structures of national cohesion; on the other hand, a consensual identity, "American," that by definition transcended the "ideological limits" of class, region, generation, and race (i.e., redefined American identity, ideologically, as a process of transcending the boundaries of class, region, etc.). As this principle applied to American literary studies in particular, the relation between text and context opened into what I came to think of as a cultural symbology: a configuration or tangle of patterns of expression, interpretation, and belief common to all areas of society, including the aesthetic. So understood, "high literature" was neither an imitation of reality nor a Platonic (or Hegelian) ladder to a higher reality. It was a mediation between both, which I thought of in terms of ideological mimesis: a representation of the volatile relations between conceptual, imaginative, and social realities that was different from, often opposed to, and yet fundamentally reciprocal with the ways of the world in which it emerged. I intended my concept of ideological mimesis to convey not only literature's multivalence but its capacities (in degree, within limits) for autonomy. Nonetheless, I again found myself at odds with the dominant models of analysis in the field, in this case the field of literary studies. I think here in particular of the New Criticism, which through the 1960's and 1970's still reined in the area of textual analysis, and of oppositional criticism, which then as now comprised the most influential literary group in American Studies.

My objections to the New Critics antedated my discovery of America. They thrived on the invisibility of context, somewhat as Kafka's narrator's ingenuities depend on his disembodiment of the music; or as the mystery he marvels at of "soaring dogs," floating on air, depends on the invisibility of whatever or whoever is holding them up. My own reading had convinced me, on the contrary, that literary texts were deeply embedded in issues of context; that this embeddedment was a central source of creative, moral, and intellectual vitality; and that to deny that source of empowerment on principle, or by professional reflex, was a form of aesthetic minimalism which drained literature of its richest meanings. It was also to instate certain cultural values under the cloak of invisibility, as embodying the transcendent unities of the text. And finally, under the guise of reverence, it was to evade the most challenging questions posed by the transhistorical qualities of literature, which center on the relation (not the dichotomy) between "trans" and "historical." Criticism may aspire to judgments of eternity, but it takes place in history. As both Kafka and Benjamin remind us, the very forms of canonization are mediated by historical consciousness; we break through its limitations only in degree, and only by recognizing that we live in history, even if we live on literature.

But of course New Critics were ipso facto not Americanists. My direct engagement was with the oppositional critics. That term is a recent coinage, designating certain post-Marxist forms of cultural praxis. But in American Studies it has a far broader import. I have in mind the adversarial stance of Americanist literary critics from the very inception of the field: the school of subversion (as it has been called) that constitutes the mainstream tradition of American Studies from Vernon Parrington and Lewis Mumford through Matthiessen and Henry Nash Smith, and that has continued to provide many of its most distinguished figures. The principles of oppositionalism, so understood, center on an essentialist conflict between an always oppressive society and an always liberating literature—a sacred-secular library of America set against the ideologies in America of racism, imperialism, capitalism, and patriarchy. My objection to this particular text-context dichotomy was more complicated in application than that to the New Critics, but it was based on a similar premise. My reading of the classic American authors convinced me that they were imaginatively nourished by the culture, even when they were politically opposed to it. Melville's famous affirmation of the subversive imperative comes in an essay extolling America's destiny; and a similar dynamic informs the cultural work of Hawthorne and Emerson, as it also underlies the multiple connections between nay-saying and representative selfhood in the adventures of George Harris, Ruth Hall, Huckleberry Finn, Frederic Henry, the Invisible Man, Oedipa Maas, and Rutherford Calhoun.[10]

In all cases, the complementarity of text and context revealed a cultural symbology which not only tolerated but elicited resistance as a staple of social revitalization. This did not mean that the literature was not subversive in some sense. My disagreement with the oppositionalists lay not in particular interpretations of texts, but in their overall tendency toward allegory. I saw this as a sort of beatification of the subversive; as a denial against all historical evidence, from every field of art, of the continuously enriching reciprocity between dominant forms of art and forms of ideological domination; as a transfer of the powers of appreciative criticism to political agency; and as a confusion, accordingly, of literary analysis with social action. It was as though (in a mirror inversion of Kafka's parable) to deconstruct the musicians' patterns of performance—or to uncover adversarial tendencies within the symmetries they enacted, or to discover different groups of performers (the music, so to speak, of Benjamin's repressed world of "anonymous toil")—were to threaten the entire world of music, and potentially to undermine the moral and social structures within which the musicians functioned.

This romance quest for the subversive seemed to me to have its roots in a venerable (though "dark" and often mystical) branch of hermeneutics, the esoteric tradition that bridges gnosticism, Cabala, and the romantic vision of Satan as the secret hero of *Paradise Lost*. And in turn that vision-ary fusion of politics and art recalled the radical aesthetics of my youth. Here again literature was invested with the spiritual values of protest, and literary criticism, by extension, raised to the status of revolutionary activ-ity. But the national emphasis in this case—the focus, positive and nega-tive, on the Americanness of American literature—called attention to a cultural difference in the very concept of radicalism. I refer to a broad tra-dition of political dissent inspired by the figural America. Its connection to literary oppositionalism, as this unfolded from the Vietnam years through the Reagan era, was both theoretical and institutional. Briefly, the student rebels of one period became the academic authorities of the other. The continuities this transformation implies—beyond, or rather *within*, the profession of "generation gap," "rupture," and "politicization"—require me to return once more to my literal-metaphorical moment of border crossing, this time into the surprising radical America of the 1960's.

It was not the radicalism that surprised me. Quite the contrary: I had expected to find the land of Sacco and Vanzetti an unincorporated America of class contradictions, residual resistance, and emergent struggle. And so it was. But the protest rendered invisible the cultural limitations that these conflicts implied. The sources of conflict persisted—indeed, according to the protesters they had deepened—but they were described in terms that reinforced this society's values and myths. The counterculture swam into my view in a series of abstractions, two by two, like the procession of le-viathans at the start of *Moby-Dick*, as the gates of Ishmael's wonder-world swing open: Freedom versus Tyranny, Opportunity versus Oppression, Progress versus Chaos; and midmost of them all, like a Janus-faced phan-tom in the air, America, real and ideal. The real faced toward doomsday. The ideal, facing the millennium, appeared sometimes in the form of na-tional representatives (Jefferson, Lincoln), sometimes as representative texts (the Mayflower Compact, the federal Constitution), sometimes in cultural key words ("equal rights," "self-realization"), or else in the ap-positional symbology of pluralism ('heterogeneity," "nation of nations").

My commonsense response was "co-optation." What else would this Americanization of utopia be but some long-ripened generational rite of passage, a ritual recycling of the energies of radical change into the structures of continuity? In this culture, I concluded, the conservatives were on the left; their characteristic strategy was to displace radical alternatives with an indigenous tradition of reform. Thus the alternative implicit in Nat Turner's revolt had been absorbed into the exemplary American protest embodied in *The Narrative of Frederick Douglass*; so, too in the long run, were the alternatives offered by Paul Robeson and Malcolm X. The quintessentially liberal programs for change that linked Elizabeth Cady Stanton to Gloria Steinem encompassed, blurred, and eventually eliminated other feminist alternatives (those which did not focus on America), from the Grimké sisters to Emma Goldman and Angela Davis. It was the cultural work of Emerson and Emersonians, from (say) William James through Paul Goodman, to obviate socialist or communist alternatives to capitalism. This form of cultural work joined Jefferson to Thoreau and both to Martin Luther King in an omnivorous oppositionalism that ingested all competing modes of radicalism—from the Fourierists to Herbert Marcuse and Noam Chomsky—in the course of redefining injustice as unAmerican, revolution as the legacy of 1776, and inequities of class, race, and gender as disparities between the theory and the practice of Americanness.

These dissenters, it seemed clear, had miscalculated not just the power but the nature of rhetoric. They had thought to appropriate America as a trope of the spirit, and so to turn the national symbol, now freed of its base historical content, into a vehicle of moral and political renovation. In the event, however, the symbol had refigured the moral and political terms of renovation—had rendered freedom, opportunity, democracy, and radicalism itself part of the American Way.[11] But the results of their miscalculations, as I traced these back through the 1900's, had unexpected consequences. What I learned from that century-long lesson in co-optation altered my views both of American protest and of the radical outlook I had brought to it. The culture, I discovered, had indeed found ways of harnessing revolution for its own purposes; but the ways themselves were volatile, even (to a point) open-ended. They tended toward subversion even as they drew such tendencies into persistent, deeply conservative patterns of culture.

In short, the issue was not co-optation or dissent. It was varieties of co-optation, varieties of dissent, and above all varieties of co-optation/dissent. America was a symbolic *field*, continually influenced by extrinsic sources, and sometimes changing through those influences, but characteristically absorbing and adapting them to its own distinctive patterns. And in the course of adaptation, it was recurrently generating its own adversarial forms. The "alternative Americas" it spawned were (like the originating symbol) ideology and utopia combined. They opposed the system in ways that reaffirmed its ideals; but the process of reaffirmation constituted a radical tradition *of a certain kind*. Hence the ambiguities that linked Douglass to King, Thoreau to Goodman, Stanton to Steinem. In all these cases, dissent was demonstrably an appeal to, and through, the rhetoric and values of the dominant culture; and in every case, it issued in a fundamental challenge to the system: racism subverted in the story of a self-made man; patriarchy subverted through a revised version of the Declaration of Independence; the authority of government subverted by a July Fourth experiment in self-reliance.

The theory of co-optation, like Benjamin's attack on empathic history, assumes a basic dichotomy between radicalism and reform, as though one *could* be for or against an entire culture; as though not to be against a culture fundamentally (whatever that means) was to be fundamentally part of it; and as though one could hope to effect social change by advocating ideas or programs that were alien to whatever held together the society at large—which is to say, to its strategies of cohesion. The radical/reformist reciprocities I discovered pointed me in a different direction. They called for a reconsideration of the entire structure of dichotomies by which I had found American protest wanting. The European forms of radicalism I had inherited were indeed opposed to that tradition, but they, too, I recognized, were couched in a rhetoric that expressed the cultures within which they had been generated. And they had given rise to forms of social action that were ambiguously liberating and/or restrictive, progressive and/or repressive, revolutionary and/or reformist.

The difference between the two traditions was not that of empirical analysis versus symbolic projection, activism versus acquiescence. It was an opposition between distinctive processes of culture formation, entailing, in each case, mixed forms of empirical (or detached) analysis and symbolic projection (or empathic understanding). And, as it happened, the opposition issued in major differences both in modes of social cohesion and in prescriptions for social renovation. Insofar as this opposition, too, was a false one—insofar as (say) *Walden* resists *The Communist Manifesto* absolutely, denies altogether the theory of historical materialism, class identity, or the socialist state—it is because each rests on a hermeneutics of transcendence. Thoreau's appeal to self-reliance, like Karl Marx's to class struggle, implies a chiliastic solution ("the only true America," "the dictatorship of the proletariat"), built on apodictic either/ors: individualism or conformity, revolution or oppression. The result is not a contrast between true and false resistance to the barbarism of one's culture. It is a wholesale transfer of agency, as in Kafka's parable, from one's culture to the imputed higher laws of nature, history, and the mind.

What did seem to me distinctive in degree about the American instance was the cultural function of radicalism. It was a strategy of pluralism everywhere to compartmentalize dissent so as to absorb it, incrementally, *unus inter pares*, into a dominant liberal discourse. But American liberalism *privileged* dissent. One reason for the impact of the Puritans was their success in making a dissenting faith the cornerstone of community; and the continuities this suggests may be traced through the rhetoric of the American Revolution and the Emersonian re-vision of individualism as the mandate both for permanent resistance and for American identity—a transcendental license to have your dissent and to make it too.

This was the context as well of oppositional criticism as I encountered it in the late 1960's; and it remains the context of American literary studies in our time of dissensus. For although dissensus involves the disintegration of certain traditional structures of academic authority, nonetheless the *conditions* of dissensus do not transcend ideology. On the contrary: they are a purer expression of the liberal marketplace than the genteel modes they superseded, which offered at least some residual resistance to the pluralist incorporation of academia. In an earlier, more innocent time, upstart ethnics could make their way into the humanities on the condition that they re-formed themselves (in dress, manner, accent, and moral outlook) as custodians of Arnoldian Culture, the preservers of literature as a transcendent "criticism of life," meaning in their case the life of liberal capitalism. Their latter-day upstart heirs demand in effect that the humanities come down from that ivory tower, comply with the conditions of American free enterprise (equal opportunity, open competition, supply-and-demand specialization), and participate in the power structures of the state, including its structures of class, mass communication, and government.

This is not to disparage the work of oppositional critics, then and now.[12] They have raised important issues, exposed the constrictions of established theories and the injustice of established practices, and properly called attention to the pressures of history not only upon the literature we interpret but upon our categories of interpretation. In these and similar ways they have been right to call their criticism subversive. But subversive in what sense, and to what ends, and for whom?

My misgiving first expressed itself in my sense of wonder at the scope and intensity of their political claims. Particular questions of interpretation apart, why were these Americanists so intent on demonstrating the subversiveness of authors who for the most part had either openly endorsed the American Way, or else had lamented American corruption as the failure of New Eden? Or mutatis mutandis, why were they so intent on asserting the regenerative powers of literary studies (their own) that were not only inaccessible but unintelligible to society at large? I recall thinking in this regard of two Thurber cartoons, which might be considered examples by contrast of the advantages of cross-cultural perspective. One of these shows a copyist sitting before Rubens's *Rape of the Sabine Women* and carefully reproducing the flowers in a corner of the scene. The other cartoon shows a woman smiling like the Mona Lisa, while the perplexed man next to her asks: "What do you want to be enigmatic *for*, Monica?" What did these oppositionalists want Edith Wharton and William Faulkner— or more strangely still, their recondite readings of Wharton or Faulkner —to be radical *for*?

For an America, I believe, that rendered invisible the interpreter's complicity in the culture. I do not mean complicity as a synonym for moral (or even clerical) treason. One may be complicitous simultaneously in various aspects of culture: those which help people rationalize their greed, those which help naturalize existing or emergent networks of power, and those which open the way to fundamental moral and social improvements. In this case, however, complicity involved a strikingly uncritical stance (considering the professional self-reflexivity of these critics) toward precisely these sorts of ambiguities. In allegorizing the powers of opposition—and in effect transcendentalizing the subversive—these critics seemed almost willfully oblivious to their own cultural function. It was as though their method had somehow recast oppositionalism itself in the image of America; as though, to recall Benjamin's thesis, they had found at the origins of the errand not the barbarism of civilized progress but the redemptive wholeness of utopia; or, in the terms of Kafka's parable, as though they had appropriated to their academic performances the radical potential of the symbology they opposed. One general symptom is the alliance between radicalism and upward mobility in the profession at large—the rites of academia encoded in writings of dissent.[13] A more telling symptom for my purposes is the cultural function of American Studies. Surely it is no ac-

cident that, of all academic specialties, this field has been the most hos-
pitable from the start to new waves of immigration from the other America
into the profession. Nor is it by accident that, in spite of its very name,
American Studies (as in *United* States) has gravitated toward a *denial*
of cohesion; that this *rhetoric* of denial has presented itself in protests
against exclusion (i.e., *for integration*); that the protest has taken the form
of hyphenated ethnicity—Italian-American, Irish-American, and Jewish-
American hand in hand with African-American, Asian-American, and Native American—and that the result has been an adversarial form of interpretation which roots subversion in institutions of culture. It makes for a
paradox that could obtain, in the old immigrant myth, only in America: a
school of subversion geared toward the harmony of political activism and
the good life, and directed (under the aegis of American literary studies)
toward a fusion of personal, professional, and national identity.

I have found in this institutionalization of dissent still another boundary demarcating the problematics of cross-cultural criticism.[14]

Toward the end of Kafka's "Investigations of a Dog," the narrator is
granted a visionary consolation. As he lies alone, near death, utterly exhausted by a long series of frustrations, suddenly, he tells us,

a beautiful creature . . . stood before me. . . . My senses . . . seemed to see or to
hear something about him [of which he himself was unaware]. . . . I thought I saw
that the hound was already singing without knowing it, nay, more, that the melody,
separated from him, was floating in the air in accordance with its own laws, and,
as though he had no part in it, was moving toward me, toward me alone.

I suppose that an analogy might be drawn to those ineffable moments of
wonder that light up the republic of American letters: Whitman's vision of
America singing what turns out to be an epic "Song of Myself"; the African
slave Phillis Wheatley's first sight of what she later learned to call "the land
of freedom's heaven-defended race"; the westward caravan at the start of
The Prairie, face to face with Natty Bumppo, towering against the sunset;
Mary Antin's Pisgah-view (from Ellis Island) of the new promised land; the
uncut forests of Long Island at the end of *The Great Gatsby*, pandering in
whispers to the last and greatest of human dreams; Perry Miller's voca-
tional epiphany at the mouth of the Congo River, a calling (he reports)
from the primal darkness to tell the story of a brave New World; John
Boyle O'Reilly's immigrant vision, at Plymouth Rock, "Of light predes-
tined" streaming from "The Mayflower's . . . chosen womb"; and before
even those mythic Puritans, the discoverer Columbus, as Emerson identi-

fies him, and with him, at the beginning of *his* career, in the opening pages
of *Nature*:

This beauty of Nature which is seen and felt as beauty, is the least part. . . .
    The presence of a higher, namely, of the spiritual element is essential to its per-
fection. The high and divine beauty which can be loved without effeminacy, is that
which is found in combination with the human will. Beauty is the mark God sets
upon virtue. . . . When a noble act is done . . . are not these heroes entitled to add
the beauty of the scene to the beauty of the deed? When the bark of Columbus nears
the shore of America;—before it, the beach lined with savages, fleeing out of their
huts of cane; the sea behind; and the purple mountains of the Indian Archipelago
around, can we separate the man from the living picture? Does not the New World
clothe his form with her palm-groves and savannahs as fit drapery?[15]

I offer this emblem of discovery as an *ultimum* of the rhetoric of transcendence—an interpretation of origins and ends that appropriates the
mysteries of gender, nature, and the Oversoul to the culturally transparent
"I." And it is worth remarking that Emerson's American Scholar fits well
into its "living picture." He, too, stands at the rhetorical "shore of America": a "New World" which he claims by naming, as being his by visionary
right, simultaneously his and not-his, a hero's trophy of beauty, virtue, sav-
agery, and representative selfhood. And the same is true of Emerson himself, standing in as the essential discoverer for Man Thinking and Columbus alike: "I do not make it; I arrive there, and behold what was there already. . . . And what a future it opens! . . . I am ready to die out of nature,
and be born again into this new yet unapproachable America I have found
in the West." That triumph of culture is perhaps the richest instance in
modern history of the dialectic Benjamin speaks of between barbarism and
civilization; the fullest modern case against empathic history, as being the
instrument of the victors: "All rulers are the heirs of those who conquered
before them. Hence, empathy with the victor invariably benefits the rulers. . . . Whoever has emerged victorious participates to this day in the
triumphal procession in which the present rulers step over those who are
lying prostrate. . . . According to traditional practice, the spoils are carried
along in the procession. They are called cultural treasures."[16]
    "The American Scholar" both mystifies the discourse of conquest and
transfers its cultural spoils to the observer-interpreter (and those he represents). Even as he renders unto Caesar the things that are Caesar's, territory and inhabitants alike, Emerson renders them transcendentally unto
God. "I arrive there, and behold what was there already": Emerson raises
the victors' *veni-vidi-vici* into the music of the spheres by investing their
"noble act" with the "presence of a higher, *namely*, of the spiritual element

essential to its perfection." And he does so, like Columbus, "without effeminacy," draped in nature's purple, as the "savages" hasten in wonder toward his figural "bark," "fleeing out of their huts of cane," as once the Magi hastened from the East to witness the Nativity. Except that the drapery, for Columbus, was the "purple mountains of the Indian Archipelago"; in Emerson's case, the prospect extends indefinitely into and across the American interior, at once toward his own "inward mountains, with the tranquil eternal meadows spread at their base," and toward the Rockies of the "continental" West. And of course the "savages" are no longer visible in "The American Scholar." In their place, Emerson paints for us an awakening "our": "the sluggard intellect of this continent . . . look[ing] from under its iron lids" toward "the postponed expectation of the world . . . a new age, as the star in the constellation Harp, which now flames in our zenith, astronomers announce, shall one day be the pole-star for a thousand years."[17]

My own America, if I may call it so, elicited a different sense of wonder. To put this in its proper prosaic terms, it elicited a critical method designed to illuminate the conflicts implicit in border crossing, and to draw out their unresolved complementarities. I spoke of this method at the start as unrepresentative, thinking of the corporate American figured in Emerson's Scholar. But the contrast itself suggests another constituency: the other America hidden from view by that interpretation; or as I called it, appropriatively, the unincorporated country of my alien namesakes, Sacco and Vanzetti, a rhetorically United States of nonetheless mainly unresolved borders—between class and race, race and generation, generation and region, region and religion, religious and ethnic and national heritage—and a constantly shifting array of cultural crossing, including those between Jewish-Canadian marginality and Emersonian dissent.

The benefits of that method still seem pertinent to me, perhaps more now than ever, with the impending Americanization of what has been called, imprecisely, our postcapitalist world. I began this present investigation, after much hesitation about theme and focus, directly after a lecture I attended by a visiting Russian economist, Stanislav Shatalin. It was a dramatic occasion, since Shatalin was then directing the marketplace transformation underway in the U.S.S.R.; and it had an added personal edge (I fancied) for me alone, since he happened to come from the same region from which my parents had emigrated at about the time of his birth. "We have been wandering in the wilderness for forty years," was Shatalin's summary of the Communist experience; "the time of ideology is over, and the time for truth has arrived"—by which, he explained, he meant free enterprise, individualism, and liberal democracy.[18] As he proceeded to outline his 500-day truth-plan, conjuring up transcendent things to come, I found my thoughts turning gradually elsewhere—drifting back, as though in accordance with a law of their own, to the process of my personal and professional discovery of New Canaan. I had had a different border-crossing experience, and I had a different, cross-cultural story to tell. My proper theme and focus, I realized, was the music of America.

"It Is Time":

The Buber-Rosenzweig Bible Translation in Context

Klaus Reichert

*W*hy does anybody wish to retranslate something, when and if that something has already become an integral part of the language and culture into which it has been translated? There may be various plausible reasons, scholarly and aesthetic: the text may reach radically different audiences, the language of the translated text may have become obsolete, and so on. Indeed, translation has an innovative force—it secures the survival of texts that otherwise may become historical blanks. Refocusing of attention seems to be next to impossible, however, with texts that have established their own tradition and have become almost completely detached from their origins. Within the German framework a good case in point is Schlegel's Shakespeare. Although many attempts were made to come closer to the original, to reproduce more adequately the syntactic and metrical jumps and breaks of its lines or its different stylistic layers, to adapt it better to changing stage conditions, Schlegel's translations have never been superseded—not because they were so good but because they were and are part of the Weimar culture which they had helped to shape, Shakespeare having become the third of Germany's classical authors.[1]

A much stronger case in point is of course Luther's German Bible. It must be borne in mind that the German into which Luther translated was to a large extent his own creation. This entailed an entire break with the languages of medieval German poetry which was almost exclusively written in the South German dialects. But it meant, above all, forming a new language out of the clumsy usage in the high German chancelleries by amalgamating it intertextually with the language actually spoken in everyday life, in the marketplace, in the nursery, by peasants and citizens, and forging it into a new literary medium.

But Luther's language—because of its imagery, its inventiveness, its concreteness, its drastic formulations, its lyrical touches, its prose rhythms—must be seen not only as the creation of codified High German but at the same time as the inception of the dominant linguistic paradigm of postmedieval German culture in general. Far into the nineteenth century the language of German philosophy and poetry had its roots in Luther's German. None of later attempts at translating the Bible—be they Protestant or Catholic—succeeded in bypassing Luther; all they did was to "improve" upon his text by minor emendations or by adapting it to changing usage. Even Jewish endeavors—beginning after spurious attempts with Moses Mendelssohn, who saw his translation as part of his emancipatory program to give his Yiddish-speaking fellow Jews access to the high German language and culture by way of the very text they had to read weekly—had to resort to the one and only language in which the German Bible had been transmitted, even though Mendelssohn tried very hard to adhere more closely to the original.[2] Gradually during the nineteenth century, with the emergence of biblical criticism, the attitude toward a Bible translation changed: scholars such as Leopold Zunz, the founder of Jewish Studies, Ludwig Philippson, Samson Raphael Hirsch, and Emil Kautzsch offered texts that were philologically correct, sober, emptied of poetic quality, interested only in rendering the alleged meaning as precisely as possible. Although these scholars were certainly aware of different historical, and hence stylistic, layers, of different voices, the merging of halakic and haggadic streams, their rendering had the plain tone of German academic discourse, using more or less automatically the Lutheran terms in a thinned-out form—that is, bereft of their context. Important in the new renderings is the addition of a commentary: after so much biblical criticism one can no longer rely on the word of God but has to explain it, to "make sense" of it—not, however in the form of question and answer or of various options as in the Mishnah or in the two Talmuds, but by way of positivist clear-cut decisions: there can only be one plausible answer to questions mainly philological.

Representative—and setting an example for Christian undertakings to come—is Ludwig Philippson's *Israelitische Bibel*, published in Leipzig in 1844, which was intended to be the Jewish "Volksbibel," emulating Luther's—it was this Bible, incidentally, which Freud had used as a child and which possibly had an influence on the shaping of his thoughts.[3] Philippson offers a bilingual edition, but the bulk of his work consists in his running commentary, which discusses, sentence by sentence, with meticulous care, the full range of problems posed by the text. It is a grand work of enlightened scholarship—and this, precisely, is its problem. There is a veil spread between text and commentary which can never be lifted. How does one respond to the alleged revelation of the text when each phrase can be dissected into its numerous layers of different provenance? It is, conversely, the commentary that reveals what the translation fails to transmit. To give just one example: In rendering Exodus 3.14, the revelation of the name of God, the enigmatic, possibly tautological "ihyeh asher ihyeh," Philippson offers practically the same solution as Luther had: "Ich werde sein, welcher ich werde sein!" (Luther had "Ich werde sein der ich sein werde.") If we turn to the Vulgate we get "Ego sum qui sum," and in the same vein the Authorized Version has: "I am that I am." Now the form "ihyeh" is a Qal imperfect (of *hayah*, to be, to become), and the Hebrew imperfect loosely corresponds to the English future tense, but it really indicates an incomplete or ongoing action that possibly has no termination and may not have had a beginning. Thus neither of the tenses chosen for translation gives an adequate rendering of what goes on: the future tense seems to postpone the revelation while the present seems to indicate a confinement, a remaining-within-Himself—aloof, *absconditus*—of the person that reveals Himself. If translation fails, all depends on the commentary.

Here Philippson displays the whole range of his erudition. He discusses all the relevant readings of the passage. Of special interest is the rendering of the Septuagint—"ego eimi ho ōn," "I am the being one (*der Seiende*)"—because it draws on the same root of the verb and yet qualifies it: the same and not the same as being in the continuous presence of the participle. The phrase at once unfolds the meaning of *hayah* and puts a rift between the terms that were two first persons singular—that is, between the one undivided being that only repeats its oneness in order to state His being identical with Himself. Yet it is precisely the Greek reading that enables Philippson to extract two meanings from the two instances of "ihyeh," for he holds that only the first is a strong term that only states His eternity, whereas the second is a subsidiary term that only states the unchangeability of the everlasting one: "The relative pronoun 'asher' draws all of the substantiality of God's being from the foregoing 'ihyeh' and connects it with the new 'ihyeh,' a 'being becoming' (ein 'Sein werden'), i.e., an eternal one." Thus it is Philippson's commentary with its subtle philosophical distinctions that captivates the reader's attention.

The translation, by contrast, is written in the style of a feigned archaic naïveté, in the style of the fairy tales and sagas that became so popular in

Germany after the great collections of the brothers Grimm and the roman-
tics. It rolls on and on, always in complete sentences even where the original does not have them, without any changes in tone, without differences
between the darker and the clearer passages, the enigmatic and the strict
narrative, in one homogeneous and compact mass. It is true that there is
some Hebraic flavoring—he keeps the names, for example: Moscheh, Jiz-
chak, even Mizrajim for Egypt—but this seems to express little more than
a reverence to the spirit of his age which had discovered the alleged exotism
of Jewish themes and characters and turned them into poetry, operas,
paintings. Philippson's translation is an act of assimilation and appropriation: he adjusts it to the existing cultural context. The archaic and simplistic surface does not hide any secrets; no force of words draws the reader
into its vortex. The gulf between commentary and translation cannot be
bridged.

This detour was necessary in order to set the scene for the entrance of
Buber and Rosenzweig. By way of transition let me add to the Philippson
discussion what Rosenzweig had to say about the translation of "ihyeh."
In the so-called working papers where he comments upon the first draft
version of the nascent translation which Buber had sent him, we read:

"To be" (sein) doesn't work. This is hopelessly platonized in German, as in all post-
platonic languages, including medieval Hebrew. Surely we don't want to transmit
the atrocities of the Septuagint. The words are not "philosophy of the Bible" but
they grow wholly out of the moment, encompassing thereby eternity too, of
course. . . . The phrase is, like all explanations of a name, not a name but a real,
a spoken sentence which is then followed by its compression into a name. The pres-
entness, the being-here, can only be expressed thus: Ich werde dasein, als der ich
dasein werde [I shall be here as the one who shall be here]—"sein" would point to
something remote, "dasein" is all presence, but comprises, in the second part of the
word, "-sein," also an everlasting existence of being.[4]

In the next verse, when God says: "Thus you shall speak to the sons of
Israel: 'ehyeh' sends me to you," only then, Rosenzweig continues, "the real
name appears, 'the' name, forging together both parts of the phrase, which
had, in their first occurrence, the form of question and answer. Now it says
in its finished or contracted form: Ich bin da [I am here]." Thus the translation ventures to give the two possible tense equivalents—future and present—one after the other or, rather, it draws the future into the present.[5]

While the other translations give here for the name of God "I am" or
"Ich werde sein" or "ho ōn" or even "Qui est," Buber and Rosenzweig
boldly state "Ich bin da," which also recapitulates the "dasein" of the first
phrase. "Da" is a rich and polyvalent word in German and became, at

about the same time, of great prominence in the work of Heidegger. It is demonstrative, points to something, gives a direction, calls attention, at the same time that it indicates a presence, a closeness or nearness. Thus the simple German phrase "Ich bin da" contracts timeless existence and actual presence, a presence that is directed at the other who hears the statement. The translation, then, is at once a perfectly correct rendering of the original and a clear statement of the redirection by which Rosenzweig approached scripture, drawing it into the ken of the everyday experience of the reader— or more specifically, the listener—now. Thus translation becomes an instance of interpretation. In this case it is part of the reformulation of Judaism within the cultural and political context of Germany after the First World War.

In 1917, while still in military service, Rosenzweig published his first educational pamphlet, "It Is Time . . . Thoughts about the Problem of Jewish Education at the Present Moment," addressed to Hermann Cohen. In it he states that though Judaism is part of the world that surrounds it, it must not be "appropriated" (*angeeignet*) in that sense.

And if Judaism is a force of the past, a peculiarity of the present—to us it is the goal of every future. And since future, therefore a world of its own, in spite of the world that surrounds us. And since a world of its own, therefore rooted in the soul of each and everyone in his or her own language. The German, also the German in the Jew, can and will read the Bible in German—in Luther's, in Herder's or Mendelssohn's versions; the Jew can only understand it in Hebrew.

And further: "Meaning depends upon language, and it is a gross underestimation of the intimacy by which Christendom and the German language have been mated since Luther and even before his time, if one believes to be able to convey Jewish contents in German without the flavoring of an alien faith." His proposal, then, to Cohen was, always with the future of Jewry in Germany in view, to renew and fortify Hebrew studies and to put them on a manageable footing. Toward the end of his pamphlet he emphasizes: "We need this new vivacity. The flame of joyous hope, with which many of us acclaimed the outbreak of the war as the dawn of a new age of German Jewry, is extinguished. From a seriously Jewish viewpoint fortunately so. Great changes must not fall as a gift gratuitously to the capable person."[6]

Thus Rosenzweig makes the case for a new, not a reformed, Judaism by going back to its roots—that is, to Hebrew. At the same time he turns his back on any assimilative tendencies which had been the hope of German Jews for over a century—an unrequited love, as Gershom Scholem termed it. Rosenzweig's, and Hermann Cohen's, conviction lay in the

direction of a two-culture theory, not along the lines of segregated Zionism or any brand of assimilated or enlightened German Jewry: what they
aimed at was to be Germans and Jews, with a capitalized AND. What would
have become of this great project if it had had a chance to unfold in history,
nobody knows. Under the heading of this "and" the Bible translation will
have to be considered. But before entering into it let me turn to Rosenzweig's translation of *Sixty Hymns and Poems* by the Jewish-Spanish medieval poet Jehuda Halevi, with notes and introductory essay published in
1924. This work may safely be called a revolutionary achievement in the
theory and practice of translation.

Rosenzweig was so bold as to introduce Hebrew structures into the
German language.[7] The task of the translator is not, he claims, to bridge
the gap between languages in such a way that the gap is filled up, to smooth
over the distance—this would simply be a communicative transfer, a transferring of content, as if content were separable from the form in which it
was expressed; the task is, on the contrary, to keep open the distances, to
expressly point to them. The task is to reshape German, to make it sound
strange, in order to make the alien sound of the other language audible.

If the voice of the Other [*die fremde Stimme*] has anything to say, then language
(the language translated into) must afterwards look different than before. . . . Language will experience a renewal. For the alien [*fremde*] poet not only breathes into
the new language what he has to say himself, but brings the heritage of the general
spirit of his own language to the new one, so that what happens is not only a renewal of language by virtue of the alien poet but by virtue of the alien or other spirit
of language [*durch den fremden Sprachgeist*] itself.[8]

Yet it is not a hybrid language, not an Esperanto Rosenzweig has in mind
when he envisages the superposition of the two spirits of language. "There
is only One language," he contends. "There are no peculiarities of one
language that do not have their counterpart in any other language, albeit
marginalized or as a remnant in dialects or in the nursery." It is these lost
or unused possibilities that the translator has to seek out, put to use and
make dominant: he speaks of the "cultivation [*Urbarmachung*] of fallow
ground."[9] Thus, what may first sound like alienation, an estrangement of
one's own language, is fundamentally held to be a renewal of that language
out of its own virtuality, which had been fully unfolded in another language. To make Hebrew audible in German at once marks the distance
between translated text and original and shows how it may be sublated by
listening to the other voice underneath or above one's own breath.

For the practical purposes of the Jehuda Halevi let me only mention
four principles Rosenzweig adhered to. First, he tried to retain the para-

tactic structure or what he calls the "cyclopic architecture" of Hebrew syntax, that hard-edged technique of stringing words together without modal words or without a smoothing out between words, and with hardly any subordinate clauses. The second principle is rhyme structure. Here he tries to retain also the consonants, not only the vowels as is customary in German. Moreover, the long rhyme chains of Halevi made it necessary, if the structure was to be kept, to make up new words by applying unusual prefixes or suffixes to a given root, or by using different inflections—a device Rudolf Borchardt resorted to in his new Dante at the same time.[10] Third, metrics: Here Rosenzweig calls in question the rigid division between musical and expiratory accent. Why should it be a fixed law in our modern languages that the word accent in prose must be the same in verse? Did not Greek and Latin poetry achieve its peculiar aesthetic tension from the nonidentity of word accent and verse accent? He reminds us that this nonidentity is, after all, not so strange to our own ears if we think of musical declamation, where it does not irritate us at all. And he points to the attempts at an evenly poised stress (*gleichschwebender Ton*)[11] of Stefan George and his circle, where a modification of fixed accents had been practiced for some decades. He could have added Schönberg's experiments with spoken songs (*Sprechgesang*). The purpose is obvious: Rosenzweig wants to reproduce as closely as possible the accumulation of heavy syllables in medieval Hebrew poetry, but at the same time he wants to liberate the sound quality of poetry from the yoke of prose accents, revitalizing possibilities that had only been in marginal use, hardly ever in the poetry that was to be read. Rosenzweig also broke new ground with a fourth principle. It is the principle of what today would be termed intertextuality. It is what Rosenzweig calls mosaic technique.[12] The medieval Jew, he claims, was so much imbued with classical texts, foremost the Bible, and at the same time so secure of his own style, that it was all one to him whether he quoted or whether he spoke in his own voice: the quotation had become part of his own thinking and feeling, it never functioned as ornament or reference to an authority. The task of the translator in this case is to point to the allusive character of this language—that is, to devise it as a network of references and cross-references. So he uses quotations that have a resonance in the ear of his German public—and takes them from Luther's Bible and Protestant chorals. At this time, in 1924, he still believed that Luther and the German Bible formed an inseparable unity—after all, he wanted to produce anamnestic effects similar to those of the original. It was more important to introduce other voices, other layers of style into his translation than to replace them by more adequate, perhaps more Jewish translations of his own. It was more important to tie the quotations to the resonances of an existing tradition than to question this very tradition. He felt it necessary to resort to a memory which necessarily engendered wrong associations, a blending of two different cultural contexts, the latter of which was based upon the appropriation and extinction of the previous one by way of translation.

This problem of balancing two fundamentally divergent traditions shows the aporia a German Jew must have been exposed to, in particular a Jew who wanted to be a German at the same time. Out of this aporia arose the need for a new Bible translation that would let the Hebrew shine through. This was a Herculean attempt to break away not only from the Lutheran tradition but at the same time from the language that had been shaped by its great authors upon Luther's foundation, and to establish nothing less than a new tradition, to *construct a memory*, to rebuild the ship while it was fully afloat. It was Buber who finally convinced Rosenzweig that the translation should be undertaken even though both were aware—the more so as the work progressed—of the fundamental untranslatability of the texts. Buber made first drafts; Rosenzweig commented upon them, corrected, proposed alternatives. The dispute over a single word—in Rosenzweig's case in written form since he could not speak—could go on for weeks. All this is well documented and has been written about at length, mainly by the translators themselves; indeed there is no translation we know so much about. It was to be a "faithful" translation—but faithful to what? A "literal" translation—but in what sense?

The major decision was to recover the oral quality of the written word, for they did not aim at translation as substitution but as reverberation. To do so they divided the text into what they called "Kola," each "Kolon" or breath unit constituting a rhythmic and semantic whole. This was not an arbitrary choice—they simply disregarded in many cases the common verse divisions that had been introduced by the Masoretic notation as well as the chapter divisions that had been taken over from the Vulgate in the sixteenth century. By breaking up the phrases of the received text and rearranging them in kolometric form they distinguished between oral and written parts of the phrases, the oral parts of course not being limited to direct speech. To give a simple example: where Luther has (Gen. 33.1) "Jakob hob seine Augen auf und sah seinen Bruder Esau kommen mit vierhundert Mann" (Jacob lifted up his eyes and saw his brother Esau come with four hundred men) the new translation has "Jaakob hob seine Augen und sah,/da, Essaw kam und mit ihm vierhundert Mann" (and he saw,/ lo and behold, Esau came). While Luther makes a smooth, grammatically correct statement in two main clauses, Rosenzweig/Buber, following the original, make a ruffled statement, using the "hineh" ("da," "lo," always an exclamatory word or a word of surprise) to draw the listener or reader into the action, to make him participate in Jacob's seeing. The dramatic effect is of course heightened by the internal rhyme absent in the original, but then the Hebrew has an abundance of [â] and [a:] sounds in the first kolon. Thus the breath units call for constant attention on the part of the reader/listener, who must be on the alert to shift ground from kolon to kolon, never knowing what is going to happen next. The text never "flows" linearly as the Lutheran and the texts in its wake do; rather it establishes a textual space with horizontal *and* vertical axes. Rosenzweig states: "this whole wealth of voices and timbres [*Klangfarben*]—once it is liberated from the muffled gray of the usual piano score—will by this notation as score become again audible, readable—audibly readable [*laut lesbar*]." And: the kola "give back to the word its free and oral breathing that had been stifled by the writtenness of scripture."[13] The translation was of course to be read aloud, in accord with Jewish practice but also in remembrance of the originally oral transmission of the word of God before it had been confined to writing.[14]

The next decision concerns what I would call structural translation. Rosenzweig and Buber knew perfectly well that the text had been written by various hands (J, E, D, P) over several centuries, and complied by bringing to the fore the various voices. Yet their authority was the final redactor who had made a coherent whole out of the many strands and layers. Thus, they held, nothing was arbitrary, nothing just a remnant from an earlier layer: coherence had been brought about by numerous cross-references, repetitions of words, word stems, whole phrases, puns, allusions, real or veiled quotations. But this was not only a question of creating a coherent whole: it was a means of achieving a permanent self-commentary of the text, one passage elucidating another by offering a counterpart, for example, or taking up a thought that had been left open in a former place, or cutting through the layers in such a way that halakic and haggadic strands were connected. Thus, such repetitions, paronomasias, and so on were not only stylistic devices but functioned as concatenations and elucidated the meaning by way of cross-references. For the reader this is of course only recognizable in a second reading, which is to say that the new Bible, like any modernist text, relies on a constant rereading, a reading backward and forward. Again, as with kolometrics, the attention and concentration expected is immense: one cannot read through the text as one does with other Bible translations, for Rosenzweig and Buber have transformed what one assumed one knew into a highly complex network of allusions and assumptions, somewhat similar in structure to *Ulysses*. The key phrase for this technique is Buber's "Leitwort" which functions in exactly the same way as Joyce's "leitmotif." And yet, what appears so modern is deeply rooted in the tradition of Midrashic interpretation. In the Midrash Rabbah, for example, we find the same method of elucidating a passage by pointing out the various parallel passages or by referring to other contexts, often using puns or etymologies as connecting links, or unfolding an image implied, but not expressed, in a word. What is dispersed, then, over the commentaries is to be drawn into the German text itself. Commentary, in the Midrashic sense, is the backbone of this translation; there is not one line that does not echo other lines.

Commentary is also the general characteristic of the semantic procedure. It shows most obviously in the handling of names which always mean something but have been taken over simply as names in the previous translations. Thus, after "Babel," they put, in apposition, "Wirrwarr" (confusion), which is used in German of confused language in particular, the alliterative form corresponding to the verb "balal." In many places they even give the full Hebrew phrasing: "Er rief seinen Namen: Noach! / denn er sprach: / Se jenachmenu—/ Der wird uns trösten" (He called his name: Noach! / for he said: / Se jenachmenu—/ He shall console us). To get down to the basic meaning of each word was the uppermost principle, to lay bare the meaning of the words in their utter concreteness, to strip them of the abstract—theological or philosophical—accretions that had made them intangible and shrouded them in terms and notions. Probably the most conspicuous example in this respect is the "ruakh elohim" of Genesis 1.2, which had been handed down as "pneuma theou," "spiritus dei," "spirit of god," and "Geist Gottes." When these renderings were first used they certainly carried the original's meaning of "wind" and "breath," even in German as Rosenzweig and Buber maintained and could prove from Hildebrand's long article in Grimm's *Wörterbuch*. But it was equally true that the renderings had since had a career as major theologoumena. In German this would reach from associations with the holy spirit ("heiliger Geist") all the way down to Hegel's *Phänomenologie des Geistes* (in English: "mind"). All of these—allegedly misleading—connotations had to be barred once and for all, and the word had to be reinstated in its primeval nakedness. What they resorted to—after considering "breath," "breeze," "wind,"[15] and so on—was finally "Braus Gottes," a word that does not echo anything but expresses the bustling, roaring, blustering, and raging of that first wind, in German also connected with the tossing of the sea: thus, the intimation of an "Urwort." And yet, the idea behind this decision being perfectly justified, the word just doesn't sound right—it is less primordial than awry. If the word is used it occurs mainly in the connection "in Saus und Braus," that is, "to revel and riot," which certainly is a wrong association for "ruakh." We may say, then, that however close Rosenzweig/Buber tried to get to the original meaning, they did not pay all that much attention to German usage, even though they intended the text to be read aloud. Nor did they want to. They intended, instead, to revitalize German from its roots, as they went back in their reading to Hebrew roots, using obsolete words alongside common ones.

Related attempts at a renewal of German had been made by Wagner, with his teutonic reverberations, were made by George, Borchardt, Heidegger, and ran into the terrible germanization of the thirties and forties. It was all in the air. The question behind it is, however, also a theoretical one: does language progress in a linear way, or is it possible that earlier—maybe forgotten, maybe discarded stages—may contribute to later ones? If the development of literature, art, and music opted for the second, why not language? Rosenzweig gave the example of a German theologian of the Enlightenment who had complained in 1794 of Luther's words becoming obsolete, at the time that they were coming back into common usage by way of the German classicist writers.[16] Did he hope for something similar to happen in the 1920's? The signs were all there, but also the reverse, as reactions such as Kracauer's, Benjamin's, and Bloch's attest.

None of the words one expects will be there: no altar, no sacrifice, no testimony, no feast of tabernacles, and so on, because all of these words had to be stripped of their Greek or Latin garments and be rethought and reshaped from German roots, or because they had become abstract concepts and lost their concreteness. Thus "altar" usually becomes "Schlachtstatt" (place of slaughtering), but in the case of the "altar of burnt offering" it becomes "Statt der Darhöhung." This is a made-up word, a portmanteau one may say, probably of "darbringen" (to offer, to present) and "erhöhen" (to raise somebody or something to a higher position). In Hebrew " 'olah" its root is still sensed: "to go up, ascend"; while our "burnt offering" or "Brandopfer" goes back to Greek "holokauston." The prefix "dar-," which implies a movement, a direction, is the old form of "da" which we have discussed in connection with the name of God ("Ich bin da") and is possibly intended to remind us of this presence.

Attempts other than those at literalism—but what does "literal" *mean* in the examples given?—concern clear interpretatory manipulation. The tetragrammaton—usually translated as "the Lord," "the Lord God," or "God"[17]—is given as "I," "He," "my," "his." Where the James version has "I am the Lord," Rosenzweig and Buber just state "ICH." The decision for the sheer personal or possessive pronoun clearly implies closeness, the readiness of here and now, the principle of the "I-and-Thou" dialogue, so pertinent to this translation. The "feasts of the Lord" become "SEINE Gezeiten" (which is misleading by common German usage, because "Gezeiten" means "tide," the ebb and flow); the "ark of the covenant of the Lord" turns out as "der Schrein SEINES Bundes," and so on. Even closer to the presence of God they include such renderings as, for the "ark of testimony," "Schrein der Vergegenwärtigung." "Testimony" would refer to something given in the past, once for all, something concluded, while the " 'ed" always implies somebody who had been there, had been present, and who can now and always bear testimony of the act he witnessed: therefore "Vergegenwärtigung" as the act of realization, of, literally translated, making something become, again, present, to call it back to mind. Similarly, "the tabernacle of the congregation" (usually "Stiftshütte" in German) becomes in the first version "Zelt der Gegenwart" ("tent of presence"), in the final version "Zelt der Begegnung" ("tent of meeting"). The closeness of "Vergegenwärtigung" and "Gegenwart" is caused by the etymological relation of " 'ed" and "mo'ed." When Buber changed the latter term to the more "correct" rendering of "Begegnung" he had probably also in mind that by way of the duplicity of the root "gegen" he could establish a relationship between words, commonly not felt or thought of in German. Rosenzweig speaks of "Wurzelsinn" ("root meaning")—a word and concept he took over from Herder—and "Wurzelsinnlichkeit" (the "sensuousness of roots") and demands: "The translator must be bold enough to dive down to these layers if he wants to discover also in the other language [i.e., the language translated into] the words that are so closely linked in the original language, words that only on the surface, in the dictionary, lie far apart but may be found out as related in a closed circle of perception and idea."[18] And this is exactly what Rosenzweig/Buber dared to do: to rethink and rewrite German from the inside, to bring up to the surface correspondences that had lain dormant in the roots of language, to open up new possibilities by recalling old or lost ones, unused potentialities. What they write is both an invented ur-German and a hebraization of German. Their Bible is German *and* Jewish, with no admixture of Christian readings. As Rosenzweig wrote in *Scripture and Luther's Translation*, which appeared in the same year, 1926, as the first three books of the Pentateuch:

One day, a miracle happens and the spirits of the two languages mate. This does not strike like a bolt out of the blue. The time for such a *hieros gamos*, for such a Holy Wedding, is not ripe until a receptive people reaches out toward the wing-beat of an alien masterpiece, with its own yearning and its own utterance, when its receptiveness is no longer based on curiosity, interest, desire for education, or even aesthetic pleasure, but has become an integral part of the people's historical development.[19]

Rosenzweig and Buber felt that the historical or "national" constellation for the Jews living in Germany had arrived in which such a mating of spirits might be achieved. Rosenzweig's motto for his educational pamphlet, "It Is Time," had been taken from Psalm 119 (126): "It is time for thee, Lord, to work: for they have made void the law" (James); the shift in Rosenzweig's own rendering is remarkable: "Zeit ists zu handeln für den Herrn—sie zernichten deine Lehre." And Rosenzweig felt sure that the work they had done would last for generations to come. As he said in a letter to Buber: "In time to come it will be said of our translation, too, that the Jews have learned from it the German language."[20]

How are we to evaluate the translation? It is not an appropriation, not an assimilation. It is perhaps foremost a twofold act of negation: a crossing out of the German—or for that matter, Christian—Bible tradition, and a revocation of the development of the German language. Also the intention is twofold: to leave the original intact, to pre- and conserve it, and to build up, or invent, an otherness as an offer of a new identity. The project is as grand as it is probably fallacious and linguistically impossible. It is nothing less than an attempt at colonizing the space between two cultures by resorting to double-edged strategies. The question is how to be self and other, how to have two voices—separated by more than two thousand years—in a single word, to exfoliate self and other as places of mutual translatability, letting the Hebrew appear as a possibility of German, the German as a transformation of Hebrew. If all translation thematizes border, certainly this one does: it permanently *points* to the original. (In the working papers we find Rosenzweig's exclamation: "O, dear reader, go and learn Hebrew!")[21] Studying the working papers one notes that every available commentary was consulted, from Onkelos and the Targums, the Talmuds and Rashi to Wellhausen, Kautzsch, and more recent ones, and whatever they found essential they tried to incorporate into their text by way of their choice or makeup of words. But one equally notes that each commentary seems to have been for them, as it were, equidistant from the text—that is, there is an absence of historical awareness, a leveling out of the distance between reader and text as if the text could and would speak to us here and now, which has of course to do with the quasi-existentialist approach to the text. ("It is not literature and it is not theology," Rosenzweig writes.) This approach can certainly be justified theoretically and has its counterparts in other fields (Heidegger, Leo Strauss). But how can it be transformed into the language of a translation? Here the skipping of tradition, the disregard for the stages of linguistic development, turns out to be a violation, an offense against the very spirit of language that they stressed so emphatically.

If their extensive use of obsolete words may be seen as a "rescue work," as a protest against oblivion, their making up of words is situated on a different plane. Is it permitted to take words apart and arrange the syllables at will? Borchardt, in a long private letter to Buber of 1930, speaks of "unreal, lifeless phrasings," of "mechanical engenderings," of their use of the "lively formative elements of language" as if they were "dead little stones in a mosaic" that could be reshuffled at will.[22] In an unpublished note by Scholem from about the same time we read: "Rosenzweig's translations live in the demonic glamor of a hybrid existence [Zwitterdasein]. His activity as a translator was determined by his magic wish for a deeper and deeper marriage with the German: a disaster for the Jewish perspective."[23] This reflects of course Scholem's totally different approach to Judaism, language, and translation, but is important in that it stresses the magical aspect of Rosenzweig's endeavor. Like demiurges the two translators arranged and rearranged the matter of creation hoping for a breath that would enliven their pages. Like any magic wish it reaches beyond itself. To have concretized the fundamental untranslatability of the text indicates this Beyond.

The reaction upon the publication of the first volumes was almost unanimously negative—from Jewish, in particular liberal, circles as well as from "profane" intellectual positions. The longest and most scathing attack came from Siegfried Kracauer in a two-part review in the Frankfurter Zeitung, April 1926.[24] He claimed that the historical situation was decidedly not one that called for a new Bible translation, certainly not for one in the style and with the assumptions of Rosenzweig/Buber. Social and economic power relations, he claimed, conditioned the spiritual structure of the present society, and exclusively spiritual endeavors would only help stabilize existing conditions. A new translation would have to be inspired by a revolutionary spirit, a spirit that got down to the profane realities of external facts with the intention of changing them. And in the language Rosenzweig and Buber use or invent Kracauer senses the utter loss of this reality. It is not an archaic language, he maintains, but the language of yesteryear, mythologizing jargon, outmoded neoromanticism of the fin-de-siècle, the passé language of bourgeois provenance. The numerous alliterations recall Richard Wagner's runes; the general tone sounds as though it was taken from George's *Stern des Bundes*—"Künder" for "prophet," for instance, bears the stamp of that self-styled high priest and his circle.[25] The most horrible accusation is that which associates this language with that of incipient Nazism: Kracauer speaks of "völkischer Tonfall," "völkische Romantik," a language, that is, of blood and soil, of a return to the glebe, as it were, a re-teutonization—implying a re-barbarization—of a language that had been molded, over the centuries, into an instrument of the greatest sophistication and subtlety.[26]

Nor was Kracauer alone in his severe criticism. Benjamin, whose own ideas about the "task of the translator" (about the "spirit of language," for example) were so close to Rosenzweig's, wrote to Kracauer to congratulate him on his review: "You have put down something truly enjoyable. Something has been done: the whole is 'classified' for us once and for all, one need not waste any time about it; . . . From the theoretical foundation of your rebuff through the comparison with Luther's German rendering of the Vulgate to the unsparing and appropriate proof of its linguistic descent from Wagner, everything seems to me pertinent in the highest degree."[27] In a letter to Scholem of the same year, who had also been hostile to the translation,[28] Benjamin writes:

I have no idea who in the whole world should be interested in a translation of the Bible into German at the present moment. Now that the contents of Judaism become topical again while the German language is at a highly critical stage and, above all, fruitful relations between both seem to me to be possible, if at all, only in a latent way, isn't the new translation in this situation a questionable exposition of things which, thus exposed, discredit themselves at once in this kind of German?[29]

Martin Jay has summarized Benjamin's position:

He rejected the major premises of the translation: no emphatic rapport between the Biblical *Künder* and the attentive listener, whatsoever his historical circumstances, could be assumed possible in the present era. The chasm between speech and writing was not capable of being bridged by naively restoring the original Hebrew. Indeed, Benjamin felt that recapturing the spoken word was not the way to overcome linguistic alienation; there was no easy return to an Edenic unity of name and thing in which meanings were perfectly expressive of a deliberate intention.[30]

At the same time it must be remembered that Benjamin had a high regard for Rosenzweig's *Star of Redemption*, where he would have found linguistic and "existentialist" tendencies similar to those he criticized in the Bible.

There are two problems, then, with the new Bible and the reactions to it: one is political, the other linguistic. Many of the people who criticized the new Bible were assimilated Jews, loosely connected with what was to become "the Frankfurt School" and its ideas. The problem of Cohen, of Rosenzweig and Buber—how to be a Jew *and* a German—was not theirs. They were living and thinking in terms of an international community of intellectuals for whom neither national nor religious ideas had any interest except as testimonies of reactionary and anachronistic minds. For them it was necessary to analyze as thoroughly as possible the ruling conditions of present society—to track down their reverberations even in art and literature—and if possible to change that very society. To them the problem of a German Jewry was a problem of the past, or if not quite, it would soon become obsolete. To them it was unimaginable that there could or should be a Jewish revival. The Bible was a historical document, and if there was to be any new translation, it had to be a scholarly one. The idea that a translation could be its own commentary, as Rosenzweig/Buber had intended, was probably incomprehensible to them. If there were Jews among these enlightened scholars who did not believe in assimilation—such as Scholem—the way for them lay in the direction of Zionism, with the possible consequence of emigrating to Palestine at once, as Scholem did. But apart from the question of a renewal of Jewry in Germany, those scholars and critics were equally doubtful that to focus on the reorientation of the individual mind could also entail a political act. They only perceived in the translation a parallel to those esoteric movements that abounded in the twenties which they held to be antipolitical but which were merely distrustful of grand external political solutions.

Of course the problem with language has a political layer as well. At the time of the translation, all nationalist movements in Germany were busy exterminating foreign influences in the language. They aimed to purify German and to get it back to its more "genuine" earlier stages, with its concomitant peasant ideology. Wagner's libretti are a good case in point, with their assumed recourse to middle-high German vocabulary and Norse types of versification which mirror the chauvinist side of Teutonic historicism, even if some of the words—for the most part they were made up—were revivals of old ones. Though Rosenzweig/Buber, in response to Kracauer's reproof, insisted that the words they used had been in existence long before Bayreuth, the question remains whether you *can* use them, after Bayreuth, as it were innocently. Can one jump out of one's historical context with impunity? However, the question may as well be turned round: should one leave an instrument such as the German language, with its wealth of possibilities, in the hands of those who abused it? Was one not obliged to expose the difference in the seemingly identical as a positioning of the Other? How else can we understand Buber's decision to follow his and Rosenzweig's course after 1933, after the Holocaust, and well into the 1950s when the translation, after many revisions, was finally finished?

Perhaps it is only possible for the afterborn—after the memory of the language of barbarity has faded—to judge impartially the enormous achievement of this work. But it was already Scholem, who in the 1920's had been among its severe critics, who emphasized the historic importance of the work after its completion in 1961. In an address to Buber he summarized:

With you clear things are clear, difficult things are difficult, incomprehensible things are incomprehensible. . . . The reader is constantly turned back upon his own reflection and must ask himself, what really is it that urges to become expressed? Nowhere have you smoothed out. . . . You have roughed up the text in order to bring it more immediately to the reader struck by such speech. . . . Your translation is not only translation, it is, without adding a word of explanation as such, commentary as well. . . . This inclusion of the commentary into the most rigorous literalness of the translation seems to me to be one of the great achievements of your work. . . . The language into which you translated was not that of everyday life, not that of the German literature of the twenties. It was a German which was contained as a possibility, feeding on old tendencies, in this language, and it was just this utopian element which made your translation so particularly exciting and inspiring.

And Scholem concludes with the question whether after what had happened, there were any Germans left who could listen to and comprehend the living sound that Buber and Rosenzweig had made audible in their language.[31]

The paradox remains, this enigma of squaring the circle: to invent a language that is at one and the same time thoroughly Hebrew and the embodiment of a German that never existed, but might come into existence, be revealed, in the act of creation. A veritable utopian design: to be a Jew *and* a German, self and other, without appropriation. Never has translation been more utopian, never has it been carried out with greater consequence. Now that we slowly begin to listen to the other voice beneath our own, this translation has perhaps, at last, a chance to be heard.

The Black Hole of Culture:
Japan, Radical Otherness, and the
Disappearance of Difference

(or, "In Japan everything normal")

K. Ludwig Pfeiffer

"Japan is no longer the hermit of the East, but the most Western of the nations of the West."[1]

"The Japanese is thoroughly oriental in his pleasures, however he may follow the West in his ambitions."

"The Japanese in their heart do hate the West, but they are sharp enough to see that no nation can be a first-class power which does not wear trousers."

Conclusion: "There is generally, it must be confessed, method in Japanese madness, but it does look very mad to the unreasoning globe-trotter."[2]

The Fun Game of Cultural Comparisons

*C*ultural observation and comparison, even in their self-trivialization, can be amusing. Nor need we be overly concerned, as long as some semblance of descriptive, analytical, or theoretical rigor is maintained, with the decline toward tautology, less-than-elegant variation, or downright contradiction that analysis and comparison seem inevitably to fall prey to. We may well believe that there is a core to cultures that will, in the last resort, control and contain the play of perceived differences, hold at bay a potentially anarchic behavioral, mental, or affective scope. This looks like a natural intuition without which we rarely operate. We may hold, with respect to American and Japanese modes of experience, for instance, that "most Americans dabbling in Zen look like Americans dabbling in Zen, and most Japanese applying Western individualism do so with a Japanese spirit underneath. The difference in the worlds is sharp and difficult to penetrate."[3] However "individualistic you are invited to be [in Japan], you are often invited to be individualistic for *somebody*." *Kosei*, for instance, the Japanese word for "individualism," would not denote western individualism (*kojinshugi*), of which the Japanese are "extremely suspicious."[4] But if there seems to exist a rocklike basis for judgments like these, the same holds true, conversely, for assertions concerning fundamental similarities. Marx was struck—without of course having ever been to Japan (but what does it matter, since Japan, according to many visitors, tends to become more, and not less enigmatic the longer you are there?)— by the similarity between Japan in the 1860's and medieval Europe: "Japan, with its purely feudal organization of landed property and its developed *petite culture*, gives a much truer picture of the European middle ages than all our history books."[5]

All this, however, instead of strengthening our belief in cultural identities and differences, might tempt us to conclude, provisionally, that, sophisticated theories and approaches concerning "transcultural understanding"[6] notwithstanding, there is hardly any difference, in principle, between Douglas Sladen's moderately witty to downright absurd aphorisms, and ambitious, serious cultural description. They become virtually indistinguishable, in particular, in authors who, precisely because of the very richness of their "intercultural" experience, are driven toward pronounced statements: The Japanese diplomat Ichiro Kawasaki, with his enormously variegated career, is a good example.[7] The almost ritualistic churning out of several-volume collections on Japan,[8] with their neat divisions into sectors like culture, society, state, economy, thought, seem to augur ill for the possibility of an escape from the sameness of and the repetitive distinctions made by cultural description.

Fatal Attractions: Givenness or Construction, Reality or Stereotype?

"Translation," linguistic or cultural, is one of the important metaphors we live by. It proceeds from a not just intuitively plausible assumption that, somehow, texts have meanings, that cultures possess identities definable, to a large extent, in terms of accumulated meanings. These may be produced by historical traditions, national or group affiliations and affinities, by the implications of rituals, practices, and the like. Translation, in this train of thought, does not aim at an integral preservation of these more or less fixed or fluid identities. But, in being conscious of its own perspectivism, in pointing out, also, layers of immanent otherness in the cultures themselves, translation will work out structures of mutuality and otherness, that is, of controlled correspondences and differences—structures to be distinguished, by virtue of the carefulness and circumspection of interpreting translations, from the frequently wholesale appropriations, deformations, from the subjection or even destruction of otherness in "real" history.

Attractive and justified as such an image of translation may be, it is unstable, both logico-semantically and historically. If we push it a little bit, we may swerve into notions of cultural dialogue and commerce preceding, or at least contemporaneous with, cultural identities. From there, it is but a small step to an image of cultural "heat" (*chaleur culturelle*), an image of "fundamental" cultural agitation, instability, turbulence, and whirlpool.[9] In such contexts, where culture is a process of transitory configurations, the usual range of connotations for "translation" will apply only intermittently—identity then being the exceptional product, and not the regular process. Instead of *cultural products and identities*, one would be interested in *conditions of cultural (image) production*, which may, or may not, have identifiable and in some way translatable entities as their result.

The preceding is a strategic, a theoretical move. It does not deny the possible "reality" of well-defined cultures. It amounts, however, to a *suspension* of cultural referentialization and, consequently, translation. It does so in the interest of a *conceptual experiment* with a "culture" traditionally held to embody a cultural essence in the highest degree—in an *enigmatic*, but, in spite and maybe because of that, *decipherable* (and by implication then *translatable*) way.

This article, in any case, is *not about* Japan. The intention is to be taken in a sense even more radical than Roland Barthes's precautions back in 1970 (warnings which, as usual, have gone largely unheeded). Barthes did not want to take the Orient and the Occident as "realities" "which one would try to approach and to oppose historically, philosophically, culturally, politically. I do not look with the eyes of a lover at an essence of Orient" (the latter, according to the experts, nonexistent anyway because of the vast "differences" between, say, China and Japan).[10]

Still, Barthes aims at the possibility of difference, mutation, indeed revolution in symbolic systems. The confrontation with "a fictive people" goes a first step toward a history of our own obscurity which might make manifest "the compactness of our narcissism." In looking at "Japan," the empire and epitome of empty signs, Barthes is not looking for different symbols, but for "the very fissure of the symbolic order." That breaking apart of the symbolic, of the deep structure of cultural difference, may not even show "on the level of cultural products."[11] The determination, however, to establish a cultural discourse of referential and comparative self-restraint, is hard to carry through. Barthes talks about cities, cuisine, haiku, theater not just in an inevitably descriptive way. He also does not try to hide that talk about "Japan" can be a form of western self-aggression. Thus, western cuisine, according to Barthes, is bent upon the domination, the "penetration" of food (the importance of knife and fork and of certain ways of using them). Japanese cuisine is devoted, on the other hand, to an art of "a nutritional circle,"[12] where the "tender" manipulations of the chopsticks both in preparation and consumption tend to (re-)create inviolate levels of life processes. Western puppet theater is haunted, if also fascinated, by the anxiety about the human automaton. Bunraku, the Japanese puppet theater (which uses large puppets with the manipulators and their actions remaining visible on the stage), looks for the "perceptible abstraction" of the human body. There is no opposition between animate/inanimate, not the hidden but basic hysteria troubling western fascination with the theater.[13] There is, finally, no transformation (or the illusionary enactment of it in western poetry) of "impression" into "expression" or "description" in the haiku. The consummation, devoutly to be wished and worked for in western languages, "the adequate relation between signifier and signified," occurs, in haiku, as an event, not as the result of an expressive effect frantically sought for. In the haiku, we recognize a repetition without origin, an event without cause, a memory without a subject, a speech act without moorings.[14]

Despite his intentions, though, Barthes's discourse waxes referential. To accept what he says would, on the other hand, seem to depend to a large, if indeterminable, degree upon the sym/antipathy one bears toward what appears, from whatever perspective, as (layers, parts of) Japanese culture. Moreover, if descriptive precision there is—and there certainly is, given our standards, a lot of it—Barthes's text also looks like a nostalgic—or, with respect to both poststructuralism and postmodernism—an anticipatory self-description of what some of us have become aware of as the deficits, the burdens of western cultural traditions. There are obvious similarities with Baudrillard's analysis particularly of the American scene and, to a lesser extent, of European contemporary cultural "realities." In those, the collapse of the distinction between the signifier and the signified is always imminent. They come close to that Japanese reality in the haiku where "meaning is refused to the real; what is more: the real cannot even dispose of the meaning of the real." Shakespeare could still write (and Barthes quotes it): "When the light of sense goes out, but with a flash that has revealed the invisible world." Japan (according to Barthes) and the postmodern West (according to its prophets) have kept producing the flashes but done away with the revelation.[15]

There can be hardly any doubt, though, that Barthes's book ranks among the most sophisticated and undogmatic versions of a type of cultural discourse which *tries to convey a sense of cultural difference without falling prey to its referential traps*. It is reminiscent of some of the writings of Lafcadio Hearn (or Koizumi Yakumo) and their large stretches of unashamed "impressionism" and judgmental restraint. In Hearn too, though, that restraint gave way, or was based upon, a self-criticism of the West which made him live and die in Japan.[16] Hearn tried to capture, indeed to imitate, that "gentleness" of Japanese culture which seemed to demand more precise descriptions and explanations only when it changed abruptly into its opposite—forms of culturally determined and yet very immediate violence (including suicidal violence against oneself) or transcendental attitudes in Zen and Buddhism felt to be diametrically opposed to western transcendent(alist) religion and thought.

It might appear, indeed, that it was the advent of "Japanology" that brought about the hardening of cultural discourse into a referential one bound to find out, in the most rigorous fashion, facts designating some givenness of cultural characteristics and differences. In what became, and probably has remained, the classic work on Japan from the point of view of "cultural anthropology," Ruth Benedict's *The Chrysanthemum and the Sword: Patterns of Japanese Culture* (1946, reprinted in paperback 1989), that tendency was carried to the extreme of taxonomies and lists of cultural givens (in particular the "schematic table of Japanese obligations and their reciprocals," that is, various kinds of duties, including feelings, to various kinds of reference groups).[17] Ezra F. Vogel, himself one of the famous Japan experts (if more so in terms of the social and economic analysis of Japan as "Number One"), has commented that "the few Western social scientists who did field work [field work being apparently thought of as the methodological remedy] in Japan in the 1950s and the 1960s felt that Benedict's work was overdrawn. It made the Japanese seem too stiff, too bound by duty and social position, too concerned with their reputation."[18] Although my argument may seem crude, I take it that one of the main reasons for Benedict's (and similar) tendencies is the "fact" that the book was produced *under pressure*: the pressure, during the later stages of the Pacific war, to "know" as much as possible about the "morale" of the Japanese (why they were willing to fight even when they were losing, why they would be ready to die rather than to be taken prisoner, why some, though, when finally living as prisoners, would cooperate with the Americans to an extraordinary degree; more generally, why and when they were both very polite and brutal, submissive and innovative, robotlike and creative, etc.).[19] Benedict does not see that she is giving away a highly problematic point: "In June, 1944, I was assigned to the study of Japan."[20] Assignments (and academic studies may be seemingly neutralized institutionalizations of such assignments) cement the idea (to some extent, especially with respect to the past, justified and unavoidable) that cultures are to be *studied as entities* rather than to be *observed and interacted with as evolving*, partly in fact *emergent systemoid patterns*. It is the dubious implications of these and other, seemingly more neutral *assignments* that cultural studies (and especially their institutions) are still laboring under. Indeed, and not surprisingly, most of the studies on Japan of that period were done under the auspices of the military. In later academic writings, not obviously motivated by the needs of such "strategic" information, the intellectual urge (the professional-practical Platonism of intellectuals, as Arnold Gehlen said) to reach a level of cultural givenness through and beyond accumulated interpretations, remains undaunted. Hijiya-Kirschnereit declares the age of the self- and other-"exoticization" of Japan to be over. But her own descriptions, in particular those of social and cultural roles of women, are inextricably tied to an ideology of givenness for cultural structures and places.[21]

I am harping, from the outset, on the pressures besetting cultural theory and description, because we know, but tend to forget, that whole scholarly disciplines owe their existence to needs for "information" on the enemy, the competitor, and the like. In—not always—mitigated forms, motivational pressures loom large as the skeletons in the cupboard of cultural studies.

However: The temptation to see cultural cores and patterns, and therefore differences, as more or less given, cannot be uninhibitedly indulged in these days. The sheer mass of "research" on Japan in the library of the University of California at Irvine (where most of the work for this article was done) covers some 25 meters of shelves. It is not just because of these quantities but certainly also because of their crushing effect that cultural studies have lost some confidence with regard to "realistic descriptions." Once a staggering amount of self-referential repetitiveness and variation is focused upon, once contradictions are seen to emanate quasi-automatically from cultural discourse, a methodological reorientation frequently imposes itself. The study of *images* of cultures and of their degeneration into stereotypes will then take precedence—alas, to no, or little, avail. The idea that cultures are nothing but images and stereotypes created around an empty reality cannot, particularly with respect to alien and therefore provocative cultures, be indefinitely tolerated. Thus, the referentiality of cultural discourse may operate more sparingly. But when it does, it cracks down again with a vengeance. Lehmann, in order to provide a controlling framework for his study of images of "modernizing" (westernizing?—this distinction is itself a difficult one) Japan from 1850 to 1905, speaks freely and indiscriminately of "cultural invasions" and "imports" from the fifth century onward—as if invasions and imports were the same (or anything definite at all), or as if their "impact" were clear.[22] The volume edited by Gregor Paul[23] aims, in its very title, at a neat separation of "cliché and reality of Japanese culture." Hijiya-Kirschnereit[24] simply keeps her descriptive passages and "theoretical" problems more or less (that is, seemingly, chapter-wise) apart.

The pressure toward reference in both descriptive and image-oriented studies has done away with more "cosmopolitan" forms of writing. "Cosmopolitanism" may, for present purposes, be defined as the *acknowledgment of difference in the absence of its givenness*—an acknowledgment, that is, of culture as transitory spaces for behavioral negotiations. We find writings of that kind in times in which the pressure to come to terms with the emerging and soon threatening world power Japan (talk of that had been going at least since the Japanese-Russian war of 1904–5) was not yet very strong or could still be handled by traditions of a cooler, yet sensitive *style* of cultural thought. Lehmann quotes highly impressive passages from the London *Times* of the first years of our century, in which differences are neither taken for granted nor denied altogether. Sir Henry Norman's book *The Real Japan* (1908) is both a serious and a humorous piece of work which, in spite of its fearsome title, navigates very intelligently between assertions of cultural cores, patterns, and differences.[25] Culture here emerges as a plurality of possibilities, as something which, apart from more or less stable organizational patterns of everyday life, will be constantly in the making—under real or imagined pressures. And even Sladen's aphoristic meanderings of 1903, of which some are quoted above, handle culture and cultural difference with ease. Witticisms, apparent self-contradictions, or paradoxes serve to encircle Japanese culture discursively, but do not describe it as reality—the rest is "experience" as an interplay of belief, expectations, impressions, and skepticism.

Modern societies, perhaps from the nineteenth century onward, have been liberating themselves progressively from the grip of rhetorical, stylistic, behavioral—in sum, binding cultural—*rules*. These, however, had not predominantly defined culture as structures of meanings extending behind habitual practices and appearances. They were meant to provide a basis for its "graceful" performance and production—or for aggression against those who looked different and followed different rules (crusades, colonialism, etc.). Defoe's main distinction, to take but one example, in *Robinson Crusoe*, divides people into human beings (mainly Europeans, whether English, Spanish or other) and savages seen more as beasts than humans. Here as elsewhere, cultural interpretations were not in demand, not even when dangerous situations did not more or less automatically rule them out. Schiller's growing skepticism with respect to the chances of "grace" in an ideal culture of play, his leaning toward value- and meaning-charged forms of dignity and duty, can then also be seen as a tacit acknowledgment of a historic transition from cultures of rules, play, and aggression to cultures of self- and other-interpretation and their more intricate and indirect ways of action. Culture, as the graceful performance of rules, or as something aggressively imposed upon, freezes into series of serious definitional efforts in which grace is lost and legitimacy has to be continuously manufactured. While it certainly has not become impossible, it probably has become, since the nineteenth century, more difficult to instantiate the "cosmopolitanism" of an artist like Händel, who, coming from what might be seen as a heavily deterministic cultural background, was able to behave in Italy like an Italian and in England like an Englishman. (The same, even more surprisingly, seems to have been true of Händel's factotum, an ex–wool merchant from Franconia, who gave up his trade and followed Händel to England where his son then lived as [or like?] an English gentleman in Bath). And, given the usual gamut of opinions on Japan, it seems also difficult to visualize persons like the Würzburg-born physician Ph. F. von Siebold today, who, working for the Dutch (and changing the "von" of his name to "van" accordingly), took the rules of life in early nineteenth-century Japan for granted and left only because he was expelled for suspicion of espionage. In his case, as in many others, a definition of Japanese culture was fabricated by its government under a largely self-imposed and therefore imaginary pressure.[26] Since the nineteenth century then, a generalized, though normally metaphorically diluted "Kulturkampf" may have encouraged, in the wake of national (military and economic) competition, substantialistic definitions of cultures. For those, especially in the academic context, linguistic and literary studies were frequently exploited. Intercultural negotiations—behavioral and otherwise—were condensed into cultural stereotypes, of which "national character" has become one of the more obnoxious forms.

A Dialectic of Sorts? The Manufacture of Identity and Difference Between Radical Otherness and the Vanishing of Difference

In this situation, we will not profit much by distinguishing layers of culture, on which stability and difference might be more easily predicated. The very term "culture" has undergone semantic evolutions, refinements, abstractions, and reconcretizations of various kinds in various "cultures." Since anything, however trivial, may be, but need not be, taken as a cultural token, equivalence or correspondence of levels and layers of various cultures appears highly improbable. Indeed, the term "everyday culture" was invented in order to handle what appeared as a collapse of the distinction between everyday life and (high) culture and therefore as a potential for the "culturization" of everything. One may—even as a man—interpret techniques and procedures of haircutting (to say nothing of hairsplitting) in Japan and Germany as culturally significant, because of obvious differences in ritualization and the corresponding psychosomatic implications. Studies have been conducted on changes in gift giving within the *changing* Japanese culture. Skiing can be viewed "cross-culturally," because differences in group behavior, body movement, and "individualism" seem to vary highly between Japanese, Koreans, and Americans.[27] The intricacies in the conceptualization and application of personal relations, in particular with respect to age, gender, and status, seem to differ as significantly as the culture-dependent forms of neurosis and its behavioral manifestations.[28] Social or psychological theories cannot explain these variations without referring to some notion of culture (or "sociability" as distinct from "society," a distinction made already by Simmel).[29] Differences, then, from everyday routines to performances and appreciations of high culture, certainly "exist." But the definite shapes they may take, the modes in which they become operative, the images into which they are manufactured and on whose strength we then tend to act, these are different matters altogether. Thus, it may occur that Japanese culture, different as it is, bestows on westerners a sense of what has been called, for want of a better expression, "psychological security," a "sense of 'belonging,'" even if one can never really participate.[30] Tomlin, the British cultural attaché, who lived in Japan for six or seven years, expects, for these opinions, reproaches of sentimentalism (similar to those addressed to Hearn). But he does not shrink from asserting—in the twentieth century and for a country which, for many, has embodied and lived its form of postmodernism for a long time— that you "feel nearer to the essence of things. You feel that there *is* a natural life and natural order, which, perpetually renewed and sanctioned, are the font and condition of human happiness."[31] Gerhard Kaiser (a "Germanist" in Freiburg) extrapolates similar perspectives from an experience of the No theatre:

Going home, the European remembers vaguely that No has exercised important influences on the European theatre of our century—on Gordon Craig, W. B. Yeats, Ezra Pound, Thornton Wilder, Paul Claudel, Bert Brecht, Marcel Marceau. Later he remembers the cultural anthropology of Herder in its humanitarian breadth. It can embrace even East Asia, perceived but dimly by its author. . . . Thus, in looking at what is alien, we are looking at potentials of ourselves. More lively than reminiscences in cultural knowledge is the anticipatory feeling of the European visitor that, once in Germany, he will feel nostalgia [*Heimweh*] for Japan.[32]

Risky as such language is, impossible even as it may seem it yet reflects the *almost paradoxical disappearance of difference in a context of its strongest presence.*

Tomlin's version of this paradox, "if it be a paradox," is that "this communal solidarity, this slightly introverted form of society, does not alienate the foreigner but attracts him."[33] Not every foreigner of course, and foreign women less so than men. In any case, the hoary question whether Japanese culture has changed but very slowly or been transformed radically under the "regular impact of culture contact—from ancient times to the present,"[34] whether there are hard and fast distinctions between authentic Japan and westernized Japan, receives Tomlin's again only seemingly paradoxical answer: "there has never been an authentic Japan which was not also a Japan avid to assimilate outside influence. That *is* the authentic Japan."[35] Periods of apparently total isolation (and this for more than 200 years under the Tokugawas) or, on the contrary, of sweeping westernization (immediately after the Tokugawas in the Meiji period) are then just extreme swings of the pendulum.

There is hardly a way to distinguish Japanese "culture" from "imports," "influences," "invasions," and the like. Chinese writing, art, ar-

chitecture, law, and administration since the fourth century, Indian Buddhism (in a time when this "religion" had declined both in India and in
China), European thought and science from the early eighteenth century
onward,[36] the wholesale "westernization" during the Meiji period, have established Japan as a test case and, indeed, continuous challenge for cultural
theory and its semantics. Assertions of its radical otherness are encountered as frequently as discoveries of a basic commonalty with at least parts
of the West (or, worse, the western and particularly the German "psyche").
There is, then, no cogent way to couch *cultural comparisons in the framework of core and difference*. It has been said, almost paradoxically again,
that the feudal, isolationist Tokugawa regime from the early seventeenth
far into the nineteenth century (when Perry's "black ships" finally broke
that "isolation," which, according to Keene, had not been isolationist after
all), "was in fact a protomodern society." "Feudal values, although they
were definitely not the product of cultural contact with Europe, made it
possible for Japan to accommodate the West and allowed the nation to
begin the process of modernization quickly."[37] Cultural comparison thus
runs into an impasse, once it tries, in its usual way, to conceptualize what
may appear as both radical otherness and vanishing difference. Christopher speaks about subtle transformations in a process of "absorption"
hard to generalize about. He sees that process at work even in the Japanese
language. There is no consensus among linguists whether Japanese belongs
to any of the established groups of languages (the most frequently made
classification is with the Altaic languages, but even in that context Japanese seems remote). Yet this language has not only adopted a writing system totally alien to its own linguistic structure but also taken over massive
numbers of foreign, particularly English, words. These words, in their Japanese use, will frequently strike foreigners as absurd; yet their use can also
be seen as "both logical and serviceable."[38] Lots of customs which appear
thoroughly and purely Japanese, are, from school uniforms (from Germany) to Pachinko (a type of gambling probably from the U.S.), not "originally" Japanese at all.

   Although the expression sounds plausible, it is still hard to see, then,
what it could mean that the Japanese today are very comfortable with
western lifestyles and cultural practice (especially in the arts) and yet are
so "at one remove."[39] As the recording of an impression, the statement appears irresistible. It may be true that, because they "borrowed" so much
over the centuries, the Japanese are afraid of losing their cultural identity.
But if this has provoked frantic efforts to define cultural identity, it cer-

tainly has not blessed these efforts with much success. There may be a comparatively high *ethnic* unity amongst the Japanese. There may exist, to be sure, a peculiar system of the individual's social obligations. But all this may be a persevering *analogy* to the role of *cultural rules* which I have attributed to a pre-nineteenth-century Europe. They need not, that is, *define* the culture, but provide a regularizing, normalizing frame for its *unpredictable, transitory production*. The Japanese may feel, "however inchoately, a great sense of commonalty." Depending on the way we see this, however, the fact that, for instance, Japanese who appear in commercials, "both live and animated, tend to have distinctly more Caucasian features than the general run of Japanese do,"[40] may appear both paradoxical, curious, or self-evident.

One can, of course, try and explain all this. The point, however, is, and is supposed to remain, that the comparative enumeration of cultural characteristics *runs into deep trouble exactly when it seems to encounter its greatest chances*. Thus, while it may be true that "few people are as fundamentally dissimilar as the Japanese and the Jews," this presupposes a notion of cultural "entity" very hard to sustain. The stronger the case for the assertion appears, the more it takes on aspects of national and cultural jokes altogether too familiar. Ben-Dasan asserts that "to Jews, the Japanese willingness to obey or disobey laws as circumstances and convenience dictate is basically unintelligible." On the other hand, "the Japanese regard the complicated regulations governing the lives of orthodox Jews as excessively strict and almost ludicrous in their irrelevance to what the Japanese consider the basic human experience."[41] This is uncomfortably close to Sladen's quip that it is "no use keeping the law in Japan. If a policeman wishes to lock a man up, he does not wait for him to be guilty, so what does it matter. The Japanese do not keep the law, they obey the police."[42] But it also neglects a massive body of opinion, both Japanese and western, that life in Japan is heavily regulated in analogous, if not identical, ways. Its rules can certainly be laid in the form of binding lawlike propositions. At the same time, of course, the laws of the legal system proper may be phrased in such a way as to allow for their continuous reinterpretation and reapplication under changing circumstances.[43] But then, similar assertions might be made with respect to the behavioral interpretation of Jewish laws which have to serve under highly different circumstances indeed. Also, on a different but probably fundamental level, the role of the mother in delineating a scope for social but also cultural behavior may be fairly similar in Jewish and Japanese culture. The definition of Japanese culture (and by implication others) looks, then, at its best as a witty and pseudo-naive *game* (which the Japanese in particular seem to indulge in with zest), or, worse, as a sadly serious and therefore fallacious enterprise.[44]

The Indeterminateness of Culture and Hypothetical Rereferentializations

Cultures—apart from everyday routines— may be said to be the invention, manufacture, and partial implementation of "fictitious" (in Bentham's sense) cores and differences under pressure. Cultural discourse and theory are products of their latter-day institutionalization. They are, as it were by definition, the overstatement of the fictions under, again, softer and harder forms of pressure. This seems to hold in particular for those "informations" on culture which we obtain from members of a particular culture itself. Statements may be homogeneous to the point of tautology, or contradictory to the point of disintegration. Japanese academic colleagues in particular seem to like to play the game both ways. The result—a literal quote—can be seen in the subtitle of this article. There is no way of determining the status of that statement. It may be the logical corollary of the famous "relativism" often attributed to the Japanese, of their reluctance to commit themselves to well-defined positions, their dread of confrontation and distaste for explicit statement[45]—but also just their playful enactment. It may testify to a sense of how easily the appearance of situations, therefore the perspectives and feelings attached to them, and consequently the situations themselves can change. In a reflexive-reflective mood, we may also become aware, though, that questioning as a form of ascertaining an illusionary givenness may drive the notion of cultural coherence and consistency, which it is supposed to establish, to disintegration.

However that may be: The impression that Japanese culture is radically different retains an almost rocklike solidity. Frustrating behavioral deadlocks in trivial or complex situations form part and parcel of the cultural experience of both Japanese and *gai(koku)jin* (foreigner, outsider). This may start with the "meaning" of smiles (a notorious example). And it may mar intellectual "exchange." As often as not, westerners may have the feeling that there is nothing to exchange because Japanese *curiosity*—a kind of mythical cultural joker—eagerly absorbs everything and gives back nothing. Therefore the notion that Japanese culture is like a black hole, devouring everything, giving back nothing in return, has gained ground.[46] There is reason to suspect that whole discursive fields like the humanities, seemingly existing in more or less identical forms in Japan and in the West, stand in totally different relations to the domains of cultural or economic behavior. Finally, the categorizations provided by the language are so different that analogous cultural differences seem to ensue by necessity.

Yet the eagerness with which people tend to capitalize on the appearance of difference should give us pause. A gap, and a big one, between western and Japanese cultures certainly exists. But on which levels does it become amenable to theory, does it orient emotions and cognition, does it impose itself on the description of experience? I choose to revert heuristically to theories of *cultural origins* in order to circumnavigate—perhaps—the theoretical deadlock. Origin theories of course do not lend themselves automatically to the analysis of modern cultures. But in some of them there seem to reside impulses that might push the problem one step ahead. Jonathan Z. Smith, in a debate with Walter Burkert and René Girard on "violent" origins of cultures, has said that "the disintegration of culture began with culture itself."[47] Cultures, from that perspective, acquire a hypothetical to fictitious origin and basis when, for whichever reasons (conflicts, catastrophes, rivalries . . .), claims and assertions of identity and difference seem to be called for. That origin *may* lie in literal violence of which quite a lot certainly remains. We are not obliged, however, to adopt (Burkertian, Girardian . . .) notions of "real" violence. In a generalized sense, assertions of identity and difference are violent, or as Edgar Morin might put it, quasi-hysterical overreactions.[48] These are transformed into provisional practices and notions of culture in situations of real or imagined behavioral pressure. Indeed, Girard's theory of original violence and scapegoating— the scapegoat being in some "extraordinary" way "different"—can be taken as a version of *claims of difference in the absence of its givenness.* There may not have been, as Renato Rosaldo warns us, that original social chaos, disorganization, disruption, disturbance which provokes scapegoating as the imposition of radical difference for Girard.[49] But it is hard to visualize "culture contacts" without forms of pressure through which confusedly perceived "differences" are pushed into fictitious clarity. And I would like to follow Burkert in his assumption that elementary and seemingly highly distinctive forms of any culture, its rituals, are not so much "expressions" of some cultural core. They are rather, to some extent, institutionalized fictions invested with "as-if" qualities to fill out, by mythical designations, the threat of cultural void. From there, culturally distinctive but basically unstable religions derive—not the other way around, where one would derive the necessity of ritual as an illustration or enactment of dogma.[50] Thus, if institutions are constructed to allow an always threatened cultural continuity to come into existence, Smith rightly questions "whether there are institutions that don't wink at all." He gives the example of the Ainu (taken to be the aborigines of Japan) who, with respect to a bear ritual, say "they actually nurse the bear. Now, surely they say yes, and surely they say no."[51]

A referentializing type of cultural description has come to dominate, it seems, because we tend to forget that cultural institutions can only be taken with a wink. But, on the other hand, even if we or cultural institutions wink at our-/themselves, fictitious and real gaps and differences do not simply vanish. A *decisionistic logic of cultural distinctions* will have to allow for *selective and hypothetical rereferentializations*. There is no discourse, though, to tell us beforehand when and how, and on which levels of our cognitive and psychic apparatus, of social or economic organization, distinctions are then made and imposed. Japanese culture, baffling and enigmatic once one tries to nail it down with descriptive consistency, may be taken as perhaps a very clear example of the *simultaneity of the absent* and the *fabricated*, the assiduously, studiously *cherished cultural core*.

I would assume, without holding strong beliefs on the matter, that there are explanatory plausibilities that may account for the types of pressure responsible for the Japanese situation. We may talk about a "natural" isolation of the islands (which went so far that for a long time even the northern island of Hokkaido was almost ignored), reinforced by an unusual absence of foreign wars over long periods.[52] This may have prompted feelings of both domestic, psychosocial security and protectiveness, anxiety with respect to the foreign cultures somewhere "out there," both an overemphasis of self-definition (*Nihonron*, *seishin*, the Japanese spirit) as well as its apparent counterpart, that insatiable curiousity—a curiosity so overriding so as to brush aside western concerns of consistency (the glaring example here being the coexistence and copractice of Shintoism, Buddhism, Christianity, and possibly more). Different standards of consistency may indeed have encouraged Japanese "philosophical" comparative studies in the relations between climate, culture, and rationality. Discredited as such approaches may have been after the eighteenth century in the West, they still seem to "teach" a lot not just about differences between the East and West, but for instance between the cultures of northern and southern Europe itself. Ben-Dasan invokes the seasonally regular pressures of a campaign-style agriculture based on rice in order to "understand" the Japanese sense of precise timing and long-term planning. With its concomitant work ethic (supported from other sources as well), this may go a long way to explain Japanese *economic* success *culturally*.[53]

We might talk of the perennial population pressures in Japan, thus explaining what looks like a culture of conformity, duty, and shame—but also a culture of social lubrication where "natural" feelings are important, although rarely "expressed" (and where, therefore, the relations between encoding and existence may take on very different forms).

Whatever we may think of that type of explanation, the very *texts of Japanese culture*, in which self-description is provoked by the voluntary or enforced observation of the other, formulate the *complementarity of radical otherness and vanishing difference* quite clearly. I am not able, unfortunately, to explore this with respect to what remains perhaps the most striking example of a *Japanese use of otherness in the service of identity*: writing. Pressures to introduce writing made the Japanese turn to the Chinese writing system. This would have been a highly unlikely move in any functional linguistic or cultural system. In terms of grammar, word formation, and so on, Chinese and Japanese are utterly dissimilar. A blending, then, occurred that would be "comparable to the result you might get if you decided to write English in Arabic script and to create compound words in spoken English by jamming together three or four syllables from medieval Arabic." For each of the roughly 1800 *kanji* (much reduced from the tens of thousands that exist theoretically) still in use, multiple pronunciations have to be learned, thus handling both the Chinese and Japanese words and syllables for which they are used. To make the situation stranger, the Chinese system, though extremely work-intensive, does not suffice. The Japanese use two more phonetic scripts of 48 symbols each dealing with inflections and connectives which do not exist in Chinese, as well as foreign names and places. From a Japanese point of view, Chinese writing ought to have represented extreme otherness. Yet it was and continues to be used for "genuinely" Japanese purposes. Given the huge amount of time and energy to be invested, it might be preserved (also, if not exclusively) for the reason that it "feeds the cherished Japanese sense of belonging to a unique and impenetrable culture."[54]

Keene has printed excerpts from the writings of Honda Toshiaki (1744–1821) in which Honda complains about, among other things, the uselessness of Japanese writing, appropriate only for "idle and elegant pursuits," not for the "recording of facts and opinions."[55] But Honda's plea for western writing may be, again, nothing more than another effort to put difference to the service of an opaque, centerless identity. Keene notes somewhat disapprovingly that Honda's admiration for the West "was always tempered by his fear that the foreigners might learn too much about Japan, and he showed himself more partial to isolationism than we would expect of so progressive a man."[56] Reading Keene's book about the Japanese "discovery" of Europe from 1720 to 1830, one is struck, above all, by the impression that, whatever the so-called cultural realities of Europe and Japan might have been, the pressures they exercised led to the *interchangeability* of "imitation" and "isolation" (i.e., identity) for Japanese culture itself.[57]

It does not help much, I think, to try and apply the jargon of systems theory to that situation—tempted as we may be to enjoy the identity and difference of identity and difference. Comparisons, however, do form part of deeply anchored intuitions. Their rephrasing, then, in terms of hypothetical rereferentializations of cultural openness under pressure may not be totally inappropriate. It is intended not only to make assertions of identity and difference more difficult, if not impossible (at least in their usual form). It should also signal caution with respect to talk about a global world culture, that degenerate form of what in former times was labeled cosmopolitanism. Sladen's remark of 1903—that Japan had become more western than the West itself, an impression certainly shared by many people strolling through the fashionable quarters of Tokyo today—is, in several senses, both true and false. In any case, it is deceptive because it remains chained to the seemingly simple point of view of the "observer." That concept may have been sanctioned by cultural anthropology and reinforced by systems theory. It may possess some epistemological and even "natural" plausibility. Still, it is a partly unfortunate concept. It distracts from the question to what extent cultures should be seen not only as objects of established descriptive or observational habits, but as loosely organized spaces for the negotiation of behavior and, by extension, of ranges of cognitive and affective orientation. For that, concepts of *cultural styles* might do better than latent or open notions of cultural meanings out there to be translated in situations of cultural contact. The negotiation of styles will not produce structures of meaning, but semipermanent, semitransitory patterns. Patterns certainly are potentials for meaning. But the amount of consistency meanings-in-situations may acquire to justify ordinary notions of culture is a matter for case studies. Cultural practices in Japan *may* provide examples for that, too.

J. D. Hodgson, former U.S. ambassador to Japan, has said: "It has been my experience that if you try to accommodate the Japanese in matters of style, they will try to accommodate you in matters of substance."[58] Cultural styles may be regarded as the conceptual successors to the *formalism* of cultural rules which—to risk a last rereferentialization—the West seems to have given up in favor of depth-interpretations of cultural meanings and values. Japanese cultural styles, on the other hand, might be seen as the negotiation, embodiment, as the implicit, therefore successful, preservation of norms.

MODELS OF
RELATIONSHIP

Border Crossings, Translating Theory: Ruth

J. Hillis Miller

Bless thee, Bottom, thou art translated!
—*A Midsummer Night's Dream*

*T*ranslation": the word means, etymologically, "carried from one place to another," transported across the borders between one language and another, one country and another, one culture and another. This, of course, echoes the etymology of "metaphor." A translation is a species of extended metaphorical equivalent in another language of an "original" text. The German words for "translation" mean the same thing: *Übertragung, Übersetzung*, "carried over" and "set over," as though what is written in one language were picked up, carried over, and set down in another place.

A work is, in a sense, "translated," that is, displaced, transported, carried across, even when it is read in its original language by someone who belongs to another country and another culture or to another discipline. In my own case, what I made, when I first read it, of Georges Poulet's work and, later on, of Jacques Derrida's work was no doubt something that would have seemed more than a little strange to them, even though I could read them in French. Though I read them in their original language, I nevertheless "translated" Poulet and Derrida into my own idiom. In doing so I made them useful for my own work in teaching and writing about English literature within my own particular American university context. This context was quite different from the European intellectual contexts within which Poulet and Derrida write. If what I did with their work would have seemed strange to them could they have known about it, something not quite what they had in mind when they wrote the works in question, I might feel the same if I could know what those who read my work in a language I do not know, for example, Chinese or Romanian, are making of it. Any words in any language, but perhaps especially within literary studies, works of theory, may be translated in this way to a different context and be appropriated there for new uses. Just how this can be and what it means for literary theory is itself a difficult theoretical question.

The most important event of the last 30 years in North American literary study is no doubt the assimilation, domestication, and transformation of European theory. This includes theory of many kinds: phenomenological, Lacanian, Marxist, Foucauldian, Derridean, and so on. This crossing of borders has been an interdisciplinary event through and through. This event has fundamentally transformed literary study in the United States from what it was when I began such study 45 years ago. Now the same thing is happening throughout the world, with both European and North American literary theory. This happening is in many ways extremely problematic. Just what is involved? Is it a good thing or a bad thing? These days, in the fields of literary and cultural studies, theory "travels" everywhere, to allude to the title of an essay by Edward Said: "Travelling Theory." In a recent lecture given at the Humanities Research Institute of the University of California, located in Irvine, he has spoken eloquently of another example, the influence of Lukács on Fanon:[1] *The Wretched of the Earth*, says Said, would not be what it is without Fanon's reading of Lukács, though Lukács did not at all have the Algerian struggle for independence in mind when he wrote *The History of Class Consciousness*. North American and European theoretical works are being translated and assimilated within many different languages and cultures: in the Far East, in Latin America, in Russia and other parts of Eastern Europe, in Australia, in Africa, and in India. In each place, of course, such translation takes place in a different way, at a different pace, and according to different protocols.

Just why it should be literary theory that seems to be carried over so easily, that crosses borders with such facility, is not immediately clear. Nor is it quite clear what it means that literary theory originally developed in Europe and the United States should now be traveling everywhere in the world, often by way of its North American versions. Why is this happening? Is it because theory is conceptual and generalized, therefore applicable in any context and to works in any language and within the local topography of any culture and time? Theory would, it might seem, in this differ from pedagogical techniques or specific readings of specific works. The latter are tied to particular sites and situations. Therefore they do not translate well or "travel" well, as they say of certain delicate wines that are best drunk where they are made. Literary theory, on the other hand, is like the vacuum-sealed box wines that travel anywhere and keep for a long time even after they are opened.

But, metaphorical joking aside, what exactly, literally, is literary theory anyway? We all think we know what it is, but this may be a mistake, possibly even a theoretical mistake. Even though we all think we know what theory is, it may be the essence of literary theory to resist definition. As Paul de Man puts this in a rather chilling formulation, "the main theoretical interest of literary theory consists in the impossibility of its definition."[2] What in the world does this mean? Why cannot literary theory, like almost anything else, be defined? If it were true that theory cannot be defined, it would not be altogether certain that literary theory could be institutionalized in scholarship and pedagogical practice so easily and so successfully as seems to have been the case in the United States with Continental theory, and as seems to be the case around the world now with North American literary theory. If it is not theory that is spreading everywhere, what is it that masquerades under that name? What I have elsewhere called the "triumph of theory" may be the triumph of mystified misunderstandings of the theories in question. That would make the triumph of theory another unconscious form of the resistance to theory. This different form would not be the loud and uncomprehending hostility to theory by those who have never read it that is so evident in American journalism today, but rather an unintentional betrayal of theory by those who have the warmest feelings toward it, who teach courses about it and attempt to "apply" it in teaching and writing. Just what that possibility might mean for the translation and assimilation of western theory in nonwestern countries is not immediately clear. This essay tries to confront that question.

It is conceivable that true literary theory, the real right thing, may be impossible to teach or to use in practical criticism. Theory may be impossible to translate in all the senses of that word, that is, impossible to transfer to another context, for example, another language. *Traduttore, traditore*: this (untranslatable)[3] Italian saying may be "true in spades," as they say, for literary theory, to use another perhaps untranslatable idiom. To translate theory is to traduce it, to betray it. Nevertheless, something called theory is now being translated from the United States all over the world. How does this happen?

The analogy between the exportation of theory and the spread of western technology is appealing, but does the analogy hold? Technology is tied to the culture of its country of origin in quite a different way from the way

literary theory is tied to its sources. There can be no doubt that technological innovations transform cultures. Walter Benjamin has argued this persuasively for photography and film in a famous essay, "Das Kunstwerk im
Zeitalter seiner technischen Reproduzierbarkeit" ("The Work of Art in the
Age of Mechanical Reproduction").[4] Photography and cinema have been
followed by transistor radios, television, jet planes, tape players, CDs,
VCRs, and personal computers as potent agents of cultural change. It
sometimes seems as if we are rapidly moving toward a single, worldwide
culture of blue jeans, portable radios, and tape players, in which everyone
is tied to everyone else by FAX machines and electronic mail.[5] Such a single,
universal culture might have the good effect of ultimately making nationalist wars obsolete, though we might have to wait a long time for that. But
having a single worldwide technological culture is likely to have bad effects
too. Benjamin defined one of these as a loss of "aura" in the artwork in
modern times. We might generalize the effect of modern communication
technologies as the weakening and uprooting of local cultural differences
everywhere, as much in my New England or California as, for example, in
Taiwan or Brazil. Such technologies are exported to nonwestern countries
to transform them into the West's own semblance, even though those nonwestern countries, like Taiwan or Japan, may outdo the United States in
innovative skill in the development of these technologies.[6]

Does literary theory participate in this uprooting and hasten it? Is literary theory no more than another western technological device, like the
jet engine, television and computer technology, or the atomic bomb? I do
not think so. Even though television and computer technology, for example, to some degree determine the uses that are made of them, as Benjamin argued for photography and film, nevertheless they are also in another sense neutral. They can be used in many different ways within a local
culture, turning it into new forms of itself, no doubt, but still into forms
of itself. It is to some degree adventitious that these technologies come
bringing western popular music, films, and videos to nonwestern countries. They can also be used, and are being used, for local filmmaking or
for recording the popular or traditional music of nonwestern countries.
Literary theory, on the other hand, in spite of its high degree of apodictic
generalization, is tied, perhaps even inextricably tied, to the language and
culture of its country of origin. Though theory might seem to be as impersonal and universal as any technological innovation, in fact it grows from
one particular place, time, culture, and language. It remains tied to that
place and language. Theory, when it is translated or transported, when it
crosses a border, comes bringing the culture of its originator with it. Quite

extraordinary feats of translation are necessary to disentangle a given theoretical formulation from its linguistic and cultural roots, assuming anyone should wish to do that. In fact, it may be impossible to do it. Those who seek to assimilate a foreign theory and put it to new, indigenous uses may have imported something like a Trojan horse or something like one of those computer viruses that turn resident programs to their own alien and disruptive uses. Just because a literary theory is *not* like a western technological innovation, it may be more dangerous, not just one more tool of industrialization but a bringer of an even more profound cultural change.

How may it be that theory cannot be translated? Paul de Man, after having said that literary theory is impossible to define, goes on a couple of pages later in the same essay not so much to define literary theory as to identify the conditions under which it arises. Though theory may not be defined, one thing about it is sure, according to de Man: it arises not through abstract speculation, but in concrete, empirical situations. It arises from a certain way of "approaching" specific literary texts. Literary theory is born, that is, from a certain kind of reading. It arises from reading that attends not to themes and meanings but to the question of how themes and meaning come to be. "Literary theory," says de Man, "can be said to come into being when the approach to literary texts is no longer based on nonlinguistic, that is to say historical and aesthetic, considerations, or, to put it somewhat less crudely, when the object of discussion is no longer the meaning or the value but the modalities of production and of reception of meaning and value prior to their establishment—the implication being that this establishment is problematic enough to require an autonomous discipline of critical investigation to consider its possibility and its status."[7] Whatever literary theory may be, according to de Man, it focuses on the power language has to generate meaning and value. "Meaning" here goes with "historical," while "aesthetic" goes with "value." The generation of meaning by literature is a historical event. The ascription of value is an aesthetic event. Literature is made of words and of nothing but words. Whatever power it has to reflect social and material reality or to make something happen in individual and social life arises from some potency in language or transmitted through language. It follows that literary theory must be language about language, in one way or another a branch of rhetoric, though rhetoric must be taken here to include also rhythmical and material aspects of language, as well as overt tropes. The focus of literary theory, to put this another way, must be on the performative powers of language, not on nonlinguistic, that is to say historical and aesthetic, considerations. De Man does not say historical and aesthetic considerations are not worthy of investigation. He just says literary theory should concern itself with the way literature generates these, not take them as givens to be explored in themselves. If literature, as one cultural artifact among many others, is to be approached theoretically, that theory must concern itself with the way specific literary works use words to change history, society, and individual lives, that is, to generate "meaning" and "value."

I have said that literary theory may be untranslatable because it cannot be detached from the local topographies of its source. Two forms of this cultural specificity or idiomatic quality of literary theory may be identified. One is the untranslatability of the conceptual words that form the core of the given theory. Examples would be the word "allegory" as Samuel Taylor Coleridge, Friedrich Schlegel, John Ruskin, Walter Pater, Marcel Proust, Walter Benjamin, Paul de Man, and I use it, or the word *Erscheinung* as used by Benjamin, or the words "parasite" and "host" as I use them in "The Critic as Host." Each of these words has a long history within western culture and cannot easily be detached from that history. That history is the history of chief previous uses of the word. *Erscheinung*, for example, means in German "appearance," or, more literally, "shining forth." "Appearance" can be said in more or less any language. But the word *Erscheinung* also carries with it, for example, the uses made of it by Hegel in his *Lectures on Aesthetics*. To use the word may be to make an allusion to the concept of art within romanticism. My use of the word "parasite" echoes the complex uses of that word by Shelley. The word "allegory" has a long genealogy, not only the sequence of its uses within romanticism and post-romanticism indicated by the authors I have cited, but, before that, a manifold history going back to the Greeks and the Christian exegetes of the Bible. Every influential work of contemporary western literary theory turns on such complex conceptual words, words that carry with them a silent history.

But western literary theory is tied to its cultural and linguistic origins in another quite different and apparently opposite way. There is no work of theory without examples. The examples are essential to the theory. The theory cannot be fully understood without the examples. These examples tie the theory not just to a specific language and culture, but to particular works within that culture. These works were themselves rooted in a particular time and place. To put this another way, literary theory is always a reading of some specific work or works. The relation of theory to reading is itself a difficult theoretical question. Though there is no theory without reading, theory and reading are asymmetrical. Reading always alters, disqualifies, or puts in question the theory used to read it, while being essential to that theory's formulation. The examples J. L. Austin gives in the course of developing his theory of performative speech acts in *How to Do Things with Words* qualify and even undermine his theoretical formulations, though the distinction Austin makes between performative and constative language cannot be understood without the examples. When the work of Jacques Derrida and Paul de Man, or my own work, is reduced to abstract theoretical formulations, it is often forgotten that those formulations in every case are attained by an act of reading. Derrida's reading of Mallarmé, for example, is the essential context of his notion of "dissemination," just as his reading of Paul Celan is the essential context of his theory in *Schibboleth* of what in a given language may not be translated. De Man's reading of Rousseau's *Julie* is essential to his mature notion of allegory. His reading of the word "fall" in Keats's *The Fall of Hyperion* is essential to his theoretical positings in "The Resistance to Theory." Passages from Thackeray, Shelley, and others are essential for my notion that the relation of parasite to host may figure the relation of critic to text. What I shall say later on here about the book of Ruth in the Bible is essential to the theoretical argument I am making in this chapter. To understand what Derrida means by dissemination you must read Mallarmé or at least read carefully Derrida's reading of Mallarmé. To understand what de Man means by allegory you must read de Man's reading of Rousseau. To understand what I mean by saying the critic is a "host," you must take into account what I say about my examples, even though I read them in relation to general theoretical clarifications to which the act of reading might lead. To understand this chapter you must take into account what I say about the book of Ruth.

Does this mean the works of theory cannot be translated, cannot be transported across the borders into a new country and a new language or into a new discipline to be effective there? On the contrary, I think such translation is entirely possible. It happens every day. I certainly hope it will happen with work of mine translated into various languages. Just as I can get on a jet plane in Los Angeles and find myself a few hours later almost anywhere in the world, in Taipei, Jerusalem, or Brasília, without much sensation of crossing a border, so works of theory nowadays are often translated and the translation published even before they appear in their original languages. But the difficulty of understanding just what is at stake in such translation should not be underestimated. The fact that border crossings and translations happen so rapidly nowadays may mislead us about what happens in translation. This is particularly the case when what is in question is translation into a language so rich, so different from English, and with such a splendid literary and intellectual tradition as, for example, Chinese.

How does this translation happen? How do works of theory get a new start in a new language and within a new culture? Just how does this transfer "take place"? How does a work of theory cross borders, occupy a new territory, and make a new place for itself in a new language? I shall try to explain this by telling a story. It is not my story but a very old one from the Hebrew Bible and the Christian Old Testament, the story of Ruth. The story will serve as an example of what I am talking about, since it has been translated into many different languages and cultures. As it happens, I can read it only in translation, not in the original Hebrew. Though it might persuasively be argued that this disqualifies me from saying anything valuable about the Book of Ruth, the fact that I try to do so anyway is an example of my theme: the possibility of translating texts, including theoretical ones, from one language, culture, or discipline to another. No translation can carry over all the subtleties of alliteration, anagrammatic echo, and repetition of words, motifs, and episodes, that organize this text in itself and also tie it by allusion to other parts of the Bible. All of the proper names in Ruth, for example, have conceptual meaning. The story also contains many references to Jewish law and custom, for example, the law of levirate marriage, or the custom that allowed the poor to gather stalks of corn left behind by the gleaners, though only two at a time. Ruth has been read in innumerable different ways over the centuries by millions of people. It is read aloud in synagogues on Shavuoth (Pentecost). Ruth carries with it, like every other book of the Bible, an immense history of interpretation and commentary in both the Jewish and Christian traditions.[8] I propose to see it, somewhat playfully, as an allegory of the traveling of theory from one cultural site to another, one language to another. To propose this allegorical reading adds one reading more to all the readings and translations that have gone before. Taking what in Protestantism is called "latitude of interpretation," I add another allegorical or, to use a more biblical word, "parabolic" reading to all the readings of Ruth. In doing that, you will note, I "translate" or transpose the text once more into a different context, that of my own theoretical research. There is much precedent within Christianity for parabolic or allegorical readings of texts from the Hebrew Bible or Old Testament, though not, of course, for quite the one I shall propose. A parabolic meaning by no means hollows out the historical, referential, or "realistic" meaning. Rather the allegory depends on the literal meaning.

The Book of Ruth tells a story of assimilation, the assimilation, one might almost say, the "translation," of a Moabite woman into Israelite culture during the time of the judges. This was some time in the latter part of the second millennium before Christ. Though every verse of this admirably economical and circumstantial text counts, the story can be quickly told. A famine has led a man of Bethlehem-Judah, Elimelech, to leave the land of Judah for the country of Moab. He dies and his two sons, Mahlon and Chilion, die, leaving his wife, Naomi, alone with two Moabite daughters-in-law. The famine passes and one of the daughters-in-law, Ruth, chooses to follow Naomi back home to Bethlehem. She utters the famous promise that foreswears her Moabite citizenship, so to speak, and decides for Israelite citizenship. I cite the King James translation, the one with most resonance for me: "Intreat me not to leave thee, or to return from following after thee: for whither thou goest, I will go; and where thou lodgest, I will lodge: thy people shall be my people, and thy God my God: where thou diest, will I die, and there will I be buried: the Lord do so to me, and more also, if ought but death part thee and me" (Ruth 1.16–17). Ruth's promise is an oath of allegiance. It is a powerful speech act dividing her life in two. She swears by the new God under whose judgment her speech act places her. Nothing is said about the language in which this promise is uttered. Hebrew and Moabite were apparently so similar as to be essentially the same language. Nevertheless, there may have been differences in pronunciation that would have marked Ruth as an alien.⁹ She was, in any case, submitting herself proleptically to the laws and customs of a new country. To be able to make a promise or swear an oath within a new culture is already to have changed oneself into another person.

In Judah Ruth goes then, again on her own initiative, to glean in barley and wheat fields belonging to Boaz, a powerful kinsman of her father-in-law. Boaz notices her. He encourages her to go on working in the fields, feeds her, and protects her from being "touched" by the young men who are harvesting: "Have I not charged the young men that they shall not touch thee?" (2.9). Harvest was a time when young men and women worked together in the fields and therefore a time of possible sexual license, as it still was in Thomas Hardy's England. Finally, after the harvest is over, following her mother-in-law's advice, Ruth uncovers Boaz's feet as he lies sleeping on the threshing floor "at the end of a heap of corn" (3.7) after a day of winnowing barley. She places herself at his uncovered feet. Later in the night, he wakes up, finds her, and promises to take her into his keeping.

The English version and the Midrashic and Rabbinical commentaries seem to agree that Ruth and Boaz do not sleep together, even though he does do what she asks: "spread therefore thy skirt over thine handmaid; for thou art a near kinsman" (3.9). The text says she rose up before they could recognize one another, that is, while it was still dark: "And she lay at his feet until the morning; and she rose up before one could know another. And he said, Let it not be known that a woman came into the floor" (3.14).

The next day, before ten elders of the city, Boaz offers, as by custom he must, to a still nearer kinsman of Elimelech the chance to "redeem" Elimelech's land, making it clear that this will mean also taking responsibility for Ruth. Here the law of levirate marriage (Deuteronomy 25.5–10) is implicitly invoked. This law declared that if a married man dies, his brother must marry his widow in order to keep his line or "inheritance" alive, to "raise up his seed." If not the brother, then another near kinsman. The other kinsman is Ruth's father-in-law's brother, her dead husband's uncle, while Boaz is one step further removed, that is, Ruth's father-in-law's nephew, her dead husband's cousin. This other kinsman, who is called only "so and so" (*Peloni Almoni* in Hebrew), refuses, so Boaz buys the land and Ruth along with it.

The transfer of land is confirmed when Boaz (or perhaps the kinsman) takes off his shoe and gives it to the kinsman.[10] Apparently by the time the story was written down, the custom was already archaic, since the text has to explain it: "Now this was the manner in former time in Israel concerning redeeming and concerning changing, for to confirm all things; a man plucked off his shoe, and gave it to his neighbour: and this was a testimony in Israel. Therefore the kinsman said unto Boaz, Buy it for thee. So he drew off his shoe. And Boaz said unto the elders, and unto all the people; Ye are witnesses this day, that I have bought all that was Elimelech's, and all that was Chilion's and Mahlon's, of the hand of Naomi. Moreover, Ruth the Moabitess, the wife of Mahlon, have I purchased to be my wife, to raise up the name of the dead upon his inheritance, that the name of the dead be not cut off from among his brethren, and from the gate of his place: ye are witnesses this day" (4.7–10). The shoe here functions as a kind of silent speech act sealing the bargain. It may have signified the power to pace out the land being transferred, measuring it by the foot, so to speak, but it has further curious resonances and implications. It is an act of graceful obeisance. To take off one shoe and give it away renders you less capable of walking, more vulnerable, just as a cowboy in a western film is vulnerable when he takes off his gun holster when entering a saloon. To give a person one of your shoes to seal a bargain is somewhat analogous to a familiar idiom in English: "I'd give you the shirt off my back." A "symbol" for the Greeks was originally an object broken and divided between two people that would confirm some commitment when the two halves were again fitted together ("thrown together," in the literal meaning of *symbolon*). In a somewhat similar way, dividing a pair of shoes between two persons confirms a bond between them. The shoe, a means of walking safely from one place to another, becomes the sign of the transfer of property from one person to another, its "changing," as the Bible says, or its "translation," as we might almost say.

The Hebrew term for Boaz's repossessing of Elimelech's land for its proper family is translated as "redeem." As any member of a farming family knows, a field is a most precious possession. Its transfer from one family to another is a major event. Such a transfer is analogous to the expansion of the territorial borders of a nation or to the change of a person from one citizenship to another. As Ruth ceases to be a Moabitess and becomes an Israelite, so Elimelech's land is redeemed for Elimelech's inheritance, and so Elimelech's genealogical line is maintained through Ruth's marriage to Boaz. Topographical distinctions are powerful carriers of meaning in this story: Moab as against Judah; Boaz's fields as against other fields; Elimelech's land unredeemed and then redeemed. The story is organized around the crossing of borders and the establishment of territorial rights. Movements of going, crossing borders, returning, and transferring tie one aspect of the story to others and underlie it as a structural matrix.

Ruth then marries Boaz and becomes the mother of Obed. Naomi nurses the child. It is in effect a child of her own, a son to carry on Elimelech's family after the death of her two sons. The last verses of Ruth tell the reader why the birth of Obed is important. They give the clue as to why this story became part of sacred scripture: "And Obed begat Jesse, and Jesse begat David" (4.22). The assimilation of Ruth the Moabitess into Israelite society was essential to the carrying on of Elimelech's bloodline. More important, it was essential to the sequence of generations that led first to King David, an essential actor in the Old Testament or Hebrew Bible story, and, for a Christian, ultimately to Jesus himself. Jesus came of the house of Jesse and David, as the elaborate genealogy at the beginning of Matthew specifies. Without Ruth, the alien, the Moabitess, there would have been no David and no Jesus, so her story must be told.

As Sir Edmund Leach has argued in a brilliant article about the genealogies in the Old Testament, far from being a somewhat boring series of adventitious "begats," these genealogies have a crucial function.[11] They testify to the continuity of Israelite culture. Its unbroken tradition is demonstrated by the continuity of its bloodlines. Beyond that, the genealogies show that there has been just the right balance of endogamy and exogamy. Too much endogamy or intermarriage is a kind of incest, leading to a weakening of the bloodlines. Too much exogamy or miscegenation would cause the purity of Israelite blood to thin out and vanish. Moabites, from the Israelite point of view, were outlandish barbarians, infamous for having refused to feed the Israelites when they were returning from Egypt to the promised land. To assimilate a Moabitess into the lineage of Israelite kings was no small thing. There must be just the right amount of marriage outside the tribe, just enough and no more, just as there must be at certain crucial points in Old Testament history something approaching incest. The commentators on the Book of Ruth often see Ruth as parallel to Leah and Rachel, also to Tamar, following the lead of Ruth 4.11–12, in which the witnesses say to Boaz: "The Lord make the woman that is come into thine house like Rachel and like Leah, which two did build the house of Israel. . . . And let thy house be like the house of Pharez, whom Tamar bare unto Judah, of the seed which the Lord shall give thee of this young woman." Just as Jacob was tricked by Laban into marrying Leah in addition to Rachel, thereby becoming father of the twelve tribes of Israel, so Tamar, disguised as a harlot, seduced her father-in-law, Judah, thereby becoming the mother of Pharez, direct ancestor of Boaz, therefore of David and, for Jews, of the Messiah to come, for Christians, of Jesus of Nazareth (Genesis 29.20–28; Genesis 38).

The story of Ruth is a strong confirmation of Leach's theory. For a time, before Ruth crossed the border from Moab into Israel, the whole of sacred history hung in the balance. Unless Ruth had made her decision and uttered her promise, "whither thou goest, I will go," that history could not have gone forward. Nevertheless, Ruth can hardly have made her decision in order to become the great-grandmother of King David and the many times great-grandmother of Jesus. A parallel would be the way Leda, in Yeats's "Leda and the Swan," could not know, as Zeus presumably did, that her rape would lead to two great cycles of stories in Greek mythology, the Trojan war and the story of Agamemnon. Yeats poses this as a question: "Did she put on his knowledge with his power . . . ?" The answer if the question is taken literally must be "no," though in the violence done to her by the intervention of the god's power she certainly learned something of what future Greek history would be like. Ruth's ignorance of the future when she makes her oath of allegiance to Naomi exemplifies an important feature of performative speech acts. In them, knowing and doing are never congruent. A speech act makes something happen, all right. It is a way of doing things with words, but just what will happen can never be clearly and exactly foreseen.

The story of Ruth can be taken as a parable of the translation of theory. In such a parabolic reading, Ruth the Moabitess is a figure of traveling theory. Whatever her original language and culture may have been, she can cross the border into Israel and be assimilated there only by translating herself, so to speak, or being translated, into the idiom of the new culture. She becomes a proper wife and mother among the Israelites. Nevertheless, she brings something of her own, something that resists full translation and assimilation. The decision to follow Naomi was her own. She shows great enterprise in putting herself in Boaz's way. Much of the initiative that makes the story happen is her own. Ruth is shown as an attractively strong-willed young woman, with a mind of her own. She is someone very much in charge of her own life. Whatever the commentators say, she does not seem simply the passive instrument of a historical or divine purpose that exceeds her and that makes use of her to gain its own ends. In a similar way, literary theory has its own stubborn and recalcitrant particularity. Its reliance on examples and its pivoting on the reinscription of conceptual words that have a long history tie it to its language and culture of origin. Nevertheless, it opens itself to assimilation within other cultures and languages. Like Ruth, it is prepared to say, "whither thou goest, I will go." Naomi, nevertheless, as Ziva Ben-Porat has observed,[12] plays an important role in the story. She serves as the mediator introducing Ruth to a new country and a new life. She tells Ruth how to behave in approaching Boaz. In my parabolic reading she would represent the necessary transmitter of theory, the teacher or translator who turns the alien theory into something that can be understood, transformed, and assimilated in the new place. In a new country a theory, like Ruth, is put to new uses that cannot be foreseen. These uses are an alienation of the theory, its translation into a new idiom, and its appropriation for new, indigenous purposes. Ruth's story is told from an Israelite point of view. What matters to those in Judah is the continuity and vitality of their own cultural heritage. They assimilate the alien, making the different into the same, but at the same time changing that same, in order to ensure that vitality, just as works of traveling theory are transformed in the new country or in a new discipline. In the new place a theory is made use of in ways the theory never intended or allowed for, though it also transforms the culture or discipline it enters. When theory crosses borders it is translated in the sense that Puck fits Bottom out with an ass's head in Shakespeare's *A Midsummer Night's Dream*. When theory travels it is disfigured, deformed, "translated."

To figure theory as the feminine within a strongly patriarchal culture reverses the usual gender ascription that sees theory as the product of a male will to mastery, even as the product of a western white male will to mastery over women, minorities, and the subject peoples of "other" cultures. My reversal of that is congruent with my claim that theory is in a complex relation to reading and to a given nation's cultural projects, a relation that might better be figured as the relation of woman to man, rather than that of man to woman. That the issues of gender and gender relations should arise in a discussion of something that initially seems to have nothing to do with them is in accordance with a general law. All our thinking is in one way or another gendered, even when it seems most removed from gender questions.

I have said that when theory travels it is deformed, "translated." This can be seen not only in Ruth's story but in what has happened to the text of Ruth. Ruth is itself a theoretical text. It exemplifies in schematic narrative form a set of theoretical presuppositions about Israelite culture at that time: the form and functions of promises, oaths, and nonverbal gestures like removing and giving a shoe; the subservience of women to the function of keeping a name and an inheritance alive, so that a woman can be "purchased" and has value just as a piece of land on which barley or wheat can be grown has value; certain complex assumptions about endogamy and exogamy in relation to the vitality and persistence through history of Israelite culture; a strong sense of territoriality. Theory here goes with example, but the example always exceeds and is to some degree incongruent with the theory, just as the independence and individual enterprise of Ruth, the pathos of her story, exceeds and to some degree contradicts the theoretical assumptions about genealogy and inheritance the story was written to exemplify. In a similar way my account of Ruth exceeds the theoretical uses to which I put my reading and to some degree goes counter to them.

If Ruth's story is a narrative of alienation and assimilation that can exemplify theoretical propositions about the travel of theory, what has happened to the text of Ruth (as opposed to what happens within the story) is also exemplary of the fate of theory. This book of the Hebrew Bible has been alienated from itself, translated from itself. It has been put to entirely new uses, uses by no means intended by the original authors or scribes. The first and most significant alienation (after all the changes that made the story of Ruth a sacred text in the Hebrew Bible) was, of course, the

assimilation of Ruth into the Christian Bible in all its subsequent translations, first into the pre-Christian Greek Septuagint, then into the Latin
Vulgate, then into almost innumerable vernacular languages. The original
writer or writers of Ruth had no intention of using it as a means of legit-
imating the claim of Jesus to be the Messiah. That, nevertheless, is its "theoretical" function in the Christian Bible. In coming to perform this function Ruth has been alienated from itself. It has been translated in the strong
sense of that word. Harold Bloom's way of putting this is to say that the
New Testament in its relation to the Hebrew Bible is the most outrageous
example of "misprision" in the history of the West, that is, of "mistakings"
or takings amiss, translations as mistranslation.

Ruth is a powerful text. Like a strong theoretical insight, it sticks in the
mind and invites further applications. Ruth has opened itself to many other
striking but less historically decisive misprisions. I shall mention only two.

One is the English folk tradition of *Sortes Sanctorum* (Latin for Oracles
of the Holy Writings) on Valentine's Day, described in detail in chapter 13
of Hardy's *Far From the Madding Crowd*. In this folk practice of divina-
tion by Bible and key, a young woman balances a Bible open at the first
chapter of Ruth on a long house key and repeats the verses beginning
"whither thou goest, I will go," while thinking about the man who attracts
her. If the Bible moves, then she will come to marry that man. This is a
mistranslation if there ever was one. The verses from the Bible are Ruth's
speech expressing her fidelity to Naomi, her mother-in-law. They have
nothing to do with her marriage to Boaz, except by unintentional prolep-
sis, since she has not even met or perhaps even heard of him yet. But the
words can be displaced with uncanny appropriateness to a new context in
which they fit perfectly. There they can have a new performative function.
This transposition is analogous to the way the "Wellerisms" in Dickens's
Pickwick Papers are forms of words that will have meaning in wildly different social contexts. It is also analogous to the way a theoretical formulation developed in the course of reading some specific work, such as
Derrida's idea of untranslatability in its relation to his reading of Celan,
may have a new effective function in an entirely new context. In the new
context it may assist in reading a work in a different language and social
situation. "Whither thou goest, I will go; and where thou lodgest, I will
lodge: thy people shall be my people, and thy God my God": this is just
what a young woman should say when she joins herself to her husband,
even though the words in their original context did not mean that at all.

Another mistranslation or violent appropriation of Ruth is those
hauntingly beautiful lines in Keats's "Ode to a Nightingale." Keats heard

the nightingale in a garden in Hampstead, a suburb of London. The poem speaks of the nightingale's song as something that has sounded the same in many different places and at many different times over the centuries. The nightingale's song ties Keats's own place and time to innumerable other places, times, and situations in which the nightingale's song has been heard. Thinking of this expands the poet's attention away from his preoccupation with his own suffering, limitation, and mortality to give him a virtual kinship with people in all those other places and times who have heard the nightingale. Hearing the nightingale is a momentary escape from the imminence of death, though also a way to experience the desire for death. Along with "ancient days" when the bird could be heard by "emperor and clown," and "magic casements, opening on the foam / Of perilous seas, in faery lands forlorn," as sites where the nightingale might have been heard, Keats includes Ruth gleaning barley in Boaz's field: "Perhaps the self-same song that found a path / Through the sad heart of Ruth, when, sick for home, / She stood in tears amid the alien corn" (ll. 64–70). This is very moving. It associates Ruth with Keats's general presentation of the human situation as forlorn, derelict, haunted by death, even "half in love with easeful Death" (l. 52). This pathos of alienation, however, has no biblical precedent. It is all Keats's invention. It is his translation, or mistranslation, of the story of Ruth for his own quite different purposes. Ruth in the Bible is not shown to have suffered one pang of homesickness for the country of Moab, nor to have dropped a single tear. In fact, her mind seems to be charmingly fixed on getting herself the best possible new husband in the new country. No nightingale is mentioned in Ruth. But just as a work of theory may be translated and put to entirely new uses, so the book of Ruth yields without apparent resistance to what Keats does with it.

I propose therefore what might be called the "Wellerism theory of traveling theory," taking the term from Dickens's *Pickwick Papers*. Just as "I'm pretty tough" fits Tony Weller's description of himself as a father contemplating the marriage of his son, but also might just as well be something "the wery old turkey remarked wen the farmer said he wos afeerd he should be obliged to kill him for the London market,"[13] so theoretical insights, though they are always generated in local acts of reading and have no use except in relation to acts of reading, can be transferred from their initial sites to innumerable other moments of reading in any language or discipline. But it is important to keep in mind the essential distortion involved in this translation, however scrupulously and accurately the theory is rendered in the new language. A theoretical formulation is a positing that can be effectively posited again or repositioned in many different situations and applied to many different texts or works in many media.

Theory's openness to translation is a result of the fact that a theory, in spite of appearances, is a performative, not a cognitive, use of language. The word "theory," which means "clear-seeing," seems to promise knowledge. Works of theory are nevertheless potent speech acts. A theory is a way of doing things with words, namely facilitating (or sometimes inhibiting) acts of reading. The performative words of the Christian marriage ceremony, "I pronounce you man and wife," are functional only in a given, unique marriage situation. They join just this man and this woman. Nevertheless, the same words can be used innumerable times to marry innumerable couples. In a similar way, though the formulations of literary theory originated in a unique act of reading, they can be effective in unpredictable new contexts. In those new contexts they enable, or perhaps distort, new acts of reading, even readings of works in languages the originator of the theory did not know. At the new site, giving an impetus to a new start, the theory will be radically transformed, even though the same form of words may still be used, translated as accurately as possible into the new language. If the theory is transformed by translation, it also to some degree transforms the culture or discipline it enters. The vitality of theory is to be open to such unforeseeable transformations and to bring them about as it crosses borders and is carried into new idioms.

The somewhat disturbing openness of theory to translation, its promiscuity, so to speak, reveals something essential about the original theory. Far from being a definitive expression of some way language or another kind of sign works, a theoretical formulation is always provisional and idiomatic, never wholly clear and never wholly satisfactory. The evidence for that is the way the formulation is amenable to having quite different effects in different contexts. A theoretical formulation never quite adequately expresses the insight that comes from reading.[14] That insight is always particular, local, good for this time, place, text, and act of reading only. The theoretical insight is a glimpse out of the corner of the eye of the way language works, a glimpse that is not wholly amenable to conceptualization. Another way to put this is to say that the theoretical formulation in its original language is already a translation or mistranslation of a lost original. This original can never be recovered because it never existed as anything articulated or able to be articulated in any language. Translations of theory are therefore mistranslations of mistranslations, not mistranslations of some authoritative and perspicuous original. This ought to cheer up those who translate theory and then use it performatively in a new situation. "Getting it right" no longer has the same urgency when it is seen to be impossible, though that by no means means we should not try our utmost to do so.

Cross-Culture, Chiasmus, and the Manifold of Mind

Sanford Budick

$\mathcal{C}$ an we picture an activity, or, let us say, a life function, of thinking together? What kind of thinking might this be called, in which the individual participant knows only part of what is being thought, indeed, does not even determine, or fully know, when a thought comes or goes? Assuming that knowing another—or getting to know another—is a significant part of what is called thinking, can we retrieve a picture of the joining together of our attempts to know and be known by another?[1]

These cannot be idle questions for an inquiry into the terms of a partnership of cultures. The possibility of sharing equally, and in equal measures of dependency, in the making of thought might well be fateful here. This is very likely the case, in fact, because if we once assign primacy or even independence of thought to any one agent in an alleged mutuality of cultures, we seem to have no option but to theorize such mutuality as, at best, a benevolent case of a master-slave relation. The fate of the slave in this relation could ultimately be no more than duplication of the master's mental life. In this relation even the cold comfort of a given slave's rebellion must prove to be merely illusory, not tragic, for the rebel's thinking could be performed only on the master's cue, however opposite to the slave's rebelliousness that cue might seem to be.

Where, I therefore ask again, might we find a picture of thinking shared by two individuals in one configuration of thinking? This would be a joint configuration such as Nietzsche himself—usually remembered for sharply distinguishing the thinking of master from slave—actually insisted must exist.[2] For a first glimpse of shared thinking I turn, in fact, to Nietzsche.

For Wolfgang Iser

Toward a Manifold of Mind

By enlarging upon a picture put on view by Goethe's Faust, Nietzsche reveals "manifold" minds—following Faust, he calls them "souls"—working in what may mistakenly be thought to be the unitary German mind: "The German soul is above all manifold, of diverse origins, put together and superimposed rather than actually constructed: the reason for that is its source. A German who would make bold to say 'two souls, alas, within my bosom dwell' would err very widely from the truth, more correctly he would fall short of the truth by a large number of souls."[3] Nietzsche challenges Faust's formula of only two souls in one by proceeding to "vivisect" the halves alleged for the German soul. He also does something more aggressive, first implicitly, then explicitly. He declares that even in the complex, divided mind of the most self-conscious German, obliviousness to the participation of certain minds, within the manifold, is a notable feature of the way the manifold thinks. Nietzsche will be highly circumstantial about this obliviousness, very possibly even pointing to the obliviousness of Goethe as well as his Faust. I will return to this possible accusation later on. But first I want to linger on the picture of the thinking manifold which Nietzsche scrutinizes in Goethe. Goethe provides Nietzsche's model, even if Nietzsche immeasurably deepens the model by recovering repressed minds within the manifold.

Nietzsche's reference to Faust's outburst is shorthand for an idea of a manifold of mind that is potent and recurring throughout Goethe's work and, I would especially emphasize, that Goethe regularly expresses in the rhetorical figure known as chiasmus. This is to say that in Goethe it is usual, or at least not uncommon, to find the elements of a manifold of mind as interactive binarisms in a relation of AB:BA. For example, in the case of Faust's declaration, which Nietzsche quotes in part, it may at first glance seem that Goethe offers the idea of a duplex mind and activates the figure of chiasmus merely to represent Faust in a pet of cross-purposes, saying, in effect, "In me two souls make one; one soul makes for two":

[A]   [B]
Zwei Seelen wohnen, ach!, in meiner Brust,
[B]   [A]
Die eine will sich von der andern trennen.
(Lines 1112–13)

Two souls dwell, alas, within my breast,
And each would separate from the other.[4]

Yet any doubt that Goethe is involved in a process of exploring—through
the form of chiasmus—the idea of the manifold mind is dispelled in advance by the closing couplet of the "Zueignung." Those signature verses
are Goethe's way of at least partially satisfying what he at first calls his
"längst entwöhntes Sehnen / Nach jenem stillen, ernsten Geisterreich"
(long forgotten yearning, / For the sweet solemn tryst those spirits keep)
(lines 25–26), as if in an elected affinity of minds of the living and minds
of the departed. The couplet that closes the "Zueignung" would super-
impose, that is, a manifold scene of thought which is quite similar to Faust's
spectacle of the two-halved soul, though it is also, in respect to other minds,
immensely different:

>   [A]   [B]
> Was ich besitze, seh ich wie im Weiten,
>   [B]   [A]
> Und was verschwand, wird mir zu Wirklichkeiten.
>   (Lines 31–32)

> All that I have stands off from me afar,
> And all I lost is real, my guiding-star.[5]

Here the manifold structure of the chiasmus includes participating frac-
tions which lie totally beyond the poet's ken, so that the work of the couplet
is to open up the possibility of precisely that affiliation with other minds—
outside a speaker's putative self—which his protagonist for the time being
refuses.

To enumerate the elements of this and other Goethean pictures of a
thinking together, I will principally focus on one distich near the close of
Torquato Tasso. This distich is spoken by Tasso at the moment he imagines
he has once again annihilated his world, this time by killing the Princess's
love for him. "Ist alles denn verloren?" (Is everything then lost?) he asks,
"Bin ich Nichts, / Ganz Nichts geworden?" (And have I become / A nothing, an absolute nothing?) (lines 3,409–16). The distich provides the complex answer:

> Nein, es ist alles da, und ich bin nichts;
> Ich bin mir selbst entwandt, sie ist es mir!

> No—it is all there still—and I am *nothing*.
> I am wrenched from myself, and she from me!
>   (Lines 3,417–18)[6]

This moment of Tasso's experience or consciousness is in fact the one I will
be meditating not only in Goethe's verses, but also in a particular distich
of Tasso's *Gerusalemme liberata* that Goethe (as we say) had in mind. To

grasp something of the significance of Goethe's distich (and Tasso's as well), we must refine our understanding of the potential of chiasmus for representing the manifold of mind in the act of thinking. I will try to suggest why chiasmus is necessarily the figure of a mind that cannot make up any kind of mind except by being beside itself, that is, by experiencing the inaccessibility of an undetermined other mind. The mental affiliations of chiasmus hang loose, open and magnetic, with a unique potentiality, which remains only a potentiality.[7]

Chiasmus in the Manifold of Mind

Occurrences of chiasmus are far more common than we may imagine. Handbooks of rhetorical terms principally say that chiasmus consists of a reversal of syntactic elements, or signs, which together form an X or *chi* in the pattern AB:BA. For one phase of chiasmus this is certainly true, and it is therefore legitimate to think of chiasmus in terms of antithesis or negation. Yet formally as well as historically considered, it is more accurate to say that a chiasmus is a movement of two sets of opposed signs (two binarisms) in which the pattern AB:BA is only one interim possibility. Because of the multiple meanings of all signs, any one reading (at a given juncture of possible combinations) of any sign—or syntactic element or binarism—is always to some extent an arbitrary decision. Within the fourfold network of signs, each binary term is always poised for a change of its sign (A into B, B into A). Henri Suhamy has recently emphasized this feature of shifting signs within the structure and movements of chiasmus. He notes that, in their mirror arrangement, the binary terms, passing from one syntactic element to the next, as much *reflect* as oppose each other.[8] This observation is useful, but a wholly different world of meanings for chiasmus is opened up by adding that the inherent doubleness of chiasmus necessarily leads beyond chiasmus itself: that is, the potential reversibility of all signs in any two pairs of binarisms can set the stage for the emergence of chiastic correspondences not only within any given individual's language but also, I would especially emphasize, in the potential chiastic relations between chiasma of different individuals who concur only in sharing materials for their symmetrical disagreement or difference. Given the interlinguistic and intertextual relations of all signs, these relations among chiasma do not simply form a class of rare birds. They are, rather, frequent occurrences in any complex writing or utterance.

I suggest that perhaps more than any other figure of language, chiasmus inevitably embodies what is called the problem of other minds. In fact, what we picture in the AB:BA of chiasmus may only be the experience of the limit of (our) being within thought itself: that is, we think *our being* [A] only at the limit of *what is not our being* (or *death*) [B]. Yet no sooner are we lost in this movement of thought, than we de facto reverse direction, now thinking from *what is not our being* [B] toward the limit of *our being* [A], and so on.

In the case of Goethe's distich in *Torquato Tasso*, we can see that even the first verse, by itself, is rendered intermittently chiastic by the doubleness of its elements. Thus in the first line—

[a]   [b]   [b]   [a]

Nein,   es ist alles da,   und ich bin nichts

—"Nein" momentarily creates a vacuum of absolute negation, even while it affirms (denies the denial of) "es ist alles da" (i.e., alles ist *nicht* verloren). So, too, the "da" that this speaker from the depths of "nichts" can grasp is as much *fort* (as Freud would say) from his zero self as it is *da*. Splayed between the progressive conjunction "und" (linking with "es ist alles da") and "nichts," the affirmative "ich bin" is totally bifurcated. Similarly, the final "nichts" certainly means "nothing," but it is also the obverse and signal of "alles." Even cursory examination of the second line of the distich shows that it invites very much the same analysis in precisely the reverse order of positive and negative elements (i.e., of being and nonbeing), each compacted of its own doubleness. Thus the full distich constitutes a larger chiasmus of jewellike intricacy in which the highest level of binarism is a movement between the limits of being and not-being:

[A]   [B]

[a]   [b]   [b']   [a']

Nein,   es ist alles da,   und ich bin nichts;

[B']   [A']

[b]   [a]   [a']   [b']

Ich bin mir selbst entwandt, sie ist es mir!

Within this larger chiasmus, as within each line, all the binary terms whirl and twist at incalculable speed. Instead of a formula of exclusion, A not B, or even a cross drawn in two indelible lines, we experience a continuous circulation of relations both direct and inverse: namely, AB, BA', A'B', B'A, AA', BB'—in addition to the smaller wheels within the larger wheels (ab, etc.) and with the larger wheels (aB, etc.)—each of which may be encountered separately and in combinations, forward and reverse. We can begin to describe the *X* experienced in chiasmus only by this illimitable circulation. By virtue of the cross-reading it sets in motion, chiasmus uncovers endless changes in its component antitheses, invariably to discomposing effect.

For the purposes of our present discussion of a shared thinking or a mutual fit of cultures, I would point out (here partly following Paul de Man)[9] that chiasmus creates a species of absences between its binary terms. These absences are not simply the antitheses or negations of the binary terms themselves. Nor can absence of this kind be identified with a particular location within chiasmus. In fact, the mobility of the apparent x-point in various historical usages of chiasmus—moved from within lines to couplets or quatrains, not to mention visually asymmetrical enjambments—highlights the fact that absence on this order cannot be located spatially. This sort of de-spatialization of relation has the effect of further unseating the apparently settled situations of the binary terms. This in turn facilitates the metamorphosis of A into B, B into A, so that it becomes inevitable in the movements of chiasmus that sameness (AB:BA; AA = BB) must interchange with constancy of difference (AB:AB; AB = AB). As a consequence, each binary term is charged with the potential of its opposite (i.e., A[b] or B[a]). In sum: the experience of any chiasmus with regard to its nonthematic absences and its binary terms is of movements of turning and counterturning totally different from the negation or appropriation effected in mere antithesis. In fact, chiasmus is as distinct from antithesis as negativity is from negation. This distinction is of vital importance.

Wolfgang Iser has highlighted just how different from negation negativity always is. He has emphasized that negativity is both an object and a condition of consciousness, both of which are unavoidable in human experience. We experience negativity whenever we come up against the implications, omissions, or cancellations that are necessarily part of any representation, or any writing, speaking, or thinking. These gaps indicate that all representations contain an unrealized dimension, so that each manifest representation has a kind of invisible, latent, dead accompaniment. Unlike negation, this inherent counterpart of representation defies representation. It forms an unrepresented and unrepresentable counterelement within every representation, every thought.[10]

Chiasmus, in fact, can come into being only by framing, and implicitly by acknowledging, the negativity or unformulated element within language. Experienced within more than one part of the chiasmus simultaneously, this is a negativity among the lines and halflines, even between the dualities of single words, that allows for the rotating countermotions of the polarities. This negativity is continually displaced from the nameless absences in the interstices of visual or audible matter to thematizations of negativity, and then back to the absences.

I propose further that in describing the potential relations of the chiasma (and their framings of negativity) of different individuals we stand on the verge of a picture of shared (divided) thinking—and of mutuality of culture. The negativity within the rotations of chiasmus results in the reaching out of that chiasmus, from incompleteness or obliviousness, toward the reachings out of other chiasma.

As an example of this phenomenon, I am claiming that Goethe's distich, quoted above, locates not only our possibility of hearing the pain of a man called Tasso, but also of finding the potentiality of a *co-subjective* chiasmus shared by Goethe ("the German")—in halves, mind beside mind—with a potential someone else, in fact, with more than one potential someone else at a time.

From this perspective, it would follow that in a given literary or artistic tradition, the thinking of individual artists of different times may form configurations that are, in relation to each other, not only strongly oppositional but also powerfully reciprocal, even what I am calling co-subjective. Elements of such reciprocal potentiality manifest themselves within matched oppositions, where such opposition is expressed both temporally backward (e.g., a later poet *contra* a remembered poet) and temporally forward (i.e., an earlier poet *contra* an anticipated poet). What is distinctive about this pattern of oppositions, however, is that it occurs within a potential of reciprocal relations that oppose opposition as such. Identifying this state of affairs is only yet another way of naming chiasmus, since chiasmus is itself a diagram of the simultaneous occurrence of opposition and reciprocity, in what we label AB:BA. It remains for me an open question (though an important one) just whose historical experience or co-subjectivity such a reciprocal symmetry of oppositions—or chiasmus—may be said to constitute, since it clearly cannot belong to any artist individually. What interests me is that it forms one kind of potentiality within thought. This potentiality is not pure and simple but hybrid and complex. My focus, then, is on the details of symmetrical correspondences—forward and backward, oppositionally and reciprocally—between individuals of different times.

Goethe in Tasso's "Zauberkreise"

I return to the moment of Tasso's experience rendered in Goethe's distich, now to note that Goethe's verses are a virtual translation of the following chiasmus, describing Tancred, in Tasso's *Gerusalemme liberata*:

> Va fuor di sé; presente aver gli è aviso
> l'offesa donna sua che plori e gema

He is beside himself; he thinks he is in the presence
of his injured lady who is weeping and lamenting.
$$(13.45.5-6)^{11}$$

For Goethe, in *Torquato Tasso*, the fact of this translation is primary in the
kind of thinking that engages him. That is, translation exists here as a mutual translation which results from the manifolds of mind posited in the
structures of the translated distich (in *Gerusalemme liberata*) and its translation (in *Torquato Tasso*). What is significant here is not any conscious or
even unconscious remembering on Goethe's part. The kind of shared thinking we witness here is not located in any one text. In any one text we encounter specific meanings of various kinds, but these meanings are only
interim with respect to the potentiality of thinking shared among such
texts.

It happens that we know a good deal about Goethe's intense involve-
ment, in 1790, in thinking through his own situation as poet at the court
of Weimar via Tasso's quandaries and thinking at Ferrara two centuries
earlier. Tasso's thinking was at Goethe's fingertips primarily in *Gerusalemme liberata*, the work that Tasso had struggled to complete at Ferrara.
Yet even without that kind of clue we could not help being struck by the
way Goethe's drama explicitly highlights Tasso's genius as a capacity for
assembling (*anziehen*) a manifold of mind—of minds thinking through
each other—as if in the "Geisterreich" longed for in the "Zueignung" to
Faust. (There are multiple parallels between that passage and the one I am
about to cite.) Speaking in a dense series of chiasma—for which I offer one
possible signposting—Leonora Sanvitale says of Tasso:

```
      A(b)               B(a)
Oft adelt er,   was uns gemein erschien,
      B(a)               A(b)
Und das Geschätzte   wird vor ihm zu nichts.
      A
In diesem eignen Zauberkreise wandelt
Der wunderbare Mann            B
                        und zieht uns an,
      B                     A
Mit ihm zu wandeln,     teil an ihm zu nehmen:
      A                     B
Er scheint sich uns zu nahn,   und bleibt uns fern;
      B
Er scheint uns anzusehn,       A
                        und Geister mögen
An unsrer Stelle seltsam ihm erscheinen.
            (Lines 165–72; emphasis added)
```

> Whatever seems
> Most ordinary to us he can at once
> Change into wonders, while what we cherish
> Means little to him. He is wonderful—
> He walks in his own magic world, and draws
> Other people in to share it—yet when
> He seems to come close, he is still far away:
> For him we could be disembodied spirits.

Leonora's first two lines exemplify Tasso's chiastic mind, especially the power of his negativity or "nichts" which is at the heart of his creative power. Tasso does not wander alone in his "Zauberkreise," but draws others in, as if they might occupy the vacancy of his "nichts." In this process of *anziehen* they share in making the world's enchantment, which itself remains a function of framing the "nichts." For Leonora this work of drawing other minds into an assembly of mind suggests the similar power of *anziehen* in the Princess and the Duke,[12] who have enabled Tasso and those around him to work this magic of the "Zauberkreise." Considered from the perspective of our discussion of chiasmus and a manifold of mind, we need to inquire into the nature of this shared thinking of *anziehen* in the "Zauberkreise" of *Torquato Tasso* and, perhaps by the same token of enchantment, of *hinanziehen* shared by the Chorus Mysticus in the closing chiasmus of *Faust*: "Da Unbeschreibliche, / Hier ist's getan; / Das Ewigweibliche / *Zieht uns hinan.*"

One way of approaching this inquiry into the workings of an *anziehen* is to ask how we might locate the linkage, through negativity, between Tasso's distich

> Va fuor di sé; presente aver gli è aviso
> l'offesa donna sua che plori e gema

and Goethe's

> Nein, es ist alles da, und ich bin nichts;
> Ich bin mir selbst entwandt, sie ist es mir!
>
> (Lines 3,417–18)

In the relation of these distichs we must take seriously their claims that the subjects or consciousnesses represented here are beside themselves. As I have said, I take this claim to mean that each consciousness is in part constituted by experiencing the inaccessibility of another consciousness. In each distich the binary halflines both thematize and create the structure of a manifold of mind that frames both accessible and inaccessible consciousnesses. In each distich, we see the staging for an affiliation of fractional selves, whether of Tancred and Clorinda or of (Goethe's) Tasso and the

Princess, in addition to presences and absences of Tasso in the first distich, and Goethe in the second. On Goethe's part, the presence of a "Tasso" in both distichs may even partly suggest a self-conscious attempt to lay the framework for a continuous, or reciprocal, thinking-through of a given thought. But how might this potentiality of linkage be created, specifically between the chiasma of these distichs? What kinetic quantity in both chiasma could facilitate a kind of thinking that is only a shared potentiality, one which lies distinctly beside the grasp of Goethe's individual mind (and Tasso's)?

A rough listing of the obvious and more or less static correspondences between these distichs is helpful, as a kind of process of elimination, in pointing toward the mysterious quantity in question. "Va fuor di sé" is matched quite closely by "Ich bin mir selbst entwandt"; "presente aver gli è aviso" by "es ist alles da"; "l'offesa donna sua" (*offesa*, "injured," very much in the sense of being severed) in "sie ist es mir" (she is divided from me). Only Tasso's fourth binary, "che plori e gema," does not find its symmetrical correspondent in Goethe's fourth binary, "und ich bin nichts." This latter is the phrase in which Goethe repeatedly names Tasso's power of negativity. In this element of his chiasmus, I want to suggest, Goethe's mind turns counter to Tasso's—even and especially in the act of representing the chiasmus of "Tasso's" mind through which he, Goethe, is also thinking. Something is at work here, I believe, between Tasso's and Goethe's verses, something neither poet fully controls. The circumstances of this interaction remain only in the interstices or potentialities of cross-culture. Experienced in history only as a configuration of possible encounters, it may be described in the following way.

Working from Tasso's chiasmus Goethe creates a kind of secular paradigm 'of what Erich Auerbach, characterizing Goethe's genius, has felicitously named "sensory truth."[13] In Goethe's chiasmus it is clear that this power over sensory truth consists in a play of intensely felt sensory presence and its equally felt absence (the "nichts"). In the distich from *Gerusalemme liberata* Tasso's play of absence against presence—indexed in the phrase "plori e gema"—is worlds apart from Goethe's in the sense that Goethe denies any need for superhuman mediation of human experience of negativity. Correlatively, Goethe is apparently oblivious to the interactions of his verses, beyond his meanings, with Tasso's Christian framing of negativity. Yet Goethe's framing of negativity, in his distich, is as unmistakable as Tasso's. What might be staged, and where, we need to ask, between these framings of negativity, in chiasma? Even to begin to provide an answer, we need more information.

Tasso's chiasmus depends upon the fact that Tancred's vision of his lady *gema*, "lamenting," is not of the affect of passion. Rather, via an allusion to Lamentations (repeated in *gemiti*, "laments," two lines later), it invokes the typological and antitypological meaning which his "l'offesa donna" carries. The antitypological other world opened up here is very much the burden of Tasso's negativity throughout the *Gerusalemme liberata*; and in these lines in particular that negativity is evoked quietly but surely: this is the liberated or opened-up world bestowed on the fallen, earthly world by Christ's dying in fulfillment of the type of Christ's crucifixion in the destruction of Jerusalem. (For the moment I refrain from considering the kind of chiasmus that Lamentations makes available for encounters with *Gerusalemme liberata* or *Torquato Tasso*, but I will broach that matter shortly.) Tasso's very next chiasmus, turning on Tancred's and Clorinda's participation in the liberating (opening) power of Christ's self-sacrifice, makes this clear. The *langue* (languishing sufferer) of these lines recalls the *infermo* (sick man) sixteen lines earlier—who is there Tancred, not Clorinda—reinforcing the manifold effect (of mutual sharers in Christ's condition) achieved in the chiasmus:

A   B

né può soffrir di rimirar quel sangue,

B   A

né quei gemiti udir d'egro che langue.

A   B

and he can no longer bear   to see that blood

B   A

or hear those laments   of a languishing sufferer.[14]

The complexity of Tasso's mind, behind Tancred's, is implicated in these lines by the fact that this representation of a Christian negativity is in itself a counterfeit vision of what exists in real form elsewhere. In Tasso's epic of Jerusalem delivered, the false Clorinda lamenting those laments evokes the Lamentations of Jeremiah for the destruction of Jerusalem. In this speaking of the false Clorinda, Tasso may thus remind us of the way Dante's fleshly screen for Beatrice explicitly evokes Lamentations in chapter 7 of the *Vita Nuova*.[15] Tasso's *Gerusalemme* other world, where laments, *gemiti*, are, among other things, necessarily sighs from the Lamentations of Jeremiah, has something to say, side by side, with Goethe's other world, in a thinking that belongs to neither Tasso nor Goethe alone.

Because each chiasmus is a motion of turning with negativity toward the negativity of another chiasmus, we experience here the impact of the unwritable history (*Das Unbeschreibliche*) of shared thinking. Such shared thinking is always only a potentiality that exists between individuals, between texts, between cultures, always, therefore, in an extratemporal dimension of history. Of course, none of us can be very comfortable with any notion of extratemporality, but we should recall that for Goethe, at least, the extratemporal was an inevitable feature of an authentic historism. Auerbach, following Meinecke, has reminded us of how closely identified the age of Goethe is with the formulation of historism, most especially with the belief in "the extratemporal spirit of history." Auerbach, however, sees this aspect of Goethe's mind as a limitation entailed in Goethe's tendency to avoid a fully developed realism and, correlatively, to insulate himself from the social realities of his own time. Auerbach's estimate of Goethe is to be sure immensely high, but, looking back on German history in 1946, Auerbach wonders whether the development of modern German culture "might have been" different if Goethe had been able to engage his age more fully "in the realm of realism."[16] Considering both the richness of Auerbach's appreciation of Goethe's genius and the immense catastrophe that contextualizes this particular remark, one cannot but be moved—to pause. Yet I wonder whether, without intending to do so, Auerbach has not made it harder to discern the kind of engagement with history—severely limited as it is—that Goethe, with the special limits and capacities of his historism, actually pursued. Undoubtedly it is only an insubstantial comfort for anyone who, like Auerbach, directly experienced the impact of modern German history, but I believe Goethe's poetry opens the door to just such an "extratemporal spirit of history," as if in a *Geisterreich* envisioned by his historism. Auerbach's listing of the limitations in Goethe's capacity for historical engagement serves, in fact, as a virtual portrait of the problematics that Goethe confronts directly in *Torquato Tasso* and that therefore form the context of the manifold of mind on which we are now focused. In light of the importance attached in *Torquato Tasso* to a kind of *anziehen*, or rotated drawing in of other minds to an extratemporal dimension of history (in the orbit of the *Zauberkreise*), it may even be to the point to say that Goethe gives a different, particular rotation or torque to these problems, which seem otherwise insurmountable, as they did to Auerbach.

Let me review the main points of Auerbach's analysis of Goethe's avoidance of history and its actualities. Turning Meinecke's praise of Goethe into a gentle form of blame, Auerbach says that those parts of history that Goethe ignored were ones he could have "mastered directly by the cognitional principles which were most peculiarly his own"—"if he had loved those parts of history." But, Auerbach laments, his aristocratic leanings caused him not to love them. Auerbach reads Goethe's own "confession" in Wilhelm's lament in *Wilhelm Meister* that in Germany only the nobleman may attain "a certain generalized personal culture": "I happen to have," says Wilhelm, "an irresistible propensity for the very kind of harmonious development of my nature which is denied me by my birth."[17] Citing a polemic essay of Goethe's, Auerbach notes Goethe's too easy acceptance of the fact that "nowhere in Germany is there a center of social *savoir vivre* where authors might congregate and, in their several domains, develop in one common manner and in one common direction." To Auerbach, Goethe seems unwilling to contemplate the revolutions that would be necessary to change this situation in Germany, as Auerbach reads in Goethe's statement in the same essay: "We shall not wish for upheavals which might prepare classical works in Germany."[18]

It would be absurd to argue that Goethe engaged history in the way Auerbach would have hoped, but Goethe's limited form of historical engagement is still of very great interest, especially since it manages to affiliate with something far beyond Goethe and German culture. The decisive difference between Goethe's and Auerbach's perspectives is that Goethe thinks in terms of the cross-cultural, the extratemporal, and the potential, while Auerbach is concerned with the responsibilities of a single culture to a single moment in history. Auerbach would have wished for Germany that which Goethe is unwilling to hope—for Germany. The manifold of mind that Goethe (as one partner in consciousness) thinks through the poetry of Tasso does answer, however, in considerable measure, to Auerbach's objections, even if that manifold did not (sufficiently) change the reality of German culture itself. The "cognitional principles" that peculiarly form that manifold, with its drawing in, or loving *anziehen*, of other minds into the *Zauberkreise* of a *savoir vivre*, closely match what Leonora, as we have seen, attributes to Tasso and the d'Este court. At Ferrara, Tasso, very much the commoner, strives to achieve within the manifold—together with the noblemen whom he draws after him—precisely a "generalized personal culture" and "harmonious development." For us as observers of Goethe's relation (from Weimar) to Tasso's poem (which Tasso struggled to complete, and left unfinished, at Ferrara) it is further clear that the manifold opened in "classical works" in which he participates cannot be a local German affair. (One may think here of Goethe's remark to Johann Peter Eckermann, upon reading Carlyle's estimate of Schiller, that a *Weltliteratur* would have to consist of artists of different cultures who would "correct" each other.)[19]

Indeed, the moment is now ripe to introduce Nietzsche's way of blaming Goethe for what he leaves out in the manifold of mind. I mentioned earlier that while Nietzsche borrows Goethe's picture of the multiplex soul he declares that even in the complex, divided mind of the most self-conscious German—"that German," he calls him—obliviousness to the participation of certain minds, within the manifold, is both an inevitable feature and a dangerous condition of the way the manifold thinks. Nietzsche is highly circumstantial, I suggested, about this obliviousness.

What Nietzsche tells us, in effect, is that one of the components of the German soul repressed even by Goethe is that of "the Jews." Speaking of the full range of his intellectual acquaintance, not merely his contemporaries, Nietzsche will soon remark, "I have never met a German who was favorably inclined towards the Jews."[20]

Nietzsche shows how "the Jews" alternately form components that are external and internal to what appears to be the unitary soul of the "Germans." The rules of the game in this manifold are always beyond self-knowledge: "Every people has its own tartuffery and calls it its virtues.— The best that one is one does not know—one cannot know."[21] In other words, the creative transactions among the diverse souls within the soul, like the diversity of souls itself, is not available for direct knowledge by any of the transactors. This is where Nietzsche's astounding tribute to, and censure of, "the Jews" comes in. That tribute-censure is expressed in Nietzsche's own characteristic chiasmus, giving with one hand what he takes away with the other. His binarisms are "Europe" and "the Jews" / "the Jews" and "Europe"; repetitions of "the best and the worst" in the worst and the best:

What Europe owes to the Jews? Many things, good and bad, and above all one thing that is at once of the best and the worst: the grand style in morality, the dreadfulness and majesty of infinite demands, infinite significances, the whole romanticism and sublimity of moral questionabilities—and consequently precisely the most attractive, insidious and choicest part of those iridescences and seductions to life with whose afterglow the sky of our European culture, its evening sky, is now aflame—and perhaps burning itself up. We artists among the spectators and philosophers are—grateful to the Jews for this.[22]

In this passage the Jews are not merely woven into the chiasmus of Europe and the Jews. Nietzsche sees the Jews as bearing a kind of intrinsic X or chiasmus of "sublimity," an equation wrought from "moral questionabilities": "infinite demands" / "infinite significances" = "dreadfulness" / "majesty."

The Hand Turning, Outside Time

I propose that in the case of Goethe and Tasso, at least, Nietzsche's remarks may help to locate the extratemporal and the cross-cultural thinking that

Goethe and Tasso share with "the Jews." To close this essay, I will try to
suggest how, in fact, a chiasmus of "the Jews" forms part of the manifold
of mind in which Goethe and Tasso participate, beyond any individual
thinking. I therefore turn to one final brief collection of verses from *Torquato Tasso*, from *Gerusalemme liberata*, and, this time, from Lamentations as well. I earlier discussed verses from the closing moment of *Torquato Tasso*. I now focus on the final instant of that same moment, which
is represented in the closing verses of the play. Here Goethe's last resort
seems to be only a mutuality of destructive cross-purposes suggestive of
Faust's "zwei Seelen" (including even the "klammernden Organen" of one
of those souls [*Faust*, l. 1115]). This, indeed, would seem to be a kind of
terminal romantic sublime which is inherently beyond identity, even beyond rational meaning. Tasso's nemesis and savior, Antonio, has stepped
toward Tasso and taken him by the hand. Tasso declares, "Ich kenne mich
in der Gefahr nicht mehr" (In this danger I no longer know myself), and
seals the play with these words:

> Ich fasse dich mit beiden Armen an!
> So klammert sich der Schiffer endlich noch
> Am Felsen fest, an dem er scheitern sollte.
>
> (Lines 3,451–53)

> A   B   (B)(A)
> I seize you   with both arms!
>   A
> So, in the end, the sailor still clings fast
> B   B   A
> To the rock on which he should have foundered.[23]

Closely mirroring the structure of the manifold of mind, which earlier suggests the *Zauberkreise*, this *Gefahr* is a milling of tentacles within the putative self, which are shown to be a relation of elements inside and outside
any mere self. As Antonio is both nemesis and savior—destroying rock and
steadfast redeemer—so part of Tasso is wrecked (reverts to "nichts") while
part of him is saved. Tasso reaches out with arms of both parts of his "zwei
Seelen" to the extended arm of Antonio which is itself doubled in horrifying ambiguity. At the heart of this redoubled doubleness is the desire, on
all sides, for something that stands outside the scenography itself, a negativity that remains framed in darkness. Yet this interaction within
Goethe's verses themselves cannot be their whole story, because these final
lines spoken by Goethe's Tasso think through (translate and are translated
by) the final verses of Tasso's *Gerusalemme liberata*. Here again we have
a mind-bending linkage in negativity.

Describing Godfrey's final act, Tasso writes,

e qui l'arme sospende, e qui devoto
il gran Sepolcro adora, e scioglie il voto.

and here hangs up his arms, and here devoutly
adores the great Sepulcher, and discharges his vow.

The "l'arme sospende" which somehow discharges Godfrey's "vow" is surely, in part, an answer to the blood-feuding of pagan history. Tasso wants us to take note of the difference between Godfrey's final act and that of Aeneas (in the final verses of the *Aeneid*), who thrusts his sword into Turnus's breast—sending him "to the Shades below"—in fulfillment of his "vow" to Evander to kill the killer of that king's son, Pallas. Although Godfrey's suspension of his killing arm is ushered in with streams of blood— the kind of upheaval that Goethe was loath to imagine, even for the salvation of German culture or for the making of classical works—Tasso seems to assert the world-changing power of this Christian suspension. This suspension is an imitation of the divine forgiveness for the killing of the Son of the King of Kings. The Christian's fulfillment of his vow is thus in the hanging up of the arms, the suspension of the killing arm. Instead of the shades below, humankind has now been liberated in a Jerusalem centered in the Holy Sepulcher of Christ's dying for the world. We can paraphrase this matching of worlds in many ways, but it seems clear, at least, that at the heart of this doubling of Godfrey's act over and against Aeneas's stands a Christian desire to exit the scenes of history for a shadow realm that is distinctly Christian (as if negativity could be given a name). This too is a negativity that remains framed in darkness. Thus for us it is already impossible not to hear a certain extratemporal whispering between this Tassovian framing of negativity and Goethe's at the end of *Torquato Tasso*.

Yet an extratemporal conversation of another kind speaks louder from the crossroads of Tasso's and Goethe's texts, because for Tasso the cross-cultural stakes are far higher than a competition of pagan and Christian. How could they be otherwise in a Christian epic reenacting the deliverance of Jerusalem, when in the view of Christian typology the "Old Testament" had prefigured that deliverance of Jerusalem in Jeremiah's Lamentations for the destruction of Jerusalem? Of necessity, in Tasso's verses we are poised on the boundaries of Christian typology.

During the last two millennia in the West, perhaps no written evidence of a manifold of mind has been more explicit than Christian typology, and none has been more inherently structured on obliviousness to "the Jews." In Christian typology, the thinking of "the Jews" themselves is frozen and subsumed in a thinking constituted by the types or anticipations of

Christ—which occur in the Old Testament and pre-Christian Jewish history—and the antitypes of the New Testament which have totally fulfilled
and closed off the types. In one sense, therefore, Nietzsche's explicit criticism of Goethe's merely duplex model of the German soul, as well as his
reminder concerning the place of "the Jews" in that soul, may both represent indirect responses to a Christian bipolar thinking. But Nietzsche's
insight goes deeper than the issue of displacements from history. His insight concerns, most of all, claims to the exclusive possession of negativity,
to the singlehanded staging of chiasmus, and to the control of thought itself. One alternative way, that is, of describing the leverage of Christian
typological imagination is to note that the antitype of Christ is defined by
his immense power of negativity, by his liberating the world in his dying
for it, so that an infinite other world is opened up within the mortal scene.
Nietzsche suggests, as we have seen, that "the Jews" open their own liberating chiasmus, equipped with their own framing of negativity, and that
this is what makes it inevitable for them to constitute one part of the German manifold of mind. Just so, in the extratemporal encounter that we are
considering, various chiasma of Lamentations become no less powerfully
silent partners than Goethe and Tasso. That is, Tasso's phrase "l'arme sospende"—suspended at the exact instant in which Jerusalem is delivered—
turns to Jeremiah no less than to Virgil. It recalls, reciprocally and oppositionally (that is, in the potentiality of chiasmus), the moment when the
hand of the Lord is "withdrawn," at the exact instant in which Jerusalem
was destroyed. Tasso would claim (or imagines he claims), that in *Gerusalemme liberata* the "l'arme sospende" fulfills in deliverance what was before an imperfect type. Among the relevant verses in Lamentations the following (2.3–4) are profoundly of that type:

וַיִּבְעַר בְּיַעֲקֹב כְּאֵשׁ לֶהָבָה . . . וַיַּהֲרֹג כֹּל מַחֲמַדֵּי־עָיִן בְּאֹהֶל בַּת־צִיּוֹן	הֵשִׁיב אָחוֹר יְמִינוֹ מִפְּנֵי אוֹיֵב נָצַב יְמִינוֹ כְּצָר

3.

[A]
he hath drawn back his
right hand [fem.] from
before the enemy,

[B]
and he burned against Jacob
like a flaming fire . . .

4.

[B]
he stood with his right
hand [masc.] as an
adversary

[A]
and slew all that were
pleasant to the eye in
the tabernacle of the
daughter of Zion

We can analyze this passage stylistically according to Nietzsche's comments on "the grand style in morality" of "the Jews"—that is, the style of "the Jews" that lies hidden, side by side, within the manifold of diverse minds in "the German" mind. As we noted, Nietzsche sees the "sublimity" of this style in its chiasmus of "moral questionabilities": "infinite demands" / "infinite significances" = "dreadfulness" / "majesty." The moment of Jerusalem's destruction in Lamentations, cited above, represents a sublime of this sort. Triumphalism, nationalistic pride, hiding of national failure, fixing the books of history are all impossible at this moment. A different sort of history is at stake here. The "enemy" is a term cast utterly into question, here implicating "the Jews" and God as much as non-Jews. In these verses the scriptures of "the Jews" show us a God of infinite significances who makes infinite demands upon them, demands which they do not meet. This God is both *withdrawn* from actuality and *standing* unyieldingly within it. He makes moral demands in the realm of this world, but at the same time he demands a worship of the infinite itself (in the tabernacle), centered only in an earthly framing of negativity. The structure of these verses also frames a cultus of negativity that is transacted solely in an extratemporal dimension, across the history of "the Jews" recorded in this scripture. This negativity of the Jews is therefore already explicitly formulated within one kind of typological matrix, although here the antitypological dimension is not closed, but rather reaches out for potential fulfillment elsewhere. For the Jews this would presumably take place in the continuing history of the Jews themselves, but clearly this opening for interpretation could also open the door to the creation of a Christian typology.[24]

In the God's-eye view of moral questionabilities represented in these verses from Lamentations the dialectic resolves nothing, creates no capital idea. The unresolved oppositions of these verses only keep open the potential significances of the immediate event in an infinite, extratemporal realm. I mention here only two of the most obvious of these oppositions, namely the hand of God which is said to be withdrawn while, in the following verse, that hand is said to be not-withdrawn or active; and the crossing (in the chiasmus) of the withdrawn hand of God with the feminine "tabernacle of the daughter of Zion" and, at the same time, the crossing of the not-withdrawn, destroying hand of God with the masculine Jacob-Israel. In the Hebrew text this contrast is highlighted by the remarkable expedient of changing the gender of the word *hand* between the two verses. Read horizontally, in each verse the violence occasioned in the destruction of Jerusalem is pictured in a gendered relation, and reversed gender relation, of God and "the Jews" (i.e., feminine to masculine, then masculine to feminine). God's negativity is outside (typographically within) the thematizations of these binarisms. Yet that negativity is rendered suggestively feminine insofar as it represents a withdrawal (like the feminine withdrawn hand) from any mere present world or temporality, such as is ideally suggested in the invisible presence within "the tabernacle of the daughter of Zion." The violence pictured in this masculine-to-feminine relation may of course also figure holy rape as well as a purely brutish force very much within temporality. For the Jews (Jacob-Israel), only God's negativity gives meaning, beyond the immediate catastrophe, to their very existence, at any moment in history. This feminine negativity can draw them to a realm beyond the present obliteration of their world.

There may well be overt features of translation between Lamentations —*Klagelieder*—and Goethe's final moment in *Torquato Tasso*. Goethe's Tasso even says here that "Natur," "ein Gott," gave him his poet's power "zu klagen" (lines 3,427–31). In addition the play of hands that Tasso pursues with regard to the moment of Jerusalem's destruction in Lamentations seems to have even deeper correlatives in Goethe's language. Tasso, who reaches out to Antonio's hand (of nemesis and salvation) with both his arms, is clearly, perhaps even shockingly (for Goethe's audience at least), the principle of a feminine negativity and creativity. When Antonio extends his hand to him, Tasso tells him what it means to be the feminine, "breast"-like "wave" breaking on Antonio's masculine "rock":

> Du stehest fest und still,
> Ich scheine nur die sturmbewegte Welle.
> Allein bedenk und überhebe nicht
> Dich deiner Kraft! Die mächtige Natur,
> Die diesen Felsen gründete, hat auch
> Der Welle die Beweglichkeit gegeben.
> Sie sendet ihren Sturm, die Welle flieht
> Und schwankt und schwillt und beugt sich schäumend über.
> In dieser Woge spiegelte so schön
> Die Sonne sich, es ruhten die Gestirne
> An dieser Brust, die zärtlich sich bewegte.
>
> (Lines 3,434–44)

> You stand there firm and quiet,
> I seem to be only the storm-tossed wave.
> But consider this, and do not presume
> Too much on your great strength: for Nature,
> Who set this rock in place, has also given
> A power of ceaseless movement to the wave.
> She sends her tempest and the wave draws back,

Rears itself up, and seethes, and overturns
In bursts of outflung spray. Yet this same wave
Once held the sun, so calmly; and all the stars
Once rested on its gently stirring breast.

Antonio may seem to be an Old Testament masculine God who inscrutably destroys and saves, but he is matched by the power of an Old Testament feminine God who "draws back" and holds the world in her bosom. The final verses of the drama therefore rotate upon a negativity which is framed in the same suggestive feminine way as it is in Lamentations. Only this *Ewigweibliche* gives meaning, beyond Tasso's immediate catastrophe, to his existence as a poet working in an extratemporal world that is potential (never actual) between texts and between minds. In effect, he is explaining to Antonio that only this feminine negativity creates a potentiality of relation between them that remains beyond their individual and even collective realization. In other words, only this feminine negativity *zieht uns hinan*.

These correspondences with Lamentations may well suggest semantic linkages. Yet, as I have said, my point in this essay is not to describe an intertextuality that is a semantic layering, thin or thick, controlled by a given mind. The relations between the chiasma of these different texts, especially between the framings of negativity in these chiasma, are only co-subjective, which means—as, I believe, Goethe and Nietzsche understood—that they are beyond any individual mind or subjectivity. Even now we, as individual readers, do not grasp the thinking of Goethe's last lines in *Torquato Tasso*. The lines themselves point to their own limitedness as thought or subjectivity in that they necessitate the manifold of mind in which the sharing of thought might occur. This shared thinking is only a rotation upon negativity between chiasma, not only of Goethe's "zwei Seelen" (Antonio's) with another "zwei Seelen" (Tasso's), but of these four minds (in chiasmus) reaching out to another four souls or minds in Tasso's typological pairings (as well as those of Godfrey and the liberating, freeing God) in the final verses of *Gerusalemme liberata*, and of Jeremiah's pairings (of God and the Jews) in Lamentations. This manifold of mind does not emerge as an entity in any moment of history but nonetheless is propelled toward potential encounters among its cross-cultural elements. It seems likely that this propulsion, or movement, is a pressing reality in everything that we call experience of history.

What occurs among these texts turning toward each other may well be suggestive, therefore, of a life function that continually creates poten-

tialities of relation which remain potentialities. The picture we have con-
templated seems to indicate that human beings are very much capable of
participating in, and even, in some measure, experiencing, shared thinking
of this kind. Yet it may also suggest that sustaining this aspect of our hu-
manness depends, among other things, upon resisting the pressures to say
what our shared thinking thinks, or to nudge this extratemporal and cross-
cultural *savoir vivre* toward a given temporality of a given culture.

The Emergence of
a Cross-Cultural Discourse:
Thomas Carlyle's *Sartor Resartus*

Wolfgang Iser

*T*he outline of a cross-cultural discourse as advanced in Carlyle's *Sartor Resartus* is a paradigm but by no means a blueprint of the telescoping of different cultures. It does, however, provide guidelines as to how such a telescoping might be conceived. It is paradigmatic insofar as a cross-cultural discourse cannot be set up as a transcendental stance under which the relationships between different cultures are subsumed. Instead of an overarching third dimension, the discourse concerned can only function as an interlinking network and will assume a shape whose generic features cannot be equated with any of the existing genres.

Historical Preliminaries

Why has translatability of cultures become an issue? As long as the interconnection of traditions—whether in terms of receiving an inheritance or of recasting a heritage—was taken for granted, the relationship of cultures did not pose a problem. Tradition was either reinterpreted or appropriated in accordance with prevailing standards or needs. This holds true up to the eighteenth century and is borne out, for instance, in the famous criticism of Nietzsche's leveled at Shakespeare, that in the Roman plays Shakespeare depicted his protagonists not as Romans but as Renaissance heroes.

The Querelle des anciens et des modernes, however, is the striking exception to this commonly accepted relationship. It was the perception of a fundamental difference between the *antiquii* and the *moderni* that brought about an awareness of distance between the cultures of antiquity and of the modern age.[1] The battle was triggered by the question of how to achieve perfection—an aim that both the moderns and the ancients shared. For the latter, perfection was achieved by imitating nature, whereas for the former the ancient models were no longer to be imitated but had to be surpassed. Such a shift was largely due to the fact that the moderns found themselves confronted with an ever-expanding, open-ended world, in contradistinction to the ancients, who entertained the idea of a closed cosmos. Consequently, progress became the guiding light for the moderns, who thus turned the inherited world order completely around by conceiving it as an irreversible advance into a future. The cyclical movement of day and night and the seasons, indicative of an ordered cosmos, was replaced by a linear ascent. Perfection, therefore, was no longer a given that required contemplation, as exemplified by the Greek *theoria*; instead, it was now something to be achieved, and as a task to be performed, it could no longer be an act of imitation.

In his *Parallèle des Anciens et des Modernes* (1688–97), Charles Perrault listed the existing differences between the two cultures.[2] This list, however, was meant to prove the superiority of the moderns, who had exceeded what the ancients had achieved. In order to substantiate such a claim, the passing of time became a frame of reference for both collating and assessing the differences, in the course of which a *history* began to unfold itself: by discovering difference as the dividing line between cultures, history as a cross-cultural discourse emerged. The moderns were now no longer dwarfs standing on the shoulders of the giants, as John of Salisbury had it, but were different. And as the ancient culture could not be dispensed with—not least as it had to provide a point of comparison for the achievements of the moderns—history as a form of cross-cultural interrelationship bears the inscription of a dual coding. On the one hand, the difference between the two cultures has to be overcome by a developing sequence, and on the other, this very difference has to be maintained in order to gauge the superiority achieved. This duality was to remain an incontrovertible structure of all cross-cultural discourse from then on.

The Querelle, however, remained a Battle of Books. Questions of how to attain perfection or perfectibility, of how to imitate nature or inherited models, or of how nature as a guiding norm is to be replaced by taste,[3] and of how the latter—no longer to be related to nature—is to be conceived, turned out to be the overriding concern of the Querelle, which thus confined itself to matters of art in the broadest sense of the term. Moreover, the moderns proved to be rather self-assertive in this process of differentiation, thereby endowing their discourse of history with a teleological direction.

What, however, happens when such optimism wanes? This stage was reached some fifty years after Perrault, when Rousseau responded to the prize competition of the Académie de Dijon in 1750 by stating that the arts and sciences had not, in actual fact, improved morals but had corrupted them. Such a devastating statement marked the beginning of what has since been known as cultural critique, sparked off by a crisis of culture that had not been in the orbit of those who had pleaded the superiority of their own culture over the ancients.

The experience of crisis splits culture itself apart, and such a process began to deepen and accelerate with the dawn of the Industrial Revolution. Fundamental differences opened up in individual cultures, not least through the experience of an all-pervading rift that divided a culture into an inaccessible past and a helplessly stricken present. A past cut off from the present is pushed back into an irredeemable pastness, thus inverting the very relationship highlighted in the evolving discourse of history as it had grown out of the Querelle. Furthermore, the Industrial Revolution divided the very nation into two nations: one that participated in the growing wealth, and another that had to bear the hardships. Crisis as a waning belief in a set of values—a belief indispensable for the stability of a culture—meant a split within the nation that eventually resolved itself into a nation of two cultures.

Thomas Carlyle was one of the first who not only had forebodings of such a situation but gave expression to his fears in order to remedy what the crisis had laid bare.[4] The rifts that had opened up in what one had been led to believe was a homogeneous culture could no longer be closed by the discourse of history, for its inherent optimism as regards achieving perfection by progress had been shattered. Consequently, a renegotiation between past and present became an issue for Carlyle, which he tried to solve by translating the past into the present and also by transposing different cultures into his own.

Progress was now placated as a glossing over of difference, whereas translating maintained the awareness of difference by simultaneously interrelating what was historically divided, be it the split between one's own cultural past and present, or between one's own culture and the alien ones to be encountered through a globally growing confrontation of cultures.

If one's own cultural past, as exemplified in Carlyle's *Past and Present* (1843), is totally alienated from the present,[5] translatability entails the effort to revitalize such an amputated past[6] by turning it into a mirror in which the present is refracted. As neither the past nor the present by itself is able to bring about such a mutual mirroring, a type of discourse has to be construed that allows for mutual interpenetration. Such a mutuality implies that the difference between past and present or between cultures can never be eliminated, for the past can never become a present again and one culture can never be totally encompassed by another. Consequently, whenever difference is eliminated, the encounter between cultures turns into a selective assimilation, guided by what is relevant for the culture concerned. In such instances no interaction between cultures occurs, and the incorporation of alien features is at best pragmatically justified.

Therefore the question arises as to the motivation underlying the translatability of cultures. If the experience of crises, issuing into a critique of one's own culture, is meant to balance out the deficiencies diagnosed, recourse to other cultures proves to be a means of therapy for a growing awareness of cultural pathology. The latter can be counteracted not just by taking over features and attitudes from different cultures, but first and foremost by instilling a self-reflexivity into the stricken culture, thus providing scope for self-monitoring. Translatability is motivated by the need to cope with a crisis that can no longer be alleviated by the mere assimilation or appropriation of other cultures.

At such a historic juncture, a cross-cultural discourse begins to emerge. A discourse of this kind is not to be mistaken for a translation, as translatability is to be conceived as a set of conditions that are able to bring about a mutual mirroring of cultures. It is therefore a pertinent feature of such a discourse that it establishes a network of interpenetrating relationships. These, in turn, allow for a mutual impacting of cultures upon one another, and simultaneously channel the impact.

Such a translatability is not motivated by assimilation, appropriation, or even understanding and communication, as each of these proves to be only a pragmatic exigency, and hence points to an ulterior purpose. In each of these instances, a specific interlinking within the network is privileged, and this narrows down the very differentiation opened up by the network of the cross-cultural discourse. These instances testify to a prevailing need, which makes them subject to evaluation. The network itself is a web of mobile structures, functioning as an interface between different cultures. It is a clearing station in which cultural differences are juxtaposed and sorted out.

Generic Features

Carlyle's *Sartor Resartus* (1836) is one of the first attempts at construing such a cross-cultural discourse. The concept-oriented philosophical culture of German idealism is to be transposed into the experience-oriented culture of British empiricism. The discourse devised for such an undertaking has to remain subservient to the transposition of cultures, and such a subservience is bound to have repercussions on the form of the discourse, not least because form exercises control and brings about determination. Consequently, such a discourse has to be permeated by a self-reflexivity, manifesting itself in the very subversion of its form.

The consequences of this undercutting are highlighted by the generic features of *Sartor Resartus*. Although dealing with a philosophical system, it is not cast as a treatise. Instead, we have an English Editor receiving from Germany several bags of notes and fragments from which he gets a rather disorderly glimpse of a highly speculative work: "Die Kleider, ihr Werden und Wirken,"[7] written by Diogenes Teufelsdröckh. This very introduction serves as a point of departure for exfoliating the density of a system in narrative terms which make *Sartor Resartus* almost appear to be a novel.[8] The narration, however, is constantly punctured by systematic expositions of this transcendental philosophy, which inhibit the narrative from unfolding. With the form of the treatise suspended and the narrative thwarted by arguments of philosophical disquisitions, *Sartor Resartus* pivots around an empty space that makes narrating and arguing constantly interchange. The narrative functions as a form of communication that strives to endow philosophical speculation with plausibility, whereas the abstractions that disrupt the narrative reveal transcendentalism as a mode of exceeding the familiar. Thus a British attitude permeates a systematic philosophy, just as German transcendentalism inscribes itself into a British disposition. Giving prominence to the empty space around which narrating and arguing revolve, Carlyle epitomizes in *Sartor Resartus* the telescoping of transcendentalism and empiricism. In doing so, he tries to make palatable to British readers the German import which, in turn, is bound to bring out something in the British readers of which they have hitherto not been aware.

The empty space as a generic feature of *Sartor Resartus* is further elaborated by an autobiographical account of Teufelsdröckh's spiritual growth,[9] to which one of the three books is devoted. Yet *Sartor Resartus* is not an autobiography either. The basic facts of Teufelsdröckh's development are grouped around his life-endangering crisis, which he eventually solves by devising his Philosophy of Clothes. There is an intimate commerce between the facts of life and the ever-changing garments that epitomize Teufelsdröckh's philosophy. The more life eludes one's grasp, the more concretely the Philosophy of Clothes takes shape.

Thus the space between is "colonized" by an array of garments, and the erstwhile self-inspecting autobiographer turns more and more into a tailor, who constantly designs new clothes, or refashions garments inherited from the past. The autobiographer becomes a philosopher of clothes because he is unable to capture himself. Such a space-between can be "bridged" only by "clothing," that is, by giving it a shape. "Clothing," however, does not mean eliminating the gap between a life lived and the attempt to fathom what that life is; instead, every garment provides a glimpse of the space-between that turns into a propellant for an endless production of garments, whose tailoring and retailoring strive to narrow down the distance between "being and having oneself."

Thus *Sartor Resartus* is neither an autobiography nor an exposition of a philosophical system, although both form basic constituents of the work. The life narrated demands a philosophy in order to cope with its crisis, and the philosophy that addresses the crisis is more than just a remedy; it keeps changing that very life itself without, however, capturing it in its totality. The space-between turns out to be a catalyst, evinced by the fact that Teufelsdröckh feeds his life into a philosophy which, in turn, feeds itself back into that life by changing it. This is the reason why *Sartor Resartus* unfolds as an unending proliferation of metaphors, which make both the life and the Philosophy of Clothes disperse into a welter of rather different designations. In such a dispersal the catalytic effect of the space-between becomes manifest, turning *Sartor Resartus* into a self-transforming piece of writing that on this microlevel already epitomizes the way in which a cross-cultural discourse is meant to function.

There are two consequences to be drawn from this interpenetration. First, as the density and accumulation of metaphors accrue into a critical mass, the metaphor indicates that it can never finally verbalize what it aims at, and consequently it accentuates the difference between itself and what it is designed to represent. It is this very difference, however, that triggers the exuberant proliferation of metaphors, which not only unfolds this difference into a multifariousness of aspects, but simultaneously indicates that representation must forever be separated from what it represents.

Second, the profusion of metaphors deconstructs the received notion of representation, not least because representation entails giving presence to what is different in terms of what seems to be familiar. In this respect the excessively proliferating metaphors delineate the space-between as a "black box"[10] by making its very inexplicability "explode" into a self-transforming welter of aspects, by means of which a life is translated into a mainspring of philosophy and the emerging philosophy into a structure of life.

What is epitomized here in a nutshell holds equally true for the cross-cultural discourse as advanced in *Sartor Resartus*. A form of writing that constantly disperses itself reveals an inherent contradiction. The trial runs of the metaphors are marked by a duality. On the one hand they strive to capture something, and on the other their density and dispersal cancel out the very representativeness they appear to have achieved. This counter-vailing movement signals that the cross-cultural discourse is not a third dimension under which the different cultures are to be subsumed. This would only be the case if the metaphors were accorded the quality of adequate representation, thereby establishing the cross-cultural discourse as a transcendental stance. The simultaneous undermining of what the discourse intends to achieve, however, imbues *Sartor Resartus* with a sense of comedy, whose ambivalence is not resolved by exposing German transcendentalism to ridicule but is meant to make the British readers see themselves in the mirror of such ridicule. The comedy is thus turned into a medium for the mutual transposition of cultures.

This duality makes it necessary for the English Editor to intervene. His intervention, however, is not meant to provide a solution.[11] Instead, the Editor retailors the systematic exposition of German transcendentalism in such a manner that it can be conveyed to a British public.

Right at the beginning Teufelsdröckh is praised for adding a new name "to the first ranks of Philosophy, in our German Temple of Honour"(p. 5), which causes the Editor to remark: "*Möchte es* (this remarkable Treatise) *auch im Brittischen Boden gedeihen!*" The famous treatise, however, was published in "*Weissnichtwo*" by "*Stillschweigen und Co*" (p. 5) and seems to be "a very Sea of Thought" (p. 6).

In spite of the Editor's intention to transplant this "remarkable Treatise" into British soil, he nevertheless reports a few facts concerning this strange philosophy that make Teufelsdröckh appear a Don Quixote *redivivus*. Thus a British perspective dominates. After a short while, however, this seemingly ridiculous philosopher, whose loquaciousness was published by *Stillschweigen und Co*, turns out to be "*ein echter Spass- und Galgen-vogel*" (p. 11) himself. This at least implies that there is no immediate need for the British Editor to poke fun at German transcendental philosophy, as Teufelsdröckh himself manifests a sense of superiority by ironizing himself.

The ludicrous Don Quixote turns unexpectedly into a Tristram Shandy, which is also borne out by his work, which is of a "labyrinthic combination, each Part overlaps, and indents, and indeed runs quite through the other" (pp. 26–27). Just as Sterne made Tristram Shandy deconstruct the history of his own life in order to liberate life from the very confinements imposed on it by form, Carlyle makes Teufelsdröckh gamble away all existing forms of writing in order to bring out the fantastic multifariousness of his Philosophy of Clothes.

Thus, Teufelsdröckh presents himself as a dual reading,[12] never coinciding totally with either a Don Quixote or a Tristram Shandy. Whenever one reading appears to become dominant, the other, lurking in the background, gradually asserts itself. This very assertion, however, which might do away with the equivocalness, is again tilted, and the salience of the displaced figure begins once more to loom large.

Tilting between incompatibles transforms Teufelsdröckh into an operator for the switches necessary when cultures have to be telescoped for the purpose of their mutual transmittance and reception. What initially appeared as an empty space manifesting itself in the constant interchange between narrating and arguing, and then as a space between a life lived and a philosophy capturing that life, now reappears as a constant tilting between mutually exclusive readings of the protagonist, thus setting cross-cultural operations in motion.

This tilting game endows the sense of comedy—which permeates *Sartor Resartus*—with a countervailing tendency. Teufelsdröckh is as much a target of comedy as he targets what has to be exposed. In this respect the "black box" between cultures assumes a different shape from those outlined so far in that it makes the ambivalence of comedy turn back on itself.

Teufelsdröckh is not only a humorist, but he also sallies forth into irony. This irony is indicative of his having pierced through the naïveté, the ignorance, the superficiality, and the delusion that dominate the world that he wants to revolutionize by the philosophy he puts forward. As a humorist, however, he knows that the situation in which he finds himself is marked by an ineluctable duality that makes his abstractions look absurd, although they are the remedy for the social ills of that very world that has made him a laughingstock.

Irony and humor, however, equally measure out the distance between a concept-oriented culture and an empirically oriented one, highlighting Teufelsdröckh's helpless superiority and the world's inherent blindness which his abstractions were meant to cure.

As far as the Editor is concerned, poking fun at German transcendentalism implicitly asserts a British attitude which allows transcendentalism to be channeled into empiricism. In the mirror of an experience-based attitude, the Philosophy of Clothes is reflected as convoluted craziness, and therefore the Editor appeals to "Experience" as "the grand spiritual Doctor" (p. 145). However, to reshuffle the abstractions of transcendentalism in terms of experience is not an easy task.[13] Although the Editor cannot think of a "work nobler than transplanting foreign Thought into the barren domestic soil" (p. 63), he has to pull up "the Diligence and feeble thinking Faculty of an English Editor, endeavouring to evolve printed Creation out of a German printed and written Chaos, wherein, as he shoots to and fro in it, gathering, clutching, piercing the Why to the far-distant Wherefore, his whole Faculty and Self are like to be swallowed up" (p. 63). The danger of being swallowed up in such an undertaking requires some kind of protection, and in this respect the sense of humor—deeply ingrained in the British attitude and brought to bear by the Editor—spells out the hope for survival.

This very hope, however, again makes the comedy leveled at that gibberish of abstractions ambivalent. The seemingly chaotic craziness is not meant to criticize the other culture but serves to protect one's own habitual attitudes, so that such a criticism says something not only about the foreignness of the other culture but also about the nature of one's own disposition. In this respect, the foreignness turns into a self-mirroring of those who encounter the alien culture.

Finally, the comic vein running through *Sartor Resartus* is in itself ambiguous.[14] Not only is Teufelsdröckh a humorist, but a great many of his statements are punctured by irony, and more often than not he says things with tongue in cheek. The English Editor is fully aware of the German philosopher's mode of writing, summing it up in the pithy observation: "Nothing but innuendoes, figurative crotchets: the typical Shadow, fitfully wavering, prophetico-satiric; no clear logical Picture" (p. 148). If this convoluted transcendentalism is permeated by streaks of satire, which the author himself intersperses in his own writings, then a satiric or ironic treatment of Teufelsdröckh's endeavors as entertained by the English Editor is on the verge of becoming pointless.

Why poke fun at a humorist? Well, the Editor who is sympathetically disposed towards German transcendentalism anticipates an entrenched British aversion toward these seemingly intangible abstractions. Ridiculing these intellectual acrobatics, however, implies that one is in command of the proper solutions that Teufelsdröckh is groping for in vain. But since the humorist is not as naive as his seemingly ludicrous efforts appear to be, the sense of comedy, as practiced by the Editor, is thus of a twofold nature. On the one hand it serves as a channel of communication through which German idealism can be transmitted into British empiricism. On the other, however, it makes the assumed superiority of satire and irony collapse in

view of the fact that the humorist does not stand in need of being either
unmasked or brought down to earth again. To frustrate an almost natural
reaction of one culture when confronted with another proves to be a strategy on Carlyle's part to open the gate for the other culture to enter.

This is the exact opposite to common cross-cultural relationships,
whose operations are first and foremost guided by projecting one's own
frame of reference onto the alien culture. By making the sense of comedy
militate against itself, Carlyle suspends the natural urge for projections operative in cross-cultural relations.

This tendency is endorsed by what gradually happens to the Editor. He
had considered it his commitment "to guide our British Friends into the
new Gold-country, and show them the mines; nowise to dig-out and ex-
haust its wealth, which indeed remains for all time inexhaustible. Once
there, let each dig for his own behoof, and enrich himself" (p. 166). Yet
this intention to provide guidance to the British reader makes the Editor
cross the boundary to the "Gold-country" himself, in the course of which
he becomes a proselyte, thereby lapsing into a metaphorical style of writing
"with which mode of utterance Teufelsdröckh unhappily has somewhat
infected us." Therefore it is not "hidden from the Editor that many a British
Reader sits reading quite bewildered in head, and afflicted rather than in-
structed by the present Work. . . . Yes, long ago has many a British Reader
been, as now, demanding with something like a snarl: Whereto does all
this lead; or what use is in it?" (p. 215). Although the Editor has apparently
been sucked into Teufelsdröckh's manner of writing, thereby losing "much
of his own English purity" (p. 234), he nevertheless raises the question as
to the purpose of the cross-cultural discourse that he meant to lay bare.

Philosophy of Clothes

In this respect it is worth noting that *Sartor Resartus* is primarily a paradigm of translatability rather than an actual translation of one culture into
another. Its paradigmatic quality has the advantage of exhibiting the workings of mutual transpositions of cultures since they are not as yet guided,
let alone determined, by a pragmatic purpose that would make the translatability subservient to a particular end, as exemplified in Carlyle's later
work *Past and Present*.

The Philosophy of Clothes as put forward by Teufelsdröckh is to be
conceived as an anatomy of representation. As representation presupposes
a given of sorts, one can distinguish different modes of representation. *Imitation* is certainly the most time-honored one, even though something is

bound to happen to the pregiven when represented. Something similar occurs if representation is conceived in terms of *depiction*. What is pregiven will have to be fashioned. But in both these instances representation is to be considered rather as a modality, whose range of molding is limited by a set of qualities the pregiven appears to have prior to its being represented.

In this respect the Philosophy of Clothes can be confined neither to imitation nor to depiction.[15] Instead, it anatomizes the process of translatability itself which, more often than not, is glossed over when imitation or depiction is the overriding concern of representation. Translatability is in itself something intangible; it does not have the nature of a pregiven object and hence can be tackled only by metaphors, as evinced in the Philosophy of Clothes. Clothing something is therefore neither a mode of imitation nor one of depiction. Although it seems that what is to be clothed must somehow preexist, this preexistence is never to be ascertained independently of its being clothed. This is why Carlyle makes it quite explicit that Teufelsdröckh is not a "new Adamite" (p. 45); instead, he promulgates: "Without Clothes, without bit or saddle, what hadst thou been; what had thy fleet quadruped been?—Nature is good, but she is not the best: here truly was the victory of Art over Nature" (p. 46).

If clothes cannot be considered forms of representation in the received sense of the term, as there is no one-way incline from something preexisting to its modes of conceivability, it would seem necessary to recast representation almost entirely. Right from the outset Carlyle keeps "regarding Clothes as a property, not an accident, as quite natural and spontaneous, like the leaves of trees, like the plumage of birds" (p. 2). No doubt such a statement clears Teufelsdröckh from a possible charge of Adamitism. And yet it remains double-edged, since human beings do not enter the world with a "plumage" as animals do. Instead, as Teufelsdröckh confesses: "While I—good Heaven!—have thatched myself over with the dead fleeces of sheep, the bark of vegetables, the entrails of worms, the hides of oxen or seals, the felt of furred beasts; and walk abroad a moving Rag-screen, overheaped with shreds and tatters raked from the Charnel-house of Nature, where they would have rotted, to rot on me more slowly!" (p. 44). Thus the apparent naturalness of wearing clothes is nevertheless a product of human tailoring and therefore definitely not something that comes naturally. What is natural in the kingdom of animals does not apply to human beings, although human beings do not exist apart from the clothes they wear. Obviously there is both identity and difference between clothes and human beings. Why stress difference, when it is made to collapse into an inseparable unity?

Representation as conceived by Teufelsdröckh's Philosophy of Clothes is two-way traffic:

For indeed, as Walter Shandy often insisted, there is much, nay almost all, in Names. The Name is the earliest Garment you wrap round the earth-visiting ME; to which it thenceforth cleaves, more tenaciously (for there are Names that have lasted nigh thirty centuries) than the very skin. And now from without, what mystic influences does it not send inwards, even to the centre; especially in those plastic first-times, when the whole soul is yet infantine, soft, and the invisible seedgrain will grow to be an all overshadowing tree! (p. 69)

Garments, though they are a metaphor for something preexisting, simultaneously pattern what they are meant to represent. This is the plasticity of human nature which, as such, not only remains intangible, but appears to offer itself to being shaped and molded into kaleidoscopically changing forms. In this respect each garment is a "plumage," although the very plasticity allows the "plumage" to be changed whenever necessity arises. Of course, such a patterning bears its own risks either by imprisoning the human being in one of the garments in which it has clothed itself, or by deliberately reifying the clothes to which it has become endeared, as practiced by the "*Dandiacal Body!*" (p. 229).

The Philosophy of Clothes is a kind of shorthand for the patterning and repatterning of human plasticity. It is initially conceived as a metaphor, because human plasticity is not accessible in itself. Yet the metaphor turns into a patterning, and thus functions metonymically, as otherwise human beings elude grasping. A metonymically functioning metaphor bears the inscription that whatever is, is constituted. Thus the Philosophy of Clothes ceases to be representation in the received sense, as a mere shifting of a pregiven into perceivability is no longer the issue. Instead, clothing itself translates the plastic human being into a definitive pattern in order to fathom what otherwise remains elusive. The metonymy, therefore, highlights the garment as a substitute that can be changed when worn out, not least in order to body forth aspects of human plasticity hitherto unthinkable.

The metonymic use of metaphors enables the Philosophy of Clothes to maintain the difference between the patterned and the patternings, and thus allows for the variability of patternings out of which human civilization arises. Simultaneously all forms of civilization are exposed to change as all the patternings that make up society can be repatterned. "Whatsoever sensibly exists, whatsoever represents Spirit to Spirit, is properly a Clothing, a suit of Raiment, put on for a season, and to be laid off.

Thus in this one pregnant subject of CLOTHES, rightly understood, is included all that men have thought, dreamed, done, and been: the whole External Universe and what it holds is but Clothing; and the essence of all Science lies in the PHILOSOPHY OF CLOTHES" (p. 58).

Thus the garment turns out to be a symbol of a special kind that presents itself as a representative of something intangible, and simultaneously shapes that very intangibility, for which it is only a substitute.[16] In Teufelsdröckh's own words: "In a Symbol there is concealment and yet revelation: here therefore, by Silence and by Speech acting together, comes a double significance" (p. 175). As far as the symbol conceals, it indicates through its visibility that "the thing Imagined, the thing in any way conceived as Visible, what is it but a Garment, a Clothing of the higher, celestial Invisible, 'unimaginable, formless, dark with excess of bright'" (p. 52). And as far as the symbol speaks, it indicates that this formless unspeakability can be translated into multifarious aspects by imposing ever-changing patternings on it. Out of this ineluctable duality arises the Philosophy of Clothes, which is an attempt at fathoming the unplumbable by translating it into a welter of perceivable symbols whose very limitations expose them to change. Changes are all the more necessary, because no particular type of garment can ever be equated with the inaccessibility it tries to capture. And therefore every garment is subject to critical inspection in order to find out the ulterior motivation operative in the patterning of the "invisible and unspeakable."

The reason for this duality of the symbol as substitute and patterning is the fact that the "secret of Man's Being is still like the Sphinx's secret" (p. 42). Such a concealment, however, is not something to be penetrated or tackled even, because the unfathomableness of the human being results from a basic ignorance of humankind:

Was Man with his Experience present at the Creation, then, to see how it all went on? Have any deepest scientific individuals yet dived down to the foundations of the Universe, and gauged everything there? Did the Maker take them into His counsel; that they read His ground plan of the incomprehensible All; and can say, This stands marked therein, and no more than this? Alas, not in anywise! These scientific individuals have been nowhere but where we also are; have seen some handbreadths deeper than we see into the Deep that is infinite, without bottom as without shore. (p. 204)

Such an impenetrableness translates itself into a Philosophy of Clothes, because human beings have to live, to interact, to establish organizations, societies, and religions, which obtain their stability by a differentiated sys-

tem of clothes. Therefore clothing itself "has more than a common meaning, but has two meanings" (p. 52). On the one hand it can conceal the
groundlessness from view, which results in a reification of the garment, and
on the other, it can heighten the awareness that, as a substitute, it is a patterning of the unfathomable, guided or caused even by pragmatic exigencies. Thus the groundlessness inscribes itself as duality into the garment.

This may have been one of the reasons that the Editor, when first encountering Teufelsdröckh, took him to be a kind of philosopher, who, if
he were to publish anything at all, would come out with "a refutation
of Hegel" (p. 10). The Editor anticipated correctly that a Philosophy of
Identity would be anathema to someone advocating a Philosophy of Difference.[17] Instead of identifying the "Spirit" with its manifestations, the
Philosophy of Clothes emphasizes difference between an impenetrable
groundlessness and the ensuing necessity to constitute human life by constantly clothing it and then retailoring the clothes.

Trying to chart what remains hidden from view turns the Philosophy
of Clothes into a systematic attempt at coping with openness. Such an attempt implies that the metonymic patterning can never be a projection,
covering up the groundlessness. It rather develops as a recursive loop feeding forward the garment in order to clothe openness—an openness which,
in turn, becomes a negative feedback loop by exposing the garments to
change when they no longer fit. Thus, the recursive loop adjusts future
clothing according to the past performance of the garments. Such a loop
keeps the Philosophy of Clothes from reifying the garments, and simultaneously activates the groundlessness as a form of retailoring.

Such a mutual translatability might be conceived as the hallmark of
culture, not least because the latter, since the advent of the modern age,
can no longer be grounded in an etiological myth. If an impenetrable
groundlessness replaces the etiological myth as the mainspring of culture,
the necessary stability can only be provided by a network of translatabil-
ities, as exemplified by the Philosophy of Clothes. The life of culture realizes
itself in such recursive loops, and it begins to dry up whenever the loop is
discontinued by elevating one of the achievements of its interchange into
an all-encompassing form of representation. Representation runs counter
to translatability, whose ongoing transformations are brought to a stand-
still by equating culture with one of its conspicuous features. The recursive
loop, however, is able to process groundlessness, and as there is no stance
beyond this loop for ascertaining what happens in its operations, the Philosophy of Clothes presents itself as a paradigm for spelling out the blueprint of culture. This paradigm has a dual coding: it makes tangible what

analytically remains ungraspable, and as a mode of translatability it provides access to what is beyond the terms of empiricism.

Validation by Personal Experience

To allegorize German transcendentalism—at least in the way in which Carlyle understood it—allows the transposition of something alien into perceivability in a mode familiar to the receiving culture. This is stressed right at the beginning by the Editor, who keeps pondering, "how could the Philosophy of Clothes, and the Author of such Philosophy, be brought home, in any measure, to the business and bosoms of our own English Nation?" (p. 6).

He tackled it basically by translating the convolutions of transcendentalism into terms of the philosopher's own life, in order to demonstrate that he did not just concoct these seeming absurdities out of nothing; instead, they arose out of personal experience. This allows transcendental speculations to be validated by what happened to their author: "But indeed Conviction, were it never so excellent, is worthless till it convert itself into Conduct. Nay properly Conviction is not possible till then; inasmuch as all Speculation is by nature endless, formless, a vortex amid vortices: only by a felt indubitable certainty of Experience does it find any centre to revolve round, and so fashion itself into a system" (p. 156). Such a linkup, however, provides a different referent for transcendentalism; it is no longer considered a holistic system but is conceived as an impact that is able to turn one's whole life around. The possibility of experiencing what appears to be speculative and of perceiving the invisible are frames of reference different from what may be considered the basic premises of German transcendentalism. The emphasis on experience makes it obvious that German transcendentalism when transposed into British empiricism has to be executed in terms the British reader is familiar with. Yet simultaneously Carlyle reflects on this familiarity, when castigating what he calls "a dead Iron-Balance for weighing Pains and Pleasures on" (p. 176), deeply ingrained in the British disposition. Much as an empirically oriented attitude prevails in order to make this constant trading in abstractions conceivable, if not palatable, to an English audience, Carlyle nevertheless battles against such an attitude, because it tends to congeal into a custom, and as "we do everything by Custom, even Believe by it," he continues quoting from the work of his hero: "Nay, what is Philosophy throughout but a continual battle against Custom; an ever-renewed effort to *transcend* the sphere of blind Custom, and so become Transcendental?" (p. 206). Such a transcendentalism is actually meant to monitor what human beings are doing and, though experience-oriented, they should nevertheless be able to distance themselves from what they are involved in, in order to be able to process that very experience.

This overriding aim is illustrated by Teufelsdröckh's life, because what happens to an individual carries much more conviction than the mere exposition of a philosophical system. Teufelsdröckh himself, although the engineer of the Philosophy of Clothes, nevertheless has reservations about abstractions that are in no way tied to the mastery of life. If being transcendental implies monitoring oneself, then German transcendentalism is turned into an instrument for processing experience as exemplified by Teufelsdröckh's life. Such a life becomes an epitome of how different cultures may be translated into one another.

Highlighting such a process in terms of an individual life is an offshoot of romanticism, which elevated the self into a be-all and end-all. What triggers the necessity of translating cultures into one another is again the moment of crisis which Teufelsdröckh experiences by moving from the stage of the *Everlasting No* through the *Centre of Indifference* to the *Everlasting Yea*. At the outset "The universe" was for him "as a mighty Sphinx-riddle," of which he knew "so little . . . , yet must rede or be devoured." And he continues: "In red streaks of unspeakable grandeur, yet also in the blackness of darkness, was Life to my too-unfurnished Thought, unfolding itself. A strange contradiction lay in me; and I as yet knew not the solution of it"(p. 102). Such a situation plunges Teufelsdröckh into a crisis and, long before Plessner and Lacan[18] described the decentered position of the human being, Teufelsdröckh made the pithy remark "WE are—we know not what" (p. 43). Such a split between being and not knowing what it is to be is at the bottom of Teufelsdröckh's crisis, which develops into an almost unmanageable duality: "It is because there is an Infinite in him, which with all his cunning he cannot quite bury under the Finite" (p. 151–52). This growing awareness that he is also the other of himself triggers the necessity to resolve the duality by translating the decentered positions into one another. Out of such an effort arises the Philosophy of Clothes, whose main thrust is not philosophical speculation, but an attempt to deal with "their *Wirken*, or Influences" (p. 40). This focus on the impact that the Philosophy of Clothes is meant to exercise arises from Teufelsdröckh's experience that his own life appears to him impenetrable, as manifested in his crisis, and consequently has neither to be explained nor to be understood but to be mastered. Such a mastering has a dual reference. On the one hand the garment patterns what it clothes, and on the other the garment exercises

an impact on the social conditions in which it is displayed. In a "Society
. . . to be as good as extinct," in which "the CHURCH [has] fallen speech-
less, from obesity and apoplexy; the STATE shrunken into a Police-Office,
straitened to get its pay!" (p. 184–85), the Philosophy of Clothes is, according to the Editor, meant to excite "us to self-activity, which is the best
effect of any book" (p. 21).

Inciting self-activity means changing worn-out clothes, and the subsequent divesting of society is simultaneously a redressing of its ills, because garments pattern what is otherwise impenetrable and, therefore, can
be exchanged for a more adequate patterning.

Teufelsdröckh's life serves as the living emblem for such a perpetual re-
juvenation. The *Centre of Indifference* is the "black box" of his own life,
a gulf that yawns between his being alive and not knowing what it means
to live. This unplumbable *Centre* that divides him off from himself defies
cognition, and thus translates itself into activity, feeding the *No* into a nascent *Yea*, whose feedback makes the *No* vanish, and this evaporation, in
turn, feeds the strength of conviction into the *Yea*. The life of Teufelsdröckh
provides a vivid illustration of the fact that even an individual life is marked
by a "black box" that may be cast as an empty space, a space-between, or
a *Centre of Indifference*, whose impenetrableness gives rise to recursive
loops of human self-fashioning. Thus, human life mirrors the very structure out of which culture arises. Yet Carlyle left no doubt that the elevated
self inherited from romanticism had to be transformed into a hero, who
testifies that only an outstanding individual is able to endure the crisis by
translating it into a mastery of life.

Conclusion

The experience of crisis gives rise to the Philosophy of Clothes in order to
process human life, whose ground is sealed off from cognitive penetration.
Just as life is unfathomable, so is culture, which in the final analysis manifests itself as a mastery of life. In proportion to a growing awareness that
the assumed fundamentals of life and culture are exposed to erosion, repair
becomes necessary, and this can no longer mean exchanging one set of fundamentals for another. Instead, life and culture have to be reshuffled: in
Teufelsdröckh's case by coming up with the Philosophy of Clothes, in Carlyle's case by designing the cross-cultural discourse of *Sartor Resartus*.

As long as there is an overriding conviction that a culture rests on a firm
foundation, the necessity for a cross-cultural discourse does not arise. For
such a self-understanding of culture, a cross-cultural discourse can only

mean a foreign intrusion. The very fact, however, that there is always a mutual assimilation, incorporation, or appropriation of cultures going on bears witness to exigencies that have to be met. This mutual commerce, however, is at best a patching up of what has been eroded or lost, and it does not substantively contribute to a revitalization of what has become defunct.

A cross-cultural discourse distinguishes itself from assimilation, incorporation, and appropriation, as it organizes an interchange between cultures in which the cultures concerned will not stay the same. A foreign culture is not just transposed into a familiar one; instead, as in the Philosophy of Clothes, a mutual patterning and repatterning is effected by such a discourse. First of all the foreign culture is modeled on conditions set by the receiving one, and thus it becomes defamiliarized. Such a defamiliarization is due to the terms imposed on otherness for its reception, as German transcendentalism is meant to resuscitate the dying culture of *laissez faire*. That is the service to be rendered in face of the crisis that has emerged in an agrarian society plunged into industrial production. In such a takeover of German transcendentalism, its very abstractions are recast. They no longer figure and delineate the manifestations of the *Spirit* on its way to becoming conscious of itself, but are transformed into tools for processing a crisis-ridden culture no longer able to cope with the situation on its own terms. Transcendentalism, therefore, is neither assimilated nor appropriated, but "clothed" in such a manner that its repatterning can serve the self-regeneration of an empirically oriented culture.

To accommodate transcendentalism for such a purpose, some kind of fashioning is necessary in order to make its transmittance feasible. Therefore the Editor pokes fun at the convoluted abstractions of this "written Chaos." However, the sense of comedy that pervades *Sartor Resartus* strangely loses its impact whenever it hits its target, thus invalidating habitual reactions to the absurd musings of German philosophy. The frustrated comedy turns into a trajectory along which the otherwise unpalatable abstractions are able to travel.

The operations of such a cross-cultural discourse are realized in transactional loops; by eclipsing the convention-bound features of the cultures concerned, they feed the crisis of a defunct society into transcendentalism and by a feedback they loop self-activity into empiricism. These transactional loops work chiastically, thus converting the "black box" between cultures into a dynamism, exposing each one to its otherness, the mastery of which results in change. In this respect the cross-cultural discourse is a means of mutually supportive self-regeneration of cultures and provides an opportunity to extend their life span. As a propellant for change, the discourse bears witness to the fact that no culture is founded on itself, which is evinced not least by the array of mythologies invoked when the assumed foundation of a culture has to be substantiated.

The interlinking of cultures brought about by a cross-cultural discourse enacts one culture in terms of the other. German transcendentalism is staged in terms of British empiricism and vice versa. Such a staging prevents one culture from dominating the other, and such a mutual enacting simultaneously implies a suspension of the frames of reference pertaining to the cultures telescoped. If empirical criteria guide the takeover of German transcendentalism, an alien set of references is applied that both dwarfs and enlarges features of transcendentalism. Something similar happens to empiricism when transcendentalism provides the criteria. Such a mutuality has repercussions for the cross-cultural discourse.

With the traditional references suspended, new ones have to be established, which is all the more difficult as the mutual enacting of cultures exposes them to change. The change appears to be necessary, as the old orientation of the respective culture has crumbled, and can no longer serve as a guideline for coping with the crisis. The Philosophy of Clothes gives a very vivid impression of such a situation. Teufelsdröckh writes: "The sight reaches forth into the void Deep, and you are alone with the Universe, and silently commune with it, as one mysterious Presence with another. Who am I; what is this ME? A Voice, a Motion, an Appearance;—some embodied, visualised Idea in the Eternal Mind? *Cogito, ergo sum*. Alas, poor Cogitator, this takes us but a little way" (p. 41).

When the inherited frameworks have become invalidated, the cross-cultural discourse has to establish its own guidelines, and such an endeavor is paradigmatic for cross-cultural discourse in general. It cannot exchange one frame of reference for another; instead, it has to establish multiple references in order to provide sufficient orientation for both the remedy of crisis and the control of change. Therefore routes of reference[19] have to be explored and linked up in chains of kaleidoscopically changing modes of reference.

Teufelsdröckh's Philosophy of Clothes is initially meant to designate German transcendentalism. However, this very designation is used to exemplify how human plasticity is to be shaped. Such a shifting of references continues when this particular exemplification serves as an expression of how a crisis is to be tackled. Designation, exemplification, and expression are no longer tied to a pregiven frame of reference, within which they exercise their function. Instead, they are made to substitute for one another, and the ensuing interchange of their referential mode produces the very guidelines along which the cross-cultural discourse unfolds its operations. Consequently, one culture designates something in another in order to ex-emplify what cannot be seen by the culture concerned, and thus it may turn into an expression of what the culture is like, and why—in view of what it is—it is liable to lapse. Designation of a crisis could then also turn into an exemplification of the remedy which, in turn, may give expression to the other culture invoked. And in doing so, it designates something in that cul-ture to which the culture itself appears to be blind.

A cross-cultural discourse has thus to bring about its own referentiality, which is indispensable as such a discourse *can* only operate within but not beyond reference. The only control to be exercised over the establishment of its own referentiality is the mutual mirroring of the cultures concerned, and this makes the cross-cultural discourse into a stage on which different cultures are enacted under mutually alien conditions. A discourse that lib-erates its referential control from any pregiven frame of reference in order to generate its own control by constantly shifting modes of reference as-sumes aesthetic features. What keeps it, however, from turning into an art-work is its amphibolic nature, as manifested by its inherent duality. It stages a mutual mirroring of cultures and disappears when it has wrought the transformation of the cultures concerned, which highlights its quality as a catalyst, emphasized at the end of *Sartor Resartus*: "Professor Teu-felsdröckh, be it known, is no longer visibly present at Weissnichtwo, but again to all appearance lost in space!" The only trace left is his last saying: "*Es geht an* (It is beginning)" (p. 236).[20]

Memory and Cultural Translation

Gabriel Motzkin

I

*I*n recent decades a new way of providing access to the past has developed; this new science is one that emphasizes memory rather than history, as if the traditional science of history were insufficient to preserve or study the past. Yet the reasons for the development of this new science are not to be found just in some postmodern dissatisfaction with the limitations of history as a discipline. Traditional historical science has found it difficult to confront the changed conditions of the survival of popular memory in the twentieth century. Technically, the task of preserving the past is simpler than ever before. At the same time, the existence of a universal media culture threatens previous forms of popular collective memory. It is paradoxical that technology has apparently made remembering easier, while the events to be remembered seem to be so extreme that there is something scandalous about these memories.

The development of a new science of memory creates new challenges for intercultural transmission. It becomes easier to experience the other's ways of remembering and commemorating the past. Yet this constant exposure to other cultures' memories places one's own identity in question. Is the process of cultural interpenetration one of cultural homogenization, a process that will result in the survival of only one universal culture? Or does it rather indicate a situation in which culture will be increasingly defined in terms of the relation to some other and less in terms of one's own cultural traditions?

The blurring of cultural boundaries obscures the task of translation. Cultural interpenetration appears to mean that the act of translation becomes less difficult. But is this so? Or does the convergence of cultures not rather make translation *more* difficult as the boundaries between the own and the other seem to fade? Does not translation rather imply that what is read, assimilated, and therefore remembered, hovers at the edge of identity, as something that is neither quite own nor quite other?

Different societies remember and commemorate their pasts in different ways. Despite cultural convergence, the different ways in which cultures deal with twentieth-century events show the persistence of the need for translation. Yet this requirement is a subtle one. Monuments are erected in similar styles: what distinguishes Holocaust monuments in Israel, America, and Germany? Only their different emplacements in their respective cultures, the identities of the individuals who confront them. Cultural translation is then not a tangible process between languages or styles, but rather an intangible one between conflicting historical experiences as contexts for similar artifacts. The styles have converged, but the histories have not.

The contemporary memorialization of historical experiences raises the question of whether commemoration really signifies a memory of events, or rather an active process of participation in transforming a past into a present and a future. Even if the rites of memory are copied from one of its temples to another, still the identity of the worshipers remains bound up with the significance of the rite. A German putting on a skullcap at Yad VaShem, the Holocaust memorial in Jerusalem, has a different memorializing experience than a Jew performing the same action. Put another way, is translation a translation of memories, or rather a translation of practices between one context and another?

Participating in the rites of memory is a quasi-religious function: it signifies acceptance of the truth of what is being remembered. I can go to a monument without believing in the memory, but my participation in its rite of memory is also an assent to the truth of the event that the monument memorializes. However, this participation does not mean that I have the same meaning-experience as others or even as the builders of the monument intended. A self-conscious critical attitude does not impugn the truth of the commemorated event but rather its significance. In this way, monuments are different from churches.

II

Otherness can survive in different ways in identity-forming memories, depending on whether the others have survived or not, and whether one's own past is seen as a foreign otherness. The memory of the existence of a long-vanished enemy, such as Amalek for the Jews, is often also a definition of self. When both sides to a cataclysmic confrontation survive, however, the continued existence of the other makes this kind of self-definition through the other more traumatic. It also makes it more difficult, as the memory of the other and the present interaction with the other diverge. For Jews, the differences between contemporary Germans and the Nazi past are as problematic as the continuities.

Even when there is no contact, the continued existence of the other poses more of a threat than if the other had ceased to exist. The other's continued existence implies the continued existence of a different point of view concerning a trauma that defines one's own identity. The other poses a threat not only to present identity, but also to that aspect of identity that stems from origins. The other's continued existence implies a war about the past, as well as about the present.

It is even more threatening when the enemies warring for the control of memory are, so to speak, the parents, where father and mother each have their own memories, and these memories are not just separate traditions but specific memories of the conflict between the two sides—that is, where the identity of each parent can be transmitted only in terms of the conflict with the other progenitor. The Norman conquest of England is a case where both sides are the progenitors of the English nation. For the English to exist as a people that is neither Norman nor Saxon, each of the two major progenitive groups had to take on the other's identity in such a way that the memory and the perspective of both was preserved. The elimination of either memory as a subjective perspective of self, that is, an identity-forming memory, would entail the destruction and disappearance of the English people as English. The balance necessary for this kind of tense neutrality between two warring memories can be maintained only through the creation of a new identity, for which both progenitors are partial ancestors.

It may also happen that one's own past becomes other. A historical chasm or a sea change in the civilization of a descendant people may be such that the memory of the original group seems to be a prememory indicating a preconscious preidentity rather than an actual memory. Yet in this case, the group often does not want to admit its lack of connection to the past, preferring to expand its identity retrospectively to include a transformed memory of the past; the past is assimilated to the group's identity through an artificial creation of collective memory. One such example is the tense relation between modern Greeks and Greek antiquity; modern Greek identity derives primarily from Christianity and from the struggle with the Turks. In a similar way, Italians view the Romans both as part and not as part of their own identity. The tension latent in the inclusion of such a past is manifested in the controversy over the otherness of the past, that is, its "closeness" to or "distance" from the present.

The possible choice of a past implies the ability to reselect one's parents and one's past enemies. While nineteenth-century historians believed that one cannot choose one's past, their practice in fact reflected this possibility. The choice of a new past often imported new contradictions into the historical definition of identity. Yet historical changes in the present often required not only a reinterpretation of the past but the creation of a new and radically different past.

Recreating the past could also make it possible to deny subsequent history in defining one's own identity. To the degree that subsequent history has been traumatic, part of the past must be denied. One way of denying the past is to remove the ugly part of history from one's identity by claiming that that part of the past happened to someone else. Often, traditionalist forces perceive the cause of revolution as being the incursion of foreign forces into the national identity. For a long time, Napoleon remained "the Corsican" to his enemies, and everybody knew that Corsica had been acquired by France only a few months before his birth. This kind of denial is a suppression of a remembered past, the conscious suppression of a past of which all are aware; the experiences that must be denied have occurred after the formation of group identity, and what they then engender is a kind of cognitive dissonance. In the nascent separation between American Jews and Israelis, one can observe both the war over possession of the past and the conflict about which aspects of the past should be denied.

III

Different cultures' acceptance or denial of historical discontinuity influences the translation of pasts from one culture to another. Is the adoption of a new past necessarily a means of emancipation from a past identity?

Historical studies were central in the formation of national identity in nineteenth-century Europe. Yet historical science could not give a uniform answer to the question of historical continuity. As a discipline, history assumes a distance between the present and the past; paradoxically, this sense of distance could vitiate the sense of national identity. Many cultures sought to conceal the sensed difference in identity between present and past. To the degree that they sought to define collective identity historically, they were skeptical about the relevance of living memory for the formation of identity. Moreover, living memory could threaten the historical contextualization of events. A hidden assumption of memory is that the continuing resonance of events is as important for the creation of group identity as the events themselves. On the other hand, the development of modern historical consciousness affected the way in which living memory is experienced.

Historical procedures introduced a new tension into the formation of group identity, for it meant that the task of forming group identity requires a critical self-understanding. Historical consciousness, by transforming the relations between memory and identity, also changed the structure of the relations between self and other. Since forgetting is not a historical category, in a historical conception of identity the other can never be obliterated or forgotten. Historical consciousness requires the preservation of the other, and hence a careful definition of the boundaries of the other as an inhabitant of our historical identity. In a historically aware culture, it is unavoidable that both sides to a war over memory absorb the other's memory as part of their own memory.

Even before the modern period, the memory of otherness was not always linked to land or language. But premodern historical memory did not make an issue of the other's perspective on one's own identity. Jewish memory was not concerned with the Spanish memory of the Jews in Spain. The Jewish bonds with the common memory of Spanish culture had been severed. Such a divorce can even signify a rejection of the other's memory. For the Spanish, on the other hand, the Jewish question survives as a historical question about Spanish national identity. Some Spanish historians even attribute a major role to the Jews in the formation of Spanish identity. The disjunction is rather one between the living Jews of the present and the dead Jews of the past, who are the Jews who live on in Spanish memory.

Spanish history reenters Jewish memory through the activity of Jewish historians of Spanish Jews. Their ideal of the complete preservation of the past implicitly introduces the history of the Spanish perspective on the Spanish past into the Jewish perspective on the Jewish past. Yet this kind of reencounter resonates because of a continuing hidden reference to the other as a defining identity in Jewish history. Memory's possibility of transcending land and language may be characteristic of the Jews, but it is a possibility implicit in the relation between memory and identity.

IV

The confluence of events that marked the Second World War emphasized tendencies in the Jewish relation to the other that were already apparent but that now became dominant.

Since World War II, a great body of literature has been engaged in a new pursuit: trying to explain the existential situation of Jews to a presumed other. The question in this literature, largely written by Jews, is not so much how Jews perceive the other, but how Jews are perceived by the other. The innovative move in this literature is the idea that Jews can change this perception by the other "as other." In that way a new dynamic of identity, of relation of self to other, is set in motion—one, however, that involves the explicit internalization of the perspective of the other as part of Jewish memory.

This kind of internalization characterizes the entire modern period of Jewish history. Whereas this internalization of otherness, however, previously implied assimilation, now it has become a way of setting off self from other: the perspective of the other on the self can be taken up as an emphasis of the difference between self and other. Such an assumption of the other's perspective as different can occur when assuming another's perspective as part of one's identity has been historically possible for enough time so that it has become a memory. Assimilation, as a border of lived Jewish experience, slips slowly into the past, and is now viewed from the very different vantage point of contemporary Jewish experience, one for which the rampant anti-Semitism of the prewar years no longer threatens or contributes to assimilation. Assuming the vantage point of the other is possible because the other's vantage point has been detached from its context. As a possibility of perceiving the past from the present, it is no longer assimilatory or based on the presumption that the other is anti-Semitic. Instead it is part of that definition of self which is made through constituting the other rather than accepting the other as given. The other can now be constituted as other because part of his otherness is mediated only by memory, so that the real disjunction to be bridged as a consequence of the constitution of the other by the self is the disjunction between the other as he was in the past and the other as he continues to exist.

The rememberer has a precious possession. He remembers the other as seen from his own perspective. Indeed, this other exists only because the other's other, the remembering self, remembers him. Insofar then as the other in turn requires the assumption of the rememberer's perspective for his own continued existence, he must gain access to that memory which is the exclusive possession of the rememberer. In order for the rememberer to remember, however, it may be that he must resolutely ignore any transformation that has taken place in the other, and must therefore deny the actual other the access to the memory that he has of him. Hegel could not foresee a situation in which reflection implies a dialectic for which no reconciliation of pasts is possible. However, the situation may also exist in which the memory of the constituted other is necessary for the definition of self, but this memory itself is so traumatic that it can only be cured through the therapeutic mediation of the transformed other. Here then memory and experience conflict, and it is an open question whether this conflict is salutary or noxious.

The situation in which Jews seek to explain themselves to others, and by doing so first create these others, is ambiguous. On the one hand, it could even be thought that the use of languages of other peoples is only coincidental, and that the true situation is a kind of Jewish memory seeking to make sense of events in its own terms. But this is not so. Jean Amery, for example, quite consciously imagines an audience that does not include only Jews. So does Paul Celan. Present is a belief that these others can understand the hermetic experiences that these writers seek to describe.

This belief that all people can understand the Jews, a belief that is rooted in the most fundamental assumptions of modern humanism, is opposed to that current opinion according to which no one can understand the most recent past. Both the film *Shoah* and the oral testimonies of survivors as described by Lawrence Langer in his book *Holocaust Testimonies: The Ruins of Memory*,[1] make the point that the postwar Jewish "memory" of the Holocaust and of World War II is quite unlike the memory of the survivors. Yet on the other hand the effort made to record survivors' memories shows that the succeeding generations are quite concerned with bridging the gap of understanding, that gap which the witnesses themselves claim is unbridgeable.

In both the book and the film, the Germans fade: in the memories of the victims, the Germans are not central protagonists; they function more like *dei ex machina* who set trains of horribly random events in motion. The moral appears to be that victims are concerned with their own reactions, and not with the motives of their persecutors.

But the luxury of distance from events has created a different situation for postwar Jews. If one looks at the chronology of the reception of the Holocaust, the first reaction was one that sought to grasp this event in universal rather than in particular terms: if anything was grasped as being peculiar and particular, it was the Nazis and not the Jews. The presumed particularity of the persecutors and the normality of the victims created a situation in which the first generations that did not themselves experience the Second World War knew as much if not more about the causes of Nazism than they did about the reactions of their forebears. The majority of books written and the weight of the educational system viewed the rise of

Nazism as the real historical riddle that had to be explained to future generations, not the historically marginal reactions of Holocaust victims. But
this mediation of memory through scholarship created a gap for the succeeding generations between the living memory of the survivors among
them and what they had learned as part of their own collective memory
of the Holocaust from books and teachers, a striking nonsimultaneity of
the simultaneous.[2] Consequently, the return to the study of the memory
of the Holocaust is replete with the evidence of this gap, where the memory of the survivors of the Holocaust must be turned into the memory of
succeeding generations on the basis of what succeeding generations already know about the Holocaust, and this knowledge has little to do with
the experience of the survivors.

In this case, the other has been so reconstituted that his identity is mediated by the self: the other for memory is no longer the same other that
existed in the concrete historical situation. Rather a transference of otherness from the refused other to the other of self has occurred. Thus otherness
can be integrated into self without confronting the absolute otherness of
the other. Memory makes other and self part of the same identity, denying
otherness to the real other. The identities discovered in history and in memory diverge completely.

V

In contrast, a different situation can arise for Germans. In the German situation the threatening situation in which the self simply becomes a mediation for the other's identity cannot arise. Rather, the self is constituted in
such a way that its identity is mediated by the memory of the other. For
German memory, self and other threaten to diverge completely, so that the
boundaries of identity cannot be set. If the Jewish other is rejected, Germans can only define identity by endorsing the Nazi past. Current disturbances in Germany show both that historical science is inadequate as a way
of defining identity, and that unwanted memories will resurface in the absence of the memory of the other as a structure for memory.

In the situation where either a gap in memory exists, or the conscious
suppression of memory is a response to the inability to deal with memory,
the memory of the other becomes necessary as a bridge to one's own past.
Germans begin with their alienation from their own recent past, and then
seek ways of establishing continuity in memory around the gap in their
history created by the Nazi years.

Yet at the same time that memory seeks to find ways around history, there is a growing number of memoirs of the Third Reich in all its aspects. While this abundance of memoirs may simply be an effect of the old age of the war generation, their function for readers is not merely purgative, as it may be for the writers, for the readers are concerned with the question of which part of their past should be denied.

The threat to German identity posed by the Holocaust, in the situation where the acceptance of the entire past is impossible, is the denial of the entire past. From the strictly historicist point of view familiar in German culture, all of the German past would point to this aporia. Unlike in prewar Germany, a strictly deterministic theory of history cannot be popular in postwar Germany. Then only their victims can serve the Germans as the mediation to their own past. Unless they can overcome the Holocaust, the German relation to the German past will always have something fictional and partial about it, for it will be a time before destruction, where destruction is metonymic for both the creation of the other and self-creation. In that case, we would have pre-Germans and Germans. Viewed historically, this statement is an exaggeration; German identity has survived breaks no smaller than the Second World War. From the point of view of memory, however, the continuity of German identity has been threatened and must be reestablished. The unrest of unification has shown the instability of memory in a situation in which history and memory conflict. Here the conflict over the role of the memory of the Jewish other is a conflict about the boundaries of identity.

The traditional solution to the problem of the fragility of memory in German culture was the recourse to history, as if a retrospective history could supply the continuous identity that was not automatically available in memory. The question is whether collective memory can provide identity despite such major historical threats, or whether it must become retrospective and historical in order to integrate and neutralize traumatic events in the collective consciousness. But if retrospective history cannot provide such a substitute identity, then collective memory, being weaker in this case, cannot help either. Hence recourse must be had to the other's memory as an aid to the memory of self, for here the memory of self is too weak to survive alone. To that degree, the Germans must assume the memories of their victims; they must become Jews in an aesthetic sense (meaning that they can only do so imaginatively and empathically and not really). Thus what was marginal for them becomes central, and their memories become less memories of their own past and more those of the other's past.

This opposition in the dynamic of relations between self and other between German and Jew is further complicated in that both share a universal memory as a consequence of belonging to one collective international culture, of which both, like other peoples, are only half-citizens, but which nonetheless creates its own dynamic of relations of self to other in universal memory, which then overlies the particular relations to the past. The memory of belonging to a world cultural community is very short, but however young it affects the different and opposed pasts of the members of that community, who then must mediate between their own particular memories and their participation in the new mass universal retrospection.

Perhaps the contemporary dialectic of self and other is as much affected by the desire to preserve particular memory in universal culture as by the particular relation of memory to the past. The definition of an ever-greater part of collective memory as universal, shared by all peoples, implies a competition for memory within the context of universal identity. Defining the memories of the past that impose identity in this altered context imparts particular significance within a context so wide that it appears as if all can be remembered. In the context of a universal culture, perhaps the only memory possible is a universal one, vitiated of any particular significance. However, the universal culture is itself a creature of time; the cult of memory may then be a way of insuring continued existence with the aim of a renewed postuniversal particularity.

The tendency to the universalization of collective memory has been present since antiquity, but it has been stimulated by the development of universalist ideologies and accelerated by historical events that impinge on all peoples. All the nations that fought in the Second World War are defined by their memory of that war, however great the differences between their memories. Except for the Germans, the Germans are the other for all the peoples who fought in the war on either side, even if the Germans are a different other for each of the respective peoples. And how do the peoples remember the Germans, irrespective of their attitude to the Germans of today? In all cases, the memory of the Germans is associated with the Holocaust. Thus they (the French, the Danes, or the Dutch) were fighting the people who murdered the Jews, irrespective of their own attitude to the Jews.

Thus the Holocaust becomes a universal event, a universal myth of origin, a universal collective memory, a founding event of the new history of the postwar period. However, this puts the Jews in a special place, one that is not completely to their liking, one that complicates their own work of memory. The Jews have entered universal history, but on quite different terms than they would wish to. Israeli Jews often link this entrance into history to the founding of the Jewish state, and so are even more uncomfortable with the Holocaust's universal aspect; they would seek, to some degree, to preserve the Holocaust as a special memory, as a particularizing memory of the Jewish people, much like the destruction of the Temple. But the centrality of the Jews in the historical self-interpretation of the post-modern period is not attributable only to the existence of the Jewish state. When books such as Reinhard Rürup's *Emanzipation und Antisemitismus*[3] interpret the history of the Jewish question in the nineteenth century as the central test for the scope and validity of emancipation (see also David Vital's *The Future of the Jews*[4] for this interpretation), they are disseminating a self-interpretation that would have been quite strange in non-Jewish prewar historiography, in which the status of the Jews was at best an issue of otherness, if not a marginal issue in the development of modernity. The Jewish question has assumed a central role in the official interpretation of the history of modern identity only in the postwar period. From the perspective of universal culture, the fate of Israel is a universal fate because of its link to the Holocaust. That situation creates a special tension for Jews, in that this universality is thrust upon them. They must somehow reconcile universal and particular memory, for the Jews also belong to the universal culture of postwar modernity and are also influenced in their views of the Holocaust by the reigning views in western culture. This reigning view of the Holocaust is, however, ambivalent about the particularity of the Jews, for part of the process of universalization is the setting of the Jew as the universal victim, and then the empathic identification with the Jew as the universal victim.

Jews perceive themselves as the universal others for others, whereas for others the Jews are universal others for selves. For Jews, the obstacle to a reconciliation with this fate is the assumption of the identity of a universal self, one for which all of history has become memory. For others, both their universality and their particularity remain possible only through the internalization of the particularity of universal others, the assumption of otherness as a concrete memory and not only as an abstract universalism.

In our time, the problem of collective memory is not which memory is particularizing, as was the case for much of Jewish history, but which collective memory can be universal. It is in that sense that the Holocaust is not marginal, as it is in many histories written about the Second World War or the Nazi movement. Since the Holocaust has become a central world memory, Germans must confront the Holocaust both as a universal memory and as a particular memory. Belonging to an international culture within which they must define their own memory, Germans must recreate their memory in terms of the universal dialectics of self and other set by that culture. Their situation is made more difficult by the requirements of the emergence of a double self as universal and as particular. Here yet another doubling takes place. On the one hand, the international culture is also an other for the national culture as self. On the other hand, the dialectic of self and other has been internalized because one is also part of the international culture as self, and so one must relate to one's own culture as other.

That is the question: to what degree can one take on the memory of the other as one's basic activity of remembering, and at what point does that stop? Traditionally, certain memories of the other were forgotten. The emergence of a universal collective memory makes such forgetting almost impossible. If suppressed memories of conquered others often revenged themselves in the discomfort of collective memory, then the emergence of a universal culture makes the problems of the memories of conquest and suppression, repression and revenge, into universal questions.

When we take over the memory of the other, we detach that memory from the other's historical experience. We have no access to the ways in which the other's children remember; they are caught in a different dialogue of approach and distancing than we are. This situation creates a tension for memory. Not only do memory and history diverge; memory is divorced from experience. The prime function of collective memory is the conferral of the identity requisite for the confrontation with experience. Here memory and experience conflict; we have recourse to the memory of the other to assuage this conflict, to redefine memory so as to render it more adequate for the task of experience. That memory, however, has been deprived of experience so as to make it serviceable for us. The turn to the memory of the other does not yet resolve the problem of the reconciliation between memory and experience, between past and present.

VI

This cultural gap between memory and experience may help explain why memory has become such a central issue in contemporary cultural self-reflection.

Memory first became an acute issue at the end of the nineteenth century because of the sensed inadequacy of history as a way of dealing with the past.[5] Philosophers became interested in the relation between personal time experienced as memory and the structure of universal time. Within historical studies, this division between the experience of time and its structure resurfaced as a division between structural (social, economic, or cultural) and narrative history. Implicitly, the analyses of history as structure and history as experience utilize different intuitions of time. The corresponding question is whether collective memory structures the cultural experience of time or is structured by it.

The analogous problem of whether the sense of time defines our view of the past, or our sense of a past structures our experience of time, became a problem for modern historical consciousness. Historical consciousness had presupposed three claims: history can subsume the personal experience of the past, making personal testimony dubious; the experience of the past can be studied by a science of the past, making collective memory superfluous; consciousness, whether of the past, the present, or the future, is historical consciousness, making individual memory secondary. For historicism, memory was significant only insofar as it contributes to the development of historical consciousness.

The ever-greater emphasis placed by historical studies on the past as a historical reality that cannot be grasped in terms of individual consciousness implies that contemporaries can only be partially conscious of their situation. In that case, however, their partial awareness of their present also limits their access to the past. Hence a history for which the inaccessibility of the past is a consequence of the relativity of the present means that history cannot provide access to the past to present-day Germans on the basis of their own experience.

The contrary development of an antihistoricist view emphasizing memory, however, did not decide the question of whether memory has a nonhistorical link to the past—that is, whether the existence of memory shows that the past is something other than its history, or whether memory is something other than the past. Memory may be a construct that follows upon the experience of pastness. Moreover, the position could be adopted that pastness is not a prime determinant of consciousness.

The consequent awareness that the study of memory is not the same as memory itself has contradictory implications. On the one hand, the study of memory can be viewed as a replacement for memory in an age in which monuments forget or are forgotten rather than remember; in an age of instant access to whatever survives of the past, the study of memory is possible because its objects are all taken to be simultaneously present. On the other hand, the study of memory may be the only remaining way of revealing the gap between the study of consciousness and consciousness itself. Most of the human sciences tend to conclude that a science of consciousness can be equated with consciousness. In historical studies, this convergence between history and the study of history has been a constant preoccupation; some have viewed this historical reflexivity as the advantage of historical consciousness. In the study of memory, however, this reflexivity is not possible, since the time- or consciousness-structure of a science of memory is clearly different from that of memory itself. The study of memory raises the question of whether the process by which a science replaces its objects with its own constructions is inevitable. Thus on the one hand the study of memory is a replacement for memory itself, and on the other hand the study of memory is that study par excellence in which the study cannot replace its object with itself, its text with its critique. The analysis of the structure of the science of memory can "never" be identical with the analysis of the structure of memory.

However, this could happen if a science of memory becomes the primary way in which we remember collectively. If the scientists of memory become the guardians of the past, the controllers of discourse, their prime salutary effect will have been vitiated, for they will then be studying themselves. Then, however, the object of the science of memory will no longer be memory, for the memory being studied will only be the memory that is constituted as the object of the science; as an object of science, such a memory-construct will no longer be the experience of memory but rather experience as it has been transformed by science.

VII

While the study of memory may perhaps determine what is remembered and thus replace collective memory, the history of memory cannot replace memory; the history of memory is continually being subverted by new forms of memory. Not only do new events replace old ones in memory, as they do in history, but also the way in which things are being remembered is constantly shifting. This constant shift in ways of memory is the precondition for the cultural variation between different ways of remembering. There are at least two kinds of variability in memory, the variability of events and the variability of ways of remembering, for otherwise the variability of events would always imply new forms of remembering.

It is this dynamism of memory in relation to the past that makes it possible for us to imagine that we remember events of which we have no personal memory. We are not remembering the events. Neither, however, are we remembering the physical act of being told about the events. The tale creates a memory, and that memory functions as a memory of the event, where there can be no memory of the event. Any memory must first remember the ways of remembering, which is not the same as remembering events or being told about them.

Collective ways of remembering must also themselves be remembered. A tradition of a way of remembering means that the events to be remembered are tied to the ways in which they are remembered, and it presupposes that individuals are taught to remember how to remember before they are told what it is that they are to remember.

However, events, texts, or monuments may require new ways of remembering: when Proust's Marcel remembers through the mediation of involuntary memory, he introduces a new way of memory, which only then can serve as the underpinning for other ways of remembering. When a monument poses the command "remember!" to a viewer, it may suggest a new way of remembering no less than a painting can educe a new way of seeing.

Ways of remembering are influenced by the different significance accorded to memory in different cultures. This different significance can affect both what is remembered and how it is remembered. However, such a variation between cultures in the ways of memory implies that the process of memory is not purely receptive. Unless we view memory as being engaged in an active dialogue with the outside world, we would have to conclude that while experience can modify memory, memory cannot modify experience. The possible modification of experience by memory, however, assumes that memory is not only an act. The idea that a memory can be communicated assumes that memory can modify experience not only as act but also as significance.

We have seen how different historical situations challenge different cultures to create new modes of remembering. What we have not considered is the issue of the global significance of memory in the formation of these cultures. Jewish culture and German culture accorded a different significance to memory in the formation of their identities. The survival of these patterns of apprehension of the past means that there exists a structural difference in the interpretation of the past that does not stem from the dialectic of self and other. This difference is not solely one of different histories, nor does it signify merely a different valuation of the past; it implies a different cultural strategy of evaluating any past. While a historicist explanation of memory would assume that the different role played by memory in different cultures is a consequence of the different histories of those cultures, the intuition of history in different cultures also varies with the different role of memory; the existence of a given way of remembering may first make a given history possible.

Why a culture remembers in a given way may be due to the importance that culture accords to memory. But it may also be the effect of exogenous forces. One such factor is the point in historical time at which a culture has shifted from one way of remembering to another. All cultures have some form of remembering, but the conscious decision to increase the cultural energy devoted to memory takes place in a context of both available technologies and available ways of remembering in the surrounding cultures. The Jewish emphasis on memory as the reenactment of written text through reading, interpreting, and observing the law should be viewed in the context of other ways of remembering in antiquity. The lack of a developed historical self-consciousness in traditional Judaism is a consequence of the existence of a sophisticated alternative technology of memory. The existence of this technology, however, impeded the adoption of a historical self-consciousness as a factor in the definition of Jewish identity.

Contemporary Jewish culture is characterized by the simultaneous existence of competing technologies of memory. Moreover, the problem of the translation from one code of memory to another has not yet been resolved. Jewish historiography and continued Jewish traditional learning coexist uneasily, affecting each other in hidden ways. In this situation, collective memory is fragmented.

In the same way, the development of a historical self-consciousness in modern Europe reflected a crisis of memory, a need for new ways of remembering. The adoption of history as a way of remembering implied a distance from the past, one that history claimed it could span. In turn, the development of academic history suppressed older ways of remembering the past.

This kind of crisis is particularly acute in oral cultures when they are accosted by European civilization. Nothing seems as artificial as the collections of collective memories of preliterate peoples published as academic tomes in the West. Such museological impositions of modern technologies of memory imply a preservation of memories at the expense of the preservation of ways of remembering. These cultures never had the experience of a prehistorical written codification of memory, and so they are unable to address the problem of the transposition of ways of remembering from oral traditions to written tradition, a problem Judaism confronted in antiquity.

The cultural adoption of history as a way of remembering the past both institutionalized memory in a new way and also institutionalized the practice of forgetting collective memories. Henceforth collective memory did not belong to history. Especially German culture adopted history as a replacement for collective memory. German historians used historiography to create a collective identity as a replacement for the nonexistent institutional continuity with the past. The consequence was the relative weakness of collective memory in German culture. This weakness is one reason that the issue of collective memory is particularly acute in postwar Germany, in a context in which historiography can no longer serve as the basis for national identity, and in which the need for collective memory is particularly pressing because of recent history and the dangerous fragility of German collective identity, a fragility that makes it possible for suppressed pasts to reappear. The past reappears not when it is forgotten, *pace* Goethe and Santayana, but when it can be neither remembered nor forgotten.

Remarks on the Foreign (Strange) as a Figure of Cultural Ambivalence

Renate Lachmann

Cultural Mechanism: The Transformations of the Foreign/Strange

*C*ultural semiotics operates with an inventory of categories and concepts for the analysis of cultural processes that is meant to describe totally the techniques of self-interpretation and self-modeling (transformation, translation, transcoding) by which a culture attempts to stabilize itself. Such categories are *self-description*; *cultural metalanguage* or *metatext*; *cultural grammar*; *dynamic mechanism*. Among these the concept of a *semantic binarism* of the "own" (the native) and the "other" (the foreign, strange or alien) seems to be the most interesting for the purpose of this essay. The typology of culture that Jurij Lotman proposes starts out with the cardinal question "what does 'to have meaning' mean?"[1] and is dependent on studies analyzing the role of the text and the role of signs in individual cultures or in individual stages of a culture's development. The sign type (text type) preferred at a given time becomes the parameter for describing culture. Such a notion of culture (understood as a unified text governed by a unified code and as the sum total of all texts governed by such codes) develops specific modes of producing meaning. In general terms, it is thus necessary to ask how a culture functioning as a semiotic system relates to the sign and to semioticity. This relation to sign and semioticity is reflected, on the one hand, in the "self-assessment" (*samoocenka*) of a culture, in its descriptive system—that is, in the grammars it develops about itself—and, on the other, in the way the texts produced by the culture or relevant to it are evaluated with regard to their functionality. The questions regarding the character of the sign type and the text type are related, for both questions are concerned with the problem of "semiotic-ity" (*znakovost'*).

Lotman's typological models are constructed as dichotomies. The op-positivity of the cultural codes that he reconstructs and that can define both the diachrony and the synchrony of a culture is founded on the following criteria: How a culture models its relationship to extraculture; which role a culture ascribes to texts; and how a culture ascribes value to signs.[2]

To the extent a culture recognizes or denies semioticity, it draws a boundary line between itself and extraculture, which it defines either as anticulture (thus having a negative semioticity) or as nonculture (having no semioticity whatsoever). Cultural mechanism—that is, the displace-ment of one cultural type by another—takes place according to the same principle. Thus, in Lotman's concept, cultural dynamism reveals itself as based on the desemiotization of areas that have been accorded semioticity in the preceding stage of a culture and in the semiotization of new areas. The basic dichotomy that fuels this dynamic process is that between the "own" and the "other."

The Russian language has at its disposal a variety of etymologically akin expressions (with proliferating connotations) that represent the se-mantic field of the "other":

other = *drugoj*; *drug* = friend
strange (unfamiliar) = *strannyj*; *strana* = country (the "other" country);
    čužoj
foreign = *inostrannyj, čužoj*
peculiar = *čudnoj*
marvelous (miraculous) = *čudesnyj*
monstrous = *čudoviščnyj*
wild = *dikij* (with the connotations of wild and strange; compare German
    wildfremd)

From *strannyj* is derived *strannik* or "wanderer." A *strannik* deliberately leaves his or her social conditions, "leaves culture." One could term this an intracultural migration in which a person rejects his or her "own" system and institutionalized life in search of an asystemic authenticity and im-mediacy. This paradigm of intracultural self-exclusion (a prominent ex-ample is the moribund Tolstoy) is tolerated from the dominant culture's point of view. This is especially true of the fool in Christo (*jurodivyj*).

Viktor Šklovskij coined *ostranenie*, his term of estrangement (defam-iliarization), from *strannyj*.

The philosophical term for alienation is *otčuždenie*, which derives from *čuždyj* (in German estrangement and alienation are closely linked etymologically: *Verfremdung/Entfremdung*).

The stranger (foreigner), *čužoj*, has an intra- and extracultural double status insofar as he or she either belongs to another country (the actual foreigner, who at the same time may be the enemy) or to the same culture. The foreigner within culture appears to be the representative of the otherworldly (as sorcerer, prophet, or shaman); he or she functions as the "other" of culture. Intracultural reactions to both—fear and defensiveness toward the "foreign" foreigner and respect and veneration toward the "native" foreigner—keep changing since the attributes of both phenomena either fuse or interchange: the sorcerer becomes an enemy; the foreigner a sorcerer. Identification of the concept of the other world as foreign country with that of the otherworldly, the beyond, makes the enemy connote the devil (*vrag*, cf. Latin *inimicus*). The axiology of "own" and "foreign" itself is subject to radical semantic shifts. "Foreign" takes on the attribute of true culture, "own" or "native" that of the precultural. This is especially true of the Kievan Rus after Christianization. The collision of native Russian (pre-) culture, its paganism, with Byzantine orthodoxy creates a generative pattern of antagonistic duality that seems to be the very matrix of Russian culture throughout the centuries. Double culture as an intracultural split paradigm is obviously a transformation of the dichotomy culture/extraculture.

In other words, Russia's contact/conflict with three foreign domains in the course of its history—Byzantium, Asia (Tartars, Mongols, later Siberia), and the West—is formally reflected within culture in such dualisms as unofficial/official, pagan/Christian, old believers/reformers, Slavophils/westernizers, political or religious orthodox thinkers/dissidents, and so on.

As far as the binarism especially of pagan and Christian is concerned, processes of mutual amalgamation (transcoding) and axiological shifts within the hierarchy of social and religious values take place in the course of which the "other" is incorporated and adopts the status of the "own." It must be noted that the pagan, as the representative of the intracultural foreign in this binary structure, axiologically fuses with alien religions (Islam and Catholicism, and, after the fall of Constantinople, even with Greek Orthodoxy), the priestly representatives of which are considered heretics. In this case, the pagan has a negative index. The positive evaluation of pagan as progressive, western, and enlightened leads to peculiar forms of social behavior, such as the institution of serf harems established by Russian landowners in the eighteenth century.

From these constant axiological shifts and amalgamations of social forms and the interpretive discourses they engender ensues a radical destabilization of the cultural system as a whole. The dominant official culture reacts to its refraction (dismemberment) by introducing unifying concepts directed in the first place toward its own communicative system. The implementation of these concepts is effected by adopting a foreign communicative grammar: western rhetoric. As a consequence, all dissident/dissenting discourses are excluded and repressed. In order to delineate this process, the following digression might be useful.

Mikhail Bakhtin introduced the opposition between *edinyj jazyk* and *raznorečie*[3] to describe the fierce competition that may be observed (within a cultural realm gravitating towards homogeneity) between an official, legalized, unified language and the sum total of noncanonized languages. This opposition can be invoked to define the dynamics of the formation and alternation of norms in language and communication processes. It should be noted that the unification of a language, which indeed implies the unification of the entire communication permitted by it, represents the fundamental accomplishment of a cultural system. This unification may be conceived of as a process resulting in the evolution of definite norms regulating language; in this process, authorities are developed that articulate these norms. We may denote as such authorities the rhetorical and stylistic doctrines that emerge as forces working toward the formulation of norms in a cultural system oriented toward the unification of its verbal media. Such forces are activated in order to oppose those "decentralizing" and "centrifugal" forces of the languages that resist unification and canonization. Yet *raznorečie* always means *raznokultur'e* as well (that is, a multiplicity of coexisting cultures not yet brought into accord), and consequently the central danger to a culture in the process of consolidation. On the other hand, *ustanovka na edinuju kul'turu* ("orientation toward a single culture") signifies *ustanovka na edinyj jazyk* ("orientation toward a single language").

The tendency toward the unification of language and culture designates a particular state in the semiotic mechanism of a culture, which Lotman defines as the increase of internal "monosemy," or as the "intensification of homeostatic tendencies."[4] It is directed against the augmentation of ambivalence, which in turn means a certain quality of a system that Lotman terms "incomplete orderedness." At the same time, this internal and incomplete orderedness of the system must be understood as providing the possibility for developing a dynamic that benefits from the "centrifugal" tendencies and for directing the system toward a state of "softening," in other words, to *raznokultur'e*.

In the attempt to decrease the polysemy, a culture develops mechanisms for description—or, more precisely, for self-description—serving mono-semy and orderedness. This polysemy-decreasing process implies, at the same time, a reduction of the system's "informationality"; the attempt to bring about total orderedness ultimately terminates in "ossification."

Rhetoric (and stylistics) can assume a crucial function in such pro-cesses, namely, in affirming the movement toward a unified language. In order to be able to fulfill its functions, rhetoric must acknowledge all the extralinguistic social, aesthetic, and other values developed by the system; these are the values that have led both to the specific quality of a given concrete unified language and to its differentiation into styles and sublan-guages, and that have determined the permissibility or impermissibility of communication forms. However, it is rhetoric that first actually articulates such values.

In the process by which a culture organizes or reorganizes itself, the rhetorical text actually achieves the status of a metatext in the form of a textbook or a treatise, and thus unquestionably is placed on the same level as those texts through which a cultural system attempts to describe itself.

Rhetoric, understood as a form of self-description of a cultural system (specifically, of its linguistic and communication systems), exercises a force that works toward both the self-organization of that system and its definite structuring as a semiotic whole. When a culture creates or adopts such me-tatexts as rhetoric in order to describe and organize itself, such an activity implies a normative claim with regard to the actual structuring—or the actual process of structuring—of the given culture.[5]

During the reign of Peter the Great, and in accordance with his re-forms, western rhetoric adopts the status of an officialized communicative system and becomes a mighty and oppressive tool of communicative dis-cipline. Deviating—dissenting—discourses are eliminated, in particular those considered to be unenlightened and schismatic.

Where the system undergoes a centripetal reorganization on the one hand, it opens to western culture on the other. The acceptance of the "for-eign," however, is subject to a strict control: The foreigners have to carry out special tasks, are assigned definite functions, and live in separate com-munities. Foreign social habits are dictated; those who reject them (the rep-resentatives of old Russia) are persecuted or eliminated. Thus, with the Petrine reforms, the dualistic pattern gains a dramatic dimension. The reformer, Peter I, becomes himself a cultural symbol of ambivalence: creator of a new Russia *and* destroyer of the old, a god of enlightenment and progress *and* the devil himself, and so on. What happens is that the canalized reception of the "foreign" foreign is fatally doubled by the inverse process concerning the "own" foreign.

The concept of a clear-cut dichotomy as a generator of patterns for intra- and extracultural interpretation (translation) of the foreign with respect to the own rules out those (discultural elements) that are not subject to a dichotomous control.

Literature seems to assume this conceptual blank by interrogating and crossing out the well-balanced dichotomy concept and by converting/subverting the axiologies at its disposal.

Literature of the Fantastic: The Foreign/Strange as *Phantasma*

The collapse of rhetoric as a totalizing system allows excluded, "forgotten" discourses to reappear: The discourses of folklore, superstition, and the supernatural; the discourses of the old believers, the sectarians, the heretics, and so on. This collapsing process culminates in the rise of the romantic literature of the fantastic, the mise en scène of the "other" of culture. What is crucial in this respect is the double function adopted by the literature of the fantastic: the function of a discourse (textual) and the function of conceptualization (metatextual).

The literature of the fantastic pursues not only the project of creating alternative worlds (the supernatural, the marvelous, the adventurous) but, as Rosemary Jackson puts it in her study *Fantasy: The Literature of Subversion*, it "characteristically attempts to compensate for a lack resulting from cultural constraints; it is a literature of desire, which seeks that which is experienced as absence and loss." And it "traces the unsaid and the unseen of culture: that which has been silenced, made invisible, covered over and made 'absent.'" Its excursion into the disorder or counterorder of extraculture "can only begin from a base within the dominant cultural order." "The literary fantastic is a telling index of the limits of that order. Its introduction of the 'unreal' is set against the category of the 'real'—a category which the fantastic interrogates by its difference."[6] Insofar as the real can be interpreted as both the presence of a functioning culture and the representation of the axiological model that controls its mechanism, the introduction of the other (the forgotten, repressed, unfamiliar, unseen) as an absence displaces its categories of presence and representation.

Fantasy could be termed the heretic version not only of the concepts of reality but also of fiction itself. It does not submit to the rules of fictional discourse a cultural system establishes or tolerates; it transgresses the exigencies of the mimetic grammar (otherness does not appear to be subject to mimesis); it disfigures the categories of time and space (fantastic chronotope) and causality. It discards and subverts the validity of fundamental aesthetic categories such as appropriateness (decorum, aptum). Furthermore, the counter- or rather crypto-grammar of the fantastic takes refuge in wild procedures of semiotic excess (hypertrophy) and extravagance (the ornamental, the arabesque, and the grotesque). Its plots abound in escalation, culmination, disruption, exorbitant happening and actions (the marvelous, the enigma, the adventure, murder, incest, metamorphosis, return of the dead). Its protagonists seem to be constantly troubled by eccentric states of mind (hallucination, anguish, fever dream, nightmare, fatal curiosity) and to be forced to face ghosts, monsters, lunatics, the return of the dead, and the horrible family secret. They become acquainted with parascience such as alchemy or esoteric knowledge and perform nonorthodox religious rituals (sorcery, etc.).

William Irwin, in *The Game of the Impossible: A Rhetoric of Fantasy*, defines fantasy as "a story based on and controlled by an overt violation of what is generally accepted as possibility; it is a narrative result of transforming the condition contrary to fact into 'fact' itself." However, the subversive function that ensues from such a violation of dominant assumptions and the overturning of rules of artistic representation can be associated already with one of the roots of the literary fantastic, which Bakhtin, in his study *Problems of Dostoevsky's Poetics*, considers to be the Menippean satire. His characterization of this genre, in the tradition of which he sees fantasists like Hoffmann, Dostoevsky, Gogol, Poe, Jean Paul, and others, might be helpful to sketch out the problem in question.

Characteristic of the Menippea [the most representative works of this syncretistic genre, in Bakhtin's view, were fictions such as Petronius's *Satyricon*, Apuleius's *Metamorphosis* and Lucian's *Strange Story*] are violations of the generally accepted, ordinary course of events and of the established norms of behavior and etiquette, including the verbal. Scandals and eccentricities destroy the epical and tragical integrity of the world, they form a breach in the stable, normal course of human affairs and events and free human behavior from predetermining norms and motivations.[7]

The Menippea mixed this world with the underworld and upperworld, upset time order, "quoted" dialogues with the dead, allowed for states of hallucination, dream, insanity, metamorphosis, and so on. Both, the Menippea and the textual transposition of this postmythical and postritualistic communal practice of carnival,[8] inform a mode of writing which, as an analogon (and double) to that of the fantastic, can be termed carnivalesque. Yet in spite of the common features both modes of writing share, there is a crucial difference to be noted. Since hypertrophy, the grotesque, exaggeration, transgression, eccentricity, uncontrollable semantic shifts, and the toppling of hierarchies and axiologies are aimed at an interaction with the existing culture (conceived of as the official), it is not primarily absence or the other with which the carnivalesque mode of writing is concerned. It rather ludistically comes to terms with the "other," "strange" or "foreign," conceptualizing it neither as a mysterious nor as a threatening force, but treating it as a mask or converting it into parodic and grotesque figurations.

The "other," which the fantastic conceptualizes, has an ambivalent status: it appears to be extracultural/cultural; repressed/returning. It reports an absence and simultaneously insists on its presence. The fantastic as the impossible, antirational, and unreal cannot exist (despite its celebration of representational or fictional misrule, its commitment to disintegration and its utopism) independently of that world of the real, possible, rational which it seems to conceive as inescapably monosemic. In Jackson's formulation, the fantastic "exists in a parasitical or a symbiotic relation to the real."[9] The decomposition and recombination of real elements into arbitrary, nonexistent forms—an exercise comparable to that of dreamwork—is threatening and disturbing not only because of the alternatives it proposes but because, as alternatives, these forms point to an occluded, covered memory (the unconscious of culture). The fantastic confronts culture with its oblivion.

All procedures of the mise en scène of the other (disproportioning, disfiguration, dislocation, dismemberment, disguising, and so on) can be reduced to the basic formal and conceptual device of *estrangement*. This, again, is an ambivalent, double-edged device which veils in order to unveil, shadows in order to uncover/rediscover. Its function is, in rendering strange and defamiliarizing conventionalized social and art structures, to trace the unseen, impalpable, and unperceivable. Its effect culminates in cognitive and aesthetic shock.

In order to highlight the disturbing and shocking effect the fantastic mode of writing exerted even on romantic readers/writers, it may suffice to quote some critical terms from Walter Scott's review of E. T. A. Hoffmann's fantasies (in particular *The Sandman*). Referring to Hoffmann's fancy, which he terms "wild" in contradistinction to a "moderate imagination," Scott foregrounds such features as "mental derangement," a "morbid degree of acuteness," an "ill-regulated tendency to the terrible and distressing," the "violation of probability and even possibility of a capricious, eccentric genius," "oddity and bizarrerie." Against the backdrop of "the severity of the English taste," Scott delineates the "attachment of the Germans to the mysterious" which has "invented another species of composition, which, perhaps, could hardly have made its way in any other country or language." This may be called, as he suggests, the "fantastic mode of writing"

in which the most wild and unbounded license is given to an irregular fancy, and all species of combination, however ludicrous, however shocking, are attempted and executed without scruple. In the other modes of treating the supernatural, even that mystic region is subjected to some laws, however slight; and fancy, in wandering through it, is regulated by some probabilities in the wildest flight. Not so in the fantastic style of composition, which has no restraint save that which it may ultimately find in the exhausted imagination of the author. This style bears the same proportion to the more regular romance, whether ludicrous or serious, which "farce" or rather "pantomime", maintained to "tragedy" and "comedy". Sudden transformations are introduced of the most extraordinary kind, and wrought by the most inadequate means; no attempt is made to soften their absurdity, or to reconcile their inconsistencies.[10]

Expressions such as "overexcited fancy" and its association with being on the verge "of actual insanity," the interrelation between fancy and the lack of right reason or sober truth, between fancy and absurdity, as well as Scott's comment on the "inspirations of Hoffmann" to "resemble the ideas produced by the immoderate use of opium"[11] suggest that in this mode of writing we can discern not only the return of repressed discourses but also the return of a repressed human faculty: *phantasia*. Phantasia accompanied by *mania* (*furor*) appears to be the wild counterpart of the sober and moderate operations of ordinary imagination.

It should be pointed out that Scott's negative concept of fantasy as excentricity and "mental derangement" set against the notion of accepted imaginative creativity encompasses all the attributes the analysis and theory of the fantastic have hitherto listed; furthermore, it anticipates the affinities of fantasy to the unconscious, a crucial topic in the psychoanalytical approach to this mode of writing.

And here again it is the binary figure of the unreal/real, absent/present, foreign/native, other/self-identical that lends itself to interpreting the gap (or the interplay) between fantastic transgressiveness and controlled fictional license. On the representational level, this interpretive figure culminates in the antagonism of *phantasma*/true image. Every image as a complex of signs is inscribed with an opposing sign, the *simulacrum*, a false or a dissimulating sign. By presenting the similar as potentially dissimilar, the simulacrum deprives the sign of the semantic legitimation stabilizing it. Thus, the simulacrum itself appears to be a split or a double sign (absent/present, false/true, invisible/visible, nonreferential/referential). Simulacrum is a concept documented in the classical rhetorical tradition ("Rhetorica ad Herennium," Cicero, Quintilian) which, together with *imago* and *effigies*, translates the Aristotelian concepts of *phantasma* and *eikon*; it participates in connotations that release both poles from the above-named opposition: simulacrum is both a true and a false image; it both refers to something and cancels that reference; it represents that which is absent and simultaneously disclaims it. By displaying its own falseness, the simulacrum always also questions its own position as representation; in other words, the image in this sense has its own touch of trompe l'oeil. (Compare the fata morgana phenomena in the literature of the fantastic: illusion, hallucination, and so on.)

The image of the other is, in the same sense, deceptive because it dissimulates that which is repressed, forgotten, or made absent by representing it in disguise or by rendering a disfigured and decomposed version of that which was or could have been a part of cultural experience. In Aristotle's treatise "On Memory and Recollection," the ambivalent representational status of the simulacrum is associated with the mnemonic dimension. The phantasma outlines an image for this absence, an image that attempts to fix and to conserve what is absent through similarity. Similarity itself, however, is characterized as a construct, an invention. The phantasma does not mean or denote what is to be remembered (what is absent) but simulates it (*similitudo* turns out to be *simulatio*). In this concept of inventing dissimilar similarities or simulacra, as resumed again by Quintilian, de-similarization is considered a *visio insana* which not only misses the object but renders it unrecognizable—that is, foreign or strange. The covert semantic affinity between the other as the repressed and forgotten and the other as the foreign and strange becomes overt in the transformation of the forgotten into a strange, mysterious, marvelous, or monstrous object, which seems to be the main topic of the literature of the fantastic. In other words, the other as phantasma adopts the function of the foreign/strange, and vice versa: the foreign/strange appears as the phantasma of otherness. That is why, in the fantastic mode of writing, most protagonists are depicted in their encounters with ghosts, specters, monsters, corpses, and mysterious foreigners/strangers (strangers from without and those from within: sorcerers, witches, magicians, and sectarians).

Though some texts of the fantastic resort to hallucination, dream, and insanity as quasi-rationalistic explanations of the apparition of the strange, this is not only an index of motivation and legitimation of the fantastic reconciling it with the accepted rules of fiction but also an index of its un-decidability (its inconceivability), its precarious status between represen-tation and nonrepresentation. (The return of the repressed would be con-ceived of as return of something that has never taken place, as the hint at a void, at an absolute absence, or the absolute strange: the other.)

Some examples from Russian literature of the fantastic (romantic pe-riod) may illustrate both: the complicity between mystery and extracul-ture; and the constant transformation of that which is forgotten or re-pressed into the heterocultural—that is, the return of the own in the guise of the foreign and strange.

The plot of Pushkin's "Pique Dame" is centered around an enigma that remains unsolved. Esoteric knowledge communicated by the French ma-gician and cabalist Chevalier de Saint Germain is introduced in the enlight-ened aristocratic society of nineteenth-century Russia. This knowledge re-fers to the secret of a card trick and is associated with the return of the dead (the apparition of the dead countess who, after having been abroad and in touch with Saint Germain had disclosed the secret) as well as with the an-imation of things (the pique dame on the playing card twinkles and thereby evokes the countess). The encounter with the mysterious causes the main protagonist Hermann (an enlightened man of German descent) to go mad and leave society.

Gogol's agent of evil force (sorcerer, devil) in "The Terrible Vengeance" is markedly characterized as the "foreigner," as someone who lived abroad, became acquainted with unknown customs and strange knowl-edge, someone who does not participate in the habits of the community of Ukranian Cossacks he returned to. (He dresses like a Muslim and eats like a Jew, and his religious ritual is pagan. Pagan too is the ritual of the Cath-olic Poles, the enemies of the Orthodox Cossacks in the same tale.) As the incarnation of cultural evil, the sorcerer tries to violate the incest taboo. As a consequence of the interference of evil, a whole Cossack family per-ishes. The narrative relates such a radical disturbance of order to past (for-gotten) events which happened abroad.

In Gogol's "Notes of a Madman," insanity is enacted as a grotesque-comic exploration of the language of nonsense, or the discourse of the other of sense. The nonsensical man imagines (fancies) himself to be the king of a foreign country (Spain).

Nearly all Dostoevsky's main protagonists are cultural eccentrics. They do not represent the standard enlightened ideology but rather intellectual disorder, an asystemic subversion of the system; they appear to be heretics, sectarians, criminals, revolutionaries, fanatics, fantasts, fools in Christo. The disorder of eccentricity they engender ensues from their being schismatic persons within culture (for instance Raskol'nikov, whose name refers to *raskol*, which means schism). All of them are mysterious characters introduced as foreigners who spent some part of their lives abroad. In the course of Russian postromantic literature, we can trace the same function of the foreigner, the émigré, and those returning from Siberian deportation. (Siberia functions as extraculture in both senses named above: as nonculture [wilderness] and as anticulture, for it represents a threatening exile of alternative thought, revolutionary ideas, and so on. Siberian extraculture as the other world is associated with the otherworldly, as in Dostoevsky's *Notes from a Dead House*.)

The transformation of the forgotten or repressed into the heterocultural, however, does not take place within the confines of a clear-cut binary model but is acted out as a permanent transgression of the boundaries between present and absent, true and false, and it is this very figure of ambivalence that makes the fantastic mode of writing a conceptual force, disturbingly interfering with the models a culture produces in order to come to terms with its "other."

Coda to the Discussion

Wolfgang Iser

$\mathcal{W}$hat usually gets lost when conference proceedings are published is the very debate triggered by the different positions of the participants. This is due largely to the multivoiced discourse which, more often than not, creates a tangle that hardly seems worth documenting. What might, however, be worthwhile is to sort out the issues raised in the discussion, not least as they represent a constantly shifting focus which, in turn, gives rise to a text of its own.

For such a text, the essays submitted provided the subtext, which exhibited an array of components pertinent to an interchange between cultures. The components featured in each of these essays were shaped by the very interrelations between them, making it impossible to isolate the components from the network that gradually emerged in the discussion. Therefore it remained hard to decide whether the components governed the relationship or vice versa. Whichever may be the case, interrelationship presupposes something "in between" what is related, and this determines the salience of the components or the positions interconnected. If the "in between" turns out to be a tilting of positions, it will change them; if it is a shifting of positions, it will create new correlations; if it is a space, it will bring about unforeseeable interconnections; if it is an unbridgeable gap, it will cause a clash. Thus patterns of this kind emerged as basic constituents of both cross-cultural and intracultural intercourse.

Translatability

This framework provided guidelines for exploring encounters between cultures in terms of translatability—a term that in itself stood in need of examination. Heuristically speaking, translatability is an umbrella concept that allows us to inspect the interpenetration of different cultures and intracultural levels without necessarily organizing these encounters.

Furthermore, translatability covers all kinds of translation, as it refers to a range of conditions that are only selectively realized in any one specific translation. The complete set of conditions comprised by this concept can never be brought to bear in any actual translation, but it will enable us to discern which conditions govern the latter. Thus translatability opens up awareness of what each translation privileges and of the extent to which assumed references shape the positions that are transposed into one another.

For a closer inspection of what translatability of cultures might entail, certain features of a linguistic, an intracultural, and a cross-cultural translation were pinpointed. If connotation in language arises out of a translation of the literal into the figurative, the literal meaning is simultaneously bracketed and yet visible in order to provide guidance for what is to be figured. What is bracketed and not meant is used to delineate what the figurative adumbrates, and this reshuffling can at best be described as a performance, arising out of the difference between the literal and the figurative. This difference eludes cognitive grasp but has to be assessed when—as in the Buber-Rosenzweig translation of the Hebrew Bible into German—an inspired language is rendered into a language that had no part in the original revelation.

Consequently, the words used for such a translation came under close scrutiny as regards both what they were supposed to mean and what they were unable to say. In order to ascertain their appropriate meaning for the purpose concerned, their roots had to be dug up, which more often than not entailed construing or even inventing an assumed etymon. However, when such made-up meanings failed to convey the spirituality of the Bible, the words one had to fall back upon served as a pointer to what remained unsayable. Thus the space between the two languages became operative, forcing unsayability into language by constantly making the meanings tilt both into their supposed roots and into their function of designating the unspeakable.

At the intracultural level, the discussion confined itself to only one instance of translatability: the resuscitation of a past in a present as manifested by religious observances in the *haredi* tradition. Translations of this kind are conditioned by historical necessities, by the different functions a recurring past is meant to exercise, and by the mechanisms applied for such a reactivation. The past to be revived is not just an available entity waiting to be channeled into the present but is variously invoked according to present exigencies. In other words, current necessities are projected onto the past in order to make it translatable into the present. This mutuality ultimately decides the nature of the past invoked. In the case of the *haredi*, the intention was to return to the pristine beginnings of religious observances in order to reinvigorate the present life of the community, thus eliminating the split that separated the latter from the spirituality of the fathers.

A return to the past entails undoing its pastness, shaping it in accordance with present needs and, in so doing, exposing the present to change. Such an interpenetration arises out of a mutuality between past and present, which regulates this relationship and also indicates that there is no stance beyond it. Instead, mutuality is both stance and regulator, functioning as a feed backward in order to create a feed forward, transforming the space between past and present into a catalyst.

At the cross-cultural level, translatability turned out to be a historically conditioned operation. Three major shifts were highlighted in the discussion. Initially existing traditions were transferred to a realm of emerging importance; then tradition was conceived as a framework within which the proliferating contexts of a cultural present had to be brought under control. A further shift occurred when cultures met and had to be transposed into one another.

In each of these instances, the inherent dualism of translatability is respecified. Receiving a tradition entails recasting the inheritance; charting the open-endedness of a cultural present makes the tradition peripheral to the now important core; translating different cultures into each other results in a recursive looping between them. This respecification of difference exemplifies cross-cultural interrelationships and also indicates the operational potential of the space between them.

Looking back on the various levels inspected thus far, we can discern a few pertinent features of translatability. In all the paradigms discussed, there is a mutual conditioning of positions, relationships, and the space between them. The positions in play do not stay the same, the relationships keep changing, and the space between is made operative according to prevailing needs. However, when these become preponderant, the space between will be either colonized or eliminated altogether. In this instance, translatability gives way to an assertion of dominance, in consequence of which the network of mutuality established is undone but nevertheless remains a foil to what has now become dominant.

Memory and Otherness

In order to trace the workings of translatability, two important spheres of human life were singled out for inquiry: memory and otherness, both of which are marked by a boundary-crossing and by a realignment of what has become separate.

Memory as an agent that interlinks what is different—be it the difference between past and present or between cultures—assumes kaleidoscopically changing shapes in accordance with what it is called upon to perform. Each exigency freezes the memory into a solid pattern, and its functions as mythmaker, as collective memory, and as displacement came under review in our discussion.

Memory turns into mythmaker when either origins or intangibles have to be shifted into the present. The ensuing effort to construe a material myth is meant to grasp the ungraspable, but there has to be a continual refashioning as the gulf can never be bridged. The myth only allows contextually varying control of the uncontrollable and, in order to equip it for such a task, memory has to freeze it into a stereotyped pattern. Stereotypes, however, when applied cross-culturally, are prone to turn into prejudices.

What has been termed collective memory is by nature something fictive, as it has no traceable location. Yet it functions as a frame for understanding, allowing us to comprehend the pastness of the past, and thus creating a historical consciousness. If the past can be made continuous with the present, it can equally be projected onto a future, thus molding retroactively not only its events but also our ways of experiencing them. This activity of the collective memory is driven by the desire to obtain a group identity which, more often than not, is liable to create its own foundations.

If memory can become tangible both as mythmaker and as a collectivizing agent, it can also function inversely by displacing what is remembered. It prevents the return of what a sign is meant to recall, so that the sign is then made to hide what it relates to. Such a function of memory highlights the blank area in all translations and makes it operative by dispersing what was meant to return.

There may be several reasons for this manifestation of memory. Blocking the recall can mean banishing the anxiety of remembering. It can equally mean remembering oblivion by non-representation—that is, making the sign deny its signification, or making it obliterate what it points to. Thus memory as displacement functions by scattering what is remembered, without which remembering would be deprived of its unforeseeable diversifications.

Memory crosses boundaries to a past; otherness crosses boundaries to an outside. If one were to specify the transpositions of the "other" that are inherent in every cultural document, one might come up with the following prominent types:

1. Encountering the other awakens awareness of a duality which results in an experience of difference;

2. bracketing, suspending or even excluding the other allows for an exploration of difference that raises the question of why there are such disparities;

3. incorporating the other aims at assimilation, which leads to a politics of cultural relationships;

4. appropriating the other highlights goals of utilization that are meant to remedy existing deficiencies;

5. reflecting oneself in the other entails heightened self-awareness, which leads to self-confrontation;

6. recognizing the other as primordial generates a call to responsibility prior to any possible knowledge of the other, and may produce an ethics based on imponderable commitment.

Such a catalog, which is by no means exhaustive, can be fine-tuned, as exemplified by the range of questions that cropped up in the discussion. What would it mean to live with a negative other inside oneself? Is such a negative other within oneself eventually to be digested, or will it upset the self when ultimately unassimilable? Is it possible to take over the memory of the other and, if not, how is the self penetrated by the other? And finally, perhaps, why is the self inclined to invent an other that has no counterpart in any given reality?

These proliferating types of otherness and the ways in which they are made to link up with the self raise the suspicion that there is no selfhood without an other. If so, it might mean that the self fashions the other in accordance with what it wants to be which, in the final analysis, appears to point to its basic groundlessness. Such a disposition of the self becomes all the more telling vis-à-vis the fantastic which, as an unassimilable otherness, defies absorption by the self and thus frustrates any attempts to that end.

What About Culture?

If a self attains its salient features through its relationship to otherness, the question arose in the discussion as to whether something similar applies to culture as well. Do cultures have to be juxtaposed in order to ascertain what makes them specific? Should that be the case, then otherness is a means of profiling a culture, which implies that the latter does not exist as a self-sufficient entity. Consequently, a culture may not be identified with a set of norms and values, or with the relationships between them, let alone with a presupposed origin out of which it has arisen. Assuming culture had a specific origin, why did this get lost and why have all efforts to recover it turned into myths? If culture consisted of norms and values, why have they been subject to change and transformation? And finally, if culture were made up of nothing but individual relationships between the factors mentioned, where do these relationships come from and what makes them operative? At best culture proves to be a kind of network that interlinks levels, positions, attitudes, and, last but not least, otherness in order to gain its individuality.

A network, however, remains a metaphor as long as it is not broken down into its modes of operation. In our discussion, binarism turned out to be an overriding schema for conceptualizing the operational intent of the network, and American culture proved to be a case in point, specifying binarism as a countervailing movement. There are high culture and low culture, which play upon each other; there is continuity and a continuous self-begetting, and there is a basic aversion to conformity in all these reciprocal relationships.

If this is a binarism in terms of levels, it could equally be conceived in terms of pairings, especially when the origins of a cultural network are focused upon. A typical pairing of this kind is groundlessness versus etiological myth. As origins are unplumbable, all supposed origins are mythological in nature, and hence the assumed origins are subjected to continual refashioning.

In contradistinction to such pairings, a binarism of core and periphery was also considered in order to spotlight the structure of relationships. Core and periphery can indicate a cultural hierarchy, but they can also be made to switch by viewing the periphery from the core and vice versa. Such a binarism results in constant shifts, thus representing the life of a culture. If the shifts themselves turn out to be the center, then core and periphery are downgraded into modes of manifestation for these interchanges, which exhibit the patterns of the network that regulates the interrelationships in a culture.

The binarisms of levels, pairings, and switches indicate that culture is not a static and definable entity but a galaxy of mobile features that dwarf every attempt at reducing culture to a conceptual point of view. Something similar occurs when culture is to be conceived in terms of commitment or beliefs. Such an approach has ontological implications, as it tends to determine what culture is. Whenever attempts of this kind are undertaken, more often than not they turn into a proliferating taxonomy of criteria that are supposed to bring out the basis of a culture, be it kinship, territory, language, myth, or syncretism, which by no means exhausts the list of such criteria. Even if the inherent inadequacy of all taxonomies is counterbalanced by hypostatizing one of these criteria to a universal constituent of culture, each of these alternatives makes culture elude cognitive grasp or simply tailors its multifariousness.

As long as beliefs concerning the substance of culture prevailed, hypotheses about the rise and the diversification of culture did not come under scrutiny. An inspection of current hypotheses of cultural beginnings and their subsequent differentiation would have meant branching out into anthropology and ethnography, thereby testifying to the fact that a culture is not a self-contained entity, but a multilayered process.

Eric Gans, for instance, has proposed an "originary scene" for which "such activities as hunting generate plausible settings," and in which "fear of conflict is the sole necessary motivation for the abortion of the original gesture of appropriation."[1] Vis-à-vis the killed animal, a ritual has to be imposed—arbitrary as it may be—so that the huntsmen do not kill each other in deciding who gets the prey. An equally primordial scene underlies Hans Blumenberg's hypothesis that it was the exit from the cave as an abandonment of natural protection that marked humankind's cultural beginnings.[2] Irrespective of the explanatory power of these and other presuppositions regarding the inception of culture, minimalistically conceived assumptions have an advantage over all kinds of etiological myth, as they do not reify the rise of culture, need no remolding, do not have to be deconstructed, and consequently make it possible to account for the self-generating ramifications of culture.

Modes of Transcultural Relations

Mutuality proved to be the dominant term when it came to pinpointing what happens in intra- and cross-cultural intercourse. In its broadest sense, it designates the ordinary give and take between cultures. More important, however, mutuality is an interrelationship, which to a large extent constitutes what it has connected. As cultures are not clear-cut givens, let alone holistic entities, their encounters inevitably result in mutual molding. In this respect, mutuality was considered to be a constitutive component of culture.

Something similar holds true intraculturally. An interlinked past and present mutually mirror one another, thus highlighting what each of them needs or lacks. Equally intertwined is the relationship between the vertical and the horizontal function of tradition. Vertically conceived, tradition is transmitted into a present in order to provide continuity and stability; horizontally conceived, its translation into a present serves to chart open-endedness. This kind of mutuality allows for all kinds of kaleidoscopic shifts and gradations which tie tradition inextricably to a present and vice versa.

Mutuality, however, should not be mistaken for a transhistorical norm, as its operations are selective regarding the features that are interconnected, not least as the interchange between cultures is always historically conditioned. The very fact that mutuality operates the interchange between cultures is due to the structure of culture itself, which is never a "unified text," but is something in the making. There are always changing relationships between levels of culture: high and low culture have an equal effect on each other, just as the arts and the fabric of social life continually intersect, producing shifts in their respective importance and dominance. At best, so it seems, culture is a matrix triggering interactions between its levels, its heritage, and its recasting, and between its invasion into and its invasion by other cultures. Thus mutuality reflects the basic workings of culture itself.

Hence modes such as fusion, conversion, assimilation, appropriation, and even syncretism are ways either of specifying cross-cultural interchanges or of reifying prominent features by elevating one of them into an umbrella concept. Mutuality, however, comprises all of these modes and simultaneously indicates that there is neither a transcendental stance nor a third dimension that would allow us to conceptualize cross-cultural interrelationships. Thus mutuality points to the fact that whenever features of culture are translated intra- or cross-culturally, a trace of untranslatability imprints itself on all such endeavors, just as a mutual understanding of cultures will encounter a certain incommensurability which, in actual fact, energizes such attempts at comprehension. Therefore, mutuality is marked simultaneously by an insurmountable difference between cultures and an interminable drive to build bridges. It also exposes all umbrella concepts used in assessing cultural encounters as reifications that eliminate difference and pose as an overarching third dimension. There is no way of grasping the ungraspable, and no final elimination of what remains intractable in these encounters. Reifications, then, turned out to be devices used to explain the inexplicable difference between cultures. Yet the refusal to categorize in such a manner—and this was an important point in our discussion—creates anxiety which, in the final analysis, inspires these cross-cultural reifications.

The way out is a recourse to bricolage, which is nothing but a set of explanations as to how one can conceive of encounters between cultures. A bricolage operates by making assertions and simultaneously trying to spotlight what they exclude. Stances have to be adopted and suspended. Frames for understanding have to be devised and at the same time marked off from what they are meant to represent, as there is no grandstand view from which to define interchange between cultures.

These considerations proved to be nascent features of a cross-cultural discourse, which would allow assessment of cultural differences, interpenetration of cultures, and perhaps even the way in which cultural features are telescoped. Mutuality appears to be a basic operating structure of such a discourse, and as culture seems to be a self-generating entity, a recursive looping between different cultures and intracultural levels would organize the mutual impact.

The need to inspect cross-cultural relations is triggered by an awareness of crisis—a topic that ran through our discussion, ranging from Babel and the Pentecostal language through the various syncretisms, the cultural critique of the eighteenth century, up to the conspicuous silence of Heidegger after 1945 and retroactively to what Emerson failed to articulate in reading "Fate." Crisis—so it seemed—is a prerequisite for knowing that one is embedded in a culture.

There remains a final remark: although we embarked upon the road toward a cross-cultural discourse, we never finally reached our destination. This may be due to the fact that a cross-cultural discourse requires a certain amount of self-effacement, perhaps a suspension of one's own stance, at least for a certain time, in order to listen to what the others are trying to say. There is an ethics inherent in a cross-cultural discourse to which Emerson alerted us when he asked that we should "rinse our words."

Reference Matter

Notes

S. Budick: Crises of Alterity

1. Unless otherwise indicated, all citations in my introduction are taken from the authors' essays in this volume.

2. A contribution to an earlier stage of our deliberations which is particularly relevant to the present collection is Jacques Derrida's "Interpretations at War: Kant, the Jew, the German" which appeared in *New Literary History* 22 (Winter 1991): 39–95.

3. Sanford Budick and Wolfgang Iser, eds., *Languages of the Unsayable*, Irvine Studies in the Humanities, no. 3 (New York: Columbia University Press, 1989).

4. *New Literary History* 22 (Winter 1991).

5. I could probably quote similar phrases in earlier works by more than one of us represented in this volume, but in this case I cite it from a recent, frequently illuminating book by Juliana Schiesari, *The Gendering of Melancholia: Feminism, Psychoanalysis, and the Symbolics of Loss in Renaissance Literature* (Ithaca, N.Y.: Cornell University Press, 1992), p. 228.

6. James Clifford, "The Translation of Cultures: Maurice Leenhardt's Evangelism, New Caledonia 1902–1926," reprinted in *Contemporary Literary Criticism: Literary and Cultural Studies*, ed. Robert Con Davis and Ronald Schleifer (New York: Longman, 1994), p. 627.

7. Ibid., pp. 636, 639. On the fantasy of a "holy mating" in both Franz Rosenzweig and Martin Heidegger, see my comments on Klaus Reichert's essay below and, more importantly, Reichert's essay itself.

8. Considering the pain of the nightingale's song it is difficult not to remember that the unvisualized status of the tongue of the bell has an unspeakable parallel in the tongue of Philomel, which is missing. In Ovid's telling of Philomel's tragedy she is raped by her sister's husband, who locks her away and cuts out her tongue.

9. Joshua Scodel, "The Affirmation of Paradox: A Reading of Montaigne's 'De la Phisionomie' (III:12)," *Yale French Studies* 64 (1983): 209–37; Jean Starobinski, "Sur l'emploi du chiasme dans 'Le Neveu de Rameau,'" *Revue de Metaphysique et de Morale* 89 (1984): 182–96.

10. *The Complete Essays of Montaigne*, trans. Donald M. Frame (Stanford, Calif.: Stanford University Press, 1965), p. 159.

11. I describe Goethe's version of this idea in my essay below.

12. *The Complete Essays of Montaigne*, pp. 242–44.

13. I have discussed this point in *The Dividing Muse: Images of Sacred Disjunction in Milton's Poetry* (New Haven, Conn.: Yale University Press, 1985), pp. 80–84.

14. *Seven Lectures on Shakespeare and Milton by the Late S. T. Coleridge*, ed. John Payne Collier (London: Chapman and Hall, 1856), p. 65.

J. Assmann: Translating Gods

1. The list of gods is just one of innumerable glossaries equating Sumerian and Akkadian words. There are also trilingual lists, giving the divine names in Emesal (a literary dialect), Sumerian, and Akkadian. The equation of gods, however, seems a rather complicated affair requiring a considerable amount of theological learning and ingenuity. For there are many more Sumerian gods or names than Akkadian ones. In these cases, translation turns into subsumption. There are some Akkadian gods who appear as equivalents for more than twenty Sumerian gods. But there are also Akkadian gods for whom there are no Sumerian equivalents because they are newcomers in the Babylonian pantheon. Marduk is a good example. In these cases, the scribes had to invent Sumerian equivalents. The task of compiling bilingual lists of gods was therefore a rather demanding one because it implied a great deal of theological insight. The most interesting of these sources is the explanatory list *Anu ša ameli* which contains three columns, the first giving the Sumerian name, the second the Akkadian, and the third the functional definition of the deity. This list gives what we have called the "referent" of divine names, making explicit the principle that underlies the equation or translation of divine names. Cf. R. L. Litke, "A Reconstruction of the Assyro-Babylonian God Lists An: Anum, Anu ša Ameli" (Ph.D. diss., Yale University, 1958). I owe this reference and much pertinent information to the kindness of Karlheinz Deller, to whom I express my sincere gratitude.

2. British Museum, tablet K 2100 ed. in: *Cuneiform Texts* XXV, 18. On the reserve there is a collection of general words for "god" in Sumerian (*dingir*), Akkadian (*khilibu* instead of *ilu*, perhaps an Emesal word), Hurritic (*ene*), Elamitic (*nap*), Amoritic (*malakhum*), Lulubaeic (a language spoken in the Zagros region), and Cassitic (*mash-khu*).

3. Kemal Balkan, *Kassitenstudien I: Die Sprache der Kassiten* (New Haven, Conn.: American Oriental Society, 1954), pp. 2 ff. The Cassite name *Nazimurutash*, for example, is rendered in Akkadian *Sil-Ninurta* (under the shadow of Ninurta), translating the word *nazi* (shadow) by *sil* and the Cassitic god *Murutash* by the Akkadian god *Ninurta*. This is the exact anticipation of the later practice of hellenizing native proper names.

4. Jean Nougayrol, *Textes Suméro-Akkadiens des archives privées d'Ugarit*, Ugaritica V (Paris: Imprimerie national, 1968), no. 137.

5. See L. Canfora, M. Liverani, and C. Zaccagnini, eds., *I Trattati nel Mondo Antico. Forma, Ideologia, Funzione* (Rome: L'Ermadi Bretschneider, 1990).

6. For the concept of the "multiplicity of languages and peoples" in the imperial ideology of the Achemenids, see Christoph Uehlinger, *Weltreich und "eine Rede": Eine neue Deutung der sog. Turmbauerzählung (Gen 11, 1–9)*, OBO 101 (Freiburg: Universitätsverlag, 1990), pp. 578–83.

7. See Elias Bickerman, *The Jews in the Greek Age* (Cambridge, Mass.: Harvard University Press, 1988), p. 104; D. Schlumberger, L. Robert, A. Dupont-Sommer, E. Benveniste, *Journal Asiatique* 246 (1958); D. Schlumberger and Louis Robert, *Comtes rendus de l'Academie des Inscriptions et Belles-Lettres* (Paris: Libraire C. Klincksieck, 1964), pp. 126–40.

8. See Erik H. Erikson, "Ontogeny of Ritualization in Man," in *Philosophical Transactions of the Royal Society* 251 B (London, 1966): 337–49; Konrad Lorenz, *Die Rückseite des Spiegels* (Munich: Piper, 1977), pp. 223–45; Irenäus Eibl-Eibesfeldt, *Krieg und Frieden aus der Sicht der Verhaltensforschung* (Munich: Piper, 1975).

9. I am indebted for this information to Professor Wulf Schiefenhövel, Seewiesen, who spent several years doing field work among the Papuas of New Guinea.

10. The following is based on Wolfram von Soden, "Dolmetscher und Dolmetschen im Alten Orient," in *Aus Sprache, Geschichte und Religion Babyloniens* (Naples: Istituto universitario orientale, Dipartimento di studi asiatici, 1989).

11. Ignaz J. Gelb, *Glossa* 2,93 ff.

12. Wolfgang Schenkel, "Dolmetscher," in W. Helck and E. Otto, eds., *Lexikon der Ägyptologie* (Wiesbaden: Harrassowitz, 1973), I:1116. See also the article "Dolmetscher" in *Reallexikon für Antike und Christentum* (Alfred Hermann on Ancient Egypt: BIa), ed. Theodor Klauser et al. (Stuttgart: A. Hiersemann, 1985–86).

13. See Peter Artzi, "The Birth of the Middle East," *Proceedings of the Fifth World Congress of Jewish Studies* (Jerusalem, 1969), pp. 120–24; Artzi, "Ideas and Practices of International Co-existence in the Third Millennium B.C.E.," *Bar-Ilan Studies in History* 2 (1984): 25–39; Moshe Weinfeld, "The Common Heritage of Covenantal Traditions in the Ancient World," in Canfora, Liverani, and Zuccagnini, eds., *I Trattati nel mondo antico*, pp. 175–91.

14. As pointed out by Erik Voegelin, *The Ecumenic Age, Order and History* (Baton Rouge: Louisiana State University Press, 1974), 4:121–32; Friedrich H. Tenbruck, "Gesellschaftsgeschichte oder Weltgeschichte?" *Kölner Zeitschrift für Soziologie und Sozialpsychologie* 41 (1989): 417–39.

15. Or rather: "cosmotheistic" religion, because cosmotheistic *monotheism* functioned quite in the same way.

16. See E. H. Spicer, "Persistent Cultural Systems: A Comparative Study of Identity Systems That Can Adapt to Contrasting Environments," *Science* 174, no. 4011 (1971): 795–800.

17. See Wilhelm E. Mühlmann, *Chiliasmus und Nativismus: Studien zur Psychologie, Soziologie und historischen Kasuistik der Umsturzbewegungen* (Berlin: D. Reimer, 1961); Vittorio Lanternari, *Movimenti religiosi di libertà e di salvezza*

dei popoli oppressi (Rome: Feltrinelli, 1960); German translation: *Religiöse Freiheits- und Heilsbewegungen unterdrückter Völker*, Soziologische Texte, Neuwied. Engl. (New York: Knopf, 1963); Peter Worsley, *The Trumpet Shall Sound: A Study of "Cargo"-Cults in Melanesia* (New York: Schocken, 1968).

18. See Michael Walzer, *Exodus and Revolution* (New York: Basic, 1985).

19. In the discussion, Marc Shell objected to the abuse of biologistic metaphors such as "immune reaction," which to his mind continues the racist and fascist tendencies to treat cultural differences as natural ones. The fascist revolt against humanism ("Humanitätsduselei") naturalized the effects of pseudo-speciation and stressed them as absolutely insurmountable and resisting any attempt at translation. But this attitude might in itself be described as an "immune reaction," this time not under minority but under majority conditions. In the same discussion, Gershon Shaked pointed out that these reactions might in fact be much more typical of majority cultures than minority ones.

In using the term "immune reaction" I am not (at least consciously) continuing the language of German racism but referring to systems theory, which treats both the (biological) immune system and the (cultural) identity system as self-referential systems processing information about the distinction between inner and outer, system and environment, own and foreign, and providing self-definitions. See F. J. Varela, "Der Körper denkt: Das Immunsystem und der Prozess der Körper-Individuierung," in H. U. Gumbrecht and K. L. Pfeiffer, eds., *Paradoxien, Dissonanzen, Zusammenbrüche: Situationen offener Epistemologie* (Frankfurt: Suhrkamp, 1991), pp. 727–43 (with bibliography).

20. See Spicer, "Persistent Cultural Systems."

21. I study these mechanisms in greater detail in my book *Das kulturelle Gedächtnis: Schrift, Erinnerung und politische Identität in frühen Hochkulturen* (Munich: C. H. Beck, 1992), esp. chap. 3 ("Identität und Ethnogenese").

22. See E. P. Sanders, ed., *Jewish and Christian Self-Definition*, vol. 1: *The Shaping of Christianity in the Second and Third Centuries* (Philadelphia: Fortress, 1980); vol. 2: A. I. Baumgarten, A. Mendelson, and Sanders, eds., *Aspects of Judaism in the Greco-Roman Period* (London: SCM, 1981); vol. 3: B. F. Meyer and Sanders, eds., *Self-definition in the Greco-Roman World* (London: SCM, 1982).

23. See Jan Assmann, *Ma'at: Gerechtigkeit und Unsterblichkeit im Alten Ägypten* (Munich: C. H. Beck, 1950), pp. 19–20, 279–80.

24. For the Hellenistic world see Gerhard Delling, *Die Bewältigung der Diasporasituation durch das hellenistische Judentum* (Göttingen: Vanderhoeck and Ruprecht, 1987).

25. Georges Posener, *La première domination Perse en Ègypte*, Bibliothèque d'Études 11 (1936).

26. Jan Bergman, *Ich bin Isis: Studien zum memphitischen Hintergrund der griechischen Isis-Aretalogien* (Uppsala: Almquist and Wiksell, 1968); Garth Fowden, *The Egyptian Hermes: A Historical Approach to the Late Pagan Mind* (Cambridge: Cambridge University Press, 1986).

27. In his commentary on C. H. XVI 2 (Collection Budé, Paris), André Jean

Festugière collects many pertinent passages from Greek and Latin sources: see n. 7, pp. 232–34.

28. I give a short paraphrase of a very long discussion. See Peter Crome, *Symbol und Unzulänglichkeit der Sprache: Jamblichos, Porphyrios, Proklos* (Munich: W. Fink, 1970); Jetske C. Rijlaarsdam, *Platon über die Sprache: Ein Kommentar zum Kratylos. Mit einem Anhang über die Quelle der Zeichentheorie Ferdinand de Saussures* (Utrecht, 1978).

29. Origenes C. Cels. 1.24–25, 28; 5.45.

30. *Corpus Hermeticum XVI*, ed. A. J. Festugière and A. D. Nock, 2:230; the translation appears in Fowden, *The Egyptian Hermes*, p. 37.

31. For the following see Arthur Darby Nock, *Conversion: The Old and the New in Religion from Alexander the Great to Augustine of Hippo* (1993; Oxford: Oxford University Press, 1963).

32. See ibid., p. 138.

33. See Oskar Grether, *Name und Wort Gottes im A. T.* (Giessen: A. Topelman, 1934), pp. 3 ff.; von Soden, *Bidel und Alter Orient* (Berlin: de Gruyter, 1985), pp. 78–88; Georg Fohrer, *Geschichte der israelitischen Religion* (Berlin: de Gruyter, 1969), pp. 63 ff.; Johannes C. de Moor, *The Rise of Yahwism* (Leuven: Uitgeverij Peeters, 1990), pp. 175, 237 ff. In the Egyptian myth of the "Heavenly Cow" there occurs a phrase that sounds like a close parallel. The god Re says "I am I" (*jw.j jm.j*), perhaps with a causal or temporal meaning: "(Because, or as long as) I am who I am, I shall not let them make rebellion." See Erik Hornung, *Der ägyptische Mythos von der Himmelskuh: Eine Ätiologie des Unvollkommenen* (Fribourg: Universitätsverlag, 1982), pp. 43, 125 n. aa (by G. Fecht); and de Moor, *The Rise of Yahwism*, pp. 174–75. In the Sybilline Oracles (1.137–140), Exodus 3.14 is quoted and then given an interpretation in the cosmotheistic sense: "I am the Being One (*eimì d'égo-ge ho ón*), recognize this in your mind: I put on the heaven as garment, I wrapped myself by the sea, the earth is the foundation of my feet, the air is around me as body and the stars encircle me" (R. Merkelbach and M. Totti, *Abrasax* [Oplanden: Westdeutscher Verlag, 1992], 2:131).

34. Augustine, *De consensu evangelistarum*, 1.22.30 and 1.23.31.

35. Rodney Needham, *Belief, Language and Experience* (Oxford: Blackwell, 1972).

36. G. W. Bowersock, *Hellenism in Late Antiquity* (Cambridge: Cambridge University Press, 1990), p. 5.

37. The term *hellenismos* first occurs in 2 Macc. 2.21 where, in opposition to *Ioudaismos*, it has an unmistakably polemical meaning. See E. Will and C. Orieux, *Ioudaismos-Hellenismos: Essai sur le judaisme judéen à l'époque hellénistique* (Nantes: Presses Universitaires de Nantes, 1986).

38. See Carsten Colpe, "Syncretism," in M. Eliade, ed., *The Encyclopedia of Religion* (New York: Macmillan, 1987), vol. 14; L. H. Martin, "Why Cecropian Minerva? Hellenistic Religious Syncretism as System," *Numen* 30 (1983): 131–45.

39. Robert Lattimore, "Herodotus and the Names of the Egyptian Gods," *Classical Philology* 34 (1939): 357–65.

40. See, similarly, Lucian, *De Dea Syria*, chap. 2: "The Egyptians are said to

be first among all the people known to us to form conceptions about the gods. Not much later the Syrians heard from the Egyptians the discourse about the gods and erected shrines and temples."

41. Morton Smith, *Palestinian Parties and Politics That Shaped the Old Testament*, 2d. ed. (London: SCM, 1987), pp. 43–61.

42. Herodotus visited Egypt in the years between 450 and 444 B.C.E., when Egypt and Athens were allies against Persia.

43. W. E. Mühlmann, *Chiliasmus und Nativismus: Studien zur Psychologie*, p. 12.

44. Marcel Mauss, "Essai sur le don: Forme et raison de l'échange dans les sociétés archaiques," in *Sociologie et anthropologie* (Paris: 1950), pp. 143–279; translated as *The Gift* (London: Cohen-West, 1969).

45. Marshall Sahlins, *Stone Age Economics* (1974; London: 1988). See also the collection of essays by Fritz Kramer and Christian Sigrist, *Gleichheit und Gegenseitigkeit* (Frankfurt, 1983), esp. "Tausch und Wert in Stammesgesellschaften." Also important is Arnold Gehlen, *Urmensch und Spätkultur* (Bonn: Athenaum-Verlag, 1956), pp. 50 ff.

Barasch: Visual Syncretism

1. See Arnaldo Momigliano, *On Pagans, Jews, and Christians* (Middletown, Conn.: Wesleyan University Press, 1987), p. 192. The literature is, of course, enormous, and not always helpful for an art historian. A typology of syncretisms that may also be of some use to the student of art (though it does not mention any work of art) is given by Françoise Dunant, "Les Syncretismes dans la religion de l'Égypte Romaine," in Dunant and P. Levèque, eds., *Les syncretismes dans les religions de l'Antiquité* (Leiden: E. S. Brill, 1975), pp. 152–85.

2. Ernst Kitzinger, *Early Medieval Art in the British Museum* (London: The British Museum, 1940), pp. 7–8. Kitzinger already used the concept in his article "Notes on Early Coptic Sculpture," *Archaeologia* 87 (1938): 181 ff., especially 202 ff., and he has summed it up recently in his *Byzantine Art in the Making: Main Lines of Stylistic Development in Mediterranean Art 3rd–7th Century* (Cambridge, Mass.: Harvard University Press, 1980), pp. 11–12, 17, 124.

3. Kitzinger, *Byzantine Art in the Making*, p. 11.

4. This style has been frequently discussed, but see particularly G. Rodenwaldt, "Römische Reliefs: Vorstudien zur Spätantike," *Jahrbuch des Deutschen Archäologischen Instituts* 55 (1940): 12–15.

5. I should like to refer to the thoughtful and still important analysis by Heinrich Schäfer, *Von ägyptischer Kunst, besonders der Zeichenkunst* (Leipzig: Hinrich, 1919), p. 41 ff.

6. This was the prevailing interpretation of Greek art, especially sculpture, in the nineteenth and early twentieth centuries, from Hegel to Worringer. In Hegel's historical system of the arts, "bodily" sculpture is the typical representative of Greek art; in Wilhelm Worringer's *Abstraktion und Einfühlung* (Leipzig: R. Piper,

1908) the emphasis on "Tiefenrelation," that is, the manifestation of volume, is a typical feature of Greek art.

7. Schäfer, *Von ägyptischer Kunst*, p. 42.

8. See ibid., p. 43.

9. I am not aware of any study of this particular problem. Modern art-historical research has the tendency, which is potentially misleading, to see techniques as isles of usually great stability against the background of an ever-changing history of the arts. Changes of technique and imagery in general no doubt proceed at a different pace, but the problem needs clarification.

10. This view is best expressed by Hans Petersen, "The Earliest Christian Inscriptions of Egypt," *Classical Philology* 59 (1964): 154–74, esp. 163–64.

11. This view is best presented by A. Hermann, "Die Beter-Stelen von Terenuthis in Ägypten: Zur Vorgeschichte der christlichen Oransdarstellung," *Jahrbuch für Antike und Christentum* 6 (1963): 112–28 and "Das Werden zu einem Falken: Eine ungewöhnliche Beter-Stele aus Ägypten," *Jahrbuch für Antike und Christentum* 7 (1964): 39–44. For this problem, see also the study by Klaus Parlasca, "Zur Stellung der Terenuthis-Stelen—Eine Gruppe römischer Grabreliefs aus Ägypten in Berlin," *Mitteilungen des Deutschen Archäologischen Instituts—Abteilung Kairo* 26 (1970): 173–98, esp. 188–89. Parlasca points out that the Terenouthis stelae as a group (that is, all the stelae) were produced over quite a long period, and this fact surely bears on the question to which religion they, or some of them, belong.

12. See Campbell Bonner, "The Ship of the Soul on a Group of Grave-Stelae in Terenuthis," *Proceedings of the American Philosophical Society* 85 (1942): 84–91, esp. 85.

13. For this gesture in Christian liturgy, see Rudolf Suntrup, *Die Bedeutung der liturgischen Gebärden und Bewegungen in lateinischen und deutschen Auslegungen des 9. bis 13. Jahrhunderts* (Munich: Fink, 1978), pp. 172–81.

14. See Tertullian *De oratione* 14.

15. See Minucius Felix *Octavius* 29.8.

16. Andre Grabar, *Christian Iconography: A Study of Its Origins* (Princeton, N.J.: Princeton University Press, 1968), figs. 59, 61.

17. Heinz Demisch, *Erhobene Hände: Geschichte einer Gebärde in der bildenden Kunst* (Stuttgart: Urachhaus, 1984), p. 70.

18. See U. Schweitzer, *Das Wesen des Ka im Diesseits und Jenseits der alten Aegypter* (Glückstadt/Hamburg: J. J. Augustin, 1956), pp. 21, 87, and fig. 2.

19. The statue is now in the Museum in Cairo. For a reproduction, see Demisch, *Erhobene Hände*, fig. 81.

20. See Cassian *Institutions* 2.10.2.

21. See ibid., 2.11.2. Jean-Claude Schmitt, *La Raison des gestes dans l'Occident medieval* (Paris: Gallimard, 1990), pp. 73–74, has called attention to Cassian's descriptions.

22. Franz Joseph Dölger, in his admirable treatment of the boat in early Christian symbolism, which we will follow (*Sol salutis: Gebet und Gesang im christ-*

lichen Altertum [Münster: Aschendorf, 1925], pp. 272–86), suggests that "in the countries of the eastern Mediterranean surrounded by the sea" this is natural. If I am not mistaken, however, in Christian fantasy the boat is more significant than in the non-Christian literatures of the same time and countries. I am not aware of a study of this interesting subject.

23. Lactantius *The Divine Institutes* 6.8. See *Ante-Nicene Christian Library* (Edinburgh: Clark, 1867–73), 21:370.

24. See Justin Martyr *Dialogue with Trypho* 138.2.

25. "Certainly, we see the sign of the cross represented in a natural manner on a ship, when it rides over the waves with swelling sails or glides along gently with outspread oars. . . ." says Minucius Felix *Octavius* 29.

26. Dölger, *Sol salutis*, p. 286.

27. See Aelian *Varia historia* 9.40.

28. The literature is too large, and the subject too well known, for any brief references. For a survey of the more important funerary inscriptions, see Richmond Lattimore, *Themes in Greek and Latin Epitaphs* (Urbana: University of Illinois Press, 1962), especially chap. 3. For pictorial renderings of the subject in earlier Greek art, see Emily Vermeule, *Aspects of Death in Early Greek Art and Poetry* (Berkeley: University of California Press, 1979), pp. 211 ff., n. 7, and p. 229, n. 57.

29. A. Moret, *Rois et dieux d'Egypte* (Paris: A. Colin, 1925). This derivation, I understand, has now been abandoned.

30. G. W. Bowersock, *Hellenism in Late Antiquity* (Ann Arbor: University of Michigan Press, 1991), p. 55.

31. Ibid.

32. See Garth Fowden, *The Egyptian Hermes: A Historical Approach to the Late Pagan Mind* (Cambridge: Cambridge University Press, 1986).

33. See Clement of Alexandria *Stromateis* V.2.20.3. And see Fowden, *The Egyptian Hermes*, p. 64.

34. See *The Hieroglyphics of Horapollo*, trans. George Boas (New York: Pantheon, 1950), with an informative introduction.

35. From the large literature on Clement of Alexandria, I shall mention only Salvatore R. C. Lilla, *Clement of Alexandria: A Study in Christian Platonism and Gnosticism* (London: Oxford University Press, 1971), esp. pp. 9–59.

36. Eusebius *The History of the Church* 6.18. I use the translation by G. A. Williamson (Harmondsworth: Penguin, 1989).

37. See *Scriptores Historiae Augustae, Alexanderi Severi vita* 29. A well-known dispute has been going on now for generations concerning the authenticity of this work. For our purpose these differences between scholars are of no great significance. All modern students agree that the *Historia Augusta* was written in the fourth or fifth century, and whether or not the separate data are correct, whether each individual vita was, or was not, composed by a contemporary and may be considered reliable, in matters of religion and culture the text truly reflects the period as a whole.

38. I have discussed this mosaic in some detail in "The David Mosaic in Gaza,"

reprinted in my *Imago Hominis: Studies in the Language of Art* (Vienna: IRSA, 1991), pp. 180–207.

Stierle: Translatio Studii and Renaissance

Unless noted otherwise, all translations are the author's own.

1. This was the device inscribed in the imperial seal.

2. The complex prehistory of *transferre imperium* is brilliantly expounded in Werner Goez's *Translatio Imperii: Ein Beitrag zur Geschichte des Geschichtsdenkens und der politischen Theorie im Mittelalter und in der frühen Neuzeit* (Tübingen: Mohr, 1958). Goez's book is basic for the history of the concept of *translatio imperii* and the various political implications of its use.

3. See *Ottonis episcopi frisingensis chronica sive historia de duabus civitatibus*, (Hannoverae et Lipsiae: Adolfus Hofmeister, 1912) bk. II, chap. 1, p. 69: "Concesso ad Medos Assyriorum regno Arbatus, qui huius translationis auctor fuerat, imperium arripuit ac per XXVIII annos tenuit. . . ."

4. See Goez, *Translatio Imperii*, p. 118: "Otto scheint also, obgleich der Gedanke des Ost-West-Wandels der Kultur ihm aus der Tradition überkommen war, den sprachlichen Ausdruck dafür in bewusster Parallele zur 'Translatio imperii' selbst gebildet zu haben." For the concept of *translatio studii*, see esp. Etienne Gilson, "Humanisme médiéval et Renaissance" (1930), reprinted in *Les idées et les lettres* (Paris: Vrin, 1955); Ernst Robert Curtius, *Europäische Literatur und lateinisches Mittelalter* (Bern/Munich: Francke, 1984); pp. 38–40; and August Buck, "Gab es einen Humanismus im Mittelalter?" *Romanische Forschungen* 75 (1963): 213–39. Whereas Gilson takes the formula of *translatio studii* as an argument for continuity between antiquity, the Middle Ages, and the Renaissance without, however, giving attention to the history of the term itself, Curtius takes it rather vaguely as a topos of the Latin Middle Ages. Buck instead insists on the difference between medieval *translatio studii* and Renaissance humanism: "Die Vorstellungen der 'translatio imperii' und der 'translatio studii' liessen das Bewusstsein für die zeitliche Distanz zur Antike überhaupt nicht aufkommen und verstellten den Weg zu der Einsicht, dass die antike Geschichte eine besondere Epoche, die antike Kultur ein in sich geschlossenes Ganzes bilden" (p. 226). What in spite of their divergences these three views on *translatio studii* have in common is their neglect of Otto von Freising's crucial importance for the history of *translatio imperii* and *translatio studii* as well.

5. *Ottonis . . . chronica*, bk. VII, chap. 35, p. 372.

6. Ibid., bk. V, chap. 36, p. 260.

7. Hugo of Saint Victor, *De arca Noe morali*, quoted in Goez, *Translatio Imperii*, p. 120.

8. Quoted in Goez, *Translatio Imperii*, p. 122.

9. See ibid., pp. 122–23.

10. Alexandre Micha, ed., *Les Romans de Chrétien de Troyes*, vol. 2, *Cligés* (Paris: Champion, 1975).

11. Micha's edition, following the copy of Guyot, has left out this verse. It is contained, however, in most of the other manuscripts and seems to be authentic—at least it reflects an authentic understanding of Chrétien's new conception of *romanz*. See Kristian von Troyes, *Cligés*, ed. Wendelin Foerster, 4th ed. (Halle: Max Niemeyer, 1921), p. 4, l. 23.

12. This political context of *translatio* as well as the speculative dimensions of *translatio studii* are not taken into consideration by Michelle A. Freeman in *The Poetics of Translatio studii and Conjointure: Chrétien de Troyes' Cligés* (Lexington, Ky.: French Forum, 1979).

13. Jean Rychner, ed., *Les Lais de Marie de France* (Paris: Champion, 1978), prologue, l. 16.

14. See *De Monarchia* 3.16.10–11: "Propter quod opus fuit homini duplici directivo secundum duplicem finem: scilicet summo Pontifice, qui secundum revelata humanum genus perduceret ad vitam eternam, et Imperatore, qui secundum phylosophica documenta genus humanum ad temporalem felicitatem dirigeret." All quotations are from *Le opere di Dante*, 2d ed., M. Barbi et al. (Firenze: Società Dantesca Italiana, 1960).

15. This is Dante's project of a "vulgare illustre" that does not yet exist but is to be instituted: "querimus vulgare illustre" (*De vulgari eloquentia* 1.14.8). See also Dante's passionate polemics in the *Convivio* against those Italians who use French as the language of literature: "A perpetuale infamia e depressione de li malvagi uomini d'Italia, che commendano lo volgare altrui e lo loro proprio dispregiano, dico che la loro mossa viene da cinque abominevoli cagioni" (1.11.1–2).

16. Translations are taken from *The Divine Comedy*, trans. Charles S. Singleton, 6 vols. (Princeton, N.J.: Princeton University Press, 1970).

17. "Non è il mondan romore altro ch'un fiato / di vento, ch'or vien quinci e or vien quindi, / e muta nome perché muta lato" (*Purgatorio* 11.100–102).

18. This is meant by Dante's formula "visibile parlare" for the divine art of sculpture: "Colui che mai non vide cosa nova / produsse esto visibile parlare" (*Purgatorio* 10.94–95).

19. This is why Virgil forbids Dante to speak himself: "Lascia parlare a me, ch'i' ho concetto / ciò che tu vuoi; ch' ei sarebbero schivi, / perché fuor greci, forse del tuo detto" (*Inferno* 26.73–75).

20. "O diluvio raccolto / di che deserti strani, / per inondar i nostri dolci campi!" (*Canzoniere*, ed. Gianfranco Contini [Torino: Einaudi, 1964], 128.28–30).

21. See Theodor E. Mommsen, "Petrarch's Conception of the Dark Ages," *Speculum* 17 (1942): 226–42.

22. See *Canzoniere* 34.5–8: "dal pigro gielo e dal tempo aspro e rio, / che dura quanto 'l tuo viso s'asconde, / difendi or l'onorata e sacra fronde, / ove tu prima, e poi fu' invescato io."

23. "Einer der frühesten völlig modernen Menschen" (Jakob Burckhardt, *Die Kultur der Renaissance in Italien* [1859], vol. 3 of *Gesammelte Werke* [Darmstadt: Wissenschaftliche Buchgesellschaft, 1955]).

24. Petrarch, *Le familiaro [epistolae familiares] a cura di Ugo Dotti* (Urbino: Argalía Editore), bk. IV, vol. I, pp. 362–77.

25. See Karlheinz Stierle, *Petrarcas Landschaften: Zur Geschichte ästhetischer Landschaftserfahrung* (Krefeld: Scherpe, 1979), pp. 22–32, and "Die Entdeckung der Landschaft in Literatur und Malerei der italienischen Renaissance" in Heinz-Dieter Weber, ed., *Vom Wandel des neuzeitlichen Naturbegriffs* (Konstanz: Konstanzer Universitätsverlag, 1989).

26. See Leonid Batkin, *Die italienische Renaissance: Versuch einer Charakterisierung eines Kulturtyps* (Frankfurt: Verlag Roter Stern, 1981), p. 308: "Die Renaissance ist die Kultur der Kommunikation der Kulturen."

27. See the contributions to Wolf-Dieter Stempel and Karlheinz Stierle, eds., *Die Pluralität der Welten: Aspekte der Renaissance in der Romania* (Munich: Fink, 1987).

28. The dialogical structure of Montaigne's essays and the plurality of cultural contexts they confront have been worked out in Hugo Friedrich's admirable *Montaigne* (Bern: Francke, 1949).

29. *Essais*, ed. Albert Thibaudet (Paris: Gallimard, 1933), bk. III, chap. 6, pp. 1,005–25.

30. See Stierle, "Vom Gehen, Reiten und Fahren: Der Reflexionszusammenhang von Montaignes 'Des coches,' " *Poetica* 14 (1982): 195–212.

31. Aesthetic experience for Steiner is based on "an irreducible subjectivity, the finality of a self whose freedom, whose *cortesia*, makes possible the recognition of the other" (*Real Presences: Is There Anything in What We Say?* [Chicago: University of Chicago Press, 1989], p. 198).

Besserman: The Translation of Biblical Poetics

1. On medieval translation theory (with valuable discussion and bibliography on medieval French and Italian theory and practice in particular), see Gianfranco Folena, " 'Volgarizzare' e 'tradurre': Idea e terminologia della traduzione dal medio evo italiano e romanzo all'umanesimo europeo," in *La traduzione: saggi e studi*, Centro per lo studio dell'insegnamento all'estero dell'italiano, Università degli studi di Trieste (Trieste: Lint, 1973), pp. 57–120. See also Louis G. Kelly, *The True Interpreter: A History of Translation Theory and Practice in the West* (Oxford: Blackwell, 1979); and W. Schwarz, "The Meaning of *Fidus Interpres* in Medieval Translation," *Journal of Theological Studies* 45 (1944): 73–78. For Chaucer's ideas about translation and his achievements as a translator, see discussion and references in Rita Copeland, "Rhetoric and Vernacular Translation in the Middle Ages," *Studies in the Age of Chaucer* 9 (1978): 41–75; R. A. Shoaf, "Notes Towards Chaucer's Poetics of Translation," *Studies in the Age of Chaucer* 1 (1979): 55–66; and Caroline D. Eckhardt, "The Art of Translation in *The Romaunt of the Rose*," *Studies in the Age of Chaucer* 6 (1984): 41–63.

2. Quotations from the *De Doctrina Christiana* follow Saint Augustine, *On Christian Doctrine*, trans. D. W. Robertson, Jr. (Indianapolis: Bobbs-Merrill,

1958). Robertson's translation is followed by Augustine's book, chapter, and paragraph numbers and the page number in Robertson, followed by the page number in the Latin text of Sancti Aurelii Augustini, *De Doctrina Christiana, De Vera Religione*, ed. Joseph Martin, Corpus Christianorum, Series Latina, XXXII, Aurelii Augustini Opera Pars IV, 1 (Turnholt: Brepols, 1962). The influence of the *De Doctrina Christiana*, from Cassiodorus to Wyclif and beyond, is surveyed in Robertson's introduction to *On Christian Doctrine*, pp. ix–xxi.

3. Gerald Bonner points out that Augustine's *Itala* appears to have been "a European version of the Old Latin translation used in North Africa in Augustine's time, but it does not seem possible to be more precise than this" (see "Augustine as Biblical Scholar," in *From the Beginnings to Jerome*, vol. 1 of *The Cambridge History of the Bible*, ed. P. R. Ackroyd and C. F. Evans [Cambridge: Cambridge University Press, 1970], pp. 541–63; quotation on p. 545). On the medieval distinction between translating "word for word" and translating "meanings," see Schwarz, "The Meaning of *Fidus Interpres* in Medieval Translation."

4. On the definition and widespread use of the term *sermo humilis* to describe the "plain" or "simple" style of the Bible, related to the *submissus* or "subdued" style that Augustine is discussing in the present passage, see the classic essay by Erich Auerbach, "*Sermo humilis*," in *Literary Language and Its Public in Late Latin Antiquity and in the Middle Ages*, trans. Ralph Manheim (New York: Pantheon, 1965), pp. 27–66 (pp. 33–39 on Augustine's treatment of biblical style in the *De Doctrina Christiana*, and pp. 49–50 for quotation and discussion of Augustine's "most complete statement" on the Bible's use of the *sermo humilis* style, in his letter to Volusianus, *Epistolae* 137.18).

5. For some links between Augustine's theory of scriptural allegory and the poetic theories of Dante, Petrarch, and Boccaccio, see Charles G. Osgood, ed. and trans., *Boccaccio on Poetry: Being the Preface and the Fourteenth and Fifteenth Books of Boccaccio's "Genealogia Deorum Gentilium"* (Indianapolis: Bobbs-Merrill, 1956), introduction, pp. xi–l. For a basic bibliography on the relationship of Chaucer to Dante, Petrarch, and Boccaccio, see *The Riverside Chaucer*, 3d ed., ed. Larry D. Benson (Boston: Houghton-Mifflin, 1987), pp. 776–77.

6. Quotations from the *Canterbury Tales* are identified by fragment and line number in *The Riverside Chaucer*.

7. For Middle English proverbial expressions about the need for words and deeds to be "cousins," see Bartlett Jere and Helen Wescott Whiting, *Proverbs, Sentences, and Proverbial Phrases, from English Writings Mainly before 1500* (Cambridge, Mass.: Harvard University Press, 1968), item W645; and for discussion of the literary and philosophical background of the saying, see Paul Beekman Taylor, "Chaucer's *Cosyn to the Dede*," *Speculum* 57 (1982): 315–27.

8. For the parallel passage, see lines 7,051–88 in Guillaume de Lorris and Jean de Meun's *Le Roman de la Rose*, ed. Félix Lecoy 3 vols., (Paris: Champion, 1965, 1979, 1982); and *The Romance of the Rose*, trans. Charles Dahlberg (1971; Hanover, N.H.: University Press of New England, 1983), p. 135.

9. This is a claim that Chaucer's Nun's Priest makes, invoking Romans 15.4 as a prooftext, at the conclusion of the beast fable he narrates later in the *Canterbury*

Tales (7.3,438–43). As we shall see, it is a claim that Chaucer hints at making for the entire *Canterbury Tales* when he, too, quotes Romans 15.4, in the "Retraction" at the end of the *Canterbury Tales*.

10. For evidence of "Christ" used in Middle English to refer to both God the author and the protagonist of the Bible, see the *Middle English Dictionary*, ed. Hans Kurath, Sherman M. Kuhn, John Reidy, and Robert E. Lewis (Ann Arbor: University of Michigan Press, 1954–   ), s.v. *Crist* n. 1 (a) and 1 (b). And on Chaucer's use of "courtly" and "bourgeois" or, alternatively, "courtly," "civic," and "rustic" stylistic levels in the *Canterbury Tales*, see, respectively, Charles Muscatine, *Chaucer and the French Tradition: A Study in Style and Meaning* (Berkeley: University of California Press, 1957); and John H. Fisher, "The Three Styles of Fragment I of the *Canterbury Tales*," *Chaucer Review* 8 (1973–74): 119–27.

11. A. J. Minnis, *Medieval Theory of Authorship: Scholastic Literary Attitudes in the Later Middle Ages*, 2d ed. (Philadelphia: University of Pennsylvania Press, 1988), p. 167. Judson Boyce Allen, *The Friar as Critic: Literary Attitudes in the Later Middle Ages* (Nashville: Vanderbilt University Press, 1971), pp. 3–28, also demonstrates that in the fourteenth century "what was done in reading the Bible was also done in reading poetic fictions, and equally elaborate poetic allegories were constructed on both sorts of texts" (p. 5).

12. Minnis, *Medieval Theory of Authorship*, p. 167. Minnis also cites analogues to Chaucer's apology from Jean de Meun's portion of the *Roman de la Rose* and Boccaccio's *Genealogia Deorum Gentilium* (ibid., p. 273, n. 24).

13. On this possible range of meanings for Christ's "broad" speaking, see the *Middle English Dictionary*, s.v. *brode* adv. 3 (a), (b), and (c).

14. The text of Chaucer's source for the "Tale of Melibee," Renaud de Louens's *Livre de Melibée et de Dame Prudence* (itself a translation of Albertano of Brescia's *Liber consolationis et consilii*), is edited with an introduction by J. Burke Severs, "The Tale of Melibeus," in W. F. Bryan and Germaine Dempster, eds., *Sources and Analogues of Chaucer's "Canterbury Tales"* (1941; New York: Humanities Press, 1958), pp. 560–614.

15. The "Knight's Tale" actually shows scant regard for "everich a word" of its source, Boccaccio's *Teseida*. As the detailed comparison of the two works by Robert A. Pratt demonstrates, the "Knight's Tale" is less than one-fourth the length of the *Teseida*—see Pratt's "The Knight's Tale," ibid., pp. 82–105.

16. The tradition of Gospel harmonies to which the *De Consensu Evangelistarum* belongs goes back to the *Diatessaron* of Tatian (d. c. 174 C.E.). For a survey of the tradition, see Elizabeth Salter, *Nicholas Love's "Myrrour of the Blessed Lyf of Jesu Christ,"* Analecta Cartusiana, 10 (Salzburg: Institut für Anglistik und Amerikanistik, Universität Salzburg, 1974), pp. 57–71. By Chaucer's time the assumption that the Gospels have a single "sentence" even when they appear to vary in their surface details had become a commonplace of biblical interpretation. See Minnis, *Medieval Theory of Authorship*, p. 167, and p. 273, nn. 25–26.

17. Quotations from the *De Consensu Evangelistarum* are taken from *On the Harmony of the Gospels*, trans. S. D. F. Salmond, ed. M. B. Riddle, in *The Works of St. Augustine*, vol. 6, A Select Library of Nicene and Post-Nicene Fathers of the

Christian Church, First Series (Grand Rapids, Mich.: Eerdmans, 1956). References
to Augustine's book, chapter, and paragraph numbers in the *De Consensu Evangelistarum* and the page number in Salmond's translation are provided in paren-
theses in the text, followed by the page number in the Latin text of *De Consensu
Evangelistarum*, ed. F. Weinrich, Corpus Scriptorum Ecclesiasticorum Latinorum
43 (Vienna: F. Tempsky, 1904).

18. In the present context, I can only mention the added influence on medieval
conceptions of the connection between secular and sacred writing of Jerome's influential statements on aspects of the subject. See, for example, Brenda Deen Schild-
gen, "Jerome's *Prefatory Epistles* to the Bible and *The Canterbury Tales*," *Studies
in the Age of Chaucer* 15 (1993): 111–30; and cf. Jerome's assertion in his *Adversus
Helvidium* that the Evangelists report not only what is literally true but also express
"the vulgar opinion which is a true law of history," cited and discussed, with specific reference to Bede, by Roger Ray, "Bede's *Vera Lex Historiae*," *Speculum* 55
(1980): 1–21 (quotation on pp. 5–6).

19. Augustine's views on literal and figurative interpretation of the Bible are
outlined by Henri De Lubac, *Exégèse médiévale: Les quatre sens de l'écriture*, 2
pts. in 4 vols. (Paris: Aubier, 1959–64), pt. 1, vol. 1, pp. 177–89. D. W. Robertson's
A Preface to Chaucer: Studies in Medieval Perspectives (Princeton, N.J.: Princeton
University Press, 1962) was a classic attempt—now judged by many to have been
a failed attempt—to understand Chaucer's poetry in the light of ideas about biblical
exegesis that were first authoritatively set forth by Augustine in the *De Doctrina
Christiana* and subsequently became commonplaces of medieval thought. For an
important evaluation of the strengths and weaknesses of Robertson's exegetical
brand of criticism, see Lee Patterson, "Historical Criticism and the Development
of Chaucer Studies," in *Negotiating the Past: The Historical Understanding of Medieval Literature* (Madison: University of Wisconsin Press, 1987), pp. 3–39.

20. The seriousness and the putative inviolability of the "doctrine" Chaucer
offers in the "Tale of Melibee" has been debated by Chaucer critics. See Traugott
Lawler, "Chaucer," in *Middle English Prose: A Critical Guide to Major Authors
and Genres* (New Brunswick, N.J.: Rutgers University Press, 1984), pp. 291–313
(pp. 294–96 on "Melibee"); and Lee Patterson, "'What Man Artow?': Authorial
Self-Definition in *The Tale of Sir Thopas* and *The Tale of Melibee*," *Studies in the
Age of Chaucer* 11 (1989): pp. 117–75. Though a detailed reading of "Melibee" is
beyond my present aim, it will suffice to note that even if the ironic antifeminist
remarks and other slight changes Chaucer introduced into his translation of his
source do not entirely cancel the tale's doctrine, they certainly do problematize it
in various ways.

21. Quoted from the Douay-Rheims version, Old Testament first published at
Douay, 1609; New Testament first published at Rheims, 1582 (this edition, 1899;
Rockford, Ill.: Tan Books, 1971).

22. Minnis, *Medieval Theory of Authorship*, pp. 205–9, discusses Chaucer's
use of Romans 15.4 in the context of similar appropriations of the verse by Nicholas
of Lyre, Ralph Higden, the anonymous author of the *Ovide Moralisé*, and William
Caxton. In a recent article, "Deconstructing Chaucer's Retraction," *Exemplaria* 3

(1991): 135–58, Peter W. Travis claims that the allusion to Romans 15.4 in the "Retraction" was, in one sense, Chaucer's way of "proffering a defense of the biblically authorized value of all poetry as an apologia pro sua arte. His own scripture is validated by Scripture; his book has been authorized by 'oure book'" (p. 144). Like Minnis, Travis also compares Chaucer's quote from Romans 15.4 to the paraphrase of the same verse in the opening passage of the *Ovide Moralisé*, but Travis stresses (rightly, I think) a number of differences between the two passages, including the significant fact that Chaucer, unlike the anonymous author of the *Ovide Moralisé*, explicitly cites the Bible as his source for the quotation (pp. 143–44).

23. On Chaucer's various biblical references, see my *Chaucer and the Bible: A Critical Review of Research, Indexes, and Bibliography* (New York: Garland, 1988).

24. For an overview of fourteenth-century developments in exegesis, see Beryl Smalley, *The Study of the Bible in the Middle Ages*, 3d ed. (Oxford: Clarendon Press, 1983); to be supplemented, and in part corrected, by William J. Courtenay, "The Bible in the Fourteenth Century: Some Observations," *Church History* 54 (1985): 176–87; and his *Schools and Scholars in Fourteenth-Century England* (Princeton, N.J.: Princeton University Press, 1987). On von Oyta, see Frank Rosenthal, "Heinrich von Oyta and Biblical Criticism in the Fourteenth Century," *Speculum* 25 (1950): 178–83. On de Lyra, see Herman Hailperin, *Rashi and the Christian Scholars* (Pittsburgh: University of Pittsburgh Press, 1963); and De Lubac, *Exégèse médiévale*, pt. 2, vol. 4, pp. 344–67.

25. On the increased knowledge of Greek and Hebrew in thirteenth- and fourteenth-century biblical scholarship, see Smalley, *Study of the Bible*, pp. 329–55. The fourteenth-century turn away from Augustine's predominantly allegorical kind of biblical exegesis toward a more literal, textually and linguistically focused method of reading and exegesis (of the Old Testament in particular) is evidenced throughout Nicholas de Lyra's influential commentary on the entire Bible, *Postilla litteralis super totam Bibliam*, written c. 1330 (see Hailperin, *Rashi and the Christian Scholars*, pp. 137–246).

26. On the fourteenth-century turn toward the Bible, see W. A. Pantin, *The English Church in the Fourteenth Century* (1955; University of Toronto Press–Medieval Academy of America, 1980), pp. 132–335; and William J. Courtenay, "Nominalism and Late Medieval Religion," in Charles Trinkaus and Heiko A. Oberman, eds., *The Pursuit of Holiness in Late Medieval and Renaissance Religion* (Leiden: E. J. Brill, 1974), pp. 26–59; Courtenay, "The Bible in the Fourteenth Century: Some Observations"; and Courtenay, *Schools and Scholars in Fourteenth-Century England*, pp. 368–69.

27. On Wyclif and the Lollard movement, see Anne Hudson, *The Premature Reformation: Wycliffite Texts and Lollard History* (Oxford: Clarendon Press, 1988).

28. On Wyclif's theory of biblical exegesis, see Michael Hurley, S. J., "'Scriptura Sola': Wyclif and His Critics," *Traditio* 16 (1960): 275–352. How Chaucer thematized elements in the Wycliffite reform program, including Wyclif's ideas on

biblical exegesis and translation, is considered by Hudson, *The Premature Reformation*, pp. 390–94.

29. On fourteenth-century religious currents that fostered Renaissance and Reformation cultural developments, see Heiko A. Oberman, *The Dawn of the Reformation: Essays in Late Medieval and Early Reformation Thought* (Edinburgh: T. & T. Clark, 1986).

30. That the Wycliffite movement played a role in bringing about the later English Reformation was argued by A. G. Dickens, *The English Reformation* (New York: Schocken, 1964), esp. pp. 22–37. The idea has now been more cautiously evaluated, and questioned, by Anne Hudson in *The Premature Reformation*.

31. A. C. Spearing's outline of the "Renaissance" features of Chaucer's poetry has much to recommend it (see *Medieval to Renaissance in English Poetry* [Cambridge: Cambridge University Press, 1985], pp. 1–14 on the definition of "medieval" and "Renaissance" cultural features, and pp. 15–58 on the various ways in which Chaucer's works display mainly the latter).

32. Two recent books that relate Chaucer's literary innovations to his social reality in diverse but equally compelling ways are Paul Strohm's *Social Chaucer* (Cambridge, Mass.: Harvard University Press, 1989), and Lee Patterson's *Chaucer and the Subject of History* (Madison: University of Wisconsin Press, 1991).

A. Assmann: The Curse and Blessing of Babel

Unless otherwise noted, all translations are the author's own.

1. After the expulsion from Paradise and the destruction by the flood, in the third story God punishes or checks the sinful and dangerous impulses of his unruly people. In these stories, the traits of the Mesopotamian God are still visible, the traits not of God as the creator or benevolent father but as the destroyer of his work. In the Mesopotamian myths, God is the cruel and violent rival of man. I owe this idea to Zwi Abush, who has summed up the common theme of these stories in a formula: "If God had his way, men would be helpless children." It is interesting to note that according to ancient Egyptian standards, the multiplication of the languages and peoples was considered not a work of confusion due to divine wrath, but a work of creation and a positive manifestation of divine power.

2. See Zechariah 14.9: "And the Lord shall be king over all the earth: on that day the Lord shall be one, and his name One"; and Zephania 3.8–9: "Wait for me, says the Lord, until the day that I rise up to the prey: for my determination is to gather the nations, that I may assemble the kingdoms, to pour upon them my indignation, all my fierce anger: for all the earth shall be devoured with the fire of my jealousy. For then I will convert the peoples to a purer language, that they may all call upon the name of the Lord, to serve him with one consent."

3. Mystics like Emanuel Swedenborg discussed the possibility of a purely spiritual language, a concept that was mocked by Herder: "If we were spirits, we would communicate directly via concepts spoken into each other's soul" (J. G. Herder, *Frühe Schriften 1764–1772*, vol. 1 of *Werke in 10 Bänden*, ed. U. Geier [Frankfurt: Deutscher Klassiker Verlag, 1985], p. 188).

4. Karl Erich Grözinger, *Musik und Gesang in der Theologie der frühen jü-dischen Literatur: Talmud, Midrash, Mystik*, Texte und Studien zum Antiken Judentum 3 (Tübingen: Mohr, 1982), p. 102; see also Peter Schäfer, *Die Vorstellung vom Heiligen Geist in der rabbinischen Literatur*, Studien zum Alten und Neuen Testament 28 (Munich: Kosel-Verlag, 1972).

5. Grözinger, *Musik und Gesang*, p. 107.

6. See Christoph Uehlinger, *Weltreich und "eine Rede": Eine neue Deutung der sogenannten Turmbauerzählung (Gen. 11.1–9)*, Orbis Biblicus Orientalis 101 (Freiburg/Schweiz and Göttingen: Vandenhoeck & Ruprecht, 1990), p. 265.

7. Origenes *Patrologia Graeca* 12.111–12, cited in Uehlinger, *Weltreich*, pp. 264–65.

8. Augustine *Enarrationes in Psalmos* 54. 11–12, cited in Uehlinger, *Weltreich*, p. 271: "spiritus superbiae dispersit linguas, Spiritus sanctus congregavit linguas." In the seventeenth century, Samuel Purchas expressed the topos in a similar way: "Mans sinne caused this, Gods mercie that: the one came from Babylon, the other from Hierusalem" (cited in David S. Katz, *Philo-Semitism and the Readmission of the Jews to England, 1603–1655* [Oxford: Clarendon Press, 1982], p. 60).

9. If monotheism is "translated" into the sphere of politics, the problems of political theology arise. See Jan Assmann, *Politische Theologie zwischen Ägypten und Israel* (Munich: Siemens Stiftung, 1992).

10. Augustine *Enarrationes in Psalmos* 271: "Volunt unam linguam, veniant ad ecclesiam; quia et in diversitate linguarum carnis, una est lingua in fide cordis."

11. For a discussion of these terms see Jan Assmann's contribution to this volume.

12. While the church fathers supplemented Hebrew by Greek and Latin, the Renaissance humanists supplemented Latin and Greek by Hebrew. It is the specific mark of western culture that it has preserved its central texts both in translation and in the original. This double method of text preservation—to have tradition both ways, in the translation and in the original—is the precondition for leaps in tradition, for cultural revivals and renaissances. Transformations and distances are possible, but the way back is always kept open. The polyphony was increased by three original languages (the title of a book written in 1524 by Thomas Wakefield, reader of Hebrew at Oxford, is *Oratio de laudibus et utilitate trium linguarum*).

13. Ernst Benz, *Geist und Leben der Ostkirche* (Hamburg: Rowohlt, 1957), p. 67.

14. On mission as a path to messianic unity, see Oscar Cullmann, *Christus und die Zeit*, 2d ed. (Zurich: Evangelischer Verlag, 1948), 143–45. I owe this to Theo Sundermeier. Borst comments on the politics of mission: "To teach all nations, to connect them with a common bond and lead them back to the one origin—here, the process of unfolding has the central aim of overcoming historical plurality" (Arno Borst, *Der Turmbau von Babel*, Geschichte der Meinungen über Ursprung und Vielfalt der Sprachen und Völker [Stuttgart: Hiersemann, 1957–67]).

15. This is expressed by, among many others, Tommaso Campanella (1568–1639) in *Realis Philosophiae epilogisticae* 1.12.7, pp. 159–60.

16. See Alison Coudert, "Some Theories of a Natural Language from the Re-

naissance to the 17th Century," in *Magia Naturalis und die Entstehung der modernen Naturwissenschaften* Studia Leibnitia, Sonderheft 7, (Wiesbaden: Steiner, 1978), p. 80.

17. This history is traced in the first half of the seventeenth century in England in Katz, *Philo-Semitism*, pp. 43–88.

18. Cornelius Agrippa, *Three Books of Occult Philosophy*, trans. J. F. (London: R. W. for Gregory Monie, 1651), 1.152.

19. Agrippa believed that knowledge of the prototype would entail the mastery of all the natural languages: "Now if there be any originall, whose words have a naturall signification, it is manifest that this in the Hebrew, the order of which he that shall know to resolve proportionably the letters thereof, shall have a rule exactly to find out any Idiome" (ibid.).

20. Jacob Boehme, *Werke*, ed. K. W. Schiebler (Leipzig: Johann Umbrosius Barth, 1922), 2:78.

21. I am grateful to Moshe Idel who stressed this point in the discussion of this paper.

22. "Cur tot sunt linguae nisi ut melius innominabile nominetur?" (quoted in Borst, *Der Turmbau*, 1,029). On the political mission of Cusanus see Edgar Wind, *Heidnische Mysterien in der Renaissance* (1958; Frankfurt: Suhrkamp, 1984), pp. 261n, 283–84.

23. "In varietate linguarum idem pronuntiatur" (quoted in Borst, *Der Turmbau*, 1,029).

24. Cusanus, *De pace seu concordia fidei* §1: "*Una religio in rituum varietate,*" quoted in Wind, *Heidnische Mysterien*, pp. 252, 283.

25. The *prisca theologia* was a Renaissance venture to revive Hellenism. Clemens Alexandrinus had called Moses the teacher of Plato. Philo saw an identity between the Platonic and the Mosaic law. Both were interested in translating individual cultural idioms into what Jan Assmann calls "a third language," the common language of the Hellenic civilization. The construction of a transcultural interlingua was founded on universalist concepts: the dissemination of divine ideas in the process of creation (the *logoi spermatikoi*), the notion of a common human heritage (the *rationes seminales* of the Stoa, the *formae exemplares* of Thomas, the archetypes of Philo), or on the lost tradition of arcane wisdom (*prisca theologia*). In the *prisca theologia* Noah became a central figure because he saved the arcane wisdom through the flood. Giovanni Nanni of Viterbo was an antiquary who in 1498 constructed a genealogy of wisdom in which Jewish, Egyptian, Greek, and Roman traditions were fused. See Wilhelm Schmidt-Biggermann, "Philosophia perennis im Spätmittelalter", in W. Haug and B. Wachinger, eds., *Originalität und Innovation in der frühen Neuzeit*, Fortuna Vitrea 7 (Tübingen: Niemeyer, 1992).

26. Johann Valentin Andreae, *Fama Fraternitatis* (1614), ed. Richard van Dülmen, Quellen und Forschungen zur Würtembergischen Kirchengeschichte, Bd.6 (Stuttgart: Cawler, 1976) 28–29. See Wilhelm Kühlmann, *Sozietät als Tagtraum: Rosenkreuzerbewegung und zweite Reformation*, (typescript, 1991), p. 12.

27. This disseminated body of tales has been diligently collected by F. Niewöhner in his study of Lessing's sources, *Veritas sive Varietas: Lessings Toleranzparabel*

und das Buch von den drei Betrügern, Bibliothek der Aufklärung V (Heidelberg: L. Schneider, 1988). For a recent discussion of Lessing's text see M. S. Abdullah, W. Jens, H. Küng, and S. Mosès, "Dogmatik, Fundamentalisten und Toleranz: Dialoge zur Ringparabel," *Sprache im Technischen Zeitalter* 30 (1992): 12–29.

28. Niewöhner, *Veritas sive Varietas,* p. 254.

29. This is the spirit of 1555, when at Augsburg peace was ensured by putting the decision about religion into the hand of the prince. Nathan, however, answers in the spirit of 1648 when at Münster peace was ensured by dissociating matters of politics from matters of religion.

30. Nathan when preparing himself for the interview knew that he had to steer a middle course; he was convinced that no extreme position would do. ("To play the orthodox Jew is impossible, to play the non-Jew is even less possible," he muses in the sixth scene of the third act.)

31. J. A. Comenius, *The Way of Light* (1668), trans. E. T. Campagnac (London: Hodder and Stoughton, 1938), p. 24.

32. Ibid., pp. 198, 202.

33. Jan-Dirk Müller, "Buchstabe, Geist, Subjekt: Zu einer frühneuzeitlichen Problemfigur bei Sebastian Franck," *MLN* 106 (1991): 656.

34. Theodor Haecker, *Vergil: Vater des Abendlands* (Munich: Hegenich, 1931), p. 17.

35. Contemporaneous to Haecker, there was also hegemonic humanism on the other side of the Rhine. Thomas Mann identified it with the French conservatism of H. Poincaré. According to Mann, he represented a political program in which nationalism and humanism were blended. The result was the claim of hegemonic priority of the Roman civilization, the politics of universal mission and world leadership.

36. Thomas Mann, "Goethe und Tolstoi" (1921), *Schriften und Reden zur Literatur, Kunst und Philosophie* (Frankfurt: Fischer, 1968), 1:216.

37. Mann, "Über die Lehre Spenglers" (1924), ibid., p. 225.

38. Ibid., p. 226.

39. Wolfgang Welsch, "Weisheit in einer Welt der Pluralität," in W. Oelmüller, ed., *Philosophie und Weisheit* (Paderborn: Schöningh, 1989), p. 241.

40. Johann Wolfgang von Goethe, "Maximen und Reflexionen No. 1336," *Hamburger Ausgabe,* ed. E. Trunz, 14 vols. (Munich, 1981), 12:543. The relation between translation and invasion is discussed by George Steiner, *After Babel: Aspects of Language and Translation* (London: Oxford University Press, 1976), pp. 296–413.

41. Hugo von Hofmannsthal, "Die Wege und die Begegnungen," *Erzählungen, erfundene Gespräche und Briefe,* in *Gesammelte Werke,* ed. B. Schoeller and R. Hirsch (Reisen, Frankfurt: Fischer, 1979), p. 161.

E. M. Budick: The Holocaust and American Literary Criticism

1. The texts that constitute this conversation are: Donald Pease, "New Americanists: Revisionist Interventions into the Canon," *New Americanists: Revisionist*

Interventions into the Canon, special issue of *boundary* 2 17 (1990): 1–37 and Frederick Crews, "Whose American Renaissance?" *New York Review of Books* (October 27, 1988): 68–81. The Trilling text central to this conversation is *The Liberal Imagination: Essays on Literature and Society* (1950; New York: Doubleday, 1953).

2. My epigraph is from Ludwig Lewisohn, *The American Jew: Character and Destiny* (New York: Farrar, Straus, & Co., 1950).

3. Among the books Crews reviews is *The American Renaissance Reconsidered: Selected Papers from the English Institute, 1982–83*, ed. Walter Benn Michaels and Donald E. Pease (Baltimore: Johns Hopkins University Press, 1985).

4. Pease, "New Americanists," p. 6.

5. Myra Jehlen, "Introduction: Beyond Transcendence," in Sacvan Bercovitch and Jehlen, eds., *Ideology and Classic American Literature* (Cambridge: Cambridge University Press, 1986), p. 2; see Russell J. Reising, *The Unusable Past: Theory and the Study of American Literature* (New York: Methuen, 1986); see also Pease's own "*Moby Dick* and the Cold War," in *American Renaissance Reconsidered*, pp. 113–55; this is in somewhat different form in *Ideology and Classic American Literature* as "Melville and Cultural Persuasion," pp. 384–417; Michael Denning, "'The Special American Conditions': Marxism and American Studies," *American Quarterly* 38 (1986): 356–80; Geraldine Murphy, "Romancing the Center: Cold War Politics and Classic American Literature," *Poetics Today* 9 (1988): 737–47; Kermit Vanderbilt, *American Literature and the Academy: The Roots, Growth, and Maturity of a Profession* (Philadelphia: University of Pennsylvania Press, 1986); and Cornel West, "Lionel Trilling: Godfather of Neo-Conservatism," *New Politics* 1 (1986): 233–42.

6. Mark Shechner, *After the Revolution: Studies in the Contemporary Jewish Imagination* (Bloomington: Indiana University Press, 1987), pp. 8–9; Gregory S. Jay, *America the Scrivener: Deconstruction and the Subject of Literary History* (Ithaca, N.Y.: Cornell University Press, 1990), pp. 298, 303; and see Mark Krupnick, *Lionel Trilling and the Fate of Cultural Criticism* (Evanston, Ill.: Northwestern University Press, 1986), pp. 97–98.

7. See, for example, "The Sense of the Past," *The Liberal Imagination*, pp. 177–79; Diana Trilling notes in her memoirs that Trilling's literary criticism was considered suspect by his colleagues at Columbia precisely because of its social orientation—see Diana Trilling, *The Beginning of the Journey: The Marriage of Diana and Lionel Trilling* (New York: Harcourt, Brace & Company, 1993), 268–69.

8. "Manners, Morals, and the Novel," *The Liberal Imagination*, p. 200.

9. *Sincerity and Authenticity* (Cambridge, Mass.: Harvard University Press, 1971), p. 125; in *Sincerity and Authenticity*, Trilling already refers to the figure who will become so crucial to Stephen Greenblatt's evolution of New Historicism, Raymond Williams, and he produces an idea of self-fashioning remarkably similar to Greenblatt's.

10. Bercovitch, "The Problem of Ideology in American Literary History," *Critical Inquiry* 12 (1986): 635.

11. "The Sense of the Past," pp. 176–79.

12. See Bercovitch's essay, "Discovering America: A Cross-Cultural Perspective," in this volume.

13. "Reality in America," *Liberal Imagination*, pp. 1–3.

14. Ibid., pp. 8–10.

15. Ibid., pp. 12–15.

16. Ibid., pp. 17–18.

17. Ibid., p. 19. Dreiser's anti-Semitism bore many of the trademarks of Nazi anti-Semitism. According to Daniel Aaron, Jews were from his point of view "unassimilable" and dangerous to society and therefore ought to occupy a national homeland separate from that of mainstream society—see *Writers on the Left: Episodes in American Literary Communism* (1961; New York: Octagon Books, 1979), p. 277.

18. Steven Marcus, "Lionel Trilling: 1905–75," in Quentin Anderson, Stephen Donadio, and Steven Marcus, eds., *Art, Politics, and Will: Essays in Honor of Lionel Trilling* (New York: Basic Books, 1977), p. 266.

19. Diana Trilling describes Trilling's Jewish upbringing in her *Beginning of the Journey*. For evaluations of Trilling's Jewishness—or lack of it—see Susanne Klingenstein, *Jews in the American Academy 1900–1940: The Dynamics of Intellectual Assimilation* (New Haven, Conn.: Yale University Press, 1991); Daniel T. O'Hara, *Lionel Trilling: The Work of Liberation* (Madison: University of Wisconsin Press, 1988); Morris Dickstein, "Lionel Trilling and *The Liberal Imagination*," *Sewanee Review* 94 (1986): 323–34; Alfred Kazin, *New York Jew* (London: Secker and Warburg, 1978); and, again, Mark Shechner, *After the Revolution* and Mark Krupnick, *Lionel Trilling and the Fate of Cultural Criticism*.

20. "Adams at Ease," *A Gathering of Fugitives* (New York: Harcourt, Brace, Jovanovich, 1956), p. 126.

21. "'That Smile of Parmenides Made Me Think,'" ibid., p. 166.

22. "James Joyce in His Letters," *The Last Decade: Essays and Reviews, 1965–1975*, ed. Diana Trilling (New York: Harcourt, Brace, Jovanovich, 1979), p. 46.

23. "A Novel of the Thirties," ibid., pp. 11–14.

24. "Isaac Babel," *Beyond Culture: Essays on Literature and Learning* (New York: Viking, 1965), pp. 119–44.

25. "A Novel in Passing," *A Gathering of Fugitives*; Trilling writes: "Far from forcing upon us an appalled realization of the dreadfulness of the recent past, it leads us to ask whether things were not really much worse than Mr. Gheorghiu says they were. This is in part the result of a literary inadequacy, but it is also the result of an inadequacy of moral sensitivity; one reason Mr. Gheorghiu's picture of the European horror falls short of the truth is that it deals in so minimal and perverse a way with the extreme example of that horror, the fate of the Jews" (p. 86).

26. Published respectively in *Commentary* 8 (1949): 368–69 and *Commentary* 12 (1951): 526–29.

27. *The Liberal Imagination*, p. 256.

28. *Speaking of Literature and Society*, ed. Diana Trilling (New York: Harcourt, Brace, Jovanovich, 1980), p. 52.

29. *The Liberal Imagination* and *The Opposing Self: Nine Essays in Criticism* (1950; New York: Viking Press, 1969).

30. See Diana Trilling, "Lionel Trilling: A Jew at Columbia," *Commentary* 67 (1979): 40. See, again, Diana Trilling, *The Beginning of the Journey.*

31. Karl Marx, *A World Without Jews*, trans. Dagobert D. Runes (New York: Philosophical Library, 1959).

32. Kazin, *New York Jew*, pp. 27, 194.

33. The term is Isaac Deutscher's, revived by Shechner, *After the Revolution.*

34. Jay, *America the Scrivener*, p. 297.

35. Ibid., pp. 297–98.   36. Ibid., pp. 302–12.

37. Ibid., pp. 185, 297.   38. Ibid., p. 285.

39. In a recent remake of Ernst Lubitsch's *To Be or Not To Be*, to take an example from popular culture, Mel Brooks makes the victims of Nazi oppression equally gypsy, homosexual, and Jew. I have discussed Morrison's novel at length in "The Mutual Displacements / Appropriations / Accommodations of Culture in the Fiction of Toni Morrison and Grace Paley," *Prospects* (1995). On the historical uniqueness of the Holocaust, see Steven T. Katz, *The Holocaust in Historical Context: The Holocaust and Mass Death before the Modern Age* (New York: Oxford University Press, 1994).

40. "Wordsworth and the Rabbis," *The Opposing Self*, pp. 136–37, 150.

41. Ibid., p. 123. On the relation between "Wordsworth and the Rabbis" and the Holocaust, see Edward Alexander, "Lionel Trilling," *Midstream* 29 (March 1983): 48–57; and my own "Lionel Trilling and the 'Being' of Culture," *The Massachusetts Review* 35 (1994): 63–82.

42. *Sincerity and Authenticity*, p. 24; compare with Mike Gold in *The New Masses*: "Are artists people?" "If you prick an artist, does he bleed? If you starve him does he faint?" (quoted by Daniel Aaron in *Writers on the Left*, p. 165).

43. Marx, *A World Without Jews*, p. 37.

44. Lewisohn, *The American Jew*, p. 13.

45. See Toni Morrison, "Unspeakable Things Unspoken: The Afro-American Presence in American Literature," *Michigan Quarterly Review* 28 (1989): 1–34.

46. Stanley Cavell, "Aversive Thinking: Emersonian Representations in Heidegger and Nietzsche," *Conditions Handsome and Unhandsome* (Chicago: University of Chicago Press, 1988), pp. 33–63, and *A Pitch of Philosophy: Autobiographical Exercises* (Cambridge, Mass.: Harvard University Press, 1994).

47. Bercovitch, "Discovering America," p. 156.

48. West, "Lionel Trilling," pp. 234, 238. West's list of those struggling for "revolutionary democracy," which prompts the critique of Trilling, notably does not include Jews (see pp. 240–41).

49. In "Racism's Last Word," Jacques Derrida deals with a similar issue. Countering the charge that in his essay he has separated history and the word, Derrida responds, "*apartheid*, the more it's talked about, the better. But who will do the talking? And how? These are the questions. Because talking about it is not enough" (in Henry Louis Gates, Jr., ed., *"Race," Writing, and Difference* [Chicago: Univer-

sity of Chicago Press, 1986], p. 355). In Derrida's view, to note racism's last word is exactly not to let racism have the last word. What, we might ask, about the word Holocaust? Who will say it, and how? What does it mean for the word not to be said? What does it mean for the word to be said only in silence?

50. I have explored some of these issues at greater length in *Engendering Romance: Women Writers and the Hawthorne Tradition, 1850–1990* (New Haven, Conn.: Yale University Press, 1994).

51. Many mainstream Communist supporters on the literary left were, after 1940, expressing similar views about the relation between literature and politics. Daniel Aaron quotes Albert Maltz, who remained within the Communist ranks after many others had defected, as follows: "The slogan 'art is a weapon' had been vulgarized to the point where its original meaning—art reflects or attacks social values—had been lost. In practice, it had come to mean 'that *unless* art is a weapon like a leaflet, serving immediate political ends, necessities, and programs, it is worthless or escapist or vicious.'" Maltz denounces the "writer who would misuse his art and betray the 'great humanistic tradition of culture' by serving 'an immediate political purpose'" (*Writers on the Left*, p. 387).

52. "Manners, Morals, and the Novel," *Liberal Imagination*, pp. 208, 213; recall here Trilling's objection to Dreiser's *Bulwark*, that "it does not include enough in its exploration of the problem of evil, and is not stern enough" ("Reality in America," *Liberal Imagination*, p. 17).

53. "Self-Reliance," *The Selected Writings of Ralph Waldo Emerson*, with an introduction by Brooks Atkinson (New York: Modern Library, 1940), pp. 147–49. Note the following statement by Quentin Anderson: "We have not . . . paid any attention to Trilling's urgent warning that the characteristic political mode among intellectuals masks our impulses from our awareness. . . . It was not Lionel Trilling who abandoned the politics of liberal democracy. . . . It was Trilling's contemporaries who, by their refusal of the human condition, and their love affair with an authoritarian politics . . . proceeded to charge Trilling with disloyalty to apocalypse. The quality of a democracy is to be measured not simply by its formal extension of rights to all, but by the capacity of its citizens to extend recognition to the full personhood of their fellow citizens. Our love of pattern and abstraction does not help us to extend this recognition, and it is disabling rather than useful when we are struggling with immediate questions like the impersonal power of such structures as oil companies and banks" ("On *The Middle of the Journey*," *Art, Politics, and Will*, pp. 261–64).

Bercovitch: Discovering America

1. Walt Whitman, "I Hear America Singing," and preface to *Leaves of Grass* (1855), in *Complete Poetry and Collected Prose*, ed. Justin Kaplan, Library of America (New York: Viking, 1982), pp. 174, 5; Ralph Waldo Emerson, "The Poet," in *Essays and Lectures*, ed. Joel Porte, Library of America (New York: Viking, 1983), p. 465; Franz Kafka, "Investigations of a Dog," trans. Willa and Ed-

win Muir, in *The Complete Stories*, ed. Nahum N. Glatzer (New York: Schocken, 1971), pp. 294, 280–81, 285–87, 315, 303.

2. This is repression in a familiar psychocultural sense: interpretation as a strategy for concealing our subjection to a master discourse. Again, the advantages are not far to seek—among these, evading the facts of subordination in ways that allow for compensatory modes of control—but the sense of reassurance this brings comes at the expense of critical awareness.

3. Douglas LePan, "A Country Without a Mythology," cited in Northrop Frye, *The Bush Garden: Essays on the Canadian Imagination* (Toronto: Anansi, 1971), p. 164.

4. What I found has sometimes given me pause: Puritanism as a venture in utopia; a group of radical idealists whose insulated immigrant enclave was meant to provide a specimen of good things to come; a latter-day Zion at the vanguard of history, fired by a vision that fused nostalgia and progress, prophecy and political action. The analogies to the rhetoric of my own past seem so striking now that it surprises me they did not occur to me at once, and stop me in my tracks. I prefer to think of it in retrospect as a happy coincidence of history and subjectivity—an example of the nontranscendent process of scholarly intuition.

5. Frye, *Bush Garden*, p. 138; Margaret Atwood, *Survival: A Thematic Guide to Canadian Literature* (Toronto: Anansi, 1972), p. 131.

6. The dominant English Protestant influence allowed for the "mosaic" concept, as distinct from the monolithic Catholic versions of other colonial myths, from Mexico through Central and South America, and to some extent including Catholic Quebec.

7. I expand upon this connection later in the essay. Here it will suffice to quote Benjamin directly, since the affinities are obvious enough between the "cultural treasures" of the "victors" and the process of socialization (as we have come to understand it) embedded in the process of canon formation: "To historians who wish to relive an era, Fustel de Coulanges recommends that they blot out everything they know about the later course of history. There is no better way of characterizing the method with which historical materialism has broken. It is a process of empathy whose origin is the indolence of the heart, *acedia*, which despairs of grasping and holding the genuine historical image as it flares up briefly. Among medieval theologians it was regarded as the root cause of sadness. Flaubert, who was familiar with it, wrote: '*Peu de gens devineront combien il a fallu être triste pour ressusciter Carthage.*' [Cf. Matthew Arnold's melancholy touchstones of Culture.] The nature of this sadness stands out more clearly if one asks with whom the adherents of historicism actually empathize. The answer is inevitable: with the victor. . . . According to traditional practice, the spoils are carried along in the procession. They are called cultural treasures, and a historical materialist views them with cautious detachment. . . . He regards it as his task to brush history against the grain" ("Theses on the Philosophy of History," *Illuminations*, ed. Hannah Arendt, trans. Harry Zohn [New York: Harcourt, Brace and World, 1968], pp. 256–57). Benjamin's contrast between empathic history and historical materialism applies in

some measure to the contrast I suggest below between aesthetic and contextual criticism.

8. I adopt D. H. Lawrence's term deliberately, to suggest the limitations of even the most brilliant cross-cultural investigations. In this respect, *Studies in Classic American Literature* is itself a model subject for cultural study: a fascinating mixture of outsider's perspective, insider's mystifications (e.g., "spirit of place"), and common transatlantic myths, notably those rooted in romanticism. Equally suggestive is Alexis de Tocqueville's *Democracy in America*, with its extraordinary mixture of French aristocratic "foreignness," rehashed American myths (ranging from Puritan origins to the "empty continent"), and common "modern" assumptions, notably those stemming from the Enlightenment.

9. Benjamin, "Theses," p. 256.

10. I am partly indebted for this (more or less random) list to a column by George F. Will, "Beyond the Literature of Protest," in the *Washington Post* of December 13, 1990 (p. A23):

Rutherford Calhoun is one of those rapscallions who have enlivened American Literature [ever] since Huck Finn decided civilization made him itch and lit out for the territories. . . . Calhoun is black.

So is his creator Charles Johnson, who teaches at the University of Washington and has written . . . an emancipation proclamation for black writers. It is his novel *Middle Passage*, the winner of the National Book Award. It is an example of triumphant individualism on the part of both Calhoun and Johnson.

Johnson noted that he is the first black male to win the award since Ralph Ellison won in 1953 for *Invisible Man*. Ellison's aim, says Johnson, was [the] creation of "a black American personality as complex, as multi-sided and synthetic as the American society that produced it. . . . Literature, he says . . . that is an extension of an ideology . . . lacks the power to change the reader's perceptions as the writer's perceptions change. . . . The novel is about—quietly about—patriotism."

"If," Calhoun muses, "this weird, upside-down caricature of a country called America, if this land of refugees and former indentured servants, religious heretics and half-breeds, whoresons and fugitives—this cauldron of mongrels from all points of the compass—was all I could right call *home*, than aye: I was of it. . . ."

Johnson anticipates in the 1990s a black fiction "of increasing intellectual and artistic generosity, one that enables us as a people—as a culture—to move from narrow complaint to broad celebration." I think he means celebration of the possibilities of American individualism. I know that his novel, and the award, are reasons for celebration.

A few notes may help situate Will's and Johnson's celebration in relation to my own views. (1) Huckleberry Finn lights out for the territory in order to go "howling after the Indians" with Tom Sawyer, and he does so after a very long episode in which his "individualism," along with Tom's, is severely questioned. (2) Patriotism, even in its "quietest" manifestations, is not an example of thought freed of ideology, and neither, for that matter, is the concept of an art free of ideology. (3) Both Ellison's "synthetic" America and Calhoun's "upside-down caricature" of it are versions of a mainstream cultural ideal. (4) Will is wrong to identify Johnson's views specifically as a movement away from the 1960's: see for example Coretta Scott King, "King's Dream . . . is really the American Dream," *Atlanta Journal and Constitution*, Jan. 5, 1986, p. 7.

11. A century before, Southern leaders had learned that "America" could not be manipulated to mean the ideals of feudal hierarchy, because it already represented something else—a set of culture-specific ideals, among these representative individualism, pluralist democracy, and the rights of personal assent. In the 1960's, as a century before, those ideals functioned through the denial of their cultural specificity; but of course there were certain adjustments now to meet new circumstances. First, "America" served to exclude the ideals of radical, rather than feudal, collectivism: it denied class identity as a century before it had denied racial hierarchy. Second, the protest leaders did not retreat into new havens of un-American resistance, as had the Southern visionaries before them, from the inventors of the plantation myth to the literary Agrarians. Some radicals, of course, may be said to have seceded into the groves of academe (there is a poignant cultural emblem in this regard in the coexistence of Southern Agrarians and neo-Marxists in New Haven during the late 1960's). But by and large this new generation of rebels did not need to secede because, unlike the Southern Agrarians, they had already identified their ideals, the very terms of their dissent, with pluralist democracy, representative individualism, and the rights of personal assent.

12. I should distinguish here between two kinds of oppositional criticism, one centered in the literature, the other in criticism itself. In what follows, my critique of the first group of critics—we might call them authorial oppositionalists—is more elaborate, because they have predominated from the beginning of American Studies. The second group of critics—we might call these self-reflexive oppositionalists—represents a more recent development. They have come (in varying degrees) to acknowledge literature's cultural embeddedment, but they then proceed to transfer the source of opposition from aesthetics to praxis, from the object to the method of study.

13. Again, I should distinguish here between two kinds of oppositionalism: the critics who self-consciously "play the system" and those who (I claim) play into it. But the two are often aligned in fact, and they often tend to blur in effect—sometimes, indeed, to blur in a pluralist concordia discors, as in the recent spectacle of Stanley Fish, representing the various branches of political correctness and multiculturalism. I quote from an article on his defense of these "adversarial positions," in the *New York Times Magazine* (May 3, 1992): 50: "And then there's his series of one-on-one debates with Dinesh D'Souza, the 30-year-old former Reagan White House policy analyst whose book about racial politics on campus graced the bestseller list for three months of last year. Prompted by D'Souza's lecture agent, Fish and D'Souza put themselves on the market—for a fee of $10,000 per debate. On five occasions in the last year the two men appeared before packed houses on college campuses to engage in orchestrated verbal fisticuffs." The author, Adam Begley, quotes D'Souza as saying: "'we can have a knockdown, drag-out debate and still have a drink afterward.'"

14. I do not claim this as a neutral territory of analysis. As I hope this essay suggests, cross-cultural criticism is not a form of cultural relativism. Nontranscendence is also a realm of ideals, however subject to contingency; of the real,

however vulnerable to interpretation; and of radical agency, within the limits imposed by the social and rhetorical construction of radicalisms.

15. Kafka, "Investigations," pp. 312–14; Phillis Wheatley, "To His Excellency George Washington" (1775), in *Collected Works*, ed. John C. Shields (New York: Oxford University Press, 1988), p. 146; John Boyle O'Reilley, "The Pilgrim Fathers," in *Old Colony Memorial: Plymouth Rock, Old Colony Sentinel*, LXVII, no. 31 (Plymouth, Aug. 3, 1889), p. 3; Emerson, "Nature," in *Essays and Lectures*, pp. 16, 17.

16. Emerson, "Experience," in *Essays and Lectures*, p. 485; Benjamin, "Theses," pp. 256–57.

17. Emerson, "The American Scholar" and "Experience," in *Essays and Lectures*, pp. 53, 485.

18. Shatalin delivered the talk on Oct. 2, 1990 (summarized in *Meeting Report* of the Kennan Institute for Advanced Russian Studies, VIII, no. 1, 1991), at the Woodrow Wilson International Center for Scholars. I am grateful to the Center for this experience, along with the many other benefits of a fellowship year.

Reichert: The Buber-Rosenzweig Bible Translation

Unless otherwise noted, all translations are the author's own.

1. See Klaus Reichert, "Im Hinblick auf eine Geschichte des Übersetzens," in *Sprache im technischen Zeitalter* (Berlin: Literarisches Colloquium, 1981), no. 79, pp. 196–206.

2. Rosenzweig sees Mendelssohn's attempt as one of the great achievements in the classical period of the German art of translation. Rosenzweig points to some audacious formulations that try to retain the original Hebrew phrasing: thus, against German usage, the covenant is not "made" but "cut apart" (*zerschnitten*), in reference to the sacrificial practice. But examples like this one are rare, and the translation seems to have had no influence anyway, partly because it was written in Hebrew characters. See Franz Rosenzweig, "'Der Ewige': Mendelssohn und der Gottesname," in Martin Buber and Rosenzweig, *Die Schrift und ihre Verdeutschung* (Berlin: Schocken, 1936), p. 185.

3. See Ilse Grubrich-Simitis, *Freuds Mosesstudie als Tagtraum* (Weinheim: Verlag Internationale Psychoanalyse, 1991), pp. 17–72.

4. Rosenzweig, *Sprachdenken: Arbeitspapiere zur Verdeutung der Schrift*, ed. R. Bat-Adam (Dordrecht: Nijhoff, 1984), pp. 93–94.

5. The only other version I know of where the two tenses are used is Zunz's: "Ich werde seyn der ich bin."

6. Rosenzweig, "Zeit ists . . . : Gedanken über das jüdische Bildungsproblem des Augenblicks," in *Zur jüdischen Erziehung* (Berlin: Schocken, 1937), pp. 8, 12, 31.

7. In his *Crisis of European Culture* Rudolf Pannwitz had demanded in 1917 that a translation should not render something into German but that it should attempt to transform German into English, Greek, etc. His statements had been

quoted by Walter Benjamin in his essay "The Task of the Translator" in 1923 (Walter Benjamin, *Gesammelte Schriften* [Frankfurt: Suhrkamp, 1971], vol. 4, pt. 1, p. 20). In his own Baudelaire translation, however, Benjamin did not adhere to this maxim. But it was precisely this that Buber and Rosenzweig tried to do.

8. Rosenzweig, *Sechzig Hymnen und Gedichte des Jehuda Halevi* (1924; Konstanz: Wöhrle, n.d.), p. 109.

9. Ibid.

10. Borchardt published specimens of his *Divina Commedia* translation as early as 1909. His complete German "Inferno" and "Purgatorio" were published in 1923. The German-Jewish critic Friedrich Gundolf, who was close to George, wrote that Borchardt's German was "roguish" (*gaunerhaft*), the "stationary German of the Russian Jew," a "Mauscheln." See Rudolf Borchardt, Martin Buber, *Briefe, Dokumente, Gespräche 1907–1964*, ed. G. Schuster and K. Neuwirth (Munich: Schriften der Rudolf Borchardt Gesellschaft, Band 2, 1991), pp. 13, 128, n. 25.

11. *Sechzig Hymnen*, p. 113.

12. Ibid., p. 115.

13. "Die Schrift und Luther," in Buber and Rosenzweig, *Die Schrift und ihre Verdeutschung*, pp. 123, 122.

14. Buber found confirmation for the fundamental concept of orality in the writings of Marcel Jousse, from whose *Le Style Oral* (published in 1925) Buber made excerpts (folder 43a in the Buber archive, Jewish National and University Library, Jerusalem). Jousse tried to reconstruct the oral and gestural quality of the written word of the Bible: "nous revivons, nous *récitons gestuellement* l'action dans ses grandes lignes" (Buber's emphasis). As far as I know, the connection between Jousse and Buber/Rosenzweig has not been noted; it certainly deserves attention. The *reconstruction* of the oral style, however, is only part of the picture. Looking at the drafts in the Buber archive, one gets the impression that many of the kolons were *made up* in consequence of the act of interpretation. (One often reads phrases like: "Here we need a Kolon and therefore we have to divide it thus . . .".) That is, the translators aimed at an orality that had in many instances no counterpart in the Masoretic text, alleging they were following traces hardly discernible in the written text, while in fact in many cases they were aiming for an orality that would function in German.

15. In Harold Fisch's new bilingual edition (Jerusalem Bible, 1989) we read: "And a wind from God moved over the surface of the waters."

16. "Die Schrift und Luther," p. 98.

17. Mendelssohn seems to have been the first to deviate from these renderings: he gives "Der Ewige" (the eternal one) throughout; so does Zunz. See Rosenzweig's article "Der Ewige."

18. "Die Schrift und Luther," p. 125.

19. This translation is taken from Nahum N. Glatzer, *Franz Rosenzweig: His Life and Thought*, rev. ed. (New York: Schocken, 1970), p. 257.

20. Franz Rosenzweig, *Briefe und Tagebücher*, 2 vols. (Dordrecht: Nijhoff, 1979), 2:1,085.

21. This repeats Stolberg's, the eighteenth-century Homer translator's, groan—"O, dear reader, go and learn Greek and throw my translation into the fire!"—quoted by Rosenzweig in a letter to Rudolf Hallo (March 27, 1922). The groan recurs in the working papers.

22. Borchardt and Buber, *Briefe*, pp. 44–60, esp. pp. 47, 54.

23. "Rosenzweigs Übersetzungen leben im dämonischen Glanz eines Zwitterdaseins. So war sein Wirken als Übersetzer von dem magischen Wunsch nach einer immer tieferen Ehe mit dem *Deutschen* bestimmt: ein *Verhängnis* für die jüdische Perspektive." Scholem's note (Scholem archive, Jerusalem) belongs either in the context of an article on Rosenzweig he planned to write at the time or to a letter he was drafting in reply to Edith Rosenzweig's request that he should translate *The Star of Redemption* into Hebrew.

24. "Die Bibel auf Deutsch," reprinted in Siegfried Kracauer, *Das Ornament der Masse* (Frankfurt: Suhrkamp, 1963), pp. 173–86.

25. Although Rosenzweig officially denied any influence of George (see his "Stefan George," in *Kleinere Schriften* [Berlin: Schocken, 1937], p. 503), he did take over some of his archaisms, e.g, "Tucht" for "Tugend" (virtue).

26. Martin Jay has summarized an unpublished exchange of letters between Ernst Simon and Kracauer from May 1926: "Kracauer claimed that his personal admiration for Rosenzweig and his courage was enormous, and he had meant him no slight; what he had found objectionable was the implied attempt to unite truth and existence in an unmediated way. As for the Zionist issue, he clearly felt that the *völkisch* description was appropriate despite factional disputes within the movement" (Martin Jay, "Politics of Translation: Siegfried Kracauer and Walter Benjamin on the Buber-Rosenzweig Bible," *Publications of the Leo Baeck Institute, Yearbook XXI* [London, 1976], p. 17).

27. Walter Benjamin, *Briefe an Siegfried Kracauer* (Marbach: Deutsches Literaturarchiv, 1987), p. 15.

28. The fundamental dissent between Rosenzweig and Scholem about the problem of translation from the Hebrew has not been analyzed conclusively. For the time being see Michael Brocke, "Franz Rosenzweig und Gerhard Gershom Scholem," in Walter Grab and Julius H. Schoeps, eds., *Juden in der Weimarer Republik* (Stuttgart-Bonn: Burg-Verlag, 1968).

29. Walter Benjamin, *Briefe,* 2 vols. (Frankfurt: Suhrkamp, 1966), 1:432.

30. Martin Jay, "Politics of Translation," p. 20.

31. Gershom Scholem, "An einem denkwürdigen Tage," in *Judaica* (Frankfurt: Suhrkamp, 1963), pp. 209, 211, 214–15. Nehama Leibowitz, who had been present in Buber's house when Scholem gave his address, remembers that Buber said to her afterward: "You know, the trouble with Scholem is that he does not believe in Germany" (private communication by Chaim Soloveitchik).

Pfeiffer: The Black Hole of Culture

1. Douglas Sladen, quoted in Jean-Pierre Lehmann, *The Image of Japan: From Feudal Isolation to World Power, 1850–1905* (London: George Allen & Unwin, 1978), p. 20.

2. Sladen, *Queer Things About Japan* (1903; Detroit: Singing Tree Press, 1968), pp. 123, 214, 16.

3. Bernice Z. Goldstein and Kyoko Tamura, *Japan and America: A Comparative Study in Language and Culture* (Rutland, Vt.: Charles E. Tuttle, 1975), p. 174.

4. Brian Moeran, "Japan's Internal Cultural Debate," in Takie Sugiyama Lebra and William P. Lebra, eds., *Japanese Culture and Behavior: Selected Readings*, rev. ed. (Honolulu: University of Hawaii Press, 1986), pp. 62–79, 75.

5. Quoted in Lehmann, *The Image of Japan*, p. 102.

6. Irmela Hijiya-Kirschnereit, *Das Ende der Exotik: Zur japanischen Kultur und Gesellschaft der Gegenwart* (Frankfurt am Main: Suhrkamp, 1988), chap. 3.

7. See Ichiro Kawasaki, *The Japanese Are Like That* (Rutland, Vt.: Charles E. Tuttle, 1955), and *Japan Unmasked* (Rutland, Vt.: Charles E. Tuttle, 1969), with 27 and 21 reprints respectively until 1987. See also the survey on the more recent literature on "transcultural understanding" in Hijiya-Kirschnereit, *Das Ende der Exotik*, pp. 139–221, particularly on "Japanese eurocentrism" and "European relativism," pp. 193–211.

8. See, for instance, Constantin von Barloewen and Kai Werhan-Mees, eds., *Japan und der Westen*, 3 vols. (Frankfurt am Main: Fischer, 1986), and Ulrich Menzel, ed. *Im Schatten des Siegers: Japan*, 4 vols. (Frankfurt am Main: Suhrkamp 1989).

9. Edgar Morin, *La Méthode 4: Les Idées: Leur habitat, leur vie, leurs moeurs, leur organisation* (Paris: Seuil, 1991), pp. 28–30.

10. Roland Barthes, *L'empire des signes* (Paris: Flammarion, 1970), p. 7.

11. Ibid., pp. 7–8.   12. Ibid., p. 42.

13. Ibid., pp. 71–72, 81.   14. Ibid., pp. 99, 104.

15. Ibid., pp. 110, 111.

16. See the interesting mixture of discourse types in Lafcadio Hearn, *Writings from Japan*, ed. Francis King (Harmondsworth: Penguin, 1984).

17. Ruth Benedict, *The Chrysanthemum and the Sword: Patterns of Japanese Culture* (1946; Boston: Houghton Mifflin, 1989), p. 116.

18. Ibid., foreword, p. xi.

19. See ibid., pp. x, 1–3.

20. Ibid., p. 3.

21. See statements like "Men and women in Japan live largely in separate worlds" (*Das Ende der Exotik*, p. 102), the statistics of polls (p. 103), and the assumption that the numbers quoted will not have changed "significantly" since—an assumption hardly corroborated, for instance, by Walter Edwards, *Modern Japan Through Its Weddings: Gender, Person, and Society in Ritual Portrayal* (Stanford, Calif.: Stanford University Press, 1989).

22. See Lehmann, *The Image of Japan*, chap. 1. See also the chapters on Yatoi

(hired foreigners), their self-images, and the Yatoi images of the Japanese in Hazel Jones, *Live Machines: Hired Foreigners and Meiji Japan* (Vancouver: University of British Columbia Press, 1980), on the one hand, and her almost statistically referential discourse on the other.

23. Gregor Paul, ed., *Klischee und Wirklichkeit japanischer Kultur: Beiträge zur Literatur und Philosophie in Japan und zum Japanbild in der deutschsprachigen Literatur: Festschrift für Toshinori Kanokogi* (Frankfurt am Main: Peter Lang, 1987).

24. Hijiya-Kirschnereit, *Das Ende der Exotik*; see chaps. 1 and 2 as contrasted with chap. 3.

25. Henry Norman, *The Real Japan: Studies in Contemporary Japanese Manners, Morals, Administration, and Politics* (1908; Wilmington, Del.: Scholarly Resources, 1973).

26. See Donald Keene, *The Japanese Discovery of Europe, 1720–1830*, rev. ed. (Stanford: Stanford University Press, 1969), pp. 137–38, 149–54.

27. See Harumi Befu, "Gift-Giving in a Modernizing Japan," *Japanese Culture and Behavior*, pp. 158–70, and Vincent R. S. Brandt, "Skiing Cross-Culturally," ibid., pp. 188–94.

28. For these topics see Takao Suzuki, "Language and Behavior in Japan: The Conceptualization of Personal Relations," and Yomishi Kasakara, "Fear of Eye-to-Eye Confrontation among Neurotic Patients in Japan," *Japanese Culture and Behavior*, pp. 142–57 and pp. 379–87.

29. See K. Ludwig Pfeiffer, "Kommunikationsformen als Lebensformen: Zum wissenschaftsgeschichtlichen Ort eines Programms," in Pfeiffer and Michael Walter, eds., *Kommunikationsformen als Lebensformen* (Munich: Fink, 1990), pp. 15–36, 30.

30. Eric W. F. Tomlin, *The Last Country: My Years in Japan* (London: Faber and Faber, 1974), pp. 28–29.

31. Ibid., p. 16. The intricate question of postmodernism and Japan has been treated in various ways in Masao Miyoshi and H. D. Harootunian, eds., *Postmodernism and Japan* (Durham, N.C.: Duke University Press, 1989), and K. Ludwig Pfeiffer, "Schwebende Referenzen und Verhaltenskultur: Japan und die Praxis permanenter Postmoderne," in Robert Weimann and Hans Ulrich Gumbrecht, eds., *Postmoderne—globale Differenz* (Frankfurt am Main: Suhrkamp, 1991), pp. 344–53.

32. Gerhard Kaiser, *Bilder lesen: Studien zu Literatur und bildender Kunst* (Munich: Fink, 1980), pp. 172–73.

33. Tomlin, *The Last Country*, p. 29.

34. Ardath W. Burks, *Japan: A Postindustrial Power* (Boulder, Col.: Westview Press, 1991), pp. 27–28.

35. Tomlin, *The Last Country*, p. 156.

36. Cf. Burks, *Japan*, pp. 34–39, and Keene, *The Japanese Discovery*.

37. Burks, *Japan*, p. 77. Burks is presenting the "Reischauer line" of argument.

38. Robert C. Christopher, *The Japanese Mind: The Goliath Explained* (Tokyo: Charles E. Tuttle, 1987), pp. 48–49.

39. Ibid., p. 181.

40. Ibid., pp. 187, 181.

41. Isaiah Ben-Dasan, *The Japanese and the Jews*, trans. Richard L. Gage (New York: Weatherhill, 1972), pp. 3, 100.

42. Sladen, *Queer Things About Japan*, p. 49.

43. See Christopher, *The Japanese Mind*, pp. 167–69.

44. See in particular Ian Buruma, *A Japanese Mirror: Heroes and Villains of Japanese Culture* (Harmondsworth: Penguin, 1984), pp. ix–xii and chap. 2; Hijiya-Kirschnereit, *Das Ende der Exotik*, p. 164.

45. Christopher, *The Japanese Mind*, p. 180; see also pp. 167–68.

46. See the use of this metaphor in Augustin Berque, "Das Verhältnis der Ökonomie zu Raum und Zeit in der japanischen Kultur," in *Japan und der Westen*, 1: 21–37, 32.

47. See Smith's remarks in Robert C. Hamerton-Kelly, ed., *Violent Origins: Walter Burkert, René Girard, and Jonathan Z. Smith on Ritual Killing and Cultural Formation* (Stanford, Calif.: Stanford University Press, 1987), p. 185.

48. Cf. Edgar Morin, *Le vif du sujet* (Paris: Seuil, 1969), pp. 143–45, and *Le paradigme perdu: La nature humaine* (Paris: Seuil, 1973), pp. 157–64.

49. See Rosaldo's "anthropological commentary" in *Violent Origins*, pp. 239–44, 241.

50. See Burkert, "The Problem of Ritual Killing," in *Violent Origins*, pp. 149–76, 154.

51. Hamerton-Kelly, ed., *Violent Origins*, pp. 186–87.

52. See Ben-Dasan, *The Japanese and the Jews*, pp. 12–19.

53. See ibid., pp. 48–49, and the very interesting book by Tetsuro Watsuji, *Climate and Culture: A Philosophical Study*, trans. Geoffrey Bownas (1961; Tokyo: Yushodo, 1988).

54. Christopher, *The Japanese Mind*, pp. 39–40, 42.

55. See Keene, *The Japanese Discovery*, pp. 207–8.

56. Ibid., p. 77.

57. See ibid., pp. 122–23, 160–61, 169–72.

58. Quoted in Christopher, *The Japanese Mind*, p. 174.

Miller: Border Crossings, Translating Theory

This essay was first published as Chapter 12 of J. Hillis Miller, *Topographies* (Stanford, Calif.: Stanford University Press, 1995).

1. "Travelling Theory," *The World, the Text, and the Critic* (Cambridge, Mass.: Harvard University Press, 1983), pp. 226–47; the later lecture has been revised and published as "Travelling Theory Reconsidered," in *Critical Reconstructions: The Relationship of Fiction and Life*, ed. Robert M. Polhemus and Roger B. Henkle (Stanford, Calif.: Stanford University Press, 1994), pp. 251–63.

2. Paul de Man, "The Resistance to Theory," *The Resistance to Theory* (Minneapolis: University of Minnesota Press, 1986), p. 3. Mentioning de Man perhaps incurs a responsibility to say something about de Man's wartime writings. I have elsewhere said in some detail what I have to say about those writings. (See "Paul de Man's Wartime Writings" and "An Open Letter to Jon Wiener," *Theory Now*

and Then [Durham: Duke University Press, 1991], pp. 359–84.) De Man's later writings, far from being continuous with the wartime writings, repeatedly attack just those positions—assumptions about literature and national identity—he held in the writings for *Le Soir*.

3. What is untranslatable is the contingent and intrinsically meaningless fact that in Italian changing a "u" to an "i" and making the "t" single rather than double changes "translate" into "traduce."

4. Walter Benjamin, *Illuminationen* (Frankfurt am Main: Suhrkamp Verlag, 1969), pp. 148–84; *Illuminations*, trans. Harry Zohn (New York: Schocken Books, 1969), pp. 217–51. My reference to this essay is an example of what I am discussing. Benjamin's essay has been widely influential in the United States. It is often cited and commented on. It has generated much new work in "cultural criticism." It may have been read more often in English than in the German original.

5. It is characteristic of our present cultural situation that this chapter in a preliminary form was sent by FAX halfway around the world, from Maine to Taipei, as soon as it was finished.

6. I have argued this in more detail in "The Work of Cultural Criticism in the Age of Digital Reproduction," in *Illustration* (Cambridge, Mass.: Harvard University Press, 1992).

7. De Man, "The Resistance to Theory," p. 7.

8. Some preliminary sense of this tradition can be gained from the entry on Ruth and *Ruth Rabbah* (the aggadic Midrash on the Book of Ruth) in the *Encyclopedia Judaica*. See also the entry by Jack Sasson on Ruth in *The Literary Guide to the Bible*, ed. Robert Alter and Frank Kermode (Cambridge, Mass.: Harvard University Press, 1987), 320–28; Yehoshua Bachrach, *Mother of Royalty: An Exposition of the Book of Ruth in the Light of the Sources*, trans. Leonard Oschry (Jerusalem: Feldheim, 1973); Edward F. Campbell, Jr., *Ruth: A New Translation with Introduction, Notes, and Commentary*, Anchor Bible Series (Garden City, N.Y.: Doubleday, 1975); Jack M. Sasson, *Ruth: A New Translation with a Philological Commentary and a Formalist-Folklorist Interpretation* (Baltimore: Johns Hopkins University Press, 1979); Evelyn Strouse and Bezalel Porten, "A Reading of Ruth," *Commentary* (Feb. 1979): 63–67; Shmuel Yerushalmi, *The Book of Ruth: MeAm Lo'ez*, trans. E. van Handel (New York: Maznaim, 1985); *The Book of Ruth; Megillas Ruth: A New Translation with Commentary Anthologized from Talmudic, Midrashic, and Rabbinic Sources*, trans. Meir Zlotowitz (New York: ArtScroll Tanach Studios, 1976). For an excellent discussion of some medieval Christian commentary on Ruth in relation to Chaucer's references to it, see Ellen E. Martin, "Chaucer's Ruth: An Exegetical Poetic in the Prologue to the *Legend of Good Women*," *Exemplaria* 3 (October 1991): 467–90.

9. I owe this knowledge to a conversation with Professor Moshe Greenberg of the Hebrew University of Jerusalem and to a helpful letter sent by Dr. Esther Beith-Halahmi of Bar-Ilan University in Israel. I cite part of Dr. Beith-Halahmi's letter for the interest of its details.

According to the only epigraphic "document" from Moab we have, the Stelle of Mesha King of Moab (2 Kings 3, Amos 2:1, and 2 Chronicles 20), which was found in Ancient Dibon by Samuel Klein in 1868 and whose fragments were bought by Charles Clermont-

Ganneau for France in 1870, the language of Moab was almost indistinguishable from Hebrew. This Stelle in basalt stone in which King Mesha immortalized his uprising against Israel, is inscribed in ancient Hebrew letters, and though we cannot know what the exact pronunciation was, it differs in spelling and vocabulary only slightly, containing a few words whose meaning differs and some others which do not appear in the Bible. In fact, after learning the ancient Hebrew alphabet, our students in Bible at Bar-Ilan read the text in class almost as easily as any ancient Hebrew text. This is not conclusive evidence of the language spoken by the Moabites since it could be argued that they might have inscribed the Stelle in the language of the enemy, but there is other evidence to support the thesis. See W. F. Albright in *The Archaeology of Palestine* (Harmondsworth: Penguin Books, 1949), pp. 130–36; 177–203, esp. p. 180. Albright writes that "the ancient Semitic tongues, outside Accadian, were so closely related to one another in grammar and pronunciation (phonetics) that each dialect had much in common with all its neighbors"; and the articles of Jacob Liver and of Hayim Rabin on Mesha (in Hebrew) and on Moab in *Encyclopaedia Biblia* (Jerusalem: Bialik Institute, 1962), 4:707–22, esp. 716–18 on Moab; and 921–29 (esp. 925–29) on Mesha and his Stelle.

10. At least I think it is Boaz, not the kinsman, who takes off his shoe to seal the bargain. The referent of the "he" is ambiguous, and the commentators disagree.

11. The essay is included in Michael Land, ed., *Structuralism: A Reader* (London: Jonathan Cape, 1970).

12. In response to an oral presentation of this chapter at a conference in Brasília.

13. Charles Dickens, *Pickwick Papers* (Harmondsworth: Penguin Books, 1972), p. 539.

14. This may be a form of the resistance of theory to itself and of that asymmetry of theory and reading of which de Man speaks at the end of "The Resistance to Theory": "To the extent however that they are theory, that is to say teachable, generalizable and highly responsive to systematization, rhetorical readings, like the other kinds, still avoid and resist the reading they advocate. Nothing can overcome the resistance to theory since theory *is* itself this resistance" (p. 19).

S. Budick: Cross-Culture, Chiasmus, and Manifold of Mind

1. I have commented on a number of related questions (especially with regard to certain Hegelian paradigms) in "The Experience of Literary History: Vulgar versus Not-Vulgar," *New Literary History* 25 (1994): 749–77.

2. Friedrich Nietzsche, *Beyond Good and Evil: Prelude to a Philosophy of the Future*, trans. R. J. Hollingdale (London: Penguin, 1990), 260. Numbers refer to Nietzsche's section divisions.

3. Ibid., 244.

4. In this instance I have offered my own literal translation, but the other translations from *Faust* included here are those of Philip Wayne (London: Penguin, 1979). Goethe's plays are quoted from the *Gedenkausgabe der Werke, Briefe und Gespräche*, ed. Ernst Beutler (Zürich: Artemis, 1962), vols. 5 and 6.

5. In *Faust* as a whole this *Geisterreich* reaches one kind of climax in the chiasmus of female and male, living and departed, sung by the Chorus Mysticus in the closing verses of the tragedy. I will have some comments to make about these lines

later in this essay. For a glimpse of Schiller's philosophical interest in chiasmus, as well as the possible reciprocal relation of this interest to Goethe's artistic practice, see Elizabeth M. Wilkinson's and L. A. Willoughby's introduction to their edition and translation of Schiller's *On the Aesthetic Education of Man: In a Series of Letters* (Oxford: Clarendon Press, 1982), especially pp. lxviii–lxxii, xci–xcv, and cxcv–cxcvi.

6. Unless otherwise noted, translations of *Torquato Tasso* are from the version of Alan and Sandy Brownjohn (London: Angel Books, 1985).

7. Some of my remarks below concerning the workings of chiasmus appear in my essay on English neoclassicism and romanticism, "Chiasmus and the Making of Literary Tradition: The Case of Wordsworth and 'The Days of Dryden and Pope,'" *ELH* 60 (1993): 961–87.

8. Suhamy's observation is cited by Thomas Mermall, "The Chiasmus: Unamuno's Master Trope," *PMLA* 105 (1990): 252.

9. De Man restrictively associates this feature of chiasmus with nonclassical usage. I have disputed this and other aspects of de Man's view of chiasmus in "Chiasmus and the Making of Literary Tradition."

10. This paragraph is adapted from Wolfgang Iser's account of negativity in *The Act of Reading: A Theory of Aesthetic Response* (Baltimore: Johns Hopkins University Press, 1980), pp. 182 and 225–29, and from a subsequent adaptation of those remarks in our introduction to *Languages of the Unsayable: The Play of Negativity in Literature and Literary Theory* (New York: Columbia University Press, 1989), p. xii.

11. The Italian text is that of *La Gerusalemme Liberata*, ed. Giovanni Getto (Brescia: La Scuola, 1967). I cite the literal prose translation of Ralph Nash, *Jerusalem Delivered* (Detroit: Wayne State University Press, 1987), though I arrange Nash's prose according to Tasso's lineation.

12. Praising the Princess and the Duke, she says, "Ein edler Mensch *zieht edle Menschen an* / Und weiss sie festzuhalten, wie ihr tut. / Um deinen Bruder und um dich verbinden / Gemueter sich, die euer wuerdig sind, / Und ihr seid eurer grossen Vaeter wert" (lines 59–63; my emphasis).

13. See Erich Auerbach, *Mimesis: The Representation of Reality in Western Literature*, trans. Willard Trask (1946; Princeton, N.J.: Princeton University Press, 1971), pp. 444–45, 451.

14. Nash translates *gemiti* as "groans."

15. I am indebted to Lawrence Besserman for showing me this parallel in Dante, especially since it raises Tasso's usage virtually to the level of a topos. In "A Note on the Sources of Chaucer's *Troilus* V, 540–613," *The Chaucer Review* 24 (1990): 306–7, Besserman has shown that in the "Proemio" to the *Filostrato* Boccaccio explicitly invokes the opening lament of Lamentations to bemoan the loss of his beloved: "O how solitary abideth the city that before was full of people and a mistress among the nations!"

16. Auerbach, *Mimesis*, pp. 444, 452.

17. Ibid., pp. 447, 449–50.

18. Ibid., p. 452.

19. Eckermann, *Conversations with Goethe,* trans. Gisela C. O'Brien (New York: Ungar, 1964), p. 121; entry for July 15, 1827.

20. Nietzsche, *Beyond Good and Evil,* 251. I flatter myself to think that this is a remark to which I myself, as a Jew, can happily take sharp exception, but the form of Nietzsche's argument in the shadow of Goethe's picture of the manifold is of gripping interest here. It also has a more general theoretical value which applies, in all directions, to the avoidances among all cultures.

21. Ibid., 248, 249.

22. Ibid., 250.

23. In this instance I have adapted the Brownjohn version to make it more literal, though even the first-level meaning of these verses is difficult to pin down.

24. In fact, it is just here that Auerbach's bias toward "realism" comes in again in our story, this time in relation to his work as one of the foremost modern explicators of the workings of Christian typology. Auerbach insisted that Christian typological interpretation was totally different from, and far superior to, the "allegorical" interpretation of the Jews, precisely because of the "dramatic actuality" of the "fulfillment" created in Christian typology (*Scenes from the Drama of European Literature: Six Essays,* trans. Ralph Manheim [New York: Meridian Books, 1959], pp. 51–55). I have elsewhere questioned whether the dimension of fulfillment in Christian typology is, in many highly significant cases, as closed or temporally located as Auerbach claims; and I have suggested some of the ways in which ancient Jewish texts already invent a typological-antitypological interpretation of the open kind which was employed in many Christian texts (see "Milton and the Scene of Interpretation: From Typology Toward Midrash," in *Midrash and Literature,* ed. Geoffrey H. Hartman and Sanford Budick [New Haven: Yale University Press, 1986], pp. 195–212). In the present instance from Lamentations we witness an ancient Jewish form of typology which suggests, ironically enough, that in his own way Auerbach too was oblivious to the mind of the Jews that is part of the manifold of mind within the German and the European mind.

Iser: The Emergence of a Cross-Cultural Discourse

1. For details see Hans Robert Jauss, "Ästhetische Normen und geschichtliche Reflexion in der *Querrelle des Anciens et des Modernes,*" in Charles Perrault, *Parallèle des Anciens et des Modernes en ce qui regarde les Arts et les Sciences,* ed. Jauss, Theorie und Geschichte der Literatur und der Schönen Künste 2 (Munich: Eidos, 1964), pp. 8–79.

2. See especially Perrault, *Parallèle,* pp. 103–64.

3. See Jauss, "Ästhetische Normen," p. 47.

4. This may be one of the reasons why Carlyle is beginning to attract interest again. G. B. Tennyson, *Carlyle and the Modern World,* The Carlyle Society, Occasional Papers 4 (Edinburgh: Carlyle Society, 1971), p. 3, started out his lecture to the Carlyle Society by saying, "I take some comfort in reporting that in the scholarly market Carlyle is now again on the upswing."

5. Cf. Ian Campbell, *Thomas Carlyle* (London: Hamish Hamilton, 1974), pp. 109–10.

6. G. Robert Stange, "Refractions of *Past and Present*," in *Carlyle, Past and Present: A Collection of New Essays* (London: Vision Press, 1976), p. 97, gives a brief outline of how Carlyle conceived of the relationship between past and present. John D. Rosenberg, *Carlyle and the Burden of History* (Oxford: Clarendon Press, 1985), p. 121, points out the "circuitous way" that governs the linkup between past and present, which clearly reveals nascent hermeneutic features unconsciously employed by Carlyle.

7. Thomas Carlyle, *Sartor Resartus: The Life and Opinions of Herr Teufelsdröckh*, vol. 1 of *Centenary Edition of the Works* (London: Chapman and Hall, 1897), p. 5. Unless otherwise specified, page references to *Sartor Resartus* are hereafter given parenthetically in the text.

8. Geoffrey H. Hartman, *Criticism in the Wilderness: The Study of Literature Today* (New Haven, Conn.: Yale University Press, 1980), p. 48, considers the "genre of the book . . . at once commentary and fiction." Carlisle Moore, "*Sartor Resartus* and the Problem of Carlyle's 'Conversion,'" *PMLA* 70 (1955): 667, quotes from Carlyle's correspondence (*Letters of Thomas Carlyle: 1826–1836*, ed. C. E. Norton [London: 1889], p. 365) that the book was to be "put together in the fashion of a kind of Didactic Novel; but indeed properly *like* nothing yet extant."

9. George Levine, "*Sartor Resartus* and the Balance of Fiction (1968)," in *Thomas Carlyle*, ed. Harold Bloom (New York: Chelsea House, 1986), finds it hard to pinpoint the generic features of *Sartor Resartus*: "I prefer, therefore, in order to avoid the confusion that the word 'novel' . . . inevitably brings with it, to consider *Sartor* as a fiction belonging to the complex class of 'confession-anatomy-romance'" (pp. 56–57).

10. I use the term "black box" as defined by Gregory Bateson, *Steps to an Ecology of Mind* (New York: Ballantine Books, 1972): "A 'black box' is a conventional agreement between scientists to stop trying to explain things at a certain point. . . . So the 'black box' is a label for what a bunch of things are supposed to do. . . . But it's not an explanation of *how* the bunch works. . . . There's no explanation of an explanatory principle. It's like a black box" (pp. 39–40).

11. Concerning the various functions of the "English Editor," cf. L. M. Findlay, "Paul de Man, Thomas Carlyle, and 'The Rhetoric of Temporality,'" *Dalhousie Review* 2 (1965): 172; Jerry A. Dibble, "Strategies of the Mental War: Carlyle and Hegel and the Rhetoric of Idealism," *Bulletin of the New York Public Library* 80 (1976): 100, and Rosenberg, *Carlyle and the Burden of History*, p. 10.

12. Lore Metzger, "*Sartor Resartus*: A Victorian Faust," *Comparative Literature* 13 (1961): 317, tends to confine Teufelsdröckh's "uneasy equilibrium between the two halves of his nature" to the antagonism of Faust and Mephistopheles, which makes him alternate between "divine inspiration of divinely begotten man and its eternal negation in the devil and the body's dross." Yet she also points out essential differences through which Carlyle diverged from Goethe (see esp. pp. 325–36). Charles F. Harrold, *Carlyle and German Thought: 1819–1834*, Yale

Studies in English 82 (New Haven, Conn.: Yale University Press, 1934), pp. 5–6, considers Teufelsdröckh as a direct offspring of Jean Paul's humorous characters. See also Dennis Douglas, "Carlyle and the Jacobin Undercurrent in German Transcendentalism," *Bulletin of the New York Public Library* 80 (1976): 108.

13. This is equally reflected in Carlyle criticism, which privileges either the idealist or the empiricist component of this cross-cultural relationship. Tom Lloyd, "Towards Natural Supernaturalism: Carlyle and Dual Vision," *Philological Quarterly* 65 (1986): 479–94, gives a rather balanced view of this situation. See also Lloyd's essay, "Madame Roland and Schiller's *Aesthetics*: Carlyle's 'The French Revolution,'" *Prose Studies* 3 (1986): 39–53. Dibble indicates why the two components of Carlyle's thought are so intimately interlinked: "The conflict between 'English' realism and 'German' idealism . . . begins in earnest with Kant's first *Critique*, and it is there one sees most readily the rhetorical dilemma out of which *Sartor Resartus* came" ("Strategies of the Mental War," p. 90).

14. Harold Bloom, introduction to *Thomas Carlyle*, ed. Harold Bloom (New York: Chelsea House, 1986), sees Carlyle "in the tradition of Rabelais, Voltaire, and Swift, so far as his genre (or non-genre) can be determined, but he is less a satirist than the seer of a grotesque phantasmagoria" (p. 13). Tennyson maintains: "As always, Carlyle's method is, by exaggeration and caricature, to call attention to the truth" (*Carlyle and the Modern World*, p. 22).

15. It is equally hard to trace the Philosophy of Clothes back to Swedenborg, as tentatively suggested by James C. Malin, "Carlyle's Philosophy of Clothes and Swedenborg's," *Scandinavian Studies* 33 (1961): 155–68. Douglas is certainly right in stating that in this respect Carlyle's "basic orientation is Kantian" ("Carlyle and the Jacobin Undercurrent," p. 107).

16. For the intimate relationship between symbol and silence, see Camille R. La Bossière, "Of Silence, Doubt, and Imagination: Carlyle's Conversation with Montaigne," *English Studies in Canada* 10 (1984): 63–64, 72. This essay appears to be one of the rare occasions in Carlyle criticism that draws attention to the circularity of Carlyle's interpretive procedure: "The thought of *Sartor Resartus* and its complex of core images take the reader on a circular odyssey, the chart of which plots the progress of the Carlylean imagination" (p. 67). However, there is still a difference between circularity and looping. For further evaluation of how Carlyle uses symbols in order to give voice to the unspeakable, see Findlay, "Paul de Man, Thomas Carlyle," pp. 176–77, 179.

17. For a different view of the assumed parallels between Carlyle and Hegel, especially between *Sartor Resartus* and *The Phenomenology of Mind*, see Dibble, "Strategies of the Mental War," pp. 97–102.

18. See Helmuth Plessner, "Die anthropologische Dimension der Geschichtlichkeit," in Hans Peter Dreitzel, ed., *Sozialer Wandel: Zivilisation und Fortschritt in der soziologischen Theorie* (Neuwied: Luchterhand, 1972), p. 160 and Jacques Lacan, *Schriften I*, ed. Norbert Haas (Olten and Freiburg im Breisgau: Walter, 1973), pp. 63–64, 67, 78.

19. Concerning the notion and function of routes or chains of reference, see

Nelson Goodman, *Of Mind and Other Matters* (Cambridge, Mass.: Harvard University Press, 1984), pp. 54–71.

20. Moore stresses Carlyle's commitment to action: "Action not only removes religious doubt, it creates faith and happiness and, in the form of work, creates order and belief in a dynamic society" ("Carlyle's 'Conversion,'" p. 674).

Motzkin: Memory and Cultural Translation

1. Lawrence L. Langer, *Holocaust Testimonies: The Ruins of Memory* (New Haven, Conn.: Yale University Press, 1991). See also Peter Hayes, ed., *Lessons and Legacies: The Meaning of the Holocaust in a Changing World* (Evanston, Ill.: Northwestern University Press, 1991); James Young, *The Texture of Memory: Holocaust Memorials and Meaning in Europe, Israel and America* (New Haven, Conn.: Yale University Press, forthcoming).

2. The phrase is Reinhard Koselleck's.

3. Reinhard Rürup, *Emanzipation und Antisemitismus* (Göttingen: Vandenhoeck & Rupprecht, 1973).

4. David Vital, *The Future of the Jews* (Cambridge, Mass.: Harvard University Press, 1990).

5. Gabriel Motzkin, *Time and Transcendence: Secular History, the Catholic Reaction and the Rediscovery of the Future* (Dordrecht: Kluwer Academic Publishers, 1992).

Lachmann: The Foreign as Figure of Cultural Ambivalence

1. Here and in the following passage I am referring to Jurij Lotman, "The Dynamic Model of a Semiotic System" (1974), *Semiotica* 21 (1977): 193–210, and Lotman and Boris Uspenskij, "On the Semiotic Mechanism of Culture," in *Semeiotike* 5 (1971).

2. See Renate Lachmann, "Value Aspects in Jurij Lotman's Semiotics of Culture/Semiotics of Text," in *Dispositio* 12 (1987): 13–33.

3. Mikhail Bakhtin, "Slovo v romane" (The Word in the Novel), *Voprosy literatury i èstetiki* (Moscow: Chudožestvennaja literatura, 1975), pp. 72–233.

4. Lotman, "The Dynamic Model of a Semiotic System," p. 204.

5. See Lachmann, "Aspects of the Russian Language Question in the 17th Century," in Riccardo Picchio and Harvey Goldblatt, eds., *Aspects of the Slavic Language Question* (New Haven, Conn.: Yale University Press, 1984), 2:125–185.

6. Rosemary Jackson, *Fantasy: The Literature of Subversion* (London: Methuen, 1981).

7. Mikhail Bakhtin, *Problems of Dostoevsky's Poetics*, trans. Caryl Emerson (Minneapolis: University of Minnesota Press, 1987).

8. Cf. Lachmann, "Bakhtin and Carnival: Culture as Counter-Culture," *Cultural Critique* 11 (1988/89): 115–52.

9. Jackson, *Fantasy*, p. 20.

10. Sir Walter Scott, "On the Supernatural and Fictitious Composition; and Particularly on the Works of Ernest Theodore William Hoffmann," in I. Williams, ed., *On Novelists and Fiction* (London: Routledge & Kegan Paul, 1968), pp. 325–26.

11. Ibid., p. 352.

Iser: Coda to the Discussion

1. Eric Gans, *The End of Culture: Toward a Generative Anthropology* (Berkeley: University of California Press, 1985), p. 20.

2. See Hans Blumenberg, *Höhlenausgänge* (Frankfurt am Main: Suhrkamp, 1989), pp. 11–81.

Index

In this index an "f" after a number indicates a separate reference on the next page, and an "ff" indicates separate references on the next two pages. A continuous discussion over two or more pages is indicated by a span of page numbers, e.g., "57–59." *Passim* is used for a cluster of references in close but not consecutive sequence.

Adams, Henry, 135
Agrippa, Cornelius, 91, 322n19
Alexander Severus, 51f
Alexander von Roes, 57
Ambrose, 72
Amery, Jean, 271
Apuleius, 31
Aristotle, 291
Artaud, Antonin, 103–4
Asoka, 27
Assmann, Aleida, 1f, 4
Assmann, Jan, 1, 14–17, 19ff
Auerbach, Erich, 233, 235f, 340n24
Augustine, Saint, 50, 56, 68–74, 78–84, 88f, 104
Austin, J. L., 104, 213

Bakhtin, Mikhail, 65, 285, 288
Barasch, Moshe, 1, 14, 16–21
Barth, Karl, 89
Barthes, Roland, 188ff
Bateson, Gregory, 341n10
Batkin, Leonid, 65
Baudrillard, Jean, 188
Beauvais, Vincent of, *see* Vincent de Beauvais
Ben-Dasan, Isaiah, 197, 200
Benedict, Ruth, 190f

Benjamin, Walter, 68, 142, 153–66 *passim*, 179, 183, 210, 212, 328n7, 337n4
Ben-Porat, Ziva, 219
Bercovitch, Sacvan, 7f, 17, 129, 131f, 142f
Besserman, Lawrence, 11, 339n15
Bloch, Ernst, 179
Bloom, Harold, 107, 221
Blumenberg, Hans, 300
Boccaccio, 72
Boehme, Jacob, 91f
Borchardt, Rudolf, 175, 179, 182
Bowersock, G. W., 33
Brown, John, 110
Buber, Martin, 12f, 18, 169, 172, 176–85, 295, 332n14
Budick, Emily Miller, 14
Burckhardt, Jakob, 64
Burkert, Walter, 199

Caracella, 55
Carlyle, Thomas, 4f, 18, 245, 247–64
Cassian, 46
Cassiodorus, 72
Cavell, Stanley, 2, 6f, 10, 141, 143f
Celan, Paul, 271
Celsus, 30, 32
Chaucer, 68f, 72–84

Library of Congress Cataloging-in-Publication Data

The Translatability of cultures : figurations of the space between /
edited by Sanford Budick and Wolfgang Iser.
    p.   cm.—(Irvine studies in the humanities)
    Includes index.
    ISBN 0-8047-2484-9 (cl.)
    ISBN 0-8047-2561-6 (pbk.)
    1. Translating and interpreting.   2. Literature, Comparative—
History and criticism.   3. Criticism.   4. Cross cultural studies.
I. Budick, Sanford.   II. Iser, Wolfgang.   III. Series.
PN241.T698   1996
418'.02—dc20   95-13052
                                                 CIP

♾ This book is printed on acid-free, recycled paper.

Original printing 1996
Last figure below indicates year of this printing:
05   04   03   02   01   00   99   98   97   96